JUSTICE

IAN ST JAMES, according to the press, was a
millionaire at the age of thirty, when the
merchant bank backing his enterprises suddenly collapsed and took his business with it.
In the years afterwards he started a management consultancy and later turned it into a
small investment house. In 1977 he retired to
write full-time. His earlier novels include
The Money Stones, *The Balfour Conspiracy*,
Winner Harris, *The Killing Anniversary* and
Cold New Dawn. He is married with three
children.

Ian St James

JUSTICE

FONTANA/Collins

First published by William Collins Sons & Co. Ltd 1988
A continental edition first issued in Fontana Paperbacks 1989
This edition first issued in Fontana Paperbacks 1989

Printed and bound in Great Britain by
William Collins Sons & Co. Ltd, Glasgow

For Pat and Brian who helped along
the way, and Marjory and Eddie
who waited so patiently.

Author's Note

The English legal profession adheres to strict codes of conduct. While acknowledging these, reasonable literary licence has been taken in writing this novel.

IAN ST JAMES

PROLOGUE

'I TAKE IT THERE ARE NO NEW INSTRUCTIONS,' said Sir Robert, 'no changes of mind, no last minute doubts.'

Doubts? I could have laughed in his face. I'd been plagued with doubts for months. If the verdict went against us, I would lose everything; my career, my home and what was left of my savings. I'd already lost what I cherished most, the girl I had planned to marry. My heart ached with doubts.

I coughed to clear my dry throat. 'No,' I said, 'there are no new instructions, Sir Robert.'

He regarded me soberly across the great leather-topped desk. The Victorian partner's desk was the room's single item of real value. The walls were peeling and the carpet was threadbare, the leather armchairs were losing their shape. Not for the first time I wondered why barristers chose to make their chambers so uncomfortable. Sir Robert Longfellow, QC, was a wealthy man. Outside in the courtyard was a new Rolls-Royce. He owned an apartment in the Albany and a large Georgian house on the out-skirts of Bath, yet some nuance of inverted snobbery dictated that all barristers fill their chambers with furniture fit for the junkyard, and not even the flamboyant Sir Robert would flout such a convention.

'Very well,' he said. 'You know we've drawn Hunter, do you?'

I nodded, having been already informed by Sir Robert's clerk that Mr Justice Hunter would preside over the trial.

'We could have done worse,' Sir Robert said to Olivia Newton beside him. She was his junior, chosen for this case from the ten in his chambers.

'Yes,' she agreed, while managing to convey doubt, 'but we could have done better. I was hoping we'd get Lewis.'

Sir Robert raised an eyebrow. He had a long, handsome face, an aquiline nose and a steady blue-eyed gaze that had disconcerted many a witness in the box. 'Perhaps,' he conceded with a shrug. 'Still, we've been given Hunter. We must do the best we can.' Turning to me, he asked, 'I suppose there's no movement from the other side? No last minute hint of a deal?'

Feeling sick with tension, I managed a wry smile. It was not unknown for a settlement to be achieved on the steps of the court. My father had used the tactic often in the past. It was the ultimate in brinkmanship and there was no better exponent of it than my father. But this case was different; he wanted this trial.

Sir Robert shrugged. 'Well, it's no more than you forecast.' I wondered if I detected grudging respect. If so I was hearing it for the first time. Although always polite, Sir Robert was very aware of the difference in our status. At fifty, he was an eminent QC and head of his chambers. Twenty years younger, I was a mere junior partner in a provincial firm of solicitors, and unlikely to be even that for much longer.

'It doesn't help,' he said, his blue eyes probing my face, 'this enmity between you and your father. You acting for one side and him acting for the other. Suppose Griffith offers me a deal in the robing room? Do I negotiate?'

Sir Emlyn Griffith, QC, was Sir Robert's opposite number. 'It won't happen,' I answered, shaking my head. 'They think they can't lose. Why should they negotiate?'

'But *if*?' persisted Sir Robert with visible annoyance. 'I must know where I stand. Forget your father, Mortlake. Think of your client.'

I ignored the rebuke. It was undeserved. I'm not even sure it was intended. Nerves were showing on Sir Robert's side of the desk as well as on mine. In an hour's time battle would commence and he was casting around for every available scrap of ammunition.

'What's Berkley's bottom line?' he demanded. 'What does he most want?'

'You know what he wants. To right a wrong. He wants justice.'

'How very romantic,' Sir Robert said with dry sarcasm. 'Even quixotic, considering the odds are against him.'

I remained silent for a moment, thinking of Nick Berkley. Finally I said, 'He's not a fighter by nature, you know that, but he has no choice.' I nearly added that the same could be said of me, but instead I offered a compliment. 'And he's got great faith in you.'

'Humph,' Sir Robert exclaimed, drumming the desk top with his fingertips.

Olivia cleared her throat. 'And how is our client bearing up?' she asked.

I was tempted to say, As well as could be expected. I had left Nick at the hotel, eating breakfast in his room, picking nervously at his bacon and eggs as if afraid they were poisoned. Nick was as twitchy as a flea, but I judged it best not to say so. 'He's a bit tired,' I said. 'Some of his fans besieged the hotel last night. They kept us awake for hours, screaming and shouting. God knows how they found out where we were staying. Fifty of them were in the lobby when I left, singing songs from his last LP.'

Olivia smiled, a discreet puckering of the lips which nonetheless drew a sharp sideways glance from Sir Robert.

'Where's Berkley now?' Sir Robert asked sharply. 'Not still at the hotel, I hope?'

I glanced at my watch 'No, he's on his way to the court. I arranged for the hotel to take him, hidden in their laundry van.'

Eyebrows twitched above those piercing blue eyes. 'Bit melodramatic, don't you think?'

'He'd be mobbed otherwise. I couldn't risk him arriving with his coat ripped and his shirt in tatters.'

'Dear God,' Sir Robert shuddered. 'Heaven save us from pop stars.'

I ignored the derision. Sir Robert enjoyed the smell of grease-paint more than he cared to admit. He hobnobbed with theatrical people at the Garrick Club and used the courtroom as his own special stage. There was a lot of the actor in Sir Robert, and no small love of the limelight. Which was why he had taken the case. With its all-star cast of international celebrities, the trial would command headlines. Sir

Robert's face would be on television news every night, his words would be on the front page of the papers every morning. For ten days or so he would be at the centre of public attention, no small attraction for a man with political ambitions, whose party was likely to regain power at the imminent General Election.

'Very well,' he said decisively, rising to his feet, 'let's go. But make no mistake. We're in for one hell of a fight.'

My pulse quickened. Olivia gave me an encouraging smile as she gathered her things, and a moment later I was holding the door for her as she swept out in the wake of Sir Robert. I followed them, through the outer office, down the steps and into the courtyard, and all the time my brain was struggling to take it all in. Had it really come to this? Even allowing for all that had happened, it was hard to believe we would all end in the High Court. Why? Where did things start to go wrong?

BOOK ONE

IT ALL STARTED IN GILL MARTIN'S PUB at the end of the fifties. Odd to look back to what we were then. London was different in those days; *we* were different, not only in the obvious ways of being younger and having less money, but we behaved differently from today's twenty-year-olds, or maybe I'm just getting too old to remember the turmoil of falling in love and its effect on some people. There was no mistaking its effect on Jack Webb.

Until then he and I had mostly used The Feathers for our pint after work. Sometimes we went to the Master Printer in Fleet Street, but we usually went to The Feathers because it was next to the office – until this particular day when we walked out into the thin light of late afternoon and Jack said, 'I'm sick of The Feathers. We always bump into the crowd from the office. Let's go somewhere else for a change.'

So of course I suggested the Master Printer, but Jack shook his head. 'That's just as bad. Old Tucker uses the place and you know what he's like.'

He brightened with a sudden idea, 'Tell you what. I met Bob Cooper last night at a pub in the Tottenham Court Road. I'll introduce you to that.'

I was reluctant. After eight hours of being cooped

up in the office, I was hot and crumpled enough without being crushed half to death on the tube. Admittedly Tottenham Court Road was on our way home, but it was at least thirty minutes away and my throat was rasping like sandpaper.

'Come on,' Jack encouraged, 'the beers are on me.'

That should have told me he was up to something. Without being mean, Jack was careful with his money. I suppose we both were, it was hard to come by in those days. Anyway, we went. A pub is a pub as far as I'm concerned, and I saw nothing immediately special. Gill Martin's was no more opulent than The Feathers. The patterned carpet was equally worn, chairs were covered with the same coloured vinyl, the sandwiches curled at the edges – just like those at The Feathers. Even the customers bore a resemblance; mainly men in business suits and conservative ties, although at The Feathers they were mostly solicitors or articled clerks, like Jack and me, whereas Tottenham Court Road was full of office equipment businesses, so the talk was about office planning instead of events in the Law Courts.

But if the difference in the venue was slight, there was no mistaking the difference in Jack. At The Feathers he always avoided the crush by grabbing a corner table, so as to bend my ear in relative privacy, whereas at Gill Martin's he shoved his way through the office equipment salesmen to get us stools at the bar. Surprised and intrigued I followed in his wake, and as I squeezed through the throng one of the office equipment crowd called – 'Give us a gin and tonic, Ann.' The girl behind the bar turned, and as she did so I caught the look on Jack's face. He was staring at her with such intensity that I shall never forget his expression. It told me at once why we were there. Van Gogh must have looked like that while painting his sunflowers or perhaps Turner's eyes shone with the same light when he worked on his seascapes. Certain things show when a man sees his version of beauty. Jack was like that. Almost awestruck. Clearing his throat, he managed to order a couple of beers, but it was perfectly clear why we were not at The Feathers.

My first good look at her came when she served our drinks. She had straight brown shoulder-length hair parted in the middle, an oval face, very dark eyes and black eyebrows. Oh, and good skin, smooth and flawless against a white blouse. Her eyes were exceptional, they were so black, with tiny specks of orange and gold. Not that many men were looking at her eyes, they were too busy admiring her figure. Don't get me wrong, I looked as well and liked what I saw. She had small rounded breasts and a slender waist. The counter spoiled my view of her legs but I guessed they were long by the grace of her movements. She was about five feet seven tall, and quietly enough dressed to look more like a secretary than a barmaid. When she served our beers, Jack said, 'Thanks, Ann. This is my pal, Tubby Mortlake.'

Ann said 'Hi, Tubby' and flashed me a smile before telling Jack to check his change. 'I'm still counting ten pennies to a shilling,' she said. 'This currency of yours is the end.'

I must have detected her American accent but can't really remember, after all it was a long time ago, and in any case Ann's accent was never very pronounced. People notice her clear diction rather than her accent. Anyway, that was how we met and after offering to buy her a drink, which she declined, Jack set about chatting her up, which was no easy matter. The bar was crowded, Ann was busy, and although friendly her manner was hardly encouraging. On top of which whenever Jack drew her into conversation, one of the office equipment salesmen joined in. Consequently little happened that first night. What I remember most is Jack on the way home. 'She's just so . . . so *different* from any girl I've known,' he kept saying. I held my tongue. It would have been churlish to point out that the girls Jack had known could be counted on one hand. Even so, there was no mistaking his interest. All the way back to the flat, he kept talking about Ann. 'Don't you think she's something?' he asked, more of himself than of me.

We shared a flat in Whitcombe Street in those days. Without being much of a place, it suited us – two bedrooms, a living room, bathroom and kitchen. In the living room bookshelves flanking the chimney-breast reflected our priorities: my side was full of Steinbeck and Maugham, with only the occasional law book, and Jack's side was one legal tome after another. They weren't just for show, either. He could quote chapter and verse when he chose. What he chose not to do – and this will surprise a lot of people – was to show an interest in music. I was the one to buy all the records. I don't pretend to be knowledgeable, but while I could spend an evening listening to Sinatra, Jack grew bored with that kind of music. 'It's old hat,' he would say, and I suppose he was right. After all, the end of the fifties was all about Elvis and rock and roll, and Jack knew a bit about that. He'd formed a skiffle group at school.

I'm not sure how good it was but I remember his enthusiasm. Then my father had a word with him about taking up the law and Jack packed it in. There were no half measures with Jack, and from then on his interest in music was virtually nil.

For recreation we watched cricket at Lord's and football at Highbury, according to the season. There was the pub on Saturday night and occasionally a party to go to. Neither of us had a steady girl. Jack was more interested in his career, and in my case my size was a deterrent to passion. I'd suffered with a weight problem since childhood, and that, together with my lack of inches, disqualified me from being the tall, dark, dashing type that women usually go for. Even Jack, taller and leaner, wouldn't have been mistaken for a film star. He became so well known later, with his picture in the papers so often, that it's interesting to recall him as he was then – all arms and legs, gangly, quick-moving, impatient and restless, a bit like a blond stick-insect. Beneath untidy straw-coloured hair, his eyes were grey and his nose slightly crooked. His expression was usually serious. 'Earnestly determined' is the best way I can sum him up – always trying to convince you of something and mostly succeeding.

So that's how we were then, Jack and me, when we were twenty-one and setting out in life. Articled clerks in my father's firm, sweating our way towards those magic qualifications. Jack was determined to qualify with flying colours and we all thought he would ... until that fateful visit to Gill Martin's pub. Nothing was quite the same after that.

*

Jack couldn't stop talking about her. It was Ann this and Ann that. We went back to Gill Martin's the next night and the night after that, until pubs like The Feathers began to dim in my memory. I would never have believed it of Jack. He'd got his whole life planned at that stage, he and my father between them. They'd always got on. Strange, really, because I grew up loathing my father. Jack was my friend and my father was my enemy, yet they were a mutual admiration society. They were like teacher and pupil together, indeed they *were* teacher and pupil when it came to the law.

My father was a brilliant lawyer, I'll say that for him. He could quote case histories the way some men say their prayers. Faced with a complicated legal problem, his eyes would light up. 'Where lies the heart of the matter?' he'd ask. Where indeed? According to my mother, my father's heart lay buried somewhere between Chancery Lane and the Law Courts, which was why she left him. 'God knows why I married him in the first place,' she confessed to me years later. She ran off when I was three, taking me with her, only for my father to prove his legal wizardry by gaining custody of me and denying her access for all of my schooldays.

I can understand my childhood from this distance. The scars have faded, but as a child, torn from my mother's arms by a father intent on keeping me as a way of punishing her, the experience left me hurt and bewildered. 'Why doesn't Daddy love Mummy?' I used to ask my aunt. That was Aunt Joan, my father's unmarried sister who moved in with us for a while. Not that she ever answered. 'Plenty of time for questions like that when you grow up,' was her usual sniffy response. Consequently my understanding of what happened was thwarted for a long time. Now the situation seems transparently clear. My mother was very young when she married, little more than eighteen, a pretty provincial girl working as a secretary to an ambitious lawyer in London. I can imagine her being dazzled by his drive and his brilliance. So she devoted herself to his needs, working late at the office and at weekends as well. Such loyalty earned a reward of sorts in that it led to a conventional marriage, whereupon she was given the role of gracing his table when he entertained clients. The marriage was still young when she became pregnant, a condition welcomed by her and resented by him as a hindrance to the upward sweep of his career. Such dramas are played out in thousands of households; even his demand that she have an abortion can't be uncommon. However, this time she refused to comply. The shock to my father must have been considerable. Everyone was expected to comply with his wishes. Thereafter the collapse of the marriage was predictable. Having lost a battle, my father remembered his defeat whenever he saw me, and since he hated defeats, he hated me too. And when my mother ran away from his harshness, choosing me over him, his anger knew no bounds. 'I'll see her in hell for creating such a spectacle,' he'd snarl, long before I understood what he was talking about, 'God damn her for making a fool out of me!' It was impressed on me early that no one, but *no one*, makes a fool of my father.

So I suffered a difficult childhood, developing into a large, awkward boy, lacking in confidence and a bit afraid of the world. Then I met Jack. Jack won a scholarship to our school. Ninety-eight percent of the boys were there because of fee-paying fathers, Jack was one of the two percent to represent the grand old school's experiment with democracy. It was Jack's working-class background and my weight problem which drew us together in the first place. Neither of us quite fitted in. His accent and my abysmal performances on the sports field marked us down as a couple of misfits. Not that we suffered for long. I helped Jack modify his speech, and he used his fists to persuade boys to call me Tubby (as opposed to less acceptable names), and by the end of the first term we'd survived most of the ragging. We'd also become friends. We spent holidays together, mostly at my house because Jack's lacked room for a spare card table let alone a spare bed. His father was a ticket clerk on South Harrow station, and the cramped semi-detached in which Jack had grown up would have fitted eight times into our house in Wimbledon. His eyes were like saucers the first time he saw it.

Taking Jack home was a big breakthrough for me. With Jack in the house, my father was less of a tyrant. He bullied me in secret of course, but never when Jack was around. Instead he contented himself by taunting me about my shortcomings. I could live with that, in fact I developed a perverse pleasure in disappointing my father. He had disappointed me by snatching me from my mother, and I was paying him back. I'm not sure I understood this at the time but it might explain some of our battles. For instance, as a boy, my father had captained the school cricket team. There was no likelihood of me doing that. He'd become president of the debating society, whereas I never saw the point of arguing for the sake of it. 'It will develop your powers of persuasion,' my father maintained, which simply made me resist all the more; having suffered his attempts to persuade me, I was determined not to inflict the same pressures on others.

Anyway, what with spending every other weekend at my place, Jack saw a lot of my father. Initially, he simply tried to please as a guest, and since he was impressed by the house, inevitably he was impressed by its owner. My father responded so readily that Jack became the son he might have wished for. After all, Jack actually did become president of the debating society. And so was born the never ending refrain, 'Why on earth can't you be more like Jack?'

Jack worried at first. I remember him asking, 'Don't you really care what he thinks of you?' Eventually I convinced him of my indifference. A lot had happened between my father and me that I kept secret even from Jack. Anyway, he had sense enough to realise he wasn't depriving me of anything by getting on with my father. And they did get on. Jack was fascinated by the law and my father had no other conversation. They talked for hours, or rather my father talked and Jack listened. 'Such an intelligent boy,' my father would say afterwards. It was his idea that Jack join Mortlake, Dingle and Barnes, which was a surprise in itself at the time. Ultra-selective about articled clerks, my father had refused to take even sons of his friends into the firm. However he wanted Jack. 'Be pleased to have you,' he told Jack, adding a conspiratoral whisper, 'and tell your father not to worry about fees.'

Of course, part of the scheme was designed to bring me to heel. At the time I had little idea of what I wanted from life. Subjects like psychology quite appealed to me. I'd once vaguely hankered to be an anthropologist until I explained it to my father. He went potty. 'That's exactly the sneaky sort of thing you would want,' he exploded, 'poking your nose into people's private affairs.' He lectured me with words like 'mucky' and 'underhand' before concluding as always with 'Why the devil can't you be more like Jack?'

In the end it was Jack who convinced me about the law. 'Once you're qualified,' he said, 'you can be any kind of lawyer you want.' I thought about that. Not for me the multi-million pound deals in which my father became involved. Jack found them exciting but they left me cold. If I was to take up the law, I planned to become a country solicitor. I saw myself living over the shop in a small provincial town. Downstairs a brass-plated door would open onto a cobbled street. A matronly receptionist would sit in the front office, with me in the back. That would suit me. That would make the law more personal than the big business law practised by my father. It would *mean* something to arrange a mortgage for Mrs Smith to enable her son to go to university, or to help old Farmer Brown with his Will. I'd get to know the people as individuals and that was important. It would have driven Jack mad, and he said so. Not that it mattered. He never interfered in my affairs and I never interfered with his. Meanwhile it would be fun to take a flat in the West End and begin our careers together. So when my father made his offer to Jack, I went along as part of the package. 'You can both join the firm at the same time,' said my father, as if I'd already agreed. 'I'll think about it,' I said in the graceless manner which characterised the war of attrition between us. We spent our lives trying to ensure that nothing either of us said gave the other an advantage. The outcome was usually a draw, as in the case of Jack and me joining Mortlake, Dingle and Barnes. No one was really the loser. 'Never lose to your father,' my mother had warned, 'or you'll end up with his foot on your neck.'

The rest is history. Jack and I became articled clerks and Jack soon began to make a name for himself. Long discussions about takeovers and mergers became the stuff of life to him. He'd burst into the room we shared at the office, hot with excitement: 'You'll never guess. Bloggs & Co have rejected the offer. By Christ, this takeover battle will hit the headlines.' He'd pace up and down, full of schemes for my father's big business clients. 'Listen to this,' he'd say, embarking on a description of reverse takeovers and asset-stripping that left my mind reeling. I was never required to say much, my function was merely to listen to him rehearse the arguments that later he would put to my father.

Jack's corporate side of the business was much too high powered for my taste. There was never any talk of us going into partnership when we qualified. What made us friends would make us unsuitable colleagues. So at the office, while Jack raced in the fast lane, I pottered along with conveyancing and locating lost relatives named in a Will. I was happy enough, and Jack was delirious when my father forecast a golden future for him at Mortlake, Dingle and Barnes. All of his energy was being poured into his career. And that was that state of his life when he met Ann Marion Elizabeth Church.

*

It took weeks to find out her full name. We kept going to Gill Martin's until it became our regular pub, even though Jack was making no headway at all. Anyone else would have retired from the contest but Jack always was very stubborn. 'I can't give up,' he said, 'there's just something about her.'

It was true. Ann looked like a starlet, lean and sleek, smart and glossy. She belonged not in the Tottenham Court Road, but up on a billboard, three times larger than life. Every man in the street could fantasise then. She wasn't Jack's kind of girl. He lacked that kind of money.

'How can you say that?' Jack snarled. 'You don't even know her. I'll tell you your trouble, Tubby. You're prejudiced. You think a girl who looks that good has got to be a mercenary little bitch. What kind of thinking is that?'

Back at the flat, he paced up and down. When baffled or worried he went on a route-march – up and down, up and down – it used to exhaust me to watch him.

'Well,' I said huffily, 'if you feel like that, go by yourself. No point in dragging me along every night.'

He slammed to a halt. 'Oh terrific! Thanks a million! You're a great help! If I go by myself it's obvious I'm chatting her up. You could at least give me some cover, ever think of that? It will seem like friendly interest if we're both there. We can draw her into general conversation.'

I was thinking about that when Jack moderated his tone. 'Besides,' he coaxed, 'people talk to you. They've only got to know you five minutes and they tell you their life story. Come on, Tubby, be a pal.'

That was Jack; first a play on my vanity, then an

appeal to our friendship. He had a way of overcoming objections. So we persevered with our visits to Gill Martin's.

The pub had two bars, a small one at the front, tended by Ann, and a larger one behind, presided over by Gill Martin himself. We also discovered that most of the regulars left at just after seven. Like many pubs in the West End, Gill Martin's was mostly patronised by office workers who used it for lunch and a drink after work. From seven thirty onwards the only customers in the front bar were courting couples, who in any case preferred to sit by themselves, leaving Jack and me alone at the counter.

Inevitably our visits attracted the attention of Gill Martin. He was about forty then, with a mass of black hair and deep-set watchful blue eyes. He soon took our measure. It was obvious that we only went into his pub to see Ann. Not that he minded. 'You help pay the bills,' he said cheerfully.

Jack never allowed him to be too condescending. 'Time you bought us a pint,' he would say. 'Regulars like us should be encouraged.'

Gill did stand us a pint now and then. The snag was he always stayed talking when we wanted him to leave us alone with Ann. Even so, he was really no problem. His main grievance in life was that having made his real money at lunch time he'd have shut at eight if he could, but the licensing laws compelled him to stay open. So he grumbled a lot, while for the most part remaining in the back bar with his cronies.

It took time to get to know Ann, several weeks actually. The first problem was that we couldn't really start until the office equipment crowd had left. 'The object,' Jack told me, 'is for *me* to get to know her, not them.' So he fidgeted on his stool, scowling, glancing at his watch, waiting for, *willing* the office equipment salesmen to go. Finally they drifted off and from eight until closing time became the most important part of Jack's day.

Even then, drawing Ann out wasn't easy. Although she was willing to pass the time, we were never encouraged, and her radiant smile froze at personal questions. Anyone less determined than Jack would have taken the hint. 'Jack,' I pleaded one night on the way home, 'this is embarrassing. The girl doesn't want to know.'

'Give it time,' was his only response.

I thought he was mad. Ann had been chatted up by experts. She could have set exams on the subject. I bet the last time she heard such a corny approach was when she was in junior high. Her accent was not very strong and in those days I expected all Americans to talk like Texans. Ann's Americanisms were mostly confined to expressions like 'junior high' and 'Crap'. The first 'Crap', made Jack choke on his beer. Girls didn't say things like that at the end of the fifties. English girls didn't, *nice* girls didn't, feminine girls didn't. Yet Ann was the most feminine girl I ever saw. And she was smart. Smart as in intelligent and prickly as in defensive, except defensive meant aggressive in her case. I remember one night, she looked at Jack and said, 'Lawyer, huh? Is that what you're training to be?'

'Right,' said Jack, pleased to have captured her interest.

'I don't like lawyers. They're crooks.'

Jack managed a smile. 'In films, perhaps, but in real life –'

'They're fun-loving guys who pick girls up in bars,' she interrupted. Her eyes slid over Jack, half amused, half contemptuous.

He kept his smile, although by now it was weaker. 'We only want to talk,' he said plaintively.

'So talk.'

Jack stalled. 'Ah, well . . . it would help to know your interests.'

'Try me. You start and I'll join in the chorus.'

Poor Jack. When he was slow to respond, Ann actually snorted. 'I know what you're thinking. Empty headed, all beauty, no brains. Right? Well, you're wrong. If it helps, I graduated with straight A's. Every subject. Okay?'

'Impressive,' said Jack.

That did it. Colour slid up her throat, bringing a blush to her cheeks. She looked gorgeous but that wasn't the point. 'Don't be so condescending,' she said in a voice colder than frost. 'It's so bad mannered, so . . . so *British!*'

See what I mean about aggressive? Afterwards Jack bawled me out. 'You were a fat lot of help,' he complained. The truth was I'd been frightened to speak. 'Give up,' I pleaded.

I was wasting my breath. Jack can be single minded. I know my opinion. I thought that the only thing to move Ann was a mink coat, a diamond brooch or cash paid into her bank. I was wrong, but that's what I thought at the time. Meanwhile I was witnessing the biggest clash since the irresistible force met the immovable object.

The next night, Jack bought flowers. I refused to

go with him. He talked me round in the end, but I insisted we delay our arrival until the office equipment crowd had left. At seven forty-five, we waltzed into Tottenham Court Road with Jack carrying this huge bouquet. 'She'll ram it down your throat,' I said fearfully, 'you should have bought chocolates.'

But I was wrong. Ann seemed to have trouble keeping a straight face.

'I bought you some flowers,' Jack said needlessly, handing them over.

She stared at him and shook her head in disbelief. Even so, there was a distinct softening in her expression. 'Well,' she said grudgingly, 'you sure are persistent.' Then she buried her face in the flowers, just as Gill came through from the other bar. 'My word,' said Gill. 'They're nice.'

Suddenly Ann's voice changed. She started talking like a Southern Belle, sounding like Vivien Leigh in *Gone with the Wind*. 'Aren't they the loveliest flowers you ever did see? Mah gentleman friend brought them. You know, the one who comes heah to talk.'

A big fat grin spread over Gill's face. 'Nice,' he repeated.

Ann turned to me. 'Oh, mah, I clean forgot. Where are mah manners? I do declare in mah excitement . . . I mean, Tubby, dear, did you have a hand in this beautiful gift?'

She fluttered her eyelashes, making me swallow my words. 'Um, no,' I mumbled. 'Er, Jack bought the flowers.'

'And don't tell me,' she purred. 'You bought me diamonds?'

I emitted a nervous, high pitched giggle.

Plucking a carnation from the bouquet, she threaded it behind her ear. 'Don't I excite you?' she asked, striking a pose. Her gaze scorched my face. With a moue of disappointment, she shrugged. 'Ah well,' she sighed. 'Maybe it's for the best. I'm all wrong for you. You'd only get hurt.'

I answered with a weak shake of my head.

Clutching the bouquet, Ann slipped out from behind the bar and stood before Jack. A puzzled look came into her eyes. 'As for you,' she said softly, 'maybe you're not such a creep. A girl likes to be chased. It's good for morale. So thank you.' Then she kissed his cheek and carried the flowers away to put them in water.

That was the breakthrough. A corny thing like flowers. No mink coat, no diamonds. Nine roses, nine carnations and a lot of green fern.

I remember being baffled by contradictions. Jack was right when he said – 'Admit it, Tubby, she's just so totally different.' She was; sexy, desirable, intelligent, educated. Younger than us by only a few months, yet I sensed she had seen a lot more of life.

I changed my mind about her a dozen times the following week. Her good looks unnerved me; I was inexperienced with girls anyway and she made me feel clumsy. My fatness became gross. And when she clowned around, I never knew how to react. My responses were slow, my jokes laboured. I could never make out when she was sending me up.

Even so, the more I got to know her, the more I liked her. I forgot my shyness and became immersed in her story. We gleaned a bit more every night. She'd grown up in New York, with parents who were both teachers. Apart from giving her a solid education,

33

especially in music, they'd imbued her with their own liberal views. Ann grew up during what became known as 'the McCarthy era'. I suppose Jack and I knew something about it from reading the papers, but since we paid no heed to politics we never questioned how McCarthyism affected ordinary people.

'It oppressed them,' said Ann flatly. 'McCarthyism was half way to Fascism. It had to be stopped.'

When she talked about politics her smile faded and such an intense look darkened her eyes that hairs stood up on the back of my neck. She would have made a marvellous barrister. I could picture her in court. Juries would melt under the lamps of her eyes, men would sit beguiled by the sound of her voice. She was never strident. On the contrary her voice was usually light and well modulated. Only when she talked of 'justice' and 'the rights of ordinary people' did her words grow husky with passion. I think I guessed her general good humour masked a tempestuous nature. She kept it under control, as if passion were a fierce dog to be kept chained for fear of wounds it might inflict, but I swear I saw it in her even then. Just as I sensed her courage, a quality inherited from parents who'd spent their lives fighting for their beliefs. For instance they organised petitions to Congress when McCarthy's anti-Communist zeal led to loyalty oaths being introduced into schools. Even students were compelled to sign in order to graduate. Ann signed, she had no option, but beneath her signature she wrote 'under protest'.

When she told us about it, I remember her saying – 'I was taught the value of our Bill of Rights and the Constitution. To have to sign an oath of loyalty to God and Country was against my civil rights.'

She was strong on civil rights. As a fifteen year old she was picketing Woolworth's, protesting about their policy of segregating blacks and whites at their lunch counters.

'It was no big deal in New York,' she admitted. 'Protestors in the South were putting their lives on the line.'

I'm not sure what her stories did to Jack, but they sent a shiver of excitement up my spine. I could imagine this bunch of idealistic kids wanting to set the world to rights. That was what the law should be about, not the multimillion-pound deals in which my father was involved. The law should make the world a better place. And a safer place. Ann's parents were involved in a organisation called SANE – for a 'sane' nuclear policy – and Ann spent many an evening collecting signatures on petitions to Ban the Bomb.

On Sundays, she and her friends would congregate in Washington Square Park to listen to various musicians. Ann mentioned a few, people like Woody Guthrie and Pete Seeger. I'd heard of some but most were new to me. She was a mine of information about music. You name it; opera, classical, jazz, blues, folk music, and she would discuss it like an expert. I was very impressed.

When she was seventeen her parents were killed in a car crash. Even three years later there was no disguising her sense of loss. She was an only child and their deaths had left her devastated. She went to live with relatives in Denver for a while, but my impression was that the experience was an unhappy one. She drifted back to New York, and stayed with various friends whose passion was to go to hootenannies and folk concerts at Carnegie Hall and such places. Over a period she met any number of the folk crowd – Ewan MacColl, Odetta and countless others. A friend took her to Gerde's Folk City where she met Judy Collins and Peter Yarrow (who later became part of Peter, Paul and Mary).

Somewhere along the line she had a love affair. Not that she said so, but she admitted to seeing a lot of a particular someone. At the time I had no idea of what happened, but when the affair ended the loss of her parents hit her harder than ever.

'I grew up in New York,' she said. 'There's a million people I know but sometimes it's the loneliest place in the world.'

So she came to London. Mary Martin, Gill's wife, was Ann's cousin. Mary wrote to New York suggesting the visit, and Ann had been in London exactly two weeks when Jack walked into the pub and set eyes on her for the first time.

Ann's name popped out whenever Jack opened his mouth. What was on his mind was never far from his lips.

'What I don't understand,' he scowled, 'is what she's got against lawyers. You know what she said last night? She even distrusts men who wear suits.'

As if I needed to be told what Ann thought about lawyers. I'd been in Gill Martin's when she said it.

'It wasn't personal,' I pointed out, reaching for the marmalade. 'She meant she didn't like the way America is dominated by lawyers.'

'Because lawyers are leeches. They grow fat from other people's misfortunes. They take more from

36

society than they put into it,' said Jack, quoting Ann word for word.

'Maybe she's right,' I said, thinking of my father.

Frowning hard, Jack rinsed two cups under the tap and set them down next to the teapot. We were at breakfast; tea and toast consumed while getting ready for the office. The kitchen resembled a rubbish tip, with the pots and pans used for last night's spaghetti bolognaise heaped on a pile of plates in the sink. Neither Jack nor I was house proud, but the squalor had been steadily worsening since we had started to spend our evenings at Gill Martin's.

'We'd better have a blitz on Saturday,' I said, 'otherwise we'll be reported as a health hazard.'

Jack might have not heard for all the notice he took. In stocking feet, he polished his shoes while waiting for the tea to brew. 'You don't think she's a Communist?' he asked, his face twitching anxiously. 'I mean it would explain all this Ban the Bomb stuff she goes on about.'

I said, 'The Reverend Donald Soper favours Banning the Bomb. He's not a communist.'

Jack looked doubtful, as if wishing for more concrete evidence. 'The problem,' he said, stepping into his shoes, 'is I don't think I'm getting anywhere with her.'

Neither did I but it would have been tactless to say so. Of course, progress of a sort had been made. I think Ann even looked forward to our visits. We were company for her from eight o'clock every evening, the courting couples were engrossed with themselves and Ann would have been bored to tears without us. But as for *getting anywhere* Jack could forget it. To my mind, he and Ann cancelled each other out. They'd never make a couple. He was half way to becoming a lawyer. She called lawyers parasites. Jack had become as conservative as my father; Ann was liberal to the core. His career was in London, she would return to New York. And although he was bowled over by her, she did nothing to encourage his further attentions. Since the episode with the flowers, she had unbent a good deal, enough to be charming and gracious . . . but she was nice to me, too.

'You don't think I stand a chance, do you?' he asked suddenly, a note of bitterness in his voice.

I chewed my toast, wondering how to respond. His impassioned outbursts every evening were a trial, I could do without them first thing in the morning. Finally I said, 'Why not ask her out? Take her to the pictures or something.'

'Don't be a bloody fool,' he snapped.

He was in a foul mood. He banged the teapot down with almost enough force to break it. Then he turned to me and I saw the desperation in his eyes. 'She's bound to say no if I ask her out now and if she does it will take weeks, possibly months for me to change her mind. I haven't got months. She goes back to New York at the end of August.'

When I remained silent he pulled a chair out from the table and sat down. 'What do you honestly think of her?' he asked, staring into my face as if I were the source of all wisdom.

'I think she's very nice.'

'Nice!' he exploded. 'For Christ's sake! What sort of word is nice? Breakfast in bed is *nice*, waking up with the sun in your eyes is *nice*. I'm talking about a girl, flesh and blood, a human being who breathes and laughs and dreams and . . .' Words failed him for a moment. Clamping his mouth shut, he regarded me with a look of disgust. Then he began to coax, 'Come on, Tubby. You're the amateur psychologist. You've heard her story. What makes her tick? Tell me about her.'

I would have preferred to read the paper, to drink my tea in silence, to gather myself for the journey into the office. I'm not a morning person. I swear my brain doesn't function until eleven. But Jack was flailing me with words, using them like whips to sting me into a reaction. 'You can't just say she's *nice*!' he said hotly. 'You can say she's beautiful, desirable, gorgeous, anything you bloody well like, but "nice" doesn't even begin to tell me what you think.'

I had to say something. If I hadn't, he'd have grabbed my lapels, and given me a good shaking. 'Very well,' I began uncertainly, 'she's all that you say, but right now I think she's been badly hurt and needs time to recover. That's why she's in London.'

'Go on,' he said, still staring at me.

There wasn't much I could add. Picturing the shadows which sometimes haunted Ann's eyes, I wondered if she mourned most for her dead parents or her lost lover. Eventually I said, 'She's been bruised by life. New York's full of painful memories, so she's come here until they fade. Meanwhile, she's sort of holding the world at arm's length, keeping free of involvements.'

'Ah!' The scowl left Jack's face for the first time that morning. 'You could be right about that. That could explain why I'm not getting anywhere.'

It was my turn to stare. The last thing I meant was to be encouraging.

'In fact you're exactly right,' he said, brightening. 'I've been rushing things. But you can't blame me for being impatient, can you?'

I choked into my tea. I doubt Ann knew the colour of his eyes. She wouldn't have missed us if we'd never set foot in Gill Martin's again.

'Oh well,' said Jack, with sudden cheerfulness. 'I'll just have to think of something. After all, faint heart never won fair lady.'

'What I like about Jack,' my father used to say, 'is the way he tackles problems. He's like a terrier with a rat. He grabs them by the throat and shakes them to death.'

I had visions of Jack charging into Gill Martin's and dragging Ann kicking and screaming into the Tottenham Court Road. Stupid really, because he wouldn't have raised a finger against her. On the other hand, the problem she posed tormented him. All the way into the office Jack was congratulating me on my diagnosis. I cursed myself for not remaining silent over breakfast. 'Of course, you're right,' he said. 'I just need to give her more time. Then a moment later his brow furrowed and I knew what he was thinking: time was against him: in three months Ann would return to New York and he would lose her forever.

I began to rack my brains for alternatives. If Jack wanted a girl, there were plenty about. Several secretaries in our office would have been interested, if not because of Jack's looks then because of his reputation. Everyone at Mortlake, Dingle and Barnes said he had a glorious future. According to my father,

Jack was 'a young man destined to succeed'. Alternatively Jack could choose from the daughters of his parents' neighbours in South Harrow. There were several pretty girls among them. Jack's mother had told me, as mothers will, that — 'our Jack could have the pick of them if he wanted. They're no end impressed about him becoming a lawyer.'

It was Jack's bad luck to pick a girl who thought lawyers were morons.

Not that I needed to worry. By lunch time he'd come up with a scheme, exactly as he would if a client had brought him a problem. The first I heard about it was over sandwiches and coffee. 'Ada,' he announced. 'That's the answer.'

As usual, we were at our desks, munching the corned beef on rye that Jack had collected from the delicatessen on the corner. The *Financial Times* lay open in front of him and I imagined he was referring to something in that. I was half-way through a new Alistair MacLean, and would have preferred to remain with my book, but Jack was insistent that I listen. 'Ada,' he repeated with conviction.

I hadn't the faintest idea what he was talking about. 'All right,' I sighed wearily. 'Who's Ada?'

'Not a person, you idiot. Initials. A.I.D.A.'

Glancing at the *Financial Times*, I took a guess. 'American Industrial Development Authority?'

He threw up his hands. 'Attention. Interest. Desire. Action. It's what they teach salesmen. It's also used as a debating technique. That's where I came across it. You gain attention, develop interest, stimulate desire, and create action.'

He grew impatient with my blank expression. 'With Ann. That's what I've got to do. Gain Attention. Develop Interest. Stimulate Desire. Create Action.'

In the Alistair MacLean book the ship was sinking, men were drowning, all was danger and excitement . . . But there was no stopping Jack.

'What are her interests?' he asked and answered before I could open my mouth. 'Music and politics, right? I can't capture her attention with politics because I don't know enough. But music is something I do know about.'

'Such as?' I asked in surprise.

'Rock and roll. Skiffle. I know about them. Country and Western. Ann likes that sort of music.'

To my certain knowledge, since giving up the school skiffle group, Jack hadn't so much as whistled.

Pulling his chair back, he began to pace up and down, a sure sign that he was about to embark upon a major dissertation. Any doubts were removed by the way he kept stopping in front of me and wagging a finger. I remember shuddering and thinking how like my father he was becoming; I half expected the words, 'Where lies the heart of the matter?' to fall from his lips. Instead he said, 'The first priority is to grab attention, and that's difficult in the pub. There's always so many people about.'

'I'll stay away,' I offered helpfully.

'No, no. You're a help. She likes talking to you. Besides, I dry up at times and you fill in the awkward pauses.'

'Thanks very much.'

'The point is, I've only got twelve weeks, so I've divided them up. Three weeks to Gain Attention, three to Develop Interest, three to Stimulate Desire, and three to Get Action.'

It's hard to believe he was serious, but I can still see his face, and the worry in his eyes contradicted by the determined set of his jaw, only helped my understanding. He was quite desperate. The thought of Ann going away and the possibility of not seeing her again was tearing him apart. It was in this mood that he had conceived his scatterbrained plan.

I said, 'What about the flowers? What about the last couple of weeks? I'd have thought you'd grabbed her attention by now. We've been in to see her every night.'

He shook his head. 'All we've done is get to know her. AIDA is a positive plan.'

By now, of course, he was pacing up and down. 'It would be easier if she didn't live at Gill Martin's,' he said. 'We could walk her home when the pub closed.'

'What's this *we*? Why bring me into it all the time? Why not just you? I told you, ask her out.'

'I can't risk it. You know I can't. You said so this morning. She's feeling vulnerable after the loss of her parents. She's holding the world at bay. Her mood is all wrong for a serious relationship.'

I stared at him while trying to remember exactly what I had said. Jack had changed the emphasis somehow.

He scowled. 'If I ask her out now, she'll back away, but if she comes out with us, if we went out as friends, that would be different.'

Even as I wondered who was the amateur psychologist, him or me, I began to see what he meant. Where Ann would shy away from a date, she might spend an evening with friends. Jack was right, there was a difference. I also noted that he blamed her mood exclusively on the loss of her parents, avoiding the reference to her love affair. He simply couldn't contemplate the idea of her with another man.

'What I suggest,' he continued, 'is that we tell her about the music at The Nucleus.'

'The where?'

'It's a club. Well . . .' pausing he added a qualification. 'Not a proper club. More a coffee bar, really. All the musicians use it. They go there after playing various gigs. They drift in, two or three at a time, all with their instruments, and sort of . . . well, extemporise I suppose you'd call it.' Embarrassed by my stare, he concluded with a burst of enthusiasm, 'They make some fabulous sounds.'

I'd never heard of the place and was quite sure Jack hadn't been there. 'Who have you been talking to?' I asked in astonishment.

He answered with a shamefaced look, 'I phoned a few people this morning. Remember Mike Osborne? He was in the skiffle group . . .'

Listening to him rattle off various names, I realised he'd spent the morning on the phone. He'd also been out of our room for a couple of hours, but that wasn't unusual, my father was always sending him to Companies House to look up lists of shareholders and things. 'Jack never fails to ferret out the facts,' my father would boast. Obviously Jack had been putting his ferreting skills to other uses.

He saw the look on my face. 'Sorry Tubby, I just can't get her out of my mind.'

God knows why he apologised. Certainly I don't. I suspect poor old Jack was as surprised as I was. The law was his life. He loved every musty corner of Companies House. It was his favourite place after the office. Admitting Ann was on his mind day and night, hearing himself say it, had come as a shock. He was ashamed of what he saw as a weakness.

To cover his embarrassment, he hurried on, 'I got the names of a few other places we might try. They all go on until the early hours. I thought . . .' he fidgeted for the right words, 'well, if we took Ann there a couple of nights a week –'

'You'd gain her attention,' I said spitefully.

For some reason, Jack's silly AIDA scheme had got to me. Perhaps I felt I was being used or perhaps I was jealous? After all, I had as much right as him to chase Ann, except my weight and girth, to say nothing of my temperament, inhibited me. I was shy and timid in those days and if truth is known, a little in awe of Ann. Her sharp brain and good looks were a bit overpowering. Even so, two weeks of propping up Gill's front bar had shored up my fragile self-confidence and given me a chance to get to know her. Listening to her talk about politics and music had been an education. I'd glimpsed the person behind the megawatt smile. I liked her, and Jack was my best friend, which was why I worried that one or both of them would be hurt by Jack's crazy scheme.

'Jack,' I said, 'this is madness. It's become an obsession.'

He actually blushed. 'I need your help, that's all,' he said, sounding totally wretched. Standing in front of my desk, the flush on his face deepened as a pained, haunted look came into his eyes. 'I don't want her to go back to New York,' he said, 'I want her to stay here. I think I want to marry her.'

*

45

Believe it or not, the first part of Jack's cockeyed scheme worked like a charm. Ann was growing bored working at Gill Martin's. Helping in the bar neither stimulated her nor left her exhausted. And apart from us she had little company. Gill's wife was a semi-invalid who rarely emerged from upstairs, and Gill himself was a home-loving man who seldom went out. They were fond of Ann in the way childless couples often are of young people, but having invited her to stay were at a loss to know what to do with her. So Jack's timing was right. 'We're going to The Nucleus for an hour later,' he said with feigned casualness as we settled ourselves at the bar that evening. 'Want to come?'

Ann's dark eyes widened as he explained that The Nucleus was a coffee bar where real musicians could be heard.

'You're kidding?' she said. 'Terrific.'

'So you'll come?' Jack asked with an eagerness which betrayed him.

Ann looked at me. There was real warmth in her eyes, tiny flecks of orange and gold floating in the deep blackness. 'You going too?'

'Yes.'

'Okay,' she said, nodding briskly. 'Sounds good. I'll ask Gill.'

Which, as if on cue, was Gill's moment to emerge from the back bar. 'Ask me what?'

Jack took over. Recovering from a faltering start, he was really smooth. His description of The Nucleus made it sound like a village hall decked out for a whist drive. 'A coffee bar?' Gill echoed. 'That's all it is?'

'That's all,' said Jack.

46

'Takes all sorts,' Gill shrugged. 'I'd rather have a pint any day.'

Despite his grumbling, he was a decent sort for after noting how few customers remained in the bar, he said to Ann, 'Give it until eight o'clock, then knock off. I can manage from then.'

'Sure?' Ann asked, looking pleased.

'Sure, I'm sure,' he answered cheerfully, 'it's the way I ran things before. I just pop out now and then to keep an eye on things after eight.'

Accepting Ann's quick peck on the cheek, he turned to us. 'Look after her properly now,' he instructed sternly, wagging a finger. He really did care for her, which was touching. I think he was relieved that Ann had fallen in with us and not the office equipment crowd. 'Fast lot, those salesmen,' he whispered to Ann while glancing slyly at me. 'You'll be safe with Tubby. If he tries anything, you can always run 'cos he'll never catch you.' He laughed, and twinkled his blue eyes as if to say he meant no offence.

So it was a good humoured Gill who delivered Ann into our hands, and an hour later we paid our first visit to The Nucleus. Actually Jack had called there at lunch time to make sure he could find the place. It also meant he could say he'd been there before. 'Only once,' he admitted to Ann, 'but I think you'll find it amusing.'

Amusing wouldn't have been my word. Loud, vibrant, exciting were all better descriptions. It was in a cellar. A flight of stone steps led down to a dimly lit cavern, furnished with rickety tables and uncomfortable chairs. The heat enveloped you as you descended and the music slammed you full in the face.

'Hey man, I don't believe this,' Ann shouted at me. 'What you got here is home.' She rolled her eyes and crinkled her nose to express her delight. Then, in an accent that made her sound totally English, she laughed, 'Do you come here often?'

I did after that. We went the next night and again the night after that. Then on Friday we tried two similar places, Gibson's Parlour and the Green Door. On the Saturday night we went to the Hole in the Wall. Aptly named, for that's all most of them were . . . holes in the wall, dimly lit steps leading to cellars full of music and smoke. Few were licensed to sell alcohol; most served very bad coffee that some customers spiked with whisky they brought with them. Not that people went there to drink. They went for the music and to meet kindred spirits. Audiences were musicians; professionals, amateurs, black, white, some with jobs, most searching for one, all mixed up with music buffs and a few daring young things out for an adventurous evening. The type of music depended upon who had the floor; mostly it was jazz, rhythm and blues, or rock – performed at a volume that shook the walls and vibrated through the soles of your shoes. Few people clapped when someone finished playing, the place was too sophisticated for that, and so hot that on our first night a girl fainted and had to be passed up through a grille to the pavement outside. You never listened to that music, you absorbed it. Waves of sound penetrated your being. You basked in it as in the rays of the sun.

Certainly Ann basked in it. Between numbers she talked to musicians. 'Great sound. Reminded me of Muddy Waters. You ever play his stuff?' She plunged right in, full of questions, comments, opinions. I hadn't heard of a tenth of the people she mentioned. Frankly I was a little anxious at first. This was a London new to me. I'd walked past some of these places in the daylight, never suspecting that by night the tiny cellars under my feet would be heaving with people. The Green Door, for instance, was scarcely larger than a decent sized living room. People were practically on top of each other, and talked to one another shouting to make themselves heard. You couldn't move for fear of knocking an instrument case. For me it was an education. For Ann it was home from home. I remember her dark eyes shining with excitement, 'Nobody told me London was like this. You got a great scene here. Some real talent.'

When we next went to the Green Door, the following Tuesday, everyone seemed to know Ann. I'd been nervous about her remarks, thinking they might be resented, but not a bit of it. A seven-foot West Indian slumped down next to her, 'Hey, you bin making sense ever since you opened your mouth. Where's a Chick like you get into our kind of music?'

That's why they took to her – that and her looks – she so obviously knew what she was talking about. By the time we left she had them mesmerised with tales of musicians she knew in the States.

The Green Door was just round the corner from our flat. In fact we had to pass our front door to get back to Gill's, so that night we invited Ann in for a plate of my special spaghetti bolognaise. As usual, the place looked like a rubbish dump but she appeared not to notice. We'd collected a couple of bottles of Chianti on the way back, and Jack was plying her with wine. He'd hit his stride by then and was talking twenty to the dozen. 'How come you're not a singer?' he wanted to know.

'You're kidding,' she giggled. 'I even sound bad in the shower.'

It felt strange to see a girl in the flat. With all the talk going on you'd have thought Jack and I entertained every night – two men about town. The truth was that Ann was the first girl to cross the threshold. We spent little time in the place, it was where we slept, ate and occasionally studied our law books. I wouldn't even have invited Ann that night but Jack had forced the issue. 'Come back for some spaghetti,' he'd said. 'Tubby will serve you his special.'

It wasn't bad. After she'd eaten, Ann pushed her chair back from the table. 'Phew,' she sighed. 'That was great, Tubby, but another meal like that and I'll have a figure like yours.' She laughed a warm, musical, kind laugh that filled me with pleasure.

'Going to the Green Door again tomorrow?' she asked.

'Sure,' said Jack.

'Okay then,' she said briskly, 'so how much do I owe you guys?'

Jack began to protest, but Ann interrupted, 'No way. Come on, you're not paying all the time. It puts me under an obligation and that's a definite no no.'

But Jack insisted, rather stuffily, saying she was our guest whether in our humble abode (he actually said 'humble abode'), or whether at the Green Door.

Ann listened, her dark eyes raking his face, cool amusement in her expression. 'Okay,' she said with the barest hint of a shrug. 'I'll call round here at about eight then, okay?'

'Fine,' we chorused, after which Jack walked her home and I washed up the dinner things. He was back before I finished and as it was late we went directly to bed.

Ann got her way in the end. The next evening, she arrived at the flat bearing a basket of shopping. 'I'm fixing dinner,' she announced, and refused to take no for an answer. Not that we argued for long. Jack's cooking was never up to much and we were both pretty tired of my spaghetti bolognaise. Ann served us a mouth-watering meal, and after that it became a regular occurrence for her to cook and eat at our place before we went out for the evening. It was her way of balancing the books.

All this happened amazingly quickly; I'm describing a period of only two or three weeks. During this time I found myself liking Ann more and more. She really was very different, what with her looks and her knowledge of music and being American. We were impressed by most things American in those days – it was a legacy of the war. America had emerged as the richest nation on earth, while Britain was still make do and mend. America was the capital of new thinking and some of their new ideas were coming our way, transmitted by newspapers and films. Every second craze originated in America – things like hula-hoops, hand-painted tiles and neon coloured socks that shone in the dark. Most lasting of all were American jeans. Ann wore the first pair I ever saw. Until then I'd only seen them on the cinema screen. They were much more exciting on Ann. She had the sauciest bottom I ever saw; men broke their necks when she walked down Tottenham Court Road. Odd really, because none of her movements were exaggerated. I suppose sweater and jeans simply showed off the youthful lines of her body, making old men feel young again and imbuing young men with a need to impress.

Which brings me to Jack. He was three people at once for a while. There was the secret Jack, the Jack he showed me, and the Jack he showed Ann. They were all different. The secret Jack was only visible when he thought no one was looking. I caught glimpses now and then, most often at the Green Door when Ann was lost in the music and unaware of Jack as he watched her. It's hard to describe the look on his face. To call it lust is to over-simplify, although lust was certainly part of it – the parted lips, the hot eyes, the tense expression spoke volumes. You sensed his hunger. It was as much as he could do to stop himself reaching over to touch her. He was crazy about her.

The second Jack, the one he showed me, was only too visible. His attitude to our flat changed completely. Until then we had been equally casual about housework. Everything changed with the coming of Ann. 'Do you think,' he'd scowl at me, 'you could clean the bath properly after you use it?' He was always complaining, 'Will you stop leaving dirty socks all over the place.' Frankly he became a pain in the arse and we had some heated exchanges.

The third Jack, the one he showed Ann, amazed me at times. After she insisted upon paying her way, his attitude became one of pretended indifference. He drew back, as if afraid of suffering another rebuff, and was very casual towards her. For instance he never helped in the kitchen. If Ann had trouble finding something, a pot or a pan, he'd call out, 'It's there somewhere', and go back to reading the paper. I'd be on my feet, helping to find it, after all it was our supper she was cooking, but Jack never stirred. He was the same about seeing her home. Since the Green Door was so close, Ann often came back at the end of the evening. It posed a dilemma for Jack. He was afraid to insist on walking her home, so we took it in turns. Some nights he even pretended to be tired – 'I'll leave you to see Ann home, Tubby,' he'd yawn, 'I'm off to bed.' Not that he ever went to bed. He was always waiting up when I returned. I suspect he actually timed me. 'Did she say anything about me?' was always his first question.

Even looking back from this distance, it was an absurd situation. On the face of it, we were just good friends, all three of us. In fact I was doing very well from the arrangement. I enjoyed Ann's company. Thanks to her I ate better and more regular meals; thanks to her contempt for lawyers Jack avoided praising my father's wheeling and dealing when she was around, but I failed to see what it was doing for Jack. After four weeks my opinion remained as at the outset. Jack was on a hiding to nothing. True, Ann obviously liked him, but she had become my friend as well. She spent time with us, not Jack by himself. And she still planned to return to America. 'I'll find a new job,' she said, 'and start a new life.' When she talked of such things, Jack turned away. Ann never saw the bleak look in his eye, but I did, and it worried me.

'I've still got seven weeks,' Jack told me at the beginning of June. 'Anything can happen in seven weeks.'

By now he was investing every ounce of energy in his idiotic AIDA scheme. He was a different man at the office. Where once he had been alert and attentive, he was now preoccupied and pensive. Such a change was bound to be noticed. It was only a matter of time before my father demanded an explanation. Meanwhile Jack's thoughts were so concentrated on Ann that we were taking her to the Green Door or the Two 'I's five nights a week. In fact we were at the Green Door that Saturday night and Jack couldn't make himself heard. He and Ann were talking to Mike Carson, a young guitarist, and they were having trouble communicating above the blast of the music. 'Tell you what,' Jack bellowed, 'come back to our place.'

Which was where we went – Jack, Ann and me, Mike Carson, his brother Ray, Ossie Davidson and Janie Marsden. They played together in a group called The Graduates and we all liked their music. Janie was great. She was blonde and bouncy with a real love of life. Her obvious joy of singing lifted your spirits. Clearly she was also a lover of Mike Carson because they sat holding hands.

'Isn't this terrific?' Janie enthused, looking round at the flat. 'Your own pad in the West End.'

But it wasn't the flat that had drawn them, it was Ann. At the Green Door, questions had poured from Mike's lips when she mentioned knowing Bob Dylan. Mike was enormously impressed. 'You mean you actually know Pete Seeger *as well*? Like he's a friend? Jesus Christ!'

It turned into a good evening. The conversation went on until late, and it was all about music. I recall Janie blushing and laughing when she talked about

The Graduates. I think she was a bit in awe of Ann, but she answered her questions. Apparently all of The Graduates came from Bristol. They'd been to school together, and when the skiffle craze boomed they'd formed a group much in the way lots of kids did at the time. When Janie left school, she became an apprentice hairdresser. She and Mike were going out by then, and they persuaded Ossie and Ray to keep the band together. They did well to begin with, winning talent contests and such like, which encouraged them to throw up their jobs and become full-time musicians. It was Ossie's task to get them bookings, and when local work proved insufficient they bought a second hand van to travel further afield. London drew them like moths to a flame and they'd been trying to make the grade for a year. Talking to us, Janie fairly bubbled with enthusiasm; even so I sensed we were only hearing part of the story, especially when she finished, with a brave little smile, 'I bet even Pete Seeger had to struggle to start with.'

'Sure,' Ann encouraged, 'but I'll tell you something. I've seen more talent here than in New York. The standard is incredibly high.'

They hung on her every word. I think that was the night when I really began to appreciate how much Ann knew about music. I'd gleaned bits and pieces, but my knowledge was too limited for me to form much of a judgement. But listening to her talk to The Graduates – who knew what questions to ask – was a revelation.

That night gave Jack the idea for his soirée, and the following Saturday he invited a whole gang of people back to the flat. Some of them became famous later. Ann was right when she said Soho's coffee bars were full of talented people. I hate mentioning names for fear of forgetting others, but I remember Terry Nelham who shortly afterwards became Adam Faith, and a part-time skiffle vocalist named Harry Webb who the following year became Cliff Richard. You could sell tickets for such a gathering now; then it was just a collection of young hopefuls from the Green Door and the Two 'I's, talking their heads off until the early hours of the morning. Our two armchairs and the hard-backed chairs brought in from the kitchen were totally inadequate. People sprawled on the floor, surrounded by a sea of plates, cups and beer bottles. I remember Jack orchestrating the conversation from a standing position in front of the fireplace, and having a go at me for liking Peggy Lee and traditional jazz. (I *still* like Peggy Lee and traditional jazz.) Jack's argument was that traditional jazz was fine when played by a lot of old black men in New Orleans but all wrong when played by Humphrey Lyttleton in London. 'It's a totally different culture,' he insisted. 'For God's sake, Tubby, Humphrey Lyttleton went to Eton! What can he know about some poor black bastard in the Deep South?'

We had a lot of laughs that evening. Ann was the star of course, talking about the music scene in the States. Even after all these years I can remember her describing an American television show called *American Bandstand* with a daily audience of twenty million teenagers and twenty million adults. Forty million people tuned in to pop music! Eyes glazed at the prospect. Ossie Davidson kept repeating, 'Forty million people', over and over again.

It was fun, but I failed to see what it was doing for Jack. By this time the 'developing interest' stage of his crazy AIDA scheme was nearly over and he was on the verge of 'creating desire'. I kept asking myself how is this 'creating desire'? I know it sounds daft, but living with Jack, seeing every day the secret Jack, the Jack he showed me and the Jack he showed Ann, was beginning to play on my mind; I had refused to believe in AIDA, and thought it was stupid and juvenile – but I couldn't help watching Ann to see what effect it was having. The answer was none. Of course we'd become friends, she obviously liked us, but it was still *us*, Jack and me, as distinct from Jack in particular. In fact, thanks to him encouraging half of Soho to look upon our place as a soup kitchen, Ann had a lot more people to like. She had a veritable fan club.

Then I realised what Jack was doing. I'd imagined 'creating desire' meant wanting Ann to desire him. I suppose it did, ultimately, but Jack was taking it a step at a time. His first priority was to persuade her not to return to the States. What he was doing – or attempting to do – was to make her feel so at home that she'd miss New York less and like London more. That's what he meant by 'creating desire'.

I thought he was mad.

Soon eight weeks had passed. Ann was still talking about going back to the States. I was sure Jack had lost. It was all over bar the shouting . . . and then came that evening when Jack seized his chance.

*

It happened after a bad night at the Green Door. For once, few of our friends were there and the music

57

was dull, so after an hour we got up and left. Outside on the street we were debating whether to go on to the Heaven and Hell, when someone called from across the road. 'Ann,' came a girl's voice, 'hang on a minute.' And Janie Marsham emerged from the shadows. You could see she had been crying as soon as she came into the lamplights; girls wore more mascara in those days and her cheeks were streaked with the stuff. Ray Carson followed, with Mike and Ossie behind him, guitar cases slung over their shoulders, and while they were mumbling some sort of greeting, Janie laid her hand on Ann's arm. 'Are you going home?' she asked, meaning our flat. 'Could we come and talk for a while?' She sounded desperate. For a moment we were too surprised to respond.

Usually so full of life, Janie sounded really despondent. Even her appearance was different. Normally she was impeccably groomed, but her hair was a mess and her coat was buttoned up wrongly.

'Please,' she implored. 'We'd like your advice.'

Few words are as seductive to a lawyer as *we'd like your advice*. They conjure up such visions of clients and meetings and fees that no lawyer can resist them. Certainly Jack couldn't. Recovering, he forgot the Heaven and Hell. 'Come on then,' he said, deciding for us.

We walked in silence, with only the noise of late night traffic and the sound of our footsteps on the night air. Jack led, with Ossie beside him, followed by the girls, then me and the Carson brothers. Now and again I saw Ossie and Mike Carson exchanged uneasy glances. The atmosphere was horribly tense. Ann asked, 'What's wrong?' only for Janie to shake her head. 'Tell you later,' she said. They were all so unresponsive that even Ann ceased to ask questions.

Once at the flat, Ann tried to lighten the mood. 'There's stew on the stove,' she said in a bright voice. 'Anyone want some?'

They all did, either from politeness or to defer explanations. Ann took bowls from the cupboard while I gathered spoons from the draining-board. Jack passed the dishes round. They ate hungrily and although they expressed appreciation, they did so with barely a smile. I swear I never saw more miserable people. When the food was finished, Jack could stand the atmosphere no longer. 'Okay then,' he said, taking charge. 'What's this advice you wanted?'

I can still see that room. Janie was perched on the arm of Ann's chair, Mike sat on the floor beneath the window, staring glumly at Ray across the room. Ossie rocked back and forth on a kitchen chair, while Jack took his usual stance against the mantelpiece. Janie was verging on tears. She tried to speak, failed, cleared her throat and then the words came tumbling out. 'Mike and Ray are going back to Bristol. The group's splitting up. We can't make a go of it.'

You could hear her disbelief. Incredulity sounded in every word. Hurt shone from her eyes.

Mike responded at once. 'We don't *want* to, but we can't make a living,' he said truculently. 'What else can we do?'

'Keep trying!' Janie retorted, unable to disguise the pain of betrayal. I remembered when she was last in the flat. She and Mike had held hands all evening. I wondered if more than the group was splitting up. 'Keep trying,' she repeated. 'We can't give up. Not after what we've been through.'

It took half an hour to get the full story. Janie did

most of the talking, hampered by interruptions from the others. Eventually we pieced it together. The struggle to make the grade had taken a toll. I heard echoes of what Janie had told us previously – they travelled a hard road, competition was tough, money was tight – but where previously hardships had been endured with defiance, now doubts had begun to creep in. Life in the provinces had promised so much, London had delivered so little. You could hear the questions. Why had they failed to repeat their earlier success? Why wasn't Ossie getting more bookings? Why weren't they earning more money? Their lives sounded appalling. They lived in a couple of rooms in Notting Hill Gate. Neighbours complained when they rehearsed, forcing them to drive to any open patch of ground where they could play without causing a disturbance. Now the van had collapsed and Mike and Ray were ready to quit.

'What's the point?' Mike asked dismally. 'We've given it all we've got. If we go home and get jobs, I can stack up some bread –'

'And get married,' Ossie sneered. 'Mr and Mrs Semi-Detached. Two screaming kids and a sodding great mortgage. Janie will go mad –'

'That's our business,' Mike snarled angrily.

Watching them, I wondered if the real squabble was over Janie's affections. Mike sat hugging his knees, exchanging black scowls with Ossie. If it came to a fight they were evenly matched. Mike was shorter but broader across the shoulders: Ossie was tall, angular and wiry. I suppose Ossie was the better looking with his thin, almost aristocratic face and pale coloured hair. Mike was lantern jawed and dark, with beetle brows and a truculent lip. He so closely resembled his younger brother that they might have been twins. Ray sat across the room, silent, slumped on the floor, the picture of dejection.

I was wrong about Janie being the cause of the trouble. She left her place next to Ann and crossed the room to sit down next to Mike. 'Hey,' she said gently, taking his hand, 'we promised, remember?'

Mike looked sick, and sweat marked his brow. Staring at the floor between his feet, he muttered, 'I just don't see the point, that's all . . .'

'You promised. We all agreed. We gave our word.'

Shuffling uncomfortably, he raised his head until he met her eyes. 'Okay,' he said reluctantly.

Janie kissed his cheek and looked up at Ossie. 'You gave your word too,' she reminded him anxiously.

'So?' said Ossie. 'Do you hear me backing out?'

Jack grew impatient. 'What's this all about?' he asked from his position in front of the fireplace.

Janie said, 'We want Ann to answer a question.'

'I thought you wanted advice,' Jack exclaimed irritably, clearly disappointed not to be consulted. It was Ann's advice they wanted.

Janie rose and returned to the arm of Ann's chair. 'We've been arguing for days,' she said. 'All we agree on is you'll tell us the truth.'

'No soft soap,' Mike interrupted sharply. 'We want the truth, the whole truth and nothing but the truth.'

Janie silenced him with a glance before returning to Ann. 'We picked you because you're so knowledgeable. I mean, we've listened to you talk about concerts in Washington Square and Carnegie Hall –'

'And about Bob Dylan,' Ossie interrupted.

Mike scrambled to his feet. 'We all agree to abide by your decision,' he said, crossing the room to stand before Ann. Ossie craned his neck, fixing his eyes on Ann's face, while Ray watched anxiously from the floor.

Janie took a deep breath. 'We either struggle on or quit now. It's up to you, Ann. You tell us. If you think we've got talent, we'll keep trying. If not, it's the end of a dream.'

I'll never forget Janie's face. It was cleaner than when we met because she had been to the bathroom and washed; the mascara had gone, but so too had every scrap of colour. She looked ill and desperately worried.

In the stunned silence that followed, Ann struggled to overcome her surprise. 'Of course you've got talent –'

'Talent to starve,' Mike interrupted bitterly, 'talent to live like pigs in shit. Two rooms, that's all we've got. We share a toilet with people downstairs who use it like animals. The place is always filthy. It's pathetic. Bloody pathetic!'

Janie stood with stricken face, her eyes begging Ann to ignore every word.

'Know what we eat?' Mike demanded, carried away by his outburst. 'Toast! We live on toast. Sometimes we get beans on it, or scrambled eggs, but mostly it's plain, boring, bloody toast!'

Remembering him wolfing Ann's stew, I realised he was hungry. They were all hungry, tired, and defeated. Even Ossie's face revealed the exhaustion of listening to Mike pour scorn on their ambitions. At that moment, only Janie continued to believe in her dream. Her eyes, big green whirlpools in her colourless face, pleaded with Ann.

Mike continued to rant, 'It's always tomorrow.

Tomorrow we'll be famous. Tomorrow we'll be rich. Tomorrow this, tomorrow that. It's a load of crap. Tomorrow never comes, does it? Especially in this business — it's all fantasy, make-believe. Well, I've had enough. Unless Ann says we can make it, definitely make it, I'm off to Bristol.'

Tears formed in Janie's eyes. She blinked them away with a flick of her eyelashes. Every hope she'd ever had was revealed in her face, her dreams, ambitions, and her love for Mike Carson.

'Well Ann?' Mike challenged. 'Will we make it or not?'

Ann flushed, 'Come on, what kind of question's that? No one can say for sure —'

'Do *you* think we will?'

She searched for the right answer, trying to offer encouragement without conveying false hope. 'Oh hell,' she said sounding wretched. 'It depends on so many things.'

'That's no bloody answer.' Mike swooped to swing his guitar case on to his shoulder. His eyes went to Janie. 'I kept my side of the bargain. Let Ann decide, that's what you said —'

'But why me?' Ann cried.

'Because we agreed on you,' Mike retorted. 'We all know you. Because Janie wanted you. Because . . .' he broke off and turned for the door. 'Oh, what the hell! I knew it was a waste of time.'

'But what can I do?' Ann protested. 'I'm not in the business —'

Janie burst out, 'You know the business. You know the people —'

'Not in London,' Ann shook her head helplessly.

'Oh, *please*,' Janie begged. 'Tell us what to do.'

I never heard a clearer cry for help. She was at the end of her tether. So was Mike. Janie remained convinced of her talent, but Mike's spirit had been eroded by life on the breadline and the public's indifference. He saw security in Bristol and only hesitated because Janie would blame him for wrecking her dream. He'd come hoping Ann would relieve him of that responsibility. But Ann shook her head, 'I can't decide what you do with your lives –'

'See,' Mike jeered at Janie. 'Satisfied? What did I tell you?'

Jack intervened with sudden sharpness, 'Stop badgering Ann. She said you've got talent. What more can she say?'

'Yes or no,' Mike retorted. 'That's all. Do we keep trying? Will we make it? Yes or no?'

A silence descended. Everyone looked at Ann. I looked as well, even though I recognised the impossibility of her situation. I hoped she'd say something positive. Which was when Jack took matters in hand. Crossing the room, he relieved Mike of his music case. 'Sit down a minute,' he said in a soothing voice. 'Relax, Mike. Of course Ann wants to help, we all do. Let's talk about it quietly and sensibly.'

From that moment on, Jack took charge, exactly as my father would have done, except his bedside manner was a hundred percent better than my father's. Jack even used an anaesthetic; taking our precious half-bottle of scotch down from the shelf, he divided the contents into our collection of glasses and cups. And he never stopped talking. Later I realised how important that was; having taken centre stage, he refused to release it. To be honest, I thought he talked a lot of guff. Platitudes and clichés tumbled over each other. Yet he sounded as if he understood the strain they were under. He sympathised with their predicament and with every word you felt the tension lessen. Credit where it's due, Jack was good that night. He even took the pressure off Ann without blaming Mike for making impossible demands.

'Ann's perfectly right,' he said in a voice of pure reason. 'She can't be responsible for your lives. On the other hand . . .' he fended off an interruption from Mike . . . 'I can understand you valuing her advice. She could help enormously.'

'Absolutely,' Ossie agreed, 'that's what Janie and I said.'

Ann shook her head. 'I don't see how –'

'How could you?' Jack reassured her. 'This has been thrown at you.' He smiled absolving her of all blame, before turning back to Mike. 'Be reasonable. You've got a problem. Okay, I understand. But you don't want the first thing that comes into Ann's head. You want a considered opinion.'

'We can't go on as we are –' Mike squirmed.

'Who asked you to? Give us a bit of time. The Graduates have been going a couple of years. Surely you can wait a couple of days?' Jack switched his attention to the others. 'What about that, Janie? Ossie? Ray? Doesn't that make sense?'

Naturally, Janie agreed. She'd have clutched any life-line thrown to her; Ossie too, judging by the eager shake of his head. Even Ray, who'd hardly uttered a word, shrugged and admitted he could wait forty-eight hours. Ann tried to intervene, but Jack pretended not to notice.

'That's settled then.'

Poor Mike. He could hardly disagree with Janie and the others begging him. He grumbled about 'hanging around until Monday', but it was clear that he would, and Jack gave him no chance to change his mind. 'I'm exhausted,' he announced, ending the meeting with an abruptness that verged on rudeness, although in all fairness, it was getting late. Not that Janie objected, she responded at once, gathering her things and shepherding the others towards the door. I think she wanted to leave in case Jack withdrew his support. In a sense she'd got what she came for – a reprieve – The Graduates had kept Mike and Ray for a while longer. 'See you Monday, then,' she said, kissing my cheek.

After seeing them out, Jack bounded back up the stairs, as if anxious to prevent a discussion proceeding without him, but Ann had gone into the kitchen where she banged cups about in what sounded like irritation – an impression confirmed when she emerged. 'Oh, Jack, what did you do that for?'

'Do what?'

'Get me involved.'

'You were involved already.'

'I was trying not to be.'

'You saw Janie's face. She'd pinned her hopes on you. You couldn't have sent her away.'

He was right. We had all seen Janie's desperation. There was no telling what would have happened if Ann had refused to help. Ann hesitated, a troubled look on her face. To avoid conceding the argument, she returned to the kitchen to pour the coffee, while Jack, as usual, began to prowl up and down. He shot me a glance. 'You haven't said much?'

I shrugged. 'What's to say. Perhaps you were right to play for time. By Monday they may have sorted themselves out.'

Ann came through the door carrying a tray. 'Crap! How can they sort themselves out? Janie's not the type to give up and Mike can't take much more of it . . . They're in love and the situation's tearing them apart.'

Jack made space on the coffee table. 'Only two questions are worth asking,' he said. 'First, do they have talent?'

Ann straightened up, a startled expression on her face. 'You know they've got talent.'

'So why are they starving?'

'Oh, Jack,' she sighed, shaking her head, as a mother might over a difficult child. She sank into the armchair, drawing her legs up under her and tugging her skirt over her knees. 'Musicians aren't lawyers. They don't pass exams. No one gives them a certificate to play Carnegie Hall. Some of them starve for years waiting for a break.'

'Maybe,' Jack sat on the arm of her chair, 'but I remember you coming out of the Green Door a week ago. You analysed The Graduates on the way home. Remember?'

I remembered. Ann had been cross because they had used so much American material. 'Why don't they play more of their own music?' she had asked. 'There's a British sound. In my opinion it could be the best in the world.'

When Jack reminded her, Ann shook her head. 'I was talking about Janie –'

'Ossie wrote the number you liked.'

'Okay, Ossie too,' she conceded irritably. 'What do you want me to say? You heard my views the other night. They could be great but they present them-selves badly. The group needs a drummer and Janie should be out front . . .' She stopped as she caught the look on Jack's face. 'Why are you grinning?'

'You've just proved my point,' he said, getting up from the chair. 'You *do* know what's wrong with their act. You *could* help them. They look upon you as their resident guru –'

'Rubbish!'

'Okay, they see you as their most knowledgeable friend.'

Jack had a point. What he said was perfectly true, and Ann knew it. I couldn't understand her reluctance; I'd seen the pain in her eyes earlier, her heart had gone out to Janie, she'd felt for her – at one stage, she'd reached for Janie's hand in a gesture of comfort. Yet she was resisting Jack's arguments, as if fearful of being driven into a corner. Suddenly she flared at Jack, 'You don't know what you're asking. You don't even know the business. I can only give an opinion. They need more than that!'

'Such as?' he persisted.

'Getting work for a start.' She threw up her hands. 'Take this thing about Ossie getting them bookings. Can you see him negotiating with club owners? They're sharks. They must eat him alive. He's a musician –'

'So they need a manager.'

'Oh sure,' Ann said sarcastically. 'Some creep in a three piece. "I'll make you a star," he says. "Sign here," he says, like the Devil in *Faust*. Next thing you know, he owns them.'

There was no mistaking her bitterness. It set me wondering about her musician in New York. Was that what had happened? Had she helped him survive the hard times, only to be thrown over when he became famous? Had a manager turned her lover against her? I was so engrossed in speculation that for a moment I lost track of the conversation, and when I rejoined it, Ann was fairly blazing at Jack. 'Why do you want to encourage them? You've got the wrong idea about the music business. People think it's so glamorous, but it's not. Months of work, colossal effort, reputation – everything is on the line every night they perform. Then crash, bang, wallop, some creep of a critic without an original thought in his head tears them to pieces. It's awful. Don't you think we should save them from that? Let Mike take them back to Bristol.' The words flew from her lips.

Standing in front of the mantelpiece, Jack was taken aback. 'Sorry, I didn't mean to upset you, but you said it yourself. Janie's not the type to give up. She'll do it anyway.'

Ann fell silent. A moment passed while she collected herself. Finally she looked up with pain in her eyes and exasperation in her voice. 'You're right, Janie won't give up. It will break her heart to lose Mike, but she will if she has to. God help her.'

I thought Jack would leave it at that, but he didn't. For some reason, not then clear to me, he persisted, asking in a gentle voice, 'So will you help her?'

Ann flared up again. 'I just told you –'

'You said they need a manager. Okay, I'll find one.'

'And where will you look? In a cess pit?' Spots of colour stood out on Ann's cheeks.

'They can't *all* be bad.' Jack sounded like a little boy wheedling to get his own way.

Maybe the act worked because Ann's scorn softened. 'Oh, Jack. You're such an innocent at times.

A creep in a three piece with a white hat. Can you imagine? That's a novel twist.'

Jack frowned. 'Where do white hats come into it?'

'Don't take it literally. Didn't you ever go to the movies as a kid? Remember the Westerns? Roy Rogers, the Lone Ranger, all that lot. You always knew the good guy. He wore a white hat.'

And Jack laughed, dispelling the earlier tension. 'That's right,' he nodded, 'I remember now. The good guy always wore a white hat.'

Not much happened after that. The silly joke about good guys in white hats cleared the air and Ann's scratchy manner gave way to her usual good humour. Jack walked her home and I went to bed. It was very late, four o'clock when I switched out the light. Consequently I overslept and didn't awake until mid-day. Rubbing my eyes, I went into the kitchen, grumbling about the stupidity of not getting more sleep.

I'd made the tea before I remembered it was my Sunday for seeing my mother. She gave me lunch every third Sunday; roast beef, Yorkshire pudding and all the trimmings, followed by spotted dick and thick yellow custard. It was her way of ensuring I had a balanced diet. The time was already twelve thirty and I was due there at one. Swallowing a mouthful of tea as I dressed, I was on my way down the stairs within fifteen minutes. Even so, I was late. Whitcombe Street to Bayswater takes at least half an hour, especially on Sunday when the tubes are at half strength.

'And who got up late, then?' asked my mother, as

if addressing her budgerigar. She never nags, but her habit of asking obvious questions always makes me feel guilty.

Bert followed her into the hall, clashing the carving-knife against the steel as if preparing to carve for five hundred. ''Allo, 'Allo,' he said, sounding like a policeman. 'Out chasing the girls again last night, eh? Hope you didn't do anything I wouldn't do.' And he laughed uproariously, causing my mother to smile.

My father always claimed it was to spite him that my mother married Bert Tanner. 'Imagine marrying someone called Bert,' he used to shudder. 'The man can't even speak decent English. God Almighty, that woman has sunk to the depths.'

He never realised how happy 'that woman' was as Mrs Bert Tanner. 'Bert likes me for what I am,' she once told me. 'Your father was never content. Either my hair was all wrong or I had to lose a few pounds. Bert says he was mad. "I don't want you losing no weight," he says, "there'd be nothing to cuddle."' She giggled. '"Statuesque", Bert calls me. I'm his Statuesque Venus, that's what I am.'

She was certainly statuesque. Some would have said she was stout. She had black wavy hair, rosy apple cheeks, blue eyes and good teeth – which was just as well because she had a voracious appetite. 'Got to keep your strength up,' she would laugh, urging me to second helpings.

I've heard it said that divorcées marry clones of their first partner. Not true of my mother. Bert Tanner and my father had less in common than a whale and a tortoise. Bert was a great lover of life. 'Enjoy yourself,' he was always advising me. 'No one can do it for you, can they? It's your life. Have a good time.'

He first met my mother when I was about six. She had been on her own for three years by then, supporting herself by working at Derry & Toms, which was where Bert was employed as a stock controller. He delighted in telling of how they met. 'One day there was this meeting upstairs in the office, and this secretary comes in to take notes. It was love at first sight. As soon as she sat down and picked up her pencil, I says to myself, Bert, this is the woman for you.'

It took him five years to convince my mother. 'Cheeky devil,' she giggled. 'He asked me to marry him the first time we went to the pictures. All we'd done was hold hands. We hadn't even kissed each other.'

Two hundred proposals later, she said yes. Because I was not allowed to see my mother until I was eighteen, they'd been married six years before I even met Bert. 'He was so worried about meeting you,' Mum told me. 'We both were. After all, it was fourteen years since I'd spoken to you. And all those years I knew your father was dripping poison, telling you what a bad woman I was. Fourteen years,' she would repeat sadly, shaking her head.

But she had seen me during those years, just as I had seen her, albeit from a distance. She would walk past the house, or stroll past the school. Sometimes I caught sight of her: often I didn't, but I always sensed she was there. I knew she would never desert me. My father had already explained what would happen if ever she tried to speak to me. 'Kidnapping is a custodial offence. I'll have her slapped behind bars.' There was a time when I had nightmares about her going to prison. Every year on my birthday, she would send me a cake made by Fortnum and Mason. They actually delivered it, in a big white cardboard box on which their name was printed in gold. My father fed those cakes to the dog. 'Damn and blast the woman,' he would roar in a frenzy of temper. The first time it happened, my Aunt Joan sided with me. 'It's the boy's birthday,' she said. 'Give him his cake.' They had an awful row. She had never stood up to him before. She never did again, either, because he sent her packing. 'If that's your attitude,' he shouted, 'get out of my house.' She did, too, the same day, and after that we had a succession of housekeepers. None of them stayed long because of my father's bad temper, but they all did as they were told when the cakes arrived. Straight into the study they went, without the box even being opened. And when my father came home, the big creamy cakes were fed to the dog. Strangely, I was only upset the first year. After that, I counted it as a small victory each time it happened. I think I was satisfied that no one would be locked up for sending a cake, and the fact that my father couldn't stop them coming made him the loser. I invented a ridiculously romantic game in which Mum and I were members of the French Resistance and my father was a Nazi general whose authority we were undermining. My biggest concern was for our labrador, Goldy, because he, like a fool, wolfed all the cream cakes and suffered with diarrhoea the next day, disgracing himself all over the house. 'That animal's senile,' my father would snarl, 'he'll have to go if this doesn't stop.'

First my mother, then my dog!

When I was eighteen, Mum wrote to me. The letter arrived on my birthday. In it, she explained that the court order forbidding her to contact me expired when I was eighteen – 'And I'd love to see you again. Would you like to come to lunch next Sunday?'

That was when I met Bert for the first time. He was as lean as my mother was plump. About five foot eight, receding brown hair, merry eyes and a heart of gold. 'I can't be your father,' he said, 'but I can be your friend. I want you to know there's always a room for you here. I'm afraid I can't offer you much, I can't help you become a solicitor like your father can, I ain't got his sort of money; but you're welcome to share whatever I've got.'

He really meant it. I settled for becoming his friend and having lunch with them every third Sunday. Just being with them taught me a lot. They were the happiest couple I've ever known. As long as they were together, they wanted for nothing. My mother still worked, and their joint income was enough for their needs. They lived well, but within their means. Every year they holidayed in the same boarding-house in Torquay in which they had honeymooned. They never stopped talking. They laughed constantly, and achieved a state of contentment that was truly enviable. Going to see them was never a chore, and I was only concerned about being late for fear of disappointing them.

'Disappoint nonsense,' said Bert. 'You're here now, aren't you. We're a bit late ourselves today, aren't we, Sheila? Come on, I'm just about to start carving.'

With which my mother took my coat, and I was led into the dining room. I was the only guest. They had other people in from time to time, but rarely

74

when I was there. 'We like you all to ourselves,' Mum had told me. 'There's always so much to catch up on.'

Catching up that day meant a report on Jack. They'd met Jack and had invited him to lunch a couple of times. They always asked after him; so that when Ann appeared on the scene, it had seemed natural to tell them.

'So,' said Mum over the beef, 'what's the latest on the romance? How's it going?' Her eyes shone with the avid interest of a regular reader of romantic fiction.

Her face clouded when I reported Jack's lack of progress. 'Oh dear,' she said. 'That is a shame.'

Bert said, 'I can't make him out. He seemed a bright enough lad when I met him. If he feels that way, why don't he pop the question. It works every time –'

'Oh does it?' said Mum indignantly. 'It took you long enough to get the right answer.'

Bert's eyes gleamed like polished buttons. 'Ah, but I knew you'd say yes in the end.'

'Jack's only got a few weeks,' she pointed out. 'It took you a few years.'

Bert refused to retreat. 'That just proves he's playing it all wrong. He should never have involved Tubby –'

'Peter, please. I've told you before,' Mum said severely. She loathed my nickname. She had christened me Peter and I would always be Peter to her. The name felt strange to me in those days. Being addressed as Peter made me feel uncomfortable, as if I'd put on someone else's coat by mistake. Everyone called me Tubby; except my father, and he never used any name at all. He simply looked in my direction when he gave me orders.

'Peter then,' Bert conceded. 'He shouldn't have involved Peter –'

'I don't see how he could help it, what with them going back to their flat every night –'

'Jack should have staked his claim,' Bert insisted. 'The girl would know where she stood then, wouldn't she? Trouble is, she don't know if she's Jack's girl or Tubb . . . I mean, Peter's.'

Mum bridled at that. 'Don't be silly. Peter's far too sensible to get involved with an American girl. She'd be forever dragging him off to New York and rushing him around. Peter's got it all worked out, haven't you?' she said with a fond look. 'After he qualifies, he's going to start a little practice down in Devon or somewhere, and find himself a nice, little farmer's daughter who'll cook him lovely meals and wait on him hand and foot.'

I was thinking there were worse fates when Bert said, 'We ought to have had Jack and this girl round to lunch. I'd have got to know her then. I'd be able to figure out the best move for Jack if –'

'Oh, hark at him,' Mum giggled. 'He's an expert all of a sudden –'

'Nothing like that,' Bert retorted, 'but I know Jack. I can't quite picture this Ann . . .' He shrugged and looked at me. 'You do make her sound a bit mysterious.'

A thoughtful look came into Mum's eyes. 'Yes,' she said slowly, 'come to think of it, you do. She sounds ever so nice and so on, but I know what Bert means. It's as if you hadn't told us the full story.'

Without accusing me of being evasive, they'd made

me feel guilty. I suppose they were right. In fact, I hadn't told them the full story. I'd told them about Ann growing up with her parents in New York, but hadn't said a word about her musician, partly because they might think less of her (attitudes were different in those days), and partly because I knew little to tell.

'Well, I think you should invite them round,' Bert concluded, 'and let the dog see the rabbit.'

'Yes, why don't we do that?' asked Mum, full of enthusiasm. 'Next weekend. Do you think you could bring them to lunch?'

I promised to try, which put a temporary end to the subject. After which we talked of all manner of things, although none could have been very important because I can't recall one of them now. What I do remember is walking up to Marble Arch at four o'clock to catch the tube. Strolling along in the afternoon sunshine, I began to fret about what would happen if Jack and Ann did come to lunch the following Sunday. After all, it would be a bit unfair on Ann – everyone would know of Jack's interest in her except Ann herself. I hoped Bert would 'look at the rabbit' with suitable discretion. I wouldn't want Ann to be embarrassed. Sitting on the tube, I found myself thinking back to when I'd met her for the first time. It seemed years, yet it was only eight weeks. Eight weeks before, I hadn't been to The Nucleus or the Two 'I's or the Green Door. I hadn't met such people as the Carson brothers and Janie Marsham. Now they were part of my life, and all because of Ann. Suddenly I realised I'd miss her when she returned to the States. I felt an unexpected pang, then guilt about Jack – which was unfair really, after all we were all friends, all three of us.

I'd intended to tell Jack about the lunch invitation as soon as I returned, but he was immersed in the Sunday papers. *All* of the Sunday papers. The place looked like a newsstand. I remember thinking we'd have enough papers to light fires for the rest of winter. 'Hello,' I said. 'Studying form?'

'Studying trends,' he answered, looking up from *The Sunday Times*.

I had to clear my armchair to sit down. On top of the pile of papers was the *Sunday Pictorial* folded open at the Entertainments section. Jack had circled an article about Tommy Steele. The familiar urchin grin peered up above the caption, 'Tommy orders egg and chips at the Ritz.' On the floor next to my chair, the *Sunday Despatch* informed me that Lonnie Donnegan was on an American tour, and that Jack had decorated the column with a series of stars. He was even using different-coloured pencils; red and blue, green and brown.

'Starting a scrap book?' I asked.

He scowled at me, 'I'll tell you what I've been doing, if you really want to know.'

Of course I wanted to know. Jack's newspaper reading was usually confined to the office copy of the *Financial Times*. He never bought papers on a Sunday.

'It was something Ann said going home last night.'

'Ah,' I said. I should have known that reading the Sunday papers was related to Ann. Everything else was, so why not that? Jack had reached the stage where his brain only functioned if Ann was involved.

'According to Ann,' he continued, 'the big record companies never realised what was happening in the States. They stuck to Sinatra and such like, without realising the kids wanted something different. Elvis, Buddy Holly, Little Richard, all signed up with tiny outfits because the big boys didn't want to know.'

I shrugged. I wanted to say, 'So what?' But I didn't.

'I've been reading the papers,' he said needlessly, 'and there's a hell of a lot about pop stars. If you ask me, there's a sort of cultural revolution going on. What happened in the States is happening here.'

I still failed to see the point.

'Another thing Ann said last night,' Jack continued. 'When we got back to Gill's, she said, "Who is there in England? Tommy Steele. Give it another few years, and there'll be ten Tommy Steeles."' Excitement lifted Jack's voice. 'And I think she's right, Tubby. She's dead right if you ask me.'

Tommy Steele was well known in Soho. He used to sing at the Two 'I's and places like that. His name was Tommy Hicks in those days. Then a New Zealander called John Kennedy saw him and persuaded him that he needed a manager. Kennedy threw up his job as a *Daily Sketch* reporter, changed Tommy Hicks to Tommy Steele and created Britain's answer to Elvis.

Looking very thoughtful, Jack said, 'Ann will help Janie, you know.'

'Ah,' I said, and for the first time began to see the drift of his thinking.

'What do you mean, "Ah"?'

'She didn't seem too keen last night.'

'She'll help if the Group get a proper manager.'

'She doesn't like managers.'

'I don't see why,' said Jack. 'There can't be much to running a pop group. What's involved? A few negotiations, drawing up contracts, that sort of thing.

Ossie's out of his depth, but it would be a piece of cake for someone with business experience.'

'And you know someone?'

'Absolutely.'

I thought of some of the people we'd met at the Green Door, a few of whom aspired to be managers. None of them struck me as very reliable, and I began to feel vaguely uneasy. Without knowing why, I had a sudden premonition that something bad was going to happen. I liked Janie Marsham and felt strangely anxious. She deserved better than to be used as a pawn in one of Jack's schemes.

I said, 'Janie's desperately serious about her career. You'll break her heart if you mess it up.'

Jack grinned. 'Don't worry,' he said, 'I'll get her a manager in a white hat.'

I awoke next morning still anxious that something unpleasant was going to happen. And sure enough it did, although Janie wasn't involved. It happened at the office, at eleven thirty, when my father poked his head into our room. 'Where's Jack?' he asked.

I avoided his eye by consulting my watch. 'Isn't he at Companies House?'

'I wouldn't ask if I knew, would I?' my father retorted, looking at me as if I were an idiot. Actually it was his usual way of looking at me. He'd smile and laugh with Jack, Jack was one of the boys, Jack was a young man destined to succeed. Tubby was the idiot son, employed on sufferance, never to be entrusted with anything important. I knew those were my father's views because he expressed them on various occasions, generally when other people were present. Belittling me was an art form with my father. He found fault with any document drafted by me. And when Dingle, his partner and my immediate boss, found reason to praise my work, my father was always quick to contradict him.

'I think Jack's at Companies House,' I lied.

'Damn and blast it. He spends his life there these days.'

'They're changing the system,' I said. 'Everything's taking much longer.'

'It's as well you're not there, then. At least Jack knows how to cut corners.'

'Shall I tell him you're looking for him?'

'You really do ask some damn fool questions at times. Of course I'm looking for him. Tell him I want to see him with the Jackson file. Got that? Write it down or you'll forget.'

Dutifully I wrote on a scratch-pad while he peered over my shoulder to make sure I could spell Jackson.

'Give it to him as soon as he comes in,' he said, withdrawing into the corridor. 'And do try not to forget,' he said, adopting a weary, long-suffering tone. 'It is rather important.'

It was such a typical encounter that I only remember it because it concerned Jack. My father never enquired how I was, or even what I was doing. If asked, he would have said that me being there proved I was still alive, and that his partner Dingle was in charge of my work. He might also have added that he was in his office to work, not to chatter. But his reasons went deeper than that, as he and I knew perfectly well.

I listened to him clump down the corridor, pushing doors open here and there, addressing the occupants gruffly or cheerfully depending upon who they were, until he reached his own room and the door slammed behind him. Then I went to the filing cabinet to search for the Jackson file. I'd just located it when Jack came in, looking pleased with himself. 'That went very well,' he said. 'They couldn't have been more obliging.'

I knew where he had been – to see the firm's bankers. He'd telephoned for an appointment first thing that morning, and had gone straight round when they'd agreed to see him at once.

'Nice to have influence,' he grinned. 'Any friend of your father's is a friend of theirs, so to speak. They fairly rolled out the red carpet, Tubby my boy.' He was fond of calling me 'my boy' when in an ebullient mood.

'What were you doing?' I asked. 'Opening an account?'

He laughed. 'Opening an overdraft. They lent me five hundred quid.'

I gaped. Five hundred pounds was a fortune. You could have bought our flat for five hundred pounds in those days. Five hundred pounds was as much as we earned in a year.

'Why should they lend you five hundred pounds?' I asked in astonishment.

'Why shouldn't they? I have excellent prospects.'

His prospects would diminish sharply if my father found out, and I was about to say so when suddenly the door opened and my father came in. He took one look at Jack and demanded, 'Has he told you I wanted you?'

'Er . . . good morning, sir,' Jack floundered. 'I beg your pardon –'

'Blast it!' My father wheeled round on me. 'Can't you pass on a simple message? You're useless, utterly useless!' Turning from me with a look of contempt, he told Jack, 'Stop gossiping with this fool. We've got to sort this Jackson thing out. Get the file and come along to my office.' With which he stormed out.

Pausing only long enough to accept the Jackson file from my hands, Jack scuttled after him, and I was left to lick my wounds, as was invariably the case after an encounter with my father. As a child I used to weep, heartbroken by his lack of fairness; but those days were long past. Over the years I'd learned to deal with him in the way the poor endure poverty, or the sick live with illness. Victory, of a sort, lay in suffering in silence. The way to triumph over unfairness is to pretend total indifference; so that after a while the skin hardens and injustice is less painful. Such, at least, was my theory, and I did my best to put it into practice by dismissing my father from my mind and busying myself with the papers on my desk. The problem was, little on my desk was of immediate importance – the lease of a shop, a piffling dispute with an insurance company, some correspondence concerning probate – everything I turned to could wait. Nothing had the same shock value as Jack borrowing five hundred pounds.

'Now what's he up to,' I groaned. I was coming to worry more and more about Jack. He was taking far too many liberties at the office. More than the Jackson file was in need of attention, he was falling behind with the rest of his work. He had got away with it because of his reputation. 'Jack's as keen as mustard,' people said. Or, 'Jack's as sharp as a razor, nothing slips past Jack.' Which it didn't in the old days, he *was* sharp as a razor when he applied his mind to his work. The trouble was, he no longer cared, all he cared for was Ann.

I realised the five hundred pounds had to be connected with Ann. Everything Jack did was connected with Ann – which was why his charade of feigning indifference was so stupid. Ann would be gone in four weeks. Then where would Jack be? Meanwhile he was borrowing vast sums of money, playing truant from the office, paying scant attention to his work, jeopardising his career, involving me in his lies . . .

I grew angry. Jack was my closest friend. I'd stand by him come what may, but he was letting himself down badly. Things had to be brought to a head. Remembering my mother's invitation, I decided to invite Jack to lunch by himself the following week. Without Ann's presence, we might make him see sense. If he refused to listen to me, surely he'd listen to Bert? The more I thought about it, the more valid the idea became. The anxious mood which had plagued me all night receded slightly. I knew Bert and Mum would add their warnings to mine on Sunday. What I didn't know was that warnings would be too late by the following Sunday.

I scarcely saw Jack for the rest of the day. After lunching with the Jackson people he and my father spent the afternoon together discussing the outcome. It must have gone well because Jack was in a buoyant mood when he returned to our room at the end of the day. 'Another day, another dollar,' he said cheerfully.

'That will please Father.'

'Oh, he's delighted,' said Jack. 'The trouble with you is you don't handle him right. He's not the ogre you make him out to be.'

I made no reply. Jack was always blinded by my father's brilliance as a lawyer, overlooking his shortcomings as a man.

We left the office together. I wanted to ask about the five hundred pounds. Having fretted about it all day, I was about to put the question when Jack stopped in his tracks. 'I've just remembered something,' he said. 'You go on and I'll catch you up. I'll be at Gill's place by the time you've sunk your first pint.'

So I went on by myself, still baffled about the five hundred pounds. Once at Gill's, I squeezed through the office equipment crowd and found a stool at the bar. The smile with which Ann greeted me was less vibrant than normal. Usually her smile made my day, but this was a strained, tight little smile. 'Where's Jack?' she asked.

'He'll be along shortly.' I could see she was worried. The shadows were back in her eyes. 'What's the matter?'

Her eyes met mine and her lips twitched into a quirky little smile. 'You don't miss much, do you, Tubby?'

I can never think of a good reply when someone says something like that, so I just sat there, looking at her. Finally she said, 'I'm worried sick about Janie. God knows what I'll tell her tonight.'

I'd almost forgotten about The Graduates; what with one thing and another the fact of us meeting them had slipped my mind.

Ann said, 'I spent all of yesterday thinking about what to say.'

'Why not say what you told Jack and me? That they need a manager and a good drummer —'

'Oh, that's no good,' she scolded. 'Mike will be on the first train to Bristol. Janie's relying on me to say something that . . .' she fumbled for the right words . . . 'well, something of immediate help.'

Again I was lost for an answer, but someone called for a round of drinks at that moment and Ann went off to serve them. I sat watching her and listening to the salesmen chat her up. One of them said something that made her blush and then laugh in spite of herself. She gave him a quick answer and he answered back, so that all of her attention was concentrated on the exchange and her worries about The Graduates were forgotten for a moment. I was glad, and cursed Jack for opening his mouth. Without his intervention, Ann might have avoided any further involvement. What on earth had prompted him to interfere? Thinking about him reminded me of the five hundred pounds. Why would he want five hundred pounds? Bert's voice came into my mind. 'Pop the question, it works every time.' Was that what the money was for? Engagement rings, wedding bells, setting up home? Unexpectedly, I felt another pang, the sort I'd felt the previous day at the thought of Ann going back to the States.

'Penny for them?' she said, rejoining me in a more cheerful mood.

I started guiltily. 'Nothing,' I said, 'I was just thinking about work.'

'No you weren't.'

I went red in the face. 'Oh?'

'Oh?' she mimicked. 'You'd better not tell me what you *were* thinking, judging by that guilty look. But don't kid me, Tubby, I know you too well.'

She laughed as she spoke, a warm, friendly, reassuring sort of laugh, but the look she gave me was coolly amused. I was taken by surprise. It was hard to imagine her analysing me. Stupid really, after all I'd had all sorts of thoughts about her. Embarrassed, I choked on my reply, 'What do you mean you know me too well. You hardly know me at all.'

'Don't be silly. You're kind, decent and honest.' Stepping back, she gave me a quizzical look. 'As a matter of fact, you've also got tremendous strength of character.'

'Me?' I nearly fell off the stool. 'Rubbish! You should hear my father.'

She shook her head. 'I make my own judgements.'

Confused, I said the first thing to come into my head. 'And what about Jack?'

She grinned. 'Oh, he's easy. He's a schoolboy who needs a lot of mothering.'

At that moment Gill emerged from the back bar. 'Hello Tubby ... You're looking all hot and bothered.'

Ann turned away, a wicked smile on her face.

Gill's arrival gave me a chance to recover. He and I talked for a few minutes, about football I think, but I doubt that I made much sense. My gaze kept straying to Ann at the other end of the bar. I glowed. *Kind, decent and honest.* The strength of character bit was wrong, Jack was much stronger than me, but I couldn't help feeling flattered. Eventually, I tried to concentrate on what Gill was saying. 'Sorry Gill, what was that?'

'I was just saying,' he said heavily, 'Ann got very upset yesterday, worrying about these people. What are they called? The Graduates?'

'Yes.'

'She told us about it,' he said, watching Ann serve a customer two vodka tonics. 'She's afraid she'll hurt their feelings.'

'It is difficult,' I admitted.

'Maybe,' he said, 'but I'm relying on you to make sure they don't give her a hard time.'

'Oh, they won't do that. They like her too much.'

'That's all right then,' he said, pulling a pint. 'In that case you can have this and I'll pour myself another.'

So I accepted Gill's pint and we talked about football again. He was a great Arsenal fan and he fancied their chances that season. Meanwhile Ann busied herself, and the office equipment crowd began to thin out. It was about seven forty-five by this time and there was still no sign of Jack.

'Working overtime, is he?' Gill asked.

'Something like that,' I said, looking at the clock over the bar.

Which was exactly the moment Jack chose to arrive. My back was to the door, so I missed his grand entrance. The first clue of something happening was when Gill looked over my shoulder and burst out laughing. Then Ann looked up and started to giggle. Laughter was one of her charms, but never before had I heard such helpless spontaneity. Her laughter grew to such a full, joyous sound that I was smiling even as I turned round. Jack was standing in the entrance, dressed in his usual dark grey office three piece suit. In his left hand was his briefcase and on his head was a hat – a huge, white, American cowboy ten-gallon stetson.

'Blimey,' Gill gasped. 'You got a licence for that?'

Jack advanced smiling to the bar. He had no need to speak. His eyes were on Ann and hers were on him. Both were remembering the joke about good guys in white hats. When he reached the bar, Ann clutched the counter and caught hold of his hand. She held it convulsively, unable to speak for laughter. And Jack laughed, and Gill laughed, and I laughed as well.

'Oh, Jack,' Ann cried when at last she could speak, 'I love you.'

There was so much excitement, such a sense of occasion. Jack faked a cowboy accent and ordered drinks all round. 'Set 'em up, pardner,' he called, slapping Gill on the back. Believe it or not, so much was going on that I missed the point of it all. I thought it was just a gag. I should have guessed as soon as I saw Jack in that stupid hat. What with him spending all day Sunday on his newspaper survey and then borrowing five hundred pounds – I should have known. There had been other clues: such as when I warned him about upsetting Janie and he'd said, 'Don't worry, I'll get her a manager in a white hat.' How could I have been so blind? But I was. Consequently I was shocked rigid when Jack made his announcement. 'I'm the new manager of The Graduates,' he said grandly.

I couldn't believe it. He was already taking liberties at the office, falling behind with his work. 'You've got to be joking,' I said, aghast.

But he wasn't.

I tried to make him see sense. I reminded him of the glorious career ahead of him at Mortlake, Dingle & Barnes. 'Don't be daft,' he said, 'I'll only be running The Graduates in my spare time.'

'How can you do that?' I argued. 'How can you get them bookings? You haven't any contacts.'

'It's only a matter of lifting the phone. Then I'll go round and see them.'

'When?'

'In the evenings. People running clubs work in the evenings, you know.'

'I don't believe it's that simple,' I said, shaking my head, and attacking on another front. 'Besides, you don't know enough about music —'

'Ann does. If she helps improve their act, I'll sell it. It's as simple as that.'

I looked to Ann for support, but she was too relieved to share my concern. She had been dreading meeting The Graduates, afraid of hurting their feelings. With Jack involved, the pressure was off. Besides she was still amused by the hat. Picking it up from where Jack had placed it on the bar, she put it on and went off to look at herself in a mirror. Meanwhile I tried to get Gill on my side, but he was listening with rapt attention to Jack describing the results of his newspaper reading. 'The growth potential is enormous,' Jack was saying. 'What's happening in the States will happen here, no doubt about that.'

'But Jack,' I kept saying, 'you can't spare the time.'

'A few phone calls,' he answered angrily. 'Nonsense, Tubby, that's no time at all.'

Gill nodded in agreement. 'There could be a lot of

money in it, Tubby, don't forget that. What's-his-name must be making a fortune out of Tommy Steele.'

Ann returned from the end of the bar where she had been laughing about the hat with a couple of the regulars. Her eyes were bright and her cheeks were flushed. Jack put his hand on her arm. 'I can draw up some really tight contracts for when they work in the clubs. That's what they need. And someone who can negotiate. I'll do a hell of a sight better than Ossie.'

Ann's eyes shone. 'Sure,' she said, 'a guy in a three piece wearing a white hat. How can you fail?'

If she was joking, Jack took her comment at face value. 'Exactly,' he said, turning to Gill. 'You wouldn't believe the way artists get ripped off. Some of the things Ann told me about managers in the States made my blood boil. Maybe it's different here, I don't know, but I'll tell you this: no one will rip The Graduates off with me as their manager.'

That was the clincher for Ann. Already flushed from laughter, her face fairly shone. I was the odd one out. Everyone thought it a good idea except me, and I couldn't express my real reservations. Jack was doing this to impress Ann. I didn't know if he could help The Graduates; maybe he could, maybe he couldn't. What worried me was what would happen when Ann went back to the States. It wasn't fair for Janie's hopes to be raised, only to be dashed when Jack lost interest. And he would without Ann, I felt sure about that.

'Tubby?' said Ann, catching my eye. 'Don't you like the idea?'

'It's not up to me,' I shrugged. 'It's between Jack

and The Graduates. We ought to wait and see what they think.'

They loved it. Oh, not to begin with. When they arrived at the flat they came in expecting to be knocked in a heap. Their hangdog expressions indicated differences that were as painful as ever. Janie's face was haunted by anxiety. Her eyes fairly pleaded with Ann. Ossie sat biting his nails, while Mike glowered out from under his eyebrows.

Their first surprise came when Jack took the floor. At once, Janie was all apprehension; her gaze kept shifting from Jack to Ann as if suspecting betrayal, as if saying, 'It was your opinion we wanted.'

Then Jack hit his stride. When it came to praise, he laid it on with a trowel. Not only did he expect them to be successful, he predicted their success would be huge. 'I can see the day,' he said, 'when you play the London Palladium.'

I could scarcely believe it. These were kids, nice decent kids who played good music, but kids for all that, kids who played coffee bars and school dances. To talk of the London Palladium was nonsense. What the hell did Jack know about the Palladium? I expected them to laugh, or jeer, especially Mike, but they lapped it up. I was witnessing artistic ego for the first time in my life. They were hungry for acclaim. Janie's green eyes rounded in wonder. She reached over to clasp Mike's hand, thrilled by what she was hearing.

And Jack played them like an angler, giving them all the line they wanted until the time came to reel them in. At one point, he turned and pointed to

Ossie. 'When does he get a chance to compose?' he asked. 'He's out searching for bookings instead of creating new music. How can he develop his talent while he's squabbling with promoters?'

'Right,' Ossie nodded, as if responding to a gospel preacher. I wouldn't have been surprised if he'd shouted 'Hallelujah!'

'And what about Mike?' Jack demanded from his place in front of the hearth. 'Most of his time is taken up with that bloody van. Anyone would think he's a mechanic. It's a waste of time.'

'Someone's got to do it,' Mike said hotly, defending himself. 'We can't afford garage bills –'

'You can't afford unreliable transport,' Jack retorted. 'That's why we're getting rid of it. Can you meet me in the morning? We're seeing a motor dealer in Warren Street. I'm buying you a new van.'

You'd have thought it was Christmas from the look on Mike's face. He was like a small boy confronted with Santa Claus. And before he could recover, Jack was plunging on with his plans, talking about hiring a hall for regular rehearsals and buying new outfits for Janie.

They were overwhelmed. *I* was overwhelmed. Suddenly I realised what the five hundred pounds was for. The thought brought me out in a sweat. So did Jack's talk about going to Warren Street in the morning. 'Jack,' I said, 'what about the office?'

'I'll only be an hour,' he said with a wink. 'Pretend it's another visit to Companies House.'

My God! He could pretend what he liked, but if my father found out there'd be hell to pay. Meanwhile The Graduates were sitting there with glazed eyes and open mouths. Any questions about Jack becoming their manager were forgotten. After all, he was spending money. No one had ever done that. After all, Jack was virtually a qualified lawyer, he was sure to know what he was talking about. I could see what they were thinking, just as I could see the occasional glances directed at Ann, as if seeking her approval . . . which she was giving, nodding her head, apparently agreeing with every word that fell from Jack's lips.

Then Jack sprang the trap. It was brilliantly done. Even I failed to see it coming, and I knew all about AIDA and the bank loan and everything. 'Of course,' said Jack, 'Ann's the key. We can't do it without her. I can run the business side, no problem, but I can't coach you to give a better performance. Without Ann, there's no deal.'

All eyes swivelled to Ann.

'What we've got to do,' Jack continued, 'is persuade her to stay in London, at least for another six months.'

Watching them, I saw their dismay. Ossie imagined himself begging for bookings all over again, Mike saw himself working on that wretched van; the lavish gowns Janie had dreamt about disappeared before she'd even tried them for size.

'Oh, Ann,' Janie cried. 'Please.'

Mike joined in. 'It was your advice we wanted in the first place.'

'Right,' Ossie agreed.

'That's why we came to see you,' said Ray.

Clever, clever, Jack. I was watching this unfold like someone seated in the front stalls at the theatre. Except with a difference. I wanted Ann to stay in London; suddenly it was important to me too.

'Please, Ann,' chorused The Graduates.

Jack let their appeals play upon her emotions, watching her wilt under their imploring gaze, then he said, 'You don't have to return for anything specific, do you, Ann?'

'But I'm only here on a visit,' she protested. 'I never intended to stay more than a few months.'

'But it's not essential you go back on a particular date?'

'Not essential, but . . .' Her voice faded as she looked from one face to another.

'We need you,' Janie implored.

'Come on, Ann,' said Ossie. 'We've got music to make.'

From that moment, I never doubted she'd stay. Jack had worked for this all evening. He'd made her laugh with his hat, excited her with his talk, programmed The Graduates to make her feel wanted.

For a split second Ann's eyes met mine, as if seeking my opinion. Seeing the answer in my face, she turned away, perhaps comparing the rejection she'd suffered in New York with being wanted in London. Perhaps she was relieved to put off facing old memories? Who knows, I could only guess at her thoughts, but I was sure of the outcome.

'Well,' she said cautiously, 'I suppose Gill might put me up for a while longer.'

'Oh, Ann!' Janie squealed. Ray jumped up from the floor, a grin spreading over his face, while Mike and Ossie cheered and applauded. They crowded round Ann, all talking at once, while Jack opened his briefcase and produced a bottle of champagne. How confident he had been! But what a moment. We toasted Ann for remaining in London and The Graduates for the success they'd enjoy. Janie was close to tears as she clung to Mike's arm. And even then Jack hadn't finished unveiling surprises. 'There's more!' he cried. 'To commemorate this auspicious occasion, I'm taking you all out to Wheeler's for a fish and chip supper.'

'Bravo!' Mike shouted at the prospect of food.

After that, all was activity. Ann and Janie disappeared to the bathroom, Ossie started to wind himself into the long woollen scarf he habitually wore, while Mike and Ray exchanged grins in which relief and delight were equally mingled.

Jack was the hero of the hour. 'Wait a minute,' he shouted, dipping a hand into the briefcase, 'I nearly forgot. We ought to make it official before we do anything else.' He handed Mike and Ray single sheets of typed paper, and passed another to Ossie. Janie took her copy as she came out of the bathroom. Jack said, 'It's a standard agency agreement. I copied the appropriate clauses out in the office. It gives me authority to act on your behalf and so forth. Sign 'em tomorrow if you like, but I must have them before I buy that new van in the morning.'

They signed there and then. They signed even before Ann emerged from the bathroom. 'Everyone ready?' she asked.

How excited they all were! At the restaurant, Jack called for more champagne, and at the end of the evening paid for it all. Ann's dark eyes came out from the shadows and flashed and sparkled. Next to her, Janie laughed and talked so much that she scarcely touched the food on her plate. Mike and Ray ate gargantuan meals, and Ossie drank a prodigious amount . . . while at the head of the table, Jack beamed contentment and nodded aproval.

Supper must have lasted a couple of hours, but I can't recall much that was said. Neither can I remember what happened afterwards: whether everyone came back to the flat or if we all went to the Green Door. I don't even know who walked Ann home, though I presume it was Jack. My strongest recollection is of crawling into bed, feeling indescribably sad. The champagne was partly responsible. Gin makes some people sad; with me it's champagne and I must have drunk well over a bottle. But it was more than the champagne, it was a feeling of saying goodbye to the past, an awareness of being overtaken by events; a great sense of loss. I couldn't explain it. After all, Ann was staying in London and that made me happy, but I suppose I knew things would be different. Until then I'd been Jack's equal with Ann. She'd been neither his girl nor mine, we'd shared her and I'd liked it that way. Now the relationship would change. Jack had got the 'Action' he wanted. To my vast surprise AIDA had worked and I was left nursing mixed feelings: a grudging admiration mingled with envy. I suppose I felt left out. The future looked like being Jack, Ann and The Graduates, with me applauding from the sidelines.

I didn't know what I felt for Ann. Love? Love was dangerous. Anyone or anything I'd loved in the past had been snatched away from me. My mother, my favourite toys, my dog and the stray cat I adopted. Love seemed to bring its own special kind of punishment. I was afraid of it.

Then there was Jack. How could I compete with Jack? Apart from being quicker and brighter than me, he was the closest friend I'd ever had. School would have been purgatory without Jack. My home life, growing up, living in the same house as my father — all would have been a hundred times worse. Jack's constant visits had kept my father at bay.

God, I was confused, and fearful. Part of the muddle in my head was that while I envied Jack, I feared for him at the same time. He was taking such risks with his career. He was misreading my father. He believed he could do no wrong in my father's eyes, which was true up to a point, but my father expected his protégé to match his own dedication. Mortlake, Dingle & Barnes was all that gave purpose to my father's life. 'More than that, no man should want,' was his motto. But Jack did want more. He had already borrowed five hundred pounds from my father's bankers. My father would be furious. Jack was already taking time off from the office. My father would go mad if he found out . . .

And so I fretted, befuddled by drink and envy and worry. Everyone else counted that night as a huge success. They saw themselves a step nearer their goals . . . whereas I saw only dangers and pitfalls.

There were surprisingly few pitfalls at the outset. Gill was delighted when Ann asked to stay. So was his wife Mary, with whom Ann spent a lot of time. 'I dunno what they find to talk about,' Gill grumbled, 'they sit there after breakfast, natter, natter, natter.'

Grumbling was Gill's way. He even teased Ann about Jack. 'I wonder what Cowboy Jack's got in store for you next?' he grinned.

Jack was 'Cowboy Jack' to Gill for a long time after the night of the hat. Jack only wore it the once, the following day it was returned to the theatrical costumier from whom it had been hired. It had served its purpose of making Ann laugh at the right moment. But Gill never tired of telling the story. All of his cronies had heard it. 'Cowboy Jack came through those swing doors like Roy Rogers,' he would laugh, embellishing the tale every time.

Meanwhile 'Cowboy Jack' was hectically busy. Mike's old van was part-exchanged for a new minibus with six seats in the front and plenty of room for the musical instruments. Jack had it painted scarlet and gold, with 'Jack Webb Enterprises' sign-written in black on the driver's door. Then he hired a rehearsal hall three afternoons a week. The hall was used by boy scouts some evenings, and the WI on others. Built mostly of wood, it was thirty feet wide and sixty feet long, with a raised stage at one end. 'No Smoking' signs were fixed all over the place and it reeked strongly of creosote. It was tucked away in the backstreets of Kentish Town. 'You need a map and compass to find it,' Mike complained with mock indignation – but the truth was that he was overjoyed, they all were. For the first time in their lives, The Graduates were able to rehearse in comfort. Ann was collected from Gill's pub three times a week. They auditioned for a drummer, and the job of transformation was started.

Jack did a lot of other things. He bought an off-the-shelf company and renamed it Jack Webb Enterprises Limited. He had stationery printed, using Gill's address as his office. ('I hope to God the brewery don't find out,' Gill grumbled when he gave his consent.) Business cards were printed – 'Jack Webb, Managing Director'. He obtained Ossie's list of contacts and spoke to them all. He increased the group's price from ten to twenty pounds a night and lost them six bookings. 'Don't worry,' he told a dismayed Ossie. 'Only monkeys work for peanuts. If they can't pay our price, they don't deserve you. I'll get something better.' And he did. Admittedly The Graduates were no better off because they worked less often and Jack took twenty-five percent of their money; but he treated them to a few more fish and chip suppers and their belief in him was sustained. Most of all, though, they believed in Ann. She was a natural coach. 'She's terrific,' Jack burbled after sneaking off to eavesdrop on a session in Kentish Town. 'She's bringing Janie on by leaps and bounds . . .'

And believe it or not, all of this happened in six weeks. I worried myself sick because Jack was always missing from the office.

'Jack,' I kept saying, 'you must spend more time here. Even Dingle has started to ask where you are. And when you are here, you're putting too many personal calls through the switchboard . . .'

Jack always had an answer. 'Just give me another few weeks,' he'd say. 'The business will run itself after that. Ann can take the bookings over the phone at Gill's place —'

'But if my father finds out —'

'Oh, Tubby, you're always so afraid of your father. You're twenty-one now. He can't eat you.'

'He can prevent me eating,' I pointed out gloomily. Not that Jack listened. We were supposed to study two nights a week, but we'd hardly done that since our first visit to Gill Martin's. I was beginning to worry for myself as well as for Jack. If he fell behind, he could probably catch up; if I fell behind, it might finish me.

Jack was only partly right about me and my father. I didn't fear him but I was careful not to give him a stick with which to beat me, and I knew that explaining Jack's absences from the office would do exactly that. The pretence about Companies House was wearing thin and the consequences of my father finding me out in the lie would be painful. He had taught me a lesson once before . . .

I must have been about seven at the time. A stray cat had found its way to our kitchen door. He was a handsome cat; grey and white with a single tip of ginger at the end of his tail, more a kitten than a cat, and I'd been feeding him for a week before my father found out. He disliked cats, especially strays. I was called into his study and he gave me a lecture. 'I will not tolerate unwanted animals about the place. If you don't feed it, it will go away. Understand?' I did understand and I stopped feeding the cat for a couple of days, but he seemed to know the exact time I set foot in the house. He was always there to greet me when I came home from school. I had to give him something. Meanwhile my father complained, 'That blasted cat's still prowling around. You're not feeding it, are you?' And I lied; I said no, when in fact I used to collect all the scraps left from dinner and take them down to the end of the garden under cover of darkness. The cat was always there, waiting. He would purr his thanks and rub himself against me after I'd fed him in secret. Then one evening, when I slipped out of the kitchen door, he failed to appear. 'Puss, puss,' I whispered, creeping from the potting shed to the back of the greenhouse. Finally I found him. He was curled up into a ball. I thought he was asleep. 'Puss,' I said in hushed tones, dropping to my knees and placing the plate by his nose. 'Puss,' I whispered, reaching out to stroke him. The small body was cold and stiff. It was a chilling shock to realise he was dead. I kept stroking him with a trembling hand. It was my first encounter with death. My eyes stung with tears. I was frightened and unsure what to do. Should I bury him? If so, how? At that age, I had yet to attend a funeral. Picking him up, I clutched him to my chest, trying to think of what to do for the best. Suddenly I heard a movement behind me. Turning, I was blinded by the sudden shining of a torch. 'Ah, there you are,' said my father's voice, high above me. 'Is that the stray cat?'

'He's dead,' I said, my voice trembling, 'the poor thing's dead.'

My father actually laughed. 'Is it. I wonder how that happened?'

He sounded pleased and triumphant. There was no surprise in his voice, so that although he pretended to wonder how it happened, I had an awful premonition that he knew, just as he had known exactly where to find me.

'And how do you think it died?'

'I don't know,' I answered tearfully, still cradling the stiffening body in my arms.

'You don't know,' he sneered. 'Well, I'll tell you. You see I came across some scraps in the kitchen last night; on a plate, hidden away under the sink; so I thought, bits of food like that might attract mice, or even rats. So I poisoned it.'

I went numb. The realisation seeped into my brain. I'd fed poisoned food to the cat. I had poisoned him. He had trusted me and I'd killed him.

'Liars mislead others at their peril,' my father continued gleefully. 'Had you told me you were feeding the cat naturally I shouldn't have poisoned the food. How was I to know you were a liar?'

'You knew,' I cried hotly. 'You've been spying on me. You knew all along!'

'My conscience is clear,' he said cheerfully, turning away and walking off up the path. 'You stole the food. You told the lies. And you poisoned the cat.'

I was left in the dark with tears streaming down my face, hating him and hating myself for what had happened.

The pain and the guilt suffered at that moment faded with the passage of time. My father inflicted so many punishments that the incident ceased to have special significance. It became one of many – or at least it did until I started to help Jack with his lies. 'Jack,' I protested, 'I can't say you're at Companies House again.' And Jack would think of an alternative. 'Okay, say I've taken some papers round to chambers. I won't be half an hour.'

But he was half an hour. Often he was an hour, sometimes two, and as the lies mounted up, the grey and white kitten came back to my mind. Ever since I was a child, my father had been able to tell when I lied. Yet he did nothing. He listened to my explanations of Jack's whereabouts without challenging a word. But I knew we were playing with fire. It was only a matter of time . . . then heaven help us!

I was alone in our room at the office when it happened. My father opened the door and entered, followed by Reece Jones, the office manager. Nobody liked Jones. He was a toady, always creeping to my father with one tale or another. His presence was a warning of trouble.

'Ah!' my father exclaimed, sounding quite jovial. 'Jack would appear to be absent. Where is he?'

Looking up, I regarded my father. He was a big man, well over six feet and weighing at least sixteen stone. His face was broad, ruddy in complexion, heavily jowled and pugnacious. As usual he wore a dark Savile Row suit and spotless white linen, with a handkerchief tucked into the cuff of his sleeve. That morning his cold blue eyes gleamed with malice, a sure sign of his being intent upon something unpleasant.

Instinct warned me against the usual excuses. 'Jack?' I said stupidly.

'Yes, Jack,' he echoed. His malice dissolved to a look of contempt. He began to tap one foot impatiently, while casting his eyes up to the ceiling.

'He's sick,' I said. It was the best excuse I could think of on the spur of the moment.

'Sick? How sick?' His eyebrows rose as he turned to Jones. 'Do you know anything about this? Is he in hospital? What's the matter with him?'

It was an old tactic. He never asked one question when he could ask more. He hurled questions in rapid succession, like a knife thrower pinning you to the wall. Turning back to me, he demanded, 'What do you mean, sick? Seriously sick?'

'Only a cold,' I managed. 'Er . . . a bad cold, but just a cold. I think he'll be in later –'

Pointing to my telephone, he said, 'Call him at home. I want to speak to him.'

I stared in dismay.

'Are you deaf as well as stupid? I suppose you know your own number?'

'Oh yes –'

'Then do as you're told.'

'Now?'

'Now!'

Having no choice, I dialled our number, knowing Jack was out. I even knew where he was. He was in Denmark Street, meeting a music publisher about a song Ossie had written.

'Ringing?' asked my father as the tone began to purr in my ear. Our eyes met. He knew Jack wasn't there, he knew I was acting out a charade. I could feel his enmity. He was pushing and I was resisting. The old battle was joined.

He turned away and walked over to the filing cabinet. Opening the drawer, he took out the Jackson folder, then the Martindale contract, followed by every file in Jack's care. My stomach lurched in alarm. Something very serious was about to happen.

'I'm afraid there's no answer,' I said. 'Jack's probably gone to the doctor.'

Without answering, my father crossed the room and stacked the files on Jack's desk. After which he sat down in Jack's chair and began to open the desk drawers. One drawer was locked. Removing a keyring from his pocket he examined his collection of keys. Horrified, I realised he had duplicates.

Swallowing hard, I said, 'Er . . . can I help you?'

'Don't you mean *may* I help you?' he said without looking up. 'Were you taught the Queen's English? Can't you even . . .' he broke off as his key turned in the lock. The drawer opened. He stared for a moment before, to my continuing horror, he lifted out a carton of notepaper. Straight from the printer, the box was still sealed, but one sheet was stuck to the top.

Even from where I sat I could see the red embossed lettering of Jack Webb Enterprises Ltd. Stupidly, I was still holding the phone to my ear. Replacing the receiver, I stared across the room, watching and waiting for a reaction. Not a muscle twitched in my father's face. Delving back into the drawer, he withdrew boxes of business cards, Ossie's list of contacts, and various other bits and pieces.

Powerless to stop him, I tried to think of a way to protect Jack. My brain seized up. My face and hands went clammy with sweat. I could think of nothing to say that might help. And I was sitting there, dry mouthed and panic stricken, when the door opened and Jack walked in.

'Ah!' My father looked up. 'And how is the patient?'

Jack stared. He saw my father, he saw the folders piled on the desk, he saw the letterheads and business cards, and he went white.

'I asked how you were,' said my father.

I tried to catch Jack's eye, but his gaze was fixed on my father's face with the intensity of a man watching his executioner.

'Did you go to the doctor?'

'Me, sir? No, sir.'

'Then you are perfectly well?'

'Yes, thank you, sir.'

I knew we were both done for. A thin smile came to my father's lips. He didn't even bother to look at me. He knew, as I knew, the consequences of my lie. If he decided Jack had transgressed, I would be found equally guilty. His judgement was not long in coming. 'This is all very interesting,' he said, tapping the pack of notepaper with his finger. 'Jack Webb

Enterprises indeed. And what have you been so enterprising about, Jack?'

'Nothing much, sir.'

'Oh, come now, don't be so modest. Letterheads, business cards, a company seal. This looks like a big organisation.'

He was playing like a cat with a mouse. I remembered the grey and white kitten with the ginger tip on its tail. I wanted to shout out, to put Jack on his guard, but my tongue clove to the roof of my mouth.

'Jack Webb Enterprises,' my father repeated.

Jack shrugged. 'It's something I do in my spare time.'

'Your time or my time?' My father raised his eyebrows.

'Mostly in the evening, sir.'

'I'm glad you said "mostly". "Wholly" would have been a lie, would it not?'

There was no menace in his voice. He spoke conversationally, almost casually. I knew it was a trick. He was at his most spiteful when using that tone, when he spoke with the voice of a reasonable man. But Jack walked right into the trap. Recovering some of his confidence, he managed a shamefaced grin. 'Well, I may have taken a few minutes off here and there –'

'A few minutes? You've taken two hours this morning.'

'Ah, well –'

'Yesterday you took two and a half hours for lunch, and the day before that you took three.'

'Oh, hardly. I mean, I don't think so –'

'I *know* so,' said my father, hardening his voice.

'I've made it my business to know. I've checked your coming and going just as I've checked your telephone calls. In fact I see some of the numbers listed here.' Picking up Ossie's list, he read aloud, 'The Blue Danube Coffee Bar, The Jaconara, the Hole in the Wall. You called them all yesterday, seeking employment for these entertainers whom you purport to represent.'

I felt sick. Again, I was reminded of when my father had set poison down for the kitten. How stealthily he had made his moves. How thoroughly he had prepared his ground. And how merciless had been the execution.

'You are guilty of theft,' he said coolly, 'theft of my time, theft of telephone calls charged to my account, theft of my office services –'

'Theft?' Jack repeated incredulously.

'Yes, theft. That's what it amounts to. And you betrayed the trust I placed in you –'

'Not theft,' Jack protested.

'Oh, don't worry, I shan't prosecute. However, you are dismissed with immediate effect. I have no intention of paying you another penny. Neither will I give you a reference. Take these,' my father gestured at Jack's belongings, 'and get out.'

Already white, Jack's face took on a greenish hue. He opened his mouth and closed it again. Clearing his throat, he finally found his voice, but my father was still speaking. 'You too,' he said, turning to me. 'You're fired. I never want to see you in this office again.'

I was expecting it but his words took Jack by surprise. 'Tubby?' he exclaimed. 'But Tubby's done nothing –'

'Except lie and cover up and generally act as your accomplice –'

'Bloody rubbish!' Jack roared, losing his temper, colour flooding back to his face. 'You can't sack Tubby. Tubby's done nothing –'

'Exactly. He's done nothing. He's lazy and indolent –'

'Balls!' Jack shouted.

'Jack!' I cried, at last finding my voice as I rose to my feet. 'That's enough.'

He looked at me in astonishment. 'You can't let him walk all over you. For Christ's sake, stand up to him for once –'

'Jack!' I shouted.

He choked on his words.

I took a deep breath. 'It's okay,' I said in the most normal voice I could muster. Perhaps my father did walk all over me, but I would never plead. That was the one satisfaction I had always denied him. And if I refused to plead, I was damned if I'd allow Jack to plead for me.

Rising to his feet, my father turned to Jones. 'Bring those folders to my office, I want them updated immediately.'

And with that they departed, my father leading the way and Jones following like a dog at his heels.

'Bastard!' Jack swore viciously as the door closed. Then he looked at me. 'Oh Christ, Tubby, I'm so sorry.'

I sat down, trembling. I suppose I had gone white. My colour usually deserted me when under attack from my father. Jack and I looked at each other. In the way of our friendship, we were each concerned for the other. Our careers were finished. My father would see to that. No other solicitor would take us without a reference. We had wasted three years of our lives. Jack's parents would be heartbroken. They were so proud of him; to listen to his mother talking about him was to hear a description of a future Solicitor General. Now Jack had been sacked. And what was almost as bad, I suddenly remembered, he'd borrowed a small fortune on the strength of his future at Mortlake, Dingle & Barnes.

He came and sat on the edge of my desk. 'I must make him see reason at least about you. Do you think he'd listen if I went to his office? He may have calmed down. If I could persuade him to have second thoughts about you –'

I shook my head. 'He doesn't need to calm down. He was icy calm just now and he never has second thoughts, especially about me –'

'So what do we do?'

Poor Jack. He couldn't accept it was all over. Until then he'd believed he could talk his way out of anything. He had truly believed in his special relationship with my father. I had never harboured such illusions. 'What can we do?' I said, opening a desk drawer to transfer personal belongings to my briefcase. 'It's his office. He told us to get out. We'll have to go.'

'You're going to accept it?' he asked incredulously.

'We've no choice. He won't change his mind. He told us to go.'

'Go?' he echoed, vacillating between shock and temper, 'I know where I'm going. I'm going to get drunk. I'm going to get really shit-faced drunk, that's where I'm going.'

Jumping up, he went across to his desk and started sweeping the clutter into his briefcase. Opening drawers, he banged and crashed, swearing throughout. 'What a bastard? What a cold-blooded, miserable, fucking bastard!'

A moment later he had finished. 'Right,' he said, breathing heavily. 'Ready?'

'I'd better say goodbye to Dingle first. And to –'

'Fuck goodbyes. That creep Jones will have told the whole building. I'm buggered if I'll have people smirking at me. I want a stiff drink.'

I hesitated. I could have used a drink myself. But old Dingle had always been very decent to me and I would have felt badly about not saying goodbye. Besides, now that I'd stopped trembling, I saw no reason to sneak off like a thief in the night. That would have played into my father's hands and I was damned if I'd do that. In fact it prompted a sudden idea. 'No,' I said shaking my head. 'Before I leave I shall say goodbye to everyone in the building.'

'You can't be serious!'

'I am. I'll say goodbye office by office, I'll even say goodbye to the girls on the switchboard.'

'You're a bloody masochist,' said Jack, shaking his head. 'I'm not having any of that. I'll see you in the pub.' He paused with his hands on the door, 'Not The Feathers though, I couldn't face that. I'll see you in the Master Printer, okay?'

'Okay.'

'And Tubby . . .'

I looked up from packing my briefcase.

'I am bloody sorry.'

'I know.'

And he walked out, not looking back. He walked

out of the building and down the front steps, anger on his face and God knows what in his heart.

Saying my goodbyes took longer than I expected. Nobody smirked, Jack had been quite wrong; most people were stunned and slightly embarrassed. They said how sorry they were and how much they would miss me. It was really quite touching. Old Dingle was especially decent. 'Come in,' he said when I knocked on his door, 'sit down, my boy, and let me get you a drink.' He must have known my father would have disapproved, but he poured me a sherry regardless. Dingle was my idea of the perfect family solicitor; kind, considerate, and very attentive to detail. He looked like a soft boiled egg in a charcoal-grey suit. His dome shaped head was completely bald, his face was plump and pink, and he had the tiny feet of a ballroom dancer. If you ever saw a drawing of Humpty Dumpty in a nursery-book, you'll be able to visualise Dingle in an instant. He said, 'I'm desperately sorry about what's happened.' Giving me a pained look, he added a note of apology, 'But, of course, you know your father.'

I said, Yes, I did know my father.

'I told him your work was excellent. I've never had cause for complaint. In my view you've a real feel for the law.'

'Thank you.'

'You mustn't give it up,' he said earnestly.

There was no point in saying I had no choice.

'What will you do now?' he asked.

I hadn't the faintest idea. Being fired had come as a bolt from the blue.

'Well, don't act hastily,' he said, shaking hands.

I promised I wouldn't, and went off to see the girls on the switchboard. They were tucked away in a little cubby-hole on the third floor and most people forgot they were there; I mean, when it was some-one's birthday and there was cake in the office, the girls on the switchboard were always forgotten. Anyway, I said my goodbyes and half an hour later I left the offices of Mortlake, Dingle & Barnes for the last time. Shock had buoyed me up until then, shock and the need to display all the dignity I could muster. But once on the street the consequences really hit me. I was out on my ear with less than thirty pounds in the bank, no job and no prospects. I admit it was hard not to feel sorry for myself as I set out to find Jack.

The Master Printer was packed with people three deep at the bar. I pushed my way through the crush and ordered a beer, craning my neck, searching for Jack. There was no sign of him. Carrying my drink into various corners, I expected to see the familiar mop of untidy blond hair, but Jack wasn't there. I wondered if he had gone to The Feathers. I was sure he'd said the Master Printer, but in his agitated state he might have reverted to habit. So I finished the beer and set off for The Feathers.

Unfortunately, The Feathers was packed with people from the office, all swilling away and gossiping about the morning's events. I was forced to suffer the embarrassment of saying goodbye all over again. Nobody had seen Jack. I set off for The Grapes, not really expecting him to be there, but at least it enabled me to escape.

Predictably, there was no sign of him at The

Grapes. I stayed long enough to drink another beer and to eat a cheese sandwich. Then I returned to the Master Printer. By now it was virtually closing time, and Jack was still not to be seen. Feeling angry and let down, I set out for home, wondering what the devil had happened.

As I turned into Whitcombe Street, I bumped into Ann. She was hurrying along, out of breath, a worried look on her face. 'Oh Tubby! Thank God. Have you seen him?'

Obviously she meant Jack. I started to tell her that I'd searched half the pubs in the City, when she interrupted, 'He was at Gill's. We couldn't get any sense out of him. He was in a terrible state. He kept saying he'd ruined your life. He said he'd let you down and got you both fired. Even before he arrived at Gill's, he'd been drinking himself silly.' Ann gasped for breath. 'He'd have emptied every bottle in the place if Gill had let him. We got some coffee down him, but you know what it's like in that place at lunchtime, it's chaos and we're working flat out. I went over to him whenever I could. I told him to sit there until closing time, then he could tell me about it. Next time I looked, he'd gone. Gill tried the men's room and he wasn't there either . . .'

By now she had taken my arm and was turning in the direction of the flat. Between catching her breath, she continued her explanation. 'He must have left just before closing time. I came as soon as Gill shut the doors. Tubby, what happened this morning?'

I was spared the need to answer by our arrival at the flat. 'He's probably sleeping it off,' I said, opening the door.

Ann raced ahead of me up the stairs and opened

the door at the top. 'He's not here,' she cried. By the time I reached the living room, she was coming out of the bathroom. We tried the bedrooms and the kitchen. Jack was not in the flat.

'We must find him,' she cried in dismay. 'You should have seen the state he was in. What in the world happened? Did you and he have a fight?'

'No,' I said, 'we didn't have a fight.' Then, possibly because I wanted to calm us both down, I went into the kitchen to make a pot of tea. I thought it likely that Jack would arrive home at any moment. Meanwhile it seemed wisest to remain where we were. Ann followed and took the kettle from my hands. 'I'll do that,' she said. 'Just tell me what happened.'

So I did. I gave her the bare bones, omitting most of the details, ending my account with the arrangements Jack and I had made to meet at the Master Printer. Ann had made the tea by the time I finished. We set the cups on the table and sat opposite each other. Her dark eyes were full of concern as she reached for my hand. 'Oh, Tubby, that's appalling. I'm so very sorry. What a rotten, stinking, unfair thing to happen.'

I don't think I answered. It was rotten and unfair, but complaining wouldn't help.

Then to my amazement, she began to reproach herself. 'Oh, it's all my fault,' she cried. 'How stupid not to see it coming. I'm such a selfish bitch at times!'

She rose from the table and hurried off into the living room, returning a moment later with her handbag. From the look on her face I thought she was about to burst into tears, but then I realised she was more angry than tearful. Opening the bag, she produced cigarettes and fumbled for a lighter.

'It's not your fault,' I said, trying to calm her as she rooted about in her handbag. She was too agitated to find the lighter, so I reached over to the gas stove for the matches and gave her a light. She tilted her head back and exhaled a long stream of smoke at the ceiling. 'I should have known this would happen.'

'I don't see how –'

'Oh, come on, Tubby, I'm not stupid. You can't believe I didn't know about Jack. I'd have to be blind.' She met my look of incredulity. 'All this business with Janie and the others. Don't you think I realised it was just to impress me?'

I stared speechlessly across the rim of my cup.

'Women do know these things, you know,' she said, turning away with a bitter laugh. 'Especially women like me.'

I sat very still. I was getting a glimpse of a different Ann, the Ann I had guessed about, the Ann whose experience of life was quite beyond mine.

She caught my expression. 'Oh, don't look like that. No matter what they say, I didn't murder anyone in New York. I made a mess of my life but I didn't actually kill anyone.'

I remained silent. She drew on her cigarette, the shadows back in her eyes and a sad look on her face. A minute passed before her expression diffused into a shadowy smile. She said, 'Then I came here and met you and Jack, and . . . I suppose the truth is I'd forgotten that people like you existed. People like Gill. Decent uncomplicated people. Innocents. You can't imagine the relief it's been –' breaking off, she cocked her head, listening. 'Is that Jack?' Jumping up, she hurried from the kitchen. I heard her open the door onto the landing. 'Jack?' she called.

Preparing to follow her, I pushed my chair back from the table and stood up. My head was spinning. I was amazed that she had known about Jack's little schemes.

'It's not him,' she said, returning. 'Oh, Tubby, where can he be? He was too drunk to stand up.'

Thinking hard, I said, 'He can't be boozing now. The pubs are shut. Perhaps he's sobering up over a coffee –'

'He won't come here,' she said with sudden conviction. 'He's afraid to face you –'

'No –'

'Yes. He said he's ruined your life. He got you fired and ruined your life. That's what he said.' She stubbed her cigarette out, twisting it savagely in the ashtray. 'This wouldn't have happened if I hadn't encouraged him. I got carried away, helping Janie and Ossie, it was fun, and . . .' she paused, meeting my eye defensively, as if I had accused her, 'I really am helping them, you know.'

'Yes, I'm sure –'

'I do know about music.'

'I know –'

'God, I'm a selfish cow.' She interrupted bitterly, 'I knew Jack was skipping his work. I should have said. I should have had the sense to see this coming –'

'Nobody saw it coming –'

'You did. You've been fretting for weeks.'

'Only because I know my father.'

'He sounds an absolute pig,' she said. Until that moment she had remained standing, hovering indecisively. Suddenly she reached a decision. 'It's no good, he won't come back here. I'm going to look for him. I've enough on my conscience. If he gets knocked down by a bus . . .' Her words trailed off as she made for the door.

'Wait for me,' I said. 'We'll both go.'

We searched for Jack all afternoon. Cafés, tearooms, coffee bars. We walked the length of Tottenham Court Road and Oxford Street and all round Soho. The grey drizzle of the morning gradually worsened into blustery showers. We plunged through puddles and sheltered in cafés from time to time. At five o'clock, weary and defeated, we went to Gill's. Ann had to be there to open the front bar at five thirty.

When we arrived, Gill was already behind the counter, replenishing stock and polishing glasses. He looked at Ann's face and knew we had failed to find Jack. Ann was afraid Jack might have had an accident. She was upset about us being kicked out of Mortlake, Dingle & Barnes, and she felt responsible. She blamed herself.

'Where the devil can he be?' Gill asked, scratching his head. 'You'll have to find him, Tubby, he was legless when he left here.' And then, because he was a soft hearted soul, Gill put a hand on my arm. 'Sorry to hear about this trouble with your father. Very sorry, Tubby, very sorry indeed.' It was a tactful way to express sympathy. 'Look here,' he said, turning to Ann, 'just help with the rush. Knock off after an hour and help Tubby find Jack.'

Thanking him, I returned to the flat, promising to wait for Ann there. Jack had still not returned. I know it sounds odd, considering we'd been searching all afternoon, but I hadn't worried over much until then. So much had happened, what with being chucked out by my father and meeting Ann so unexpectedly – and, I knew Jack of old, he always bounced back. But when I found myself alone in the flat, the need to find him loomed larger. I kept asking myself, 'Where the hell can he be?'

I telephoned the police and the two local hospitals. Thankfully, Jack had neither been locked up nor involved in a traffic accident. I hesitated about telephoning his mother. If he wasn't with her she'd ask questions, and I had no intention of breaking the news about events in the office. Even so, bereft of any other ideas, I was about to call her when the door-bell rang. I hurried down the stairs and opened the door. It was Ann. 'He's in a pub in Warren Street,' she said breathlessly, 'Gill just heard from the landlord.'

I got my coat and we set off. Like a lot of other places, Warren Street was different in those days. It was the centre of London's used car trade and every second shop was a car showroom. Most of the vehicles parked in the street were for sale. Not that we paid much attention as we hurried along. Ann was telling me about the landlord at The George. 'You must know him,' she said. 'Len Thomson. He's often in Gill's. Short man with wavy black hair. He said Jack's round there spending money like a drunken sailor.'

We soon found The George. Like Gill's place, it had two bars, so Ann and I separated. The bar I chose was crowded and smoke-filled, but I saw Jack at once. It was the first time I ever saw him with a cigar in his mouth. Some people believe he was born smoking a cigar, but they only know Jack from newspaper photographs. Believe me that evening in Warren Street was the first time he ever set a light to a cigar. Not that it was alight. It had been, his shirt front was covered in ash, but when I arrived the cigar was quite out.

'Tubby!' he greeted me with a beaming smile. 'Come and sit down.'

He'd wedged himself behind a corner table. As I pulled out a chair, he shouted, 'Landlord! More champagne for my friend.'

Only then did I see the up-turned bottle protruding from the ice bucket at Jack's feet. I said, 'Cigars and champagne, Jack? What's this, a celebration?'

'Certainly,' he agreed, waving his glass and slopping its expensive contents over the rim, ''Course it's a celebration. It's a great day, Tubby my boy. A red letter day if ever there was one.'

Apart from slurring his speech and showering me with saliva, he seemed fairly sober. Removing the cigar from his mouth, he stared at it, but made no attempt to re-light it. Instead he began to use it as a conductor might use a baton. He sat upright in his chair. His face was flushed, his eyes were bright, he was in excellent spirits, but not drunk. Neither, of course, was he completely sober. He was in between; in that comforting state in which all good things are possible and miracles are certain to happen. 'Are you all right?' I asked.

''Course I'm all right,' he said, momentarily solemn. Lowering his voice, he confided, 'I am now, but I got pie-eyed at lunchtime. Pissed as a newt. Staggering all over the place, I was. People thought I was drunk.'

'I was looking for you –'

'I was *here!*' he shouted, waving a hand at the bar. Then he squinted at the gold lettering on the window. From where we sat, the word 'Saloon' was spelt backwards. Jack's lips moved in silent concentration and a frown came to his brow. Finally a gleam lit his eye. 'Not this actual place, understand? Not where we are now. Coffee bar down the road. Met a magnificent fellow –'

Ann emerged at that moment, pushing her way through the throng, with Len, the landlord, grinning beside her.

'Ann,' Jack exclaimed, pushing himself up from the table, 'you're here too! Marvellous. Tubby, Ann's here.'

'Yes,' I said.

Looking at Ann, I thought she looked even more worried. 'Thanks, Len,' she said to the landlord. 'Let's get him home.'

'Champagne!' Jack bellowed. 'Landlord, I ordered another bottle –'

'Home,' Ann repeated firmly, snuggling against him before he had a chance to sit down. 'Put your arm over my shoulders, Jack, that's right. Tubby, give me a hand.'

Pulling the table clear, I was beginning to squeeze a path through to the door when Len whispered to me, 'It's beautiful. Credit to Jack. He knows a good thing when he sees one. I bet it goes like a bomb.'

I hadn't the faintest idea what he was talking about. Seeing my expression he said, 'The car. I was just telling Ann.'

At that moment we emerged on to the pavement. 'There it is,' said Len, pointing. 'Ain't it a beauty?'

Parked at the kerbside was the raciest looking

sports car I ever saw. Green paintwork and polished chrome shone in the lamplight. A battery of head-lamps adorned the radiator. Twin exhausts testified to the roar of the engine. With a number painted on the side it would have been ready for the twenty-four hour race at Le Mans.

'It's mine,' Jack crowed proudly. 'All part of the new image.'

I'd have called him a liar except for the look on Ann's face.

'It's true,' she said, 'Len told me just now. One of his regulars sold it to Jack this afternoon. Two hundred pounds down and so much a month –'

'Jack hasn't got two hundred pounds.'

'He did have. He wrote out a cheque and they cleared it especially. I've got the keys and the log book in my purse. Len just gave them to me.'

'Oh no.' I looked in horror at Jack. It must have been the last of the five hundred pounds he'd bor-rowed from the bank.

'Jack!' I cried. 'What on earth came over you. My father just fired us –'

'Best thing that ever happened.' Jack wagged his cigar. 'Greater things await us than toiling away at Mortlake, Dingle & Barnes. Don't worry, Tubby, my boy, I've worked it all out.'

I had ceased to listen. Instead I erupted in temper. 'Jack,' I spluttered, 'you can't drive. Remember? You need to take lessons and pass a test before you can drive. You've spent money you don't have on a car you can't drive!'

Suddenly Ann started to giggle. Perhaps out of relief from finding Jack, I don't know. All I know is that I saw no reason for laughter. I glared at her.

Someone had to take a responsible attitude, and I was doing my best when Len grinned, 'Is that right? Can't he drive, then?'

'No, he bloody well can't.'

'Oh, my word,' Len began to chuckle. Turning to Ann, he pulled a face which caused her to giggle even more, so that a moment later they were clinging to each other in convulsions.

'I don't see what's so funny,' I complained. I'd have said more, but I had to lunge at Jack to stop him from walking out into traffic. Having failed to open the doors on our side, he had stepped off the kerb without looking.

Ann wiped her eyes. 'Oh, Tubby, I'm sorry. I wouldn't have let Jack behind the wheel anyway. Here you are, you'd better drive.' Opening her bag, she held out some keys.

I backed away. 'I can't drive either.'

Goggle-eyed, Ann glanced at Len, who collapsed in hysterics. I fought the urge to join in. After all, I was angry. Angry with Jack, angry with some smart-arse salesman for taking advantage, angry with a fool of a banker for lending Jack money, angry with Ann and Len for their irresponsible laughter. But their hysteria was infectious. Next moment I was as convulsed as they were. Then Jack started, and we swayed and brayed and stamped helplessly around the car, slapping our thighs and each other's backs like drunken Indians.

Len drove us home, and Ann and I got Jack up to the flat. My hysterics had worn off by then. As far as I was concerned it had been a disastrous, exhausting, mixed-up crazy day and I was on the verge of collapse. But Jack was made of sterner stuff. Seemingly recovered from his drinking bout, he wanted to talk.

'Jack,' I pleaded, 'let's leave it till morning.'

'No,' he said, sinking into my armchair, 'I want to talk now. I have some very good news.'

'I don't think I can stand any more,' I said.

Ann put her hand on my arm. I think she feared an argument; rightly so, because I was exasperated and worried. I needed to think. I would have gone directly to bed except it was still quite early.

'I'll get some coffee,' I said. It only took a moment because I'd left the coffee percolator on when I rushed off to find Jack.

When I returned from the kitchen, I was amazed to see that Jack had taken his usual stance in front of the mantelpiece. He swayed a bit, making me wonder if I'd overestimated his powers of recovery. At least we'd be spared the pacing up and down, and I muttered as much to Ann, but she gave me a stern look to remind me of what she'd said about him being afraid to face me because of his guilt.

Jack began by saying, 'Bad day today, until I got a grip of myself. Then I said, Think; that's what I said, Think!'

'Was that before or after you got pissed?' I asked, losing patience.

He gave me a reproachful look but continued. 'The only cure,' he asserted. 'Booze numbs the shock until you can face the problem –'

'Of spending money you don't have on a car you can't drive –'

'Tubby!' Ann scolded. She really looked very cross, too. I subsided into silence, feeling a bit ashamed of myself.

Jack thanked her with a smile, then he said, 'I must tell you my news. I've sold one of Ossie's songs to a publisher. Isn't that terrific?'

'Oh, Jack.' Ann's face glowed. 'That's wonderful.'

He had the look of a hero back from the war. His eyes lingered on Ann for a moment, drawing encouragement, then he turned to me. 'That's what started me thinking,' he said. 'There's a lot of money in this pop business, more than people realise. I've got hundreds of ideas. Janie and The Graduates are only the start. What we need is a whole stable of entertainers. And the talent's there, Tubby. Ask Ann, she'll tell you. London is buzzing. All we've got to do is sign these people up. Ann will groom them, and you and I'll fix 'em up with gigs and publishing deals . . .' He paused before plunging on. 'We'll make a fortune if we work full time. You and me, fifty fifty. I'm giving you half the shares in Jack Webb Enterprises. We'll re-name it if you like. Webb and Mortlake. Mortlake and Webb. Whatever you like. Forget about being a solicitor. We'll make a fortune when we get going.'

Poor Jack. Jack Webb Enterprises boasted an overdraft, some letterheads and a sports car that neither of us could drive. Even as solicitors we had not contemplated working together; now, with this folly, Jack wanted me as a partner. *Wanted* was wrong. He felt obligated. He was offering me all he had, even if it was half of a loss. He was saying sorry while trying to salvage his pride.

Ann gave me an urgent, pleading look. I knew what she was saying: Don't kick him when he's down.

'Well?' Jack asked eagerly. 'What do you say? Are we partners?'

'It's very generous,' I replied, choosing my words with care. 'Let's sleep on it –'

'Sure, sure, but in principle. Do you agree in principle?'

'We'll always be partners, Jack,' I smiled.

There was such relief in his face that I realised Ann had been right when she talked about his feelings of guilt. He advanced across the room to grab my hand. 'Hear that?' he said, turning to Ann. 'Isn't it terrific? And you'll still help, won't you? I need you more than ever.'

Ann smiled. 'Yes, I'll help.'

He reached for her hand while continuing to shake mine. 'Funny,' he said, 'I thought it was the end of the world earlier. Now it's the beginning.' He grinned, knowing how mawkish he sounded but not caring as long as we knew he was grateful. Releasing us, he weaved back to the mantelpiece. 'Know something?' he asked. 'Suddenly I feel tired. Very tired.'

Indeed, at last he did show signs of exhaustion. I suspect waiting for my reaction to his offer had drained the last of his reserves. 'Would you mind if Tubby sees you home?' he asked Ann. 'I really must get to bed.'

And without waiting for a reply, he set off across the room. Eyes on the floor, his expression was a study in concentration. The coffee table almost brought him down, but he managed to reach the door to his bedroom. Pausing, he turned and looked back at me. 'I like what you said about us always being partners. Sums it up nicely,' he said. With which – and what I can only describe as a theatrical bow – he backed into his room and closed the door behind him.

Next minute a tremendous crash shook the whole flat. Something heavy fell in Jack's room. There was a muffled exclamation – 'Bugger it!' – followed by silence.

When I looked at Ann, she seemed intent on swallowing her handkerchief. Her hand was in her mouth and she shook with another fit of giggles. Just as she had started me off before, so I began to chuckle, but she shook her head. 'Sssh,' she choked as she rose from the chair. Grabbing her bag, she hurried out on to the landing and by the time I joined her, she was hanging over the banisters, shaking with laughter. 'Poor Jack,' she gasped as I closed the door. Recovering enough to put on her coat, she giggled helplessly as we descended the stairs.

Outside, Jack's ridiculous car was parked where Len had left it at the kerbside.

'Would madam prefer to drive?' I suggested.

All that pent-up laughter was released in one joyous whoop. She threw back her head and laughed with that vibrancy which is such a part of her. Then she cuddled into my side, hugging my arm, and we set off for Gill's. We'd scarcely gone fifty yards, when she stopped. Facing me, she flung her arms round my neck and kissed me full on the lips. 'Oh, Tubby,' she said breathlessly when she pulled away, 'you're the nicest guy who ever lived.'

It was a delicious moment. I'd have made more of it, except that before I could respond she had linked arms again and resumed the walk back to the pub. 'I know you hated Jack's idea,' she said. 'I was terrified you'd say so. It would have destroyed him.'

'Jack's indestructible.'

'Rubbish, that's not true.'

'Okay.'

'He was trying to make amends,' she said.

'I know.'

We walked in silence for a minute, then she said, 'He could pull it off you know. Why not think about his idea?'

My silence was sufficient answer. An evening at the Green Door was amusing, but the prospect of spending a lifetime in that atmosphere appalled me. Anyway, the idea was absurd. Jack Webb Enterprises couldn't support Jack Webb, let alone Tubby Mortlake.

'You're too sane,' said Ann, squeezing my arm. 'Everyone's a bit crazy in the music business.'

I was wondering if she meant I was dull, when she asked, 'So what will you do?'

Old Dingle had asked that. I was still lost for an answer.

'Haven't you any ideas?' Ann asked gently.

I really hadn't had time to consider. I shrugged. 'I suppose I might get a job in the legal department of a large organisation. After all, I do have some legal training.'

Then she said a very nice thing. 'Don't worry. People won't let your kind of integrity go to waste . . . You'll soon get some sort of offer.'

I tried to console myself with Ann's words after seeing her home. As I climbed the stairs back at the flat, my brain was still trying to absorb what had happened. After spending so long planning to be a solicitor in a small country town, I found it impossible to visualise anything else. Then another thought struck me, making my situation even worse. How could I explain that I'd been fired by my own father? A prospective employer would suspect me of all manner of crimes. 'He must be a thoroughly bad lot,' I could hear people say.

Once in bed, I tossed and turned, worrying and wondering if I could eke my money out until I found some sort of job. But finally I dozed off and had the most delicious dreams about Ann.

The odd thing was she was right about my future. My father had not been alone in making decisions about me that day. Other men had made up their minds. Telephone calls had been exchanged. I had been assessed in my absence. Ann was never more right than when she encouraged me by saying, 'You'll soon get some sort of offer.'

The telephone rang at nine fifteen the next morning. Jack was still sleeping off the effects of his drinking, but I'd been up over an hour. I'd even been out to buy the papers, less to read the news than to examine the 'Situations Vacant'. By nine fifteen my worst fears were confirmed; even jobs outside the profession were for qualified people. Grim-faced, munching toast and sipping tea, I was working my way through the column in the *Telegraph* headed 'Legal Assistants' when the telephone rang. It was old Dingle. Humpty Dumpty from the office. 'Hello,' he said, 'I'm glad I caught you before you went out.'

I had nowhere to go, but there seemed no point in reminding him. I imagined he had been through my files and was calling about a minor query, but not a bit of it. 'Would you be free to meet me this morning?' he asked. 'Say at about eleven thirty?'

'At the office?'

'No,' he said mysteriously. 'Actually I had the Great Western Hotel in mind. Do you know it?'

'It's at Paddington Station,' I said.

'That's right. I'll be lunching near there, but if you could be at the hotel by eleven thirty we could have coffee.'

'Fine.'

'I'll have someone with me. Tom Weston, an old friend of mine. He'd quite like to meet you.'

Jack was still sleeping when I left. There seemed no point in waking him. I'd been through the papers and none of the pop groups were advertising for a manager.

When I arrived at the Great Western, Dingle was already seated at a corner table in the cavernous lounge, talking to a man who was a complete stranger to me. I was fifteen minutes early so I thought it best to withdraw, and I was doing exactly that, intending to walk round the block for ten minutes, when Dingle looked up and saw me. He waved me over. 'Ah,' he said. 'Come and meet Tom Weston.'

Dingle never referred to me as Tubby. I suppose being on the plump side himself had given him an aversion to such names. Tom Weston, however, had no such inhibitions. 'Hello Tubby,' he said, shaking hands with a grip that would have crushed walnuts, 'Jumbo Weston. Silly name, but I'm used to it now. Got it at school and it stuck. I suppose you were christened Tubby in the same way. Kids aren't very original, are they?'

He grinned with appealing good humour. In his

early forties, he was of medium height, strongly built, with a fresh complexion and merry brown eyes. His brown hair was worn in a short-back-and-sides that did nothing to conceal the large ears that had earned him his nickname. He wore a pale brown suit in Prince of Wales check, brogue shoes, a lovat-green knitted tie; smart clothes, but not those of a professional man. He resembled my idea of a prosperous farmer, so I was surprised to learn he was a solicitor.

He laughed. 'They don't appreciate grey pin-stripes in Taunton. Formal clothes would frighten them off. Not that ours is a big firm. Nothing so important as Mortlake, Dingle & Barnes. We're just country bumpkins.'

Dingle smiled. 'With a first class reputation.'

'We try not to let people down,' Weston said modestly, looking at me. 'Now then, let's talk about you. I heard about yesterday. Only one way to look at something like that, it's your father's loss and not yours. Don't brood about it, right? What I want to know is, if you've made any plans? If not, would you like to join us? Come down and finish your articles, and if you're any good I might make you a partner when you qualify.'

Such directness was typical of Jumbo, as I was to learn. If he respected someone's opinion he backed it to the hilt. And he respected old Dingle, which is why I was there.

'This man,' Jumbo said, placing a large hand on Dingle's shoulder, 'says you'll make my kind of lawyer. So we can take that as read. What else do you do?'

His directness was so startling that I fumbled my answer. I said the usual things about liking books and listening to music, but he waved a hand impatiently. 'We all read books. But what else? Do you drink beer?'

'Well . . . yes.'

'Splendid. You don't look a namby pamby gin and tonic type. What about sports? Play anything?'

'I'm afraid not.'

'Pity,' he frowned, before asking, 'But you don't dislike sport? You're not one of those who sneer at grown men chasing a little ball around?'

'Oh no.'

'Good. What about cricket? Do you like cricket?'

'Yes. I spend half the summer at Lord's.'

His delighted grin stretched between his large ears. 'Excellent. We could use a new scorer. You sound just the chap.'

Old Dingle coughed discreetly. 'Tom played for Somerset, you know.'

'Oh?' I said, wondering if I'd seen him play.

'Before your time,' said Jumbo, reading my mind. 'Only village green stuff these days, but damn good cricket. Our lot are mustard-keen.' He sat back and grinned hugely. 'I'm going to make a speech now. I'll only make it once, so I want you to concentrate. If it sounds right, you'll be happy with us. If it sounds wrong, you'll be better off somewhere else. Got it? It's all a matter of horses for courses. Take me for example. I'd be no bloody good up here. London's for specialists. Look at the big firms like Mortlake, Dingle & Barnes. Specialising like mad. Taxation, company law, libel, probate, divorce. Agree?'

I nodded, agreeing without understanding where he was leading.

'It's the same in medicine,' he said. 'Go to Harley

Street and you'll find a consultant in everything from galloping clap to ingrowing toenails. Specialists. Stay in London if that's what you want. Learn more and more about less and less and you'll make a bloody fortune.'

He grinned his engaging grin. 'I don't spend much time dispensing the law. I'm much more interested in people.'

My interest quickened.

'The way I see it,' he said, 'is, people pay me to keep them out of trouble, and I can only do that by becoming a people expert. Any fool can look up the law. It's merely a matter of knowing the right book. But show me a book about people. Show me a book that says I'd be a fool to believe old Farmer Giles when he complains that Farmer Jones is running cattle over his land. Show me a book that says the truth is Giles and Jones have been friends for years, and their real grievance is over a woman. Show me a book that says the woman will marry Smith in a year, and that if I'd brought action against Jones in the meantime, he and Giles would be enemies the rest of their lives.'

Old Dingle cleared his throat. 'Every solicitor must exercise common sense –'

'Oh? And where do they find it? Common sense has been bred out of them. Giles tells a specialist about Jones and what does the specialist do? Issues a writ. Bloody fool. I earn a living by making Giles laugh with a story about a foolish man being led up the path by a skirt. He can't wait to re-tell it to Jones, and they both laugh so much they forget about going to court. That's what I mean by keeping people out of trouble. You can't get that out of a law book.'

Even Dingle chuckled, but he was far from convinced. 'You can't expect to know all the ins and outs of a client's life –'

'I can,' Weston interrupted. 'What's more, I insist on it. I don't want clients who're just names on a file. I want their whole lives. A man has a son. There's his education to think of. I set up a Trust. The man buys a house, I do his conveyancing. He goes into business, I advise about partnerships and limited companies. His wife has an accident, I get her compensation. His business expands, I help raise more capital. See what I mean? I'm part of his life. I'm not a solicitor, I'm a bloody Dutch Uncle.'

He burst out laughing, and would have gone on had we not been interrupted by a page boy calling, 'Mr Weston. Mr Tom Weston. Telephone call.'

'That's me,' said Jumbo, jumping up. 'Someone's in trouble. Lead me to the phone, young man,' he said eagerly to the page boy, and followed him off to the reception desk.

Old Dingle watched him go, then cocked his head at me. 'Well? Have I chosen the right man?'

I was overwhelmed. 'Do you mean it?' I stammered. 'I mean, does *he* mean it? Will he really take me on?'

'He made you a serious offer,' Dingle said gravely.

'I can't believe it,' I gasped.

'I assure you, Tom Weston isn't the type to joke about the people he employs.'

Expressing thanks was beyond me. I'd liked Jumbo Weston from the first moment. I was to go to my country town and continue with the law after all. Overjoyed, I sat shaking my head, dumbfounded by my change of fortune. A full minute passed before I could think straight. Then I thought of Jack and my happiness faded. How could I walk out on Jack? How could I rush back to the flat, full of excitement, delighted with my luck, and leave Jack alone, broke, and out of work? It seemed so unfair.

Dingle noticed the change in my expression. 'Is anything wrong?'

I hesitated, not wishing to appear ungrateful. 'I was just thinking of Jack,' I said. 'Would Jumbo give him a chance too?'

From his thoughtful expression, I imagined Dingle was considering it, but I was wrong. 'Correct me if I'm in error,' he said in that polite way of his, 'but wasn't Jack the reason you joined Mortlake, Dingle & Barnes? Your father offered Jack a place and you came along as part of the package?'

'Something like that.'

'And now Jack is the reason you are leaving.'

'I suppose so.'

Dingle smiled. 'Don't take offence, none is intended, but let me tell you how you strike me. You survived a childhood under a tyrannical father. I can only guess at what you endured, but you lived through it without becoming a weakling or a bully. That's to your immeasurable credit. You've an inner strength to which people respond. Of course, Jack helped you survive, I don't doubt that for a second, but you and Jack Webb are not destined for the same place. Yesterday's events merely hastened the inevitable. Jack Webb would not be happy with Jumbo. Jumbo would not be happy with Jack. Even to think along those lines is a mistake. Your father and Jack are both parts of your boyhood. Now is the time to move on.'

He had never spoken in such terms before. His references to my tyrannical father amazed me, but what most caught my mind was his statement about Jumbo and Jack. I knew he was right. They wouldn't get on. Even so, I might have argued had Jumbo not rejoined us at that moment.

'Sorry about that,' he said, dropping into his chair. 'Never mind, where were we?'

'I was just saying,' said Dingle with a glance at his watch, 'I really ought to be going.'

'Me too,' said Jumbo, clapping his hands for the bill. 'Now then, Tubby my lad, what's it to be? Fame and fortune in London, or getting your hands dirty with me?'

I accepted his offer without hesitation. After thanking him, I thanked Dingle for arranging the introduction and for making everything possible. Perhaps I should have said that working with Jumbo sounded like a dream come true, but I was too shy to do that. The words eluded me.

'That's all settled then,' said Jumbo, rising to his feet. Fishing through his pockets, he found some silver coins which he left next to his saucer as a tip. 'So when can you start?' he asked me. 'What about Monday?'

'Next Monday?' I said, taken aback.

'Why not?' he grinned. 'You'll only form bad habits lazing about.' Taking out his wallet, he gave me his card. 'Make it Monday morning, eh? Get the nine thirty from Paddington and you'll get a good breakfast on the train. I recommend the kippers. Don't worry about finding digs. I'll fix that up and someone will meet you at our end.'

Getting into his coat, old Dingle paused long enough to give me a wink.

Thus the arrangements were made. The interview, if it could be called an interview, had lasted less than an hour. I felt dazed, excited and a bit apprehensive. We all shook hands and went our separate ways. I'd scarcely had a chance to catch my breath, so much had happened so quickly. Yet so much more was to happen that day that it looms as long as a week in my memory. Incident was to fall upon incident with bewildering rapidity, although none of that was known to me as I rode the escalator down to the tube.

Anyone travelling from Paddington to Tottenham Court Road on the underground has to change at Notting Hill Gate, and what with the escalators and waiting for trains, the journey is probably one of the few across London accomplished quicker by cab. Not that such a thought occurred to me, I rarely used cabs in those days, so up and down the escalators I went with my mind fairly bursting. Even all these years later, I can recall my excitement. I was dizzy, overwhelmed by my good fortune. What a colossal debt I owed Dingle! How kind of him. If I'd been offered the choice of a hundred solicitors, I'd have chosen to work for Jumbo Weston. How lucky I was, how happy. In fact so happy that I travelled with a grin on my face, unknowingly, until people started to give me strange looks. One lady, a blonde wearing mascara an inch thick, actually smiled back. 'Hello Dearie, going my way?' And I told her that I was going to Tottenham Court Road before it dawned on me that she was plying her trade. I felt such a fool. Blushing furiously, I leapt out at Lancaster Gate to make my escape. 'You won't get far that way, Dearie,' she called after me, although whether she meant far with her or far on my journey, I never found out.

Perhaps I needed that to bring me down to earth. In any event, waiting at Lancaster Gate gave me a chance to collect myself. I began slowly pacing up and down the platform – and perhaps it was the very act of pacing that reminded me of Jack. Suddenly I felt that it just wouldn't do to go racing back to the flat, full of my news, without giving a damn for his feelings. Not with Jack nursing a hangover and worrying himself sick over his future. So I got to thinking about how to break the news gently, and of course Ann came to mind. Ann would help me tell Jack. Then I realised I wanted to tell Ann in any case . . . I wanted to share my excitement with her . . .

So when the train arrived and took me to Tottenham Court Road, instead of going to the flat, I walked up to Gill's. It was my first proper visit at lunch time. The pub was far busier than in the evenings, but at two-fifteen the big rush was over. People were returning to their offices, the crowd at the bar was thinning out. 'Cheerio, Ann,' they called on their way to the door. 'See you tomorrow.'

Ann threw them a quick smile, her hands moving swiftly to serve the next drink. Watching her made me realise that even without a sign on the door, the small front bar had become simply 'Ann's Bar'. Dozens of men chose it every day, merely to see Ann. 'Just like Jack,' I thought, before admitting, 'and me.'

I was so busy watching Ann that it was a moment

before I saw Gill collecting glasses up from a nearby table. After my encounter with the blonde, I thought I'd got my face under control, but I was wrong, because Gill said, 'Hello, Tubby. You look as if you've lost a tanner and found a tenner.'

Hearing my name, Ann glanced up. Her eyes brightened. 'Hey,' she said, 'you look pleased with yourself.'

I must have that sort of face. 'Yes,' I replied, 'I'll tell you later.'

So we exchanged looks and she pulled me a pint. I wanted to tell her immediately, but there were still too many people around. So I drank my beer and ate a sandwich, struggling all the time to curb my impatience. Eventually Gill called, 'Last orders', and Ann locked the door behind the final customer. Gill went off to the other bar and Ann took the stool next to me. 'Well?' she asked eagerly.

I poured out my story. I told her all about old Dingle telephoning and me rushing over to Paddington to meet Jumbo Weston. Ann listened with shining eyes, and when I finished she kissed me, for the second time in two days.

Which was when Gill returned from the back bar. 'Hello then, what's going on here?'

So we told him, with Ann seemingly as excited as I was. Gill seemed pleased too. Then he frowned. 'Taunton? That's a long way off.'

'Is it?' Ann's eyebrows rose. 'I thought it was in London.'

I should have realised an American could make that sort of mistake. After all, if I were in New York and Ann talked of Easthampton, I wouldn't have a clue where it was. So I explained that Taunton was in Somerset, three or four hours away on the train. 'Oh,' she said, and all the shadows returned to her eyes.

'So you'll move down there?' said Gill.

'Yes. I go on Monday.'

'Monday?' Ann echoed with unmistakable dismay.

Which was when I got all muddled up. I'd been walking on air until then. Meeting Jumbo Weston promised to be a turning point in my life. True, I'd grown a bit anxious about Jack, but only about how best to tell him. It hadn't occurred to me that it would be a wrench to leave Ann. Until that moment.

In a feeble sort of voice, I said, 'I'll get up to town now and then. A weekend here and there –'

She interrupted with a brittle laugh. 'Oh, fantastic. We'll hang out the flags!' Blushing, she turned away. Then she shrugged. 'Well, I've got things to do. Mike will be here soon to take me to Kentish Town. Meanwhile I'll go up and see Mary.'

Avoiding my eye, she hurried from the bar, leaving me staring after her. 'Ann?' I called as she closed the door.

Gill made a noise between a sigh and a groan. 'Oh, blimey, I'll pour us a pint.'

'What's up with Ann?'

Giving me a curious look, he went behind the counter. 'Women,' he shrugged, 'who can tell?'

'I don't understand.'

'Who does,' he said, putting my pint on the bar. 'What does Cowboy Jack think of your news?'

I explained that Jack didn't know as yet.

'Oh dear,' said Gill. 'Will your friend Dingle be able to fix him up?'

I shook my head. 'No, I did ask, but he and Jack never had a lot of time for each other.'

'So you reckon Jack's finished with the law for good?'

Nodding gloomily, I described the future that Jack had thrown away; all the great expectations about him becoming the youngest partner ever at Mortlake, Dingle & Barnes.

'Poor old fellow,' Gill sighed. He rubbed his jaw thoughtfully and a minute must have passed before he brightened. 'I'll tell you something though,' he said. 'Sometimes things work out for the best. I reckon Cowboy Jack's found something he likes more than the law.'

I wondered if he meant Ann, but Gill continued, 'This business with The Graduates could make a lot of money.'

'It's costing a lot of money,' I pointed out, 'and you couldn't call it a proper career.'

'I could,' he grinned. 'You couldn't because you want to be a solicitor, but you've got to remember that not everyone wants the same thing in life.'

All the time we were talking I was waiting for Ann to return. My gaze kept straying to the door which led to the upstairs apartment. Gill read my mind. 'If you ask me,' he said, 'your news knocked her all of a heap. She's gone upstairs to catch her breath. Take my advice and leave her alone for a bit.'

Disappointment got the better of me. 'I don't understand,' I said coldly.

Eyeing me carefully, he glanced over his shoulder. 'Between you and me,' he said, lowering his voice, 'she was up half the night about what happened yesterday. You and Jack getting the push. She kept

141

going on about it being her fault. It was three o'clock before Mary and I got her to bed. Terribly upset she was.'

I remembered Ann's comments while we were searching for Jack.

'And these Graduates,' Gill continued, 'Ossie and his crowd. Ann would have helped them anyway, but now she feels obligated. Know what she said last night? "Now I've *got* to help for Jack's sake. I'll hate myself otherwise." Then she said, "Thank God Tubby's around. He's a sheet anchor."' Gill stared until he saw what he took as a glimmer of understanding in my eyes. 'Now you arrive with your news about going off down to Taunton, and . . . well, see what I mean? She's been knocked all of a heap.'

I grew upset. 'You mean I've let her down?'

'Not let her down,' Gill sighed. 'She understands what your career means to you. She was pleased for you, you saw the way her face lit up. But . . .' he struggled to find the right words . . . 'She's got to cope with Jack by herself now, hasn't she? You don't realise how much she likes having you around. She's got confidence in you. Like she said, you're her sheet anchor. And now you won't be there, will you?'

It was turning into the most confused day of my life. One minute I had everything I wanted, the next minute my happiness was leaking out of my shoes. I walked back to Whitcombe Street bemused. I kept seeing that reproachful look in Ann's eyes. The thought of letting her down tormented me. Yet I wasn't letting her down. She had no claim on me, I had no claim on her. Ours wasn't that kind of relationship. 'Damn and blast,' I muttered, 'it isn't *any* kind of relationship. We're friends, that's all!' Was I hoping for more? How could I? Jack had seen her first. Was guilt part of my confusion? 'What kind of rubbish is that?' I snarled under my breath. Yet my confusion persisted even when I reached the flat. Earlier, I would have run up the stairs, now I trudged up like a man ascending the scaffold.

'Hello,' said Jack. 'Where have you been?'

I would have liked more time to collect myself, but there was Jack looking at me, waiting for me to say something. So I sat down and told him about Dingle's phone call and my meeting with Jumbo Weston. Jack had been reading a copy of *Music Weekly* when I arrived. As I related the story he set the paper aside and gave me his full attention. He remained silent until I finished, then, very quietly, he said, 'It's what you always wanted, Tubby. What's the matter? You don't seem very excited.'

'What about you?' I asked. 'What will you do?'

'Me? Christ, I'm all right. I've got Jack Webb Enterprises.' He stared for a moment, then his eyes lit up with understanding. 'Ah! I get it. You're tossing up between being part of that and becoming a solicitor. I see the problem.'

And would you believe it, he stood up and began to pace the room. It was so typical I should have expected it. Once Jack got an idea, he could think of nothing else. As with AIDA, so now with Jack Webb Enterprises. The shock of yesterday's events had worn off. Being fired was old news. Even wanting to be a solicitor was history. I bet he'd even convinced himself that he'd never wanted to take up the law. I sat flabbergasted as he set out my options. 'In the long run,' he said, 'you'll make more money with JWE. There's no –'

'JW what?'

'JWE,' he repeated, startled. 'Jack Webb Enterprises.'

I should have realised Jack Webb Enterprises was already a mammoth organisation in Jack's mind. It was only fitting that, like ITT and ICI, even the BBC, it should be referred to by initials.

'Of course, money will be tight to begin with,' he admitted, 'but equally you won't be making a fortune in Taunton.' He stopped pacing long enough to stand directly in front of me. 'Therefore it's the long term you've got to consider. Right?'

I nodded. My brain was numb. During the past twenty-four hours I'd hurtled up and down my emotional scale like a yo-yo. I'd experienced fear, anger, disappointment, excitement, joy and God knows what. And at that moment, I was suffering another emotion. Self-disgust. The truth is, I felt an absolute shit. It didn't matter that I thought Jack's precious JWE was doomed to failure. He believed in it, and as my friend was doing his level best to advise me on my future. And while he was doing this, I was thinking about Ann. Some friend I was turning out to be.

'The question,' Jack said, getting to the heart of the matter, 'is, where lies your future happiness? Staying in the law or making money with me? If we answer that, your choice will become clear. Right?'

I nodded again, feeling like Judas. Of course I wanted to stay in the law, and since the opportunity lay in Taunton that's where I'd go. Jack's extravagant prospectus for JWE left me cold. I wasn't really considering his alternatives. I was sitting there heavy-hearted at the thought of leaving Ann.

'Money's all very well,' Jack was saying, 'but you've got to consider job satisfaction. After all, we don't all want the same things from life.'

'That's what Gill said.'

'Oh?'

Jack's surprise fuelled my guilt even further. I invented a lame excuse. 'I thought you might have gone out, so I called in there on the way back from Paddington.'

'And what did Gill make of your news?'

'I think he was pleased for me.'

'And Ann?' He gave me such a strange look that I had trouble meeting his eye. Did he suspect I would miss her? Was he wondering if she'd miss me?

To avoid his eye, I got up. 'Ann was pleased, too,' I said, on my way to the kitchen.

'There you are, then,' he said, following me, 'and that's the opinion of people who know you. Hell's bells, Tubby, I know you better than anyone, and I *know* you're cut out for the law.'

After filling the kettle, I reached for the teapot.

'In view of what's happened,' he said, with the manner of making an important announcement, 'I don't think I ought to hold you to our partnership agreement.'

My jaw dropped. I nearly asked, 'What agreement?' but Jack was standing there, beaming good will, and thank God I had the grace to splutter, 'Are you sure?'

'You are a fool,' he said, slapping me on the back. 'The moment you walked through the door I could see you were embarrassed. Of course I release you from our agreement. Fancy you doubting it! Naturally you must go to Taunton. It's a wonderful opportunity, exactly the right thing for you.'

He was clearly delighted for me. He kept slapping my back and grabbing my hand until eventually I found myself laughing as well, partly from relief, so that I responded by slapping *his* back and we did a little jig in embarrassed celebration.

'That's it, then,' he said finally. 'That's settled.'

I suppose it was, except for my confusion, and I felt too guilty to sort that out while talking to Jack. As soon as we'd finished the tea, I made my escape. It was five thirty and my mother would be on her way home from Derry & Toms. 'I'd better go and see her,' I told Jack, 'I don't want her hearing about yesterday from anyone else. Besides, I need to tell her about Taunton.'

Even that wasn't the strict truth. The chances of Mum finding out about me being fired were one in a million. She never telephoned Mortlake, Dingle & Barnes. And while she would have to know about Taunton, the news could have waited a day.

The truth was I wanted to escape for a while. I wanted a chance to think. So a few minutes later I left the flat and set out for Bayswater. It was half on my mind to ask Mum's advice about Ann. I don't think I would have really, I was far too shy. In the event, what Mum was to tell me put thoughts even of Ann out of my mind.

'Whatever's the matter?' she cried when she opened the door. Even Bert, emerging behind her in the hall, looked a shade agitated.

I'd never called upon them in the week – Sundays

were our days for seeing each other – and I suppose the fact that it was Wednesday aroused their misgivings. After being ushered into the sitting room, I tried to set their minds at rest by saying, 'I've got some good news.' Then I told the story backwards, beginning with Jumbo Weston and Dingle before explaining that Jack and I had been fired.

Unexpectedly, Mum burst into tears. Bert was at her side in an instant, with an arm around her shoulder. 'There, there, old girl, he's all right.'

I was astonished.

Mum sobbed her heart out. I went over and sat on the sofa, the other side from Bert, and we did our best to provide comfort, but there was no stemming the flood of tears. Her bosom heaved and she choked and sobbed. Finally Bert led her off to their bedroom, leaving me feeling bewildered and wretched.

He returned after a couple of minutes and I jumped to my feet. 'I am sorry. I didn't mean to –'

''Course you didn't,' he said, waving me back down on to the sofa. 'Don't worry. It's good news. You don't know the half of it, Tubby. It's better news than you can ever imagine.'

Mystified and upset, I watched him open the sideboard and withdraw a half-bottle of brandy.

'It's the relief,' he said, pouring large measures into three glasses. 'All that tension, all these years.' Handing me a glass, he picked up one of the others. 'She's much better now. I'll just give her this. I won't be a minute.'

And true enough, he returned very quickly, meeting my bewildered look with a cheerful one of his own. 'She's just washing her face. She'll be in shortly.' He picked up his own glass and drank deeply. 'By jove,' he said, as if celebrating something, 'that's a weight off my mind. After all these years. Thank God. You've made your Mum very happy, and me, very happy indeed.'

'I don't understand,' I began, only to break off as Mother returned. She had indeed washed her face. She had also changed from her dress into a kimono, and instead of shoes she wore little flat slippers. The effect was to make her look smaller and rather vulnerable. Still a bit sniffy, she smiled sheepishly and drew me down beside her on the sofa. 'Silly of me to give way like that. It was the shock of you leaving –' She stopped abruptly and looked me full in the face. 'You have left him? There's no going back? He's got no hold over you?'

'No, I mean yes, I have left him, and I'm not going back.'

Her hand tightened on mine. 'Thank goodness. I can hardly believe it.'

Bert looked at me and cleared his throat, 'There are things you don't know. We didn't tell you before because . . .' he shrugged . . . 'well, you were eighteen by the time I met you and we thought it best to let sleeping dogs lie. Mind you, we worried, especially when you said you were going to work for your father. But the way we figured it was that at least you were no longer under his roof, and you and Jack were together. And of course, we saw you pretty often ourselves after that.'

I looked at him and waited. He ignored the armchairs flanking the fire and joined us on the sofa, so that we sat like the three wise monkeys, with Mum in the middle – and it was Mother, not Bert, who took up the story. Previously she'd said very little of what happened during my childhood, and she rarely mentioned my father. An odd comment escaped her lips now and then, enough for me to know she detested him, but she'd said little of our years apart. Bert was responsible for that. The first time I met him, he said, 'What's past is past. Looking back's a waste of time. I want us to enjoy being together.' At the time I'd imagined he'd said it because of his cheerful disposition. Generally he was so jolly that it was easy to overlook the serious side to his nature. But Bert had had another reason for wanting to shut off the past. Consideration for my mother.

She'd had a much harder time than I imagined. After the initial court battle in which she had lost custody of me, she had tried again and again. The courts always found against her, and always for the same reasons: she had deserted the family home, her income was meagre – by comparison my father was wealthy and widely respected. It was argued that by remaining with him I would live in a fine house and attend a good school.

'Even the solicitor, *my* solicitor, tried to talk me out of it,' she said wearily. 'I think he was afraid of your father.'

I could understand that. Few solicitors have much taste for suing a professional colleague. When I asked the name of her solicitor, I learned that his was a small one-man firm. Privately I thought that pitting him against James Mortlake of Mortlake, Dingle & Barnes was asking a minnow to swallow a whale; but I remained silent while Mother continued. 'Then Joan Mortlake came to see me,' she said, 'your father's sister. Do you remember her?'

'Aunt Joan.' I nodded, amazed by this revelation.

Aunt Joan had been terrified of my father. He would have regarded any contact between her and my mother as rank treachery.

'I was living in a bed-sit in Putney then,' Mum continued, 'I don't even know how she found me. Frightened the life out of me, she did, going on about your father mistreating you. I was in tears when she finished.'

My last recollection of Aunt Joan was of her intervening over my birthday cake. I'd been grateful for that. Now it seemed I had other reasons to thank her. However, Aunt Joan's courage had fallen short of going to the authorities.

'She wouldn't even see my solicitor,' said Mum, 'so, of course, he said it was all stuff and nonsense. According to him, Joan was being spiteful because she'd fallen out with her brother.'

From that day on Mum never relaxed. 'It wasn't easy because I had a living to earn,' she said, 'but I used to get down to Wimbledon whenever I could and watch out for you. When I stood outside the house, he'd see me and go potty, but there was nothing he could do, so long as I didn't speak to you, and I never did that. I just wanted him to know I was there, as a sort of warning.'

'I knew too,' I said, remembering the times I'd seen her and had fought the urge to run to her. 'He said if I ever spoke to you, he'd send you to prison.'

I regretted the words as soon as they were uttered, for her eyes glistened with tears, and it was some minutes before she could continue. Bert encouraged her softly. 'There, there, don't take on so, it's all over now.' Finally she resumed in such a quiet voice that I had to lean forward to catch her words. Apparently, eighteen months or so after Aunt Joan called, Mum had another visitor. 'Mabel Hopkins. She was his housekeeper for a while. Remember her?'

My mind went back over the years to a plump, matronly type who had lasted barely three months. 'Father sacked her,' I said.

'That's right, because she stood up for you over something.'

Mabel Hopkins was made of sterner stuff than Aunt Joan. Not only did she call on my mother, but she went with her to the solicitor and then on to the local authority, complaining that I was being cruelly treated. 'We actually got the Child Care Inspector into the house that time,' said Mum with the tiniest hint of satisfaction. 'I think he made three or four visits. Do you remember?'

I remembered my father black with rage. I remember him cursing her interference. And I remember the threats – 'You say one word, just one, about being unhappy and I'll have that woman behind bars.' Always the same threat, always the same blackmail. It worked every time. Hearing my mother's story made me realise how often I'd let her down.

'The Inspector gave up in the end,' she said sadly. 'He used to examine you for marks. On your body, to see if your father had beaten you.'

I remembered. There were never any marks. My father's punishments were more subtle than that.

Mother sighed. 'According to the Inspector, you were content with your father. We knew it wasn't true because of what Mabel told us, but there wasn't much more we could do.'

Yet she did do more. She maintained her vigil

whenever she could, and then she met Bert. 'He changed my whole life,' she said with a sideways smile. 'When I got to know him better, I told him about you. I don't think he believed me to begin with. It was Mabel who convinced him. Then he organised a positive army.'

I was hearing this for the first time. I listened in amazement to the steps Bert had taken. The first thing he did was to contact the local milkman. 'Bert found out what pub he used and met him there for a drink.' Within a few months, Bert had engaged an army of spies – the milkman, the postman, the baker, the grocer – all keeping an eye on me when they called at the house. Bert chuckled. 'Your father got wind of it and wrote to Sheila's solicitors saying he'd bring an action for defamation. But I never defamed him. All I said to Harry Oakes – he was the milkman – and the others was that Sheila was concerned about her little boy.'

Listening to Bert brought the smile back to Mum's face. A minute or two later she was actually laughing as they recounted the ways in which they had watched over me. Not a weekend passed without one or both of them spending some time near the house. 'We never did it in secret,' said Mum, 'that wouldn't do. He had to know we were there. He had to be aware we were keeping an eye on you, and that we'd be back with the Child Inspector at the first sign of trouble.' She ended with a note of defiance, 'He may have taken you away from me, but I refused to let go.'

All those years and I'd never known! And yet . . . I'd always sensed she was there. Even while enduring my father's cruelties, something had told me she would eventually stop him. Perhaps he too had known? Perhaps he realised that while he had controlled my actions, he'd never won control of my mind. All those battles; month after month, year after year, his will against mine.

Trying to tell my part of the story was difficult. I did my best, but describing what it had been like was made harder by my reluctance to recall specific incidents. I'd no wish to live through them again, and they would only have upset Mum, who had brightened considerably.

'It was the shock,' she said, 'that's why I burst out crying. The shock of hearing you were finally free of him. Oh, Peter, I can't describe the relief. He can't hurt you ever again.'

And we hugged each other, and she might have gone all weepy again but for Bert. He was her strength. He rallied her by making her laugh, and by making her look to the future. 'Let's celebrate!' he cried, pouring more brandies. 'Let's celebrate the defeat of a tyrant!'

As Mum dabbed her eyes and drank up, Bert made his plans. 'I propose,' he cried, waving his glass, 'that we go out to dinner on Saturday. What about that, Sheila?'

'The three of us? Oh, lovely —' she began, but Bert interrupted. 'Hang on, I haven't finished,' he said, looking at me. 'What you need young man, is a couple of good country suits as a going away present. We've got just the thing at Derry & Toms. Now if you come over tomorrow —'

'No, really,' I protested.

'Oh, Bert that's a lovely idea,' cried mother, turning to me. 'No arguing, we get a staff discount, so we can afford it. Besides,' she added, smiling, 'I want you to look the part when you go down to Taunton . . .'

Away she went, aided and abetted by Bert, planning lunch at Derry & Toms the next day, and telling me to ask for a Mr Wiggins in the Gentlemen's Outfitters department. Nobody would have realised she'd been in tears an hour before. Indeed, nobody would have believed the life she'd led. Colour had returned to her cheeks and the sparkle was back in her eye. Once again, Bert had got her laughing and joking. It was easy to see why she said he'd saved her life . . . indeed from what I'd just heard he'd possibly saved mine . . .

We made quite a night of it in the end. It was too late to cook an evening meal so we shared a cold supper of cheese and pickled onions, red cabbage and mustard pickles – all washed down with the last of the brandy.

I said nothing about Ann. Even to have tried to discuss my confused state of mind would have been futile; besides, it might have upset Mum who'd got my future clear in her mind – 'We can come down for the occasional weekend,' she said eagerly. 'You must find us a nice hotel, nothing too grand, somewhere small and quiet would be best . . .'

It was late when I left. Warmed by the brandies and full of fond family feelings, I set off for the tube. What a day it had been. A day and a half! Even more, it had been forty-eight hours of non-stop surprises. Mum's unexpected revelations had been the shattering finale. I felt as if I'd seen an album of fading photographs. For the first time I understood where everyone fitted in and how it had all come about. I think I felt better for knowing, for even though memories of past battles with my father had been revived, I told myself those battles were over. 'Over for good,' I heard myself say.

Old Dingle came into my mind. I remembered him saying something about my father being part of my boyhood, and that now was the time to move on.

Effectively that evening ended my time in London. Not that I left immediately for Taunton; as arranged I waited until the following Monday, and the intervening days were busy and full – but nothing happened to change the course of events. I lunched with Mum and Bert on the Thursday, we bought two tweed suits at Derry & Toms, and dined out on Saturday – but the die was cast. I was about to say goodbye to part of my life.

Jack gave me a party on the Sunday. Appropriately enough, he held it at Gill's place. The front bar was closed to the public and a sign announcing 'Private Function' was affixed to the door. Everyone came – Janie and The Graduates, the crowd from the Green Door, friends from the Two 'I's and the Heaven and Hell, even some of the girls from the office – my old office that is, at Mortlake, Dingle & Barnes. And Mary, Gill's wife, came downstairs and joined in for part of the evening. The Graduates were delighted with Jack's new status as their full-time manager, and they couldn't get over his car. They were dazzled. Ossie and Ray argued about who would be chauffeur. Ossie won, because he drove Mum and Bert home in the car at the end of the evening. So everyone came to the party, although of course most important of all was my best friend Jack, and our mutual friend, Ann.

I'd scarcely seen Ann since the Wednesday when she'd run out of the bar. We'd not been alone since, and clearly another chance wouldn't arise. I was glad and sorry about that; sorry because I wouldn't have an opportunity to express what I felt, glad because I would have embarrassed us both. So we smiled and laughed a lot, and talked of everything except what was in our hearts and our minds.

And there was Jack. My best friend Jack. 'The ex-Solicitor General,' he laughed when we found ourselves in adjacent stalls in the lavatory. 'In fact,' he added as we washed our hands, 'I'll also be the ex-tenant of the flat at the end of the month.'

'Oh?'

'It's too expensive by myself, and well . . .' he shrugged to disguise his embarrassment . . . 'it was sort of our place. I wouldn't feel right sharing with someone else.'

'Don't be daft,' I said, pretending to remain unaffected.

He grinned. 'It's true, daft or not. Anyway, Gill's got a spare room and it makes sense to use it.'

'You're moving in here?'

'That's right. At the end of the month. I fixed it with Gill yesterday.'

How quickly everything was changing!

Later Jack gave a speech, telling everyone how long we had known each other and what a tremendous friend I was. Then everyone sang 'For he's a jolly good fellow' and we all got drunk.

And so, bleary-eyed and hung-over, to Paddington Station the next morning. Just the three of us: me and my best friend Jack, and our mutual friend, Ann.

Jack wrung my hand. 'You'll make the best damn solicitor the world's ever seen.'

Ann came into my arms and kissed me full on the lips. 'Take care of yourself,' she said, her eyes darker than ever.

I boarded the train. 'Stay in touch,' I cried, waving from the window.

They waved back; Jack, tall, gangly and fair-haired; Ann, slender and dark, with eyes full of shadows. Then Jack took her arm and led her away.

BOOK TWO

IF ANYTHING MADE ME REALISE my feelings for Ann it was that painful goodbye at Paddington. Even though I squirmed and shied away from difficult questions, such as if I could no longer deceive myself, could I deceive Ann? Could I deceive my old buddy Jack, who'd laid claim to Ann from the moment he saw her, and thrown up his career to keep her in London, Jack who'd saved my hide on countless occasions?

What anguish I endured on the train. Unable to think straight, I was in an emotional mess. Finally I realised that I had to go to Taunton to sort myself out. It was an escape, whether temporary or permanent would be for me to decide later. Ironically, until then I would have seen it as an escape from my father. Instead it became an escape from my friends.

It's embarrassing to remember such fanciful thoughts. From this distance, my resolutions seem completely ridiculous, like something out of *Beau Geste*. Admittedly my plans fell well short of joining the French Foreign Legion, just as I fell well short of being Beau Geste, but I promised myself I'd stay in Taunton until I'd got Ann out of my system. I'd not set foot in London again until I could look Jack in the face. Such then were my thoughts as I travelled down to Taunton; a large, untidy young man, nursing a bad conscience, so long ago.

If Jumbo had known, how he'd have laughed. I can imagine him bawling me out – 'You stupid young idiot. Making a fool of yourself. Pull yourself together and stop mooning about.'

Luckily I had no time for mooning. Jumbo saw to that. I could write a lot about him, except that this isn't really his story, it's Jack's and Ann's, and I suppose my story, too. It's about how we met and what happened to us, for our lives were irrevocably linked despite my fine resolutions.

Even so, Jumbo had such an effect on my life that it's impossible to ignore him. He was old Dingle's nephew, by the way, although I forget when I came to know that. Not that it mattered, Dingle would have got on with Jumbo anyway, most people did. He was a folk hero in that part of England. Whenever talk turned to cricket, Jumbo's name came to their lips. In the pubs they'd chuckle with glee, savouring memories along with their pints. 'I saw him make a hundred and thirty against Yorkshire,' one would recall, 'and that was when Fred Trueman was *really* Fred Trueman.'

Being a local hero was an obvious help when Jumbo joined his father's law firm, but what made his reputation was the way he cared for people. Rich or poor, struggling or successful, a client of Jumbo's was really looked after. Not that he was a respecter of persons. Never one to suffer fools, he had a hell of a temper. He once gave the richest man in Somerset a dressing down in a manner a drill sergeant would have envied. 'You great steaming idiot!' Jumbo roared. 'What are you? Go on, say it. Repeat after me, I'm the biggest prat in the world.' And the man repeated it like a parrot, and I know why. He'd landed himself in an appalling mess, he'd been really stupid – but he knew Jumbo would rescue him when he calmed down. And Jumbo did, even though he and I had to work every weekend for a month on the case.

'We work farmer's hours down here,' he told me when I joined. 'Seven days a week and nights, too, when we have to.'

Which wasn't to say we worked all the time, far from it. We played golf and went fishing, and played snooker and darts at the pub. Farmer's hours meant working flat out when necessary, but following a more leisurely pace the rest of the time. Every other night Jumbo was out at a Rotary dinner, or a rugby club booze-up, or a cricket club dance. And as often as not I went with him, even though I had trouble getting up in the morning. Jumbo had the country-man's knack of early rising; no matter what time he went to bed, he rose at six, and his three protégés – Martin Juffs, Austen Nicholson and I – were required at the office by eight. Eight o'clock! It was pitch dark in the winter. I was horrified to begin with. I remember trying to explain I wasn't a morning per-son, but Jumbo simply went deaf. For Martin, Austen and me, it was always an eight o'clock start. The rest of the staff commenced at nine thirty, by which time we were ready with a mountain of work. 'Right,' Jumbo would grin, clapping his hands together, 'that's the day organised, now I'm off on my rounds.' Martin, Austen and I took turns to go with him and it's hard to imagine more enjoyable days. Jumbo's 'rounds' were whatever came into his head. We might call on a couple of clients, have lunch with a third, play nine holes in the afternoon and end up drinking at the cricket club. On the surface the days were pure pleasure, yet they did have a purpose. Jumbo was playing shepherd to his flock. He kept his eyes and his ears open to such effect that he could spot trouble even before it arose. Sadly, meetings and commitments prevented him from doing rounds every day, but he usually managed a couple a week.

There were no partners at Weston & Weston; instead Jumbo's retired father, Joshua, acted as consultant. He never came to the office so we went to him; every week Austen, Martin and I had to discuss our current work with the old man – separately; Jumbo never allowed us to go together. And old Josh would quiz us until our brains seized up. He insisted on knowing the ins and outs of every case on our files; we might have been young barristers pleading a case. It was excellent training. It was the way Jumbo had trained. No wonder he knew the law, for his father knew it backwards.

Jumbo was unmarried. 'Never had time,' he claimed, which in his case was possibly true. 'Besides, I'm too young. Fifty's the age to marry. A man knows his own mind at fifty. I'll take a wife then.'

Meanwhile he lived with his father in a large country house, waited on hand and foot by a housekeeper and three live-in servants, all of whom were of pensionable age. Women friends – 'Crumpet' Jumbo called them – were seen on his arm now and then, although rarely in Taunton. Occasionally word filtered back from Bristol or beyond that Jumbo had been seen with a woman, but the descriptions always varied so there must have been several.

Working for him absorbed most of my time, except that 'working' conveys the wrong impression. I would have been hard pressed to say if I was working or playing. Was it work to spend summer weekends at the cricket club? Or to attend the Hunt Ball? Were three days spent strolling around the County Show considered work? Jumbo saw everything as part of the whole. Martin, Austen and I were merging into the community, mixing with clients, many of whom became friends — although we rarely equalled Jumbo's ability to spot when one tried to pull the wool over our eyes. 'I hear what he says, but are those his real reasons?' Jumbo would ask, making us think. He was a genius at that. 'Everyone puts a gloss on their actions,' he'd say, 'it's human nature. But we can't protect them unless we know the full story.' And of course he was right. He was the perfect Dutch Uncle.

Certainly he was a Dutch Uncle to us. He organised my first driving lesson and lent me the cash for a car. When we qualified, he helped us with mortgages. 'Put some roots down,' he urged. 'It gives people confidence if you buy property in the district.' He and his father were always ready to help, so that one way and another I was more than content. Martin once said, 'It's not a career, it's a way of life.' And that summed it up.

Inexplicably I'd always known it was a way of life to suit me, yet I knew little of country ways until I went to Taunton. Perhaps escaping my father had something to do with it. Rarely absent from London, he was a city man through and through. 'Smart men live in cities,' old Joshua once joked, 'wise men live in the country.' I was neither smart nor wise, simply determined to be different from my father.

Which isn't to deny I was homesick, especially to begin with when I was living in digs. To be honest, I'm not sure if I missed Jack more than Ann or Ann more than Jack. Obviously my thoughts about them were different. Apart from anything else, Jack and I had shared so much, and Ann and I so little, that while thoughts of Jack revived memories, thoughts of Ann generated frustrations.

Work was a help. Jumbo drove me hard during those early months. I think he was testing me. Of the three disciples – as Martin, Austen and I became known – I was the last to join, so I had to establish myself. I was glad to be busy, and grateful to be still in the profession. I wanted to pay my father back for firing me from Mortlake, Dingle & Barnes. 'I'll show the old bastard,' I told myself, and I suppose I did in a way.

Having to work Saturday mornings was also a help. Everyone trooped into the office in sports jackets and flannels instead of everyday suits. Saturday mornings were a sort of up-dating session, reviewing the week that had ended and preparing for what was to come. At lunch time we adjourned to the pub, or the rugby club, or the cricket club . . . so before you knew it, Saturday was over and half the weekend with it.

To begin with I heard nothing from Jack. That too, in a way, did me no harm. Had he been in touch I might have felt restless to get back to London. However, the complete silence – no phone calls or letters, even though I'd sent him the address of my digs – began to worry me. Had he cottoned on to my feelings for Ann? Not much escaped him. So I fretted a bit. I did hear from Mum, suggesting, 'Surely you can come home for a weekend?' But I didn't, I knew as soon as I set foot in London I'd be straight round to Gill's to see Jack and Ann. More time had to pass, so I remained rooted in Taunton.

Then, after about six weeks, came a long letter from Jack, full of apologies for not writing before. He'd been working flat out for The Graduates. He wrote about the gigs they were playing, that sort of thing. There were no recriminations, not one. I breathed a sigh of relief, especially when the letter ended with, 'Ann and Gill and the rest of the gang send love and best wishes'.

Things were fine after that. I felt a hundred percent better. It lifted the guilt from my shoulders. I sent Jack my news and the old camaraderie was stronger than ever. Believe me, it was a relief. After all, what's life without friends? And Jack had been my best friend for half of my life.

There was, however, one small nagging worry. Reading between the lines of his letters made me wonder how he was coping. Certainly he wasn't making much money. I got to thinking about that. I was enjoying Jumbo's tutelage so much that I wished it for Jack. I was convinced he was wasting his life. He had such a good brain, it was tragic to spend three years pursuing a career, then give it all up. 'Okay,' I reasoned, 'he and Jumbo mightn't get on, but I bet someone would take him under their wing.' So I wrote to him, suggesting he try to resume his career.

His reply fairly bristled. Steam rose from the note-paper. 'No way,' he wrote. 'JWE will come good. Besides, I've got responsibilities. I can't walk out on

Janie and the others . . . and there's Ann to consider.'

Ann! I nearly wrote back saying, 'Forget about Ann. Dammit, she feels responsible for *you*! That's her only reason for helping. It would be a weight off her mind if you quit.'

That's what I *nearly* wrote. Of course, I wrote nothing of the kind. Once I calmed down I remembered Beau Geste and stayed out of it. No point in quarrelling. Jack would do what he would do, irrespective of me.

Luckily he struck pay-dirt shortly after that. He got The Graduates a six week tour of the north of England, playing the old Moss Empires. I don't suppose they exist now. They weren't doing very well then. Jack went along for part of the tour and sent me a postcard from Tyneside. 'It's a different country up here,' he wrote. 'You wouldn't believe these music halls, yet they're the only live entertainment there is. Live? Christ, you should see these acts. They've got singers still doing Chu Chin Chow. When I talk about rock and roll the management look as if they want to call the police. I spend most of each day rehearsing lighting cues and sweeping cobwebs from the loudspeakers. Everything closes down at ten thirty . . .'

I had to grin. Things were like that in Taunton. The only 'live' entertainment was in the bar of the cricket club when Jumbo did his Fats Waller impressions.

Jack soon got sick of touring. He returned to London at the end of ten days and wrote saying, 'Janie and the others can manage without me . . . I tell them it's all good experience . . .'

Experience for what, I wondered? True, The Graduates were working, so they must have been earning, which meant some income, although I doubt it was much. I still thought Jack was wasting his life.

But Jack was Jack. As my father once said, Jack's way of dealing with problems was to shake them to death – which sometimes made them worse before they got better. A week after he returned to London, he telephoned me to tell me he'd signed a new singer. 'A big Welsh lad, boyo. Straight from the valleys. Rough as a lump of coal but a voice like velvet. Girls go weak at the knees –'

'Hang on,' I interrupted. 'What about The Graduates? You're not dropping them are you?'

''Course I'm not dropping them. I'm a professional manager. You've got to understand this business, Tubby. One act hardly gets my foot in the door. Get me a whole string and I'll smash the bloody door down.'

It sounded risky to me. My thinking ran along conventional lines of mastering something before embarking on new commitments.

We talked of this and that for a while, until I could no longer restrain myself. 'How's Ann?' I asked.

'Great. She sends her love.'

'Is she still going back to the States?'

'What? Oh, yeah, she mentioned something the other week, but now we've got Dai on the books . . . well she's knocked out with his potential . . .'

I couldn't help thinking of AIDA. Was this another of Jack's schemes? Was that why he'd signed a new act? I wondered if that would be his response whenever Ann talked of New York. Some men kept them barefoot and pregnant, others bought them furs. Jack went out and signed a new act. Anything to keep the little woman happy.

Still playing Beau Geste, I told myself to mind my own business. And that's what I did, resisting all of Jack's suggestions to go up to London, determined to stay in Taunton until I was good and ready. Time was passing. Then Jack telephoned one day, full of excitement. 'You really must come up for a weekend,' he said. 'I've got Janie and The Graduates a month at the Stork Club.'

Even I recognised a breakthrough. After the Moss Empire tour, The Graduates had been playing dance halls for about twenty pounds a night. Dave Thomas had joined them by this stage, so there were five of them. They worked maybe only one night in four, and Jack took twenty-five percent of their money, and there were expenses to pay . . . so no one was making a fortune. But the Stork Club! Noel Coward played the Stork Club. So did Marlene Dietrich. The Stork Club was class.

I'd been in Taunton four months. Four months made seventeen weeks, or a hundred and nineteen days. I reckoned I was ready for London, so I went to Jumbo and arranged a weekend off; not a complete weekend, I was still required at the office on Saturday morning, but that didn't matter. Suddenly I was really excited. Don't misunderstand, I'd become absorbed with Jumbo's way of life: Martin, Austen and I had become friends, everything was working out fine; but it was still a thrill to contemplate that weekend. To see Jack again, to see Janie and the others, even to see Gill . . . Deliberately, I put Ann bottom of the list, although of course it would be great to see her. And Mum. I phoned her to arrange lunch with her and Bert on the Sunday. She wanted me to stay with them on the Saturday night, but Jack took care of that on the phone. 'Don't stay at your mother's,' he said. 'It will be a late night and you'll disturb her when you go in. Stay at Gill's and I'll run you to Bayswater on Sunday morning.'

I remember packing my case. Three weeks previously I'd bought my first dinner-jacket. Black tie was obligatory at the Hunt Ball. I'd been tempted to hire, then I said, 'What the hell!' and went out and bought one.

With my case packed, I caught the lunch-time train, consumed with excitement. Soon Somerset was left behind and we charged on across the green plains of Wiltshire. Jack had promised to meet me at Paddington. I could scarcely wait.

I've been to other reunions since, and been disappointed. You go expecting someone you know, and instead find somebody different. People's lives move on, what was important once no longer concerns them. And of course, you change too, often more than you realise. But meeting Jack again that day was exciting. I saw him from the window as the train drew into Paddington. He still resembled a blond stick-insect, all arms and legs and straw-coloured hair; pacing the platform as restless as ever, craning his neck, searching the train as it rolled to a halt. As I climbed down from the carriage, I glimpsed his green sports car parked at the end of the platform. Then he came striding up. 'Tubby! Good to see you,' he said, slapping my back and wringing my hand.

'And you! You're looking terrific.'

'Not half,' he said, taking my case.

The weekend really took off then. So did we, in Jack's flying-machine. I don't know who taught him to drive, the man who invented stock car racing, I think. Not that we hit anything, but Jack did his best.

'Where's the fire?' I protested.

'Relax,' he shouted. 'You're back in the big city now. The pace is faster, remember? It will blow the straw out of your hair.'

I clung on as we zig-zagged through the back-streets. Finally we squealed to a halt outside Gill's place. I was heartily glad to get out. Jack jerked a thumb at the pub. 'In you go,' he said, ushering me through the door. Then, taking me by surprise, he put his hands to his mouth. 'Ta ra!' he trumpeted. 'Here he is, folks! The boy from the sticks! Let's hear a big welcome for Tubby!'

And there they all were, waiting – Ann and Janie, the Carson brothers, Ossie, Dave Thomas, and Gill himself. And Mum and Bert. Looking plumply smart in a new yellow dress, Mum was as excited as a girl on a date. 'What are you doing here?' I gasped as she kissed me.

'Jack fetched us,' she laughed, 'in that hot rod of his.'

'Hot rod,' Bert echoed scornfully. 'Just hark at her. It's all these American films –'

'Nothing wrong with Americans!' Jack shouted.

Bert pumped my hand while Mike Carson slapped my back. Then Ann came towards me, her arms open wide. 'Tubby!' she cried, hugging me. Taking my hands, she rocked back on her heels. 'Hey, let's get a good look at you.'

Looking at her was a treat. There were no shadows in her eyes, instead they shone with excitement. The flush on her cheeks was like the bloom on a peach. I forgot my resolutions. Words fell from my lips. 'You look marvellous,' I said and blushed like a schoolboy.

'Like this?' she laughed, pulling a face at her sweater and skirt. 'I'm going up to change in a minute.' Fluttering her eyelashes, she wiggled her bottom. 'Catch me later, big boy.'

'I'll catch him first,' Janie interrupted, kissing my cheek. 'Hi, Tiger,' she grinned, 'I'll save you a dance at the Stork Club.'

Mike pushed her aside, his face alive with excitement. 'Isn't it fantastic? Us at the Stork Club? We still can't believe it.'

They all clustered round and introduced Dave. 'You've got a fan club,' he grinned. My only reply was a bewildered shake of the head. It took me a minute to reach Gill at the bar. 'You look well,' he said, shaking hands. 'The beer must agree with you in the country.'

Overwhelmed, I just stood there, feeling warm and happy, an inane grin on my face. Then I saw the sign behind the bar, 'Welcome Home Tubby' in red letters a foot high. Mum saw me looking. 'Ann did that,' she said, 'just before you came in.'

You'd have thought I was back from the war instead of from working in Taunton. I wanted to buy everyone drinks, but even that wasn't allowed. 'These are on me,' said Gill, handing me a pint.

Of course the excitement wasn't just about me. It was just as much about The Graduates. 'Jack did invite us to the Stork Club,' said Mum with a smile, 'but it goes on a bit late. We'll see you at lunch time tomorrow.'

I was glad she was there, otherwise I might have felt guilty about spending the whole evening with friends, especially when Bert said, 'We were beginning to think you'd emigrated.' And Gill leant across the counter. 'That's right, next time don't leave it so long.'

'No,' I promised, and meant it. I was glad to be back, especially on such an occasion. They were all so excited about the Stork Club, so anxious to give each other credit. 'Ann's made all the difference,' said Ray. 'We were going nowhere until we met her.' Ann shook her head. 'What about Jack? He got you the booking.' Mike shouted agreement, but Jack shouted back, 'We're a team, aren't we? You've worked, I've worked, Ann's worked, and tonight's the big night.'

I'm not sure how long we stayed in the bar, but after an hour or so The Graduates had to leave to collect their gear and get ready, and Ann was anxious to go up for her bath. 'I'd be there now except for you,' she scolded, to tease me. Mum and Bert took their cue. 'See you tomorrow,' said Mum as I kissed her. Bert grinned. 'And don't be late for lunch,' he said, wagging a finger.

As soon as they departed, Jack picked up my case. 'Come on,' he said, 'I'll settle you in.'

We left Ann and The Graduates making their arrangements. Ann was going with them to the Stork Club, to be with them backstage, holding their hands. Beneath their excitement, they were all very nervous.

It was my first time behind the scenes at Gill's place. We went through the door, up to a first floor landing, then up again. 'Bit of a climb, I'm afraid,' Jack grinned over his shoulder. 'It's okay for Ann, her room's on the first floor with Gill and Mary, but I'm up in the attic.'

I saw what he meant when we got there. The sloping ceilings were clearly the underside of the roof. There were only three rooms, Jack's bedroom, a bathroom, and the room usually used as his office.

'Here you are, old buddy,' he said. 'Welcome to the headquarters of JWE.'

It was a good-sized room. Most obvious from the door was a wooden desk under the window, attended by a swivel chair and flanked by two armchairs, one of which was overflowing with yellowing copies of *Music Week*. The single bed ('My casting couch' Jack grinned wolfishly) was set opposite a wardrobe and teak bookcase. On the floor a faded blue and yellow rug covered the dark boards.

Jack dumped my case on the bed. 'Not the Ritz,' he admitted, 'but it'll do for a night.'

'It's fine,' I assured him.

It was just like old times, except that I was still trying to get used to Jack puffing a cigar. 'My trade mark,' he grinned. 'Makes me look prosperous, don't you think?'

'Part of the image,' I said, settling into the empty armchair.

'Exactly,' he agreed, opening a drawer. Taking out two bottles, he removed the caps by jamming them under the lip of the desk and jerking them upwards. 'Beer now, champagne later,' he said. 'In fact, Tubby my boy, it'll be champagne all the way from now on.'

'Great,' I said, accepting a beer.

Inevitably he began to pace up and down, bottle in his right hand and cigar in his left. He was so keen to tell me his news. The plans spilled out one after the other, an endless cascade of schemes and ideas. From time to time he waved at some photographs over the desk. 'See that kid,' he said of a young man our age but much better looking. 'That's Dai. I told you about him. Once I've changed his name and Annie's given him the treatment, we'll have a superstar on our hands. He'll be worth his weight in gold in another couple of years . . .'

His excitement was irresistible. In full spate, Jack could raise a pulse from a corpse.

'I've got five acts now,' he said, 'and they'll all be top liners. Give them time and you'll really see something.'

He had such a positive vision of the future. Of course his confidence had been boosted by getting The Graduates into the Stork Club, but he'd never lacked faith in himself.

'Nobody teaches you in this business,' he said. 'No sir. I can't run to someone like this Jumbo of yours and check on the rules. You make the sodding rules up as you go. I decide, there and then. Get it right, and Janie plays the Stork Club. Get it wrong, and her career takes a dive.'

'That's a big responsibility,' I said, slightly facetiously, nettled by his remark about me running to Jumbo. I suppose I'd brought it on myself in a way. After all, I'd written implying Jack was wasting his life, suggesting he got back into the law. He was proving me wrong. I was glad to be wrong but niggled by that remark. I paid him back ten minutes later when he realised we ought to get ready. As I began to unpack, he saw my dinner jacket. 'Ah,' he said. 'Well done, I meant to remind you to hire one.'

'That's not hired, it's mine. Jumbo and I spend our lives at black tie functions.'

His eyes bulged. 'No shit?' he said, visibly impressed.

'Sure.' I picked up my shaving kit and made for the bathroom. Of course it was a lie, but I felt I'd struck a blow for country bumpkins the world over.

Ann had already gone when we got downstairs. 'Ossie's like a cat on hot bricks,' Gill grinned. 'Ann's got her work cut out trying to calm him down. She said she'll see you when you get there.'

So, with Gill's good luck wishes ringing in our ears, Jack and I went to the Stork Club to see Janie and The Graduates. That's how they were billed by the way, not *The Graduates*, but *Janie and* The Graduates. The début at the Stork Club was the first time Janie received separate billing; after that she never received anything less. That night she was tremendous. You'd never have thought she was nervous. She looked good, too. Her blonde hair had been pulled back, giving her a sophisticated look, and the mass of blue chiffon she wore did things for her eyes. What with her voice and the new sound from the band, I felt they had to succeed. That was the first time I'd heard the new sound, and the power Dave added on the drums made all the difference. They opened with 'Volare', which had been a big hit for Domenico Modugno. That got the audience going. Then came 'Sound of the Mountains', a new song written by Ossie, melodic and slow-tempo, before Janie revved the place up again with 'That'll be the Day'. The band belted it out behind her with the foot-tapping panache of The Crickets. Anyway, they did a forty-five-minute spot and the audience loved them.

During the performance, Ann joined us at the table, looking radiant in a silver sheath of a dress. Alive with excitement, she twisted and turned in her chair, intent on catching audience reaction, exchanging triumphant little grins with Jack, clearly delighted. It must have been a proud moment. It was her performance as much as the group's; she'd helped arrange the numbers, she'd recruited Dave and given Janie star billing, she'd helped bring them all the way from the Green Door to the Stork Club. And at the end, when people applauded and rose from their seats, she couldn't wait to rush backstage.

Later they all came to our table and we made a real night of it. Still on a high from the performance, Mike was incredibly funny. Ray egged him on, and Janie and Ann greeted each joke with peals of laughter. The talk never stopped and we all got a bit tight. I remember thinking how sophisticated we all looked, us in dinner-jackets and the girls in evening dresses. I felt a few pangs for Ann; more than a few, to be honest. It was the first time I'd seen her really dressed up. I'd never seen anyone so lovely. I felt a whole lot of envy for Jack. He and Ann had clearly become closer. Inevitably I suppose, working together and sharing so much. Even so, I kept a tight hold on myself, telling myself all the right things, that they were my friends, both of them, which was how I intended to keep it. So I joined in the laughter and shared in a successful evening.

It should have ended there, with all those laughing faces at the table. A good night to remember – the reunion at Gill's, followed by the triumph of Janie and The Graduates, then all of us drinking and laughing. But it didn't. Half an hour later I ruined the whole night.

It happened as we were leaving. Janie and the others had gone backstage to collect their things, and Jack and I were in the lobby, waiting for the commissionaire to organise a couple of cabs. We were both in good spirits, still laughing and joking.

'Great night, Tubby, my boy,' Jack beamed through a haze of cigar smoke.

'Great,' I agreed.

'Weren't they terrific?'

'Terrific,' I chorused.

Then he slid his arm over my shoulder in a gesture of friendship and suddenly it all went wrong. He said something to make my blood boil. A red mist enveloped my brain. Putting his mouth to my ear, he whispered, 'I offered you half of JWE. You blew a great opportunity. Don't you see what you missed?' He raised his hand, palm upwards, and slowly closed his fingers into a fist. 'I own Janie and The Graduates, I own Dai Evans. I own the Blackwood Trio –'

'Piss off!' I shouted, shaking myself free. Suddenly I saw myself as a fat little boy again. It wasn't Jack standing there, but my father. We were arguing about my weight, my unhealthy surplus pounds and my incessant craving for food. My father was shouting, 'You can't be hungry. If I catch you stealing from this kitchen again –' And I lashed back, 'It's my kitchen too.' At his full height, my father was a giant. 'Yours?' he roared. 'Nothing's yours. Get that into your head. This is *my* kitchen, *my* house, *my* food. I own them. I own everything.' He reached out a hand, palm upwards, and closed his fingers into a tight ball. 'I even own you,' he shouted. 'Understand? I own you.' And I screamed back, 'No! You'll never own me. You can't own people.'

'You can't own people!' I shouted at Jack, shaking with uncontrollable fury.

Then the red mist cleared and I realised where I was. Jack backed away, looking shaken. A man and a woman entered the lobby. They looked at me, shock in his eyes, distaste in hers. 'Fellow's drunk,' the man muttered, drawing her quickly away. Other people stared as I turned back to Jack.

'Steady on,' he said. 'It was only an expression.'

Staggering slightly, I put a hand to the wall. 'Sorry,' I muttered and tried to stop shaking.

Jack's shock gave way to concern. He was at my side in an instant. 'Okay? It's the heat,' he said. 'Damn stuffy in here. Let's get some air.'

What a way to end the evening. Of course it wasn't the heat. It was bad memories. Jack's words had struck a chord. How was he to know? I didn't even try to explain, I'd behaved badly enough without comparing him to my father. 'Sorry, Jack,' I said outside on the pavement. 'Dunno what came over me.'

'You look a bit better now,' he said, sounding relieved. 'I thought you were going to pass out.'

'I'm all right,' I muttered, feeling a fool.

The others emerged from the entrance at that moment, while beyond them the commissionaire had been successful in his search for cabs; two stood at the kerbside, empty and waiting.

Janie rushed up, still full of high spirits. 'We're going on to the Green Door, for old time's sake.'

Ann arrived. 'Tubby?' she said, peering into my face. 'You okay?'

Jack laughed. 'One jar too many.'

'Tired, that's all,' I said, and tried to make a joke of it by adding, 'Us country bumpkins don't have your stamina.'

'It's past two o'clock,' Ann pointed out in an understanding voice, 'and you did say you were working this morning. Shall we scrub the Green Door?'

But I couldn't do that. Ossie, Dave and Ray were already in one of the cabs, calling to us to hurry. So we went, and I did my best to pull myself together. I wasn't too bad, either; I did manage to shout above the music to Ann about my life in Taunton. Even so, I was glad when she'd had enough and wanted to go. We left the others still celebrating, and Jack, Ann and I walked back through the silent streets to Gill's place, as we had so often before.

'One hell of a night,' Jack sighed as he opened the door.

'Yes,' I agreed. But his chance remark had unlocked a store of old memories, and later I awoke, covered in sweat, seeing my father's face as I sat up in bed. 'You can't own people,' I choked into the darkness.

What with the late night and being plagued by nightmares, I woke the next morning with a sore head. Even so, it was at a fairly respectable hour; ten o'clock, which was a relief. Resisting the urge to turn over, I got up and went to the bathroom. Hearing Jack snoring, I left him in peace, there seemed no point in waking him when I had to leave in an hour. So, washed and shaved, dressed and packed, I crept down the stairs in search of some coffee. Which was when I bumped into Gill. Clad in dressing-gown and slippers, he was coming through the darkened bar with the Sunday papers under his arm. 'Bloody hell, Tubby. You made me jump.'

He was even more startled to see the case in my hand. 'Are you off? Blimey lad, don't you want breakfast? At least stay and have a cup of tea. Besides, I want to hear about last night.'

So I settled for tea, several cups actually, while I told him about Janie's début. There was no mistaking his pleasure. 'I am glad,' he beamed. 'Glad for Ann and Cowboy Jack an' all. They've worked hard, you know. This gig didn't fall off the back of a lorry.'

After that we talked of various things, including my life down in Taunton. 'Funny,' he said, 'I knew it suited you as soon as you walked in yesterday. A blind man could see that. I reckon it did you good to get away. No matter how close you are, working with family ain't always easy.'

Soberly, I agreed.

He wanted to rouse Ann and Jack to say goodbye, but I wouldn't hear of it. 'Let them sleep on. I'll give them a buzz later from Mum's place.'

He cocked an eyebrow. 'You going back to Taunton today?'

'After lunch.'

'You'll keep in touch?'

''Course I will.'

He seemed anxious that I should. 'They miss you, you know,' he said, jerking his head at the ceiling. 'Especially Ann. After what happened in the States . . .' he shrugged and a faint smile came to his face, 'well, you know, I reckon you helped her. Know what she calls you? Her gentle man. Not gentleman, but a gentle man. Two words –'

'What happened in the States?' I asked, instantly curious.

He hesitated, swirling the tea around in his cup. 'Ann,' I prompted, 'and some musician.'

Gill shrugged. 'The bastard let her down, didn't he.'

'I don't know. That's why I'm asking.'

For a moment I thought he was going to tell me. I knew Ann had run away from something, she as good as said so the day we were searching for Jack. But Gill rose to his feet. 'Water under the bridge,' he said. 'She might tell you herself one day.' He put his hand on my shoulder. 'All I'm saying is, come and see us more often. Don't bury yourself in the country.'

'I'm not burying myself. I work there.'

He nodded genially. 'I'm only saying we miss you.'

He wasn't *only* saying that. He was changing the subject, steering me away from talk of Ann's past. He refused to be drawn and I fell short of pressing him further. After all, what was it to me? I was going back to Taunton, to continue my role as Beau Geste.

Thankfully that Beau Geste nonsense was short lived. Ann phoned on the Monday, to say she was sorry we'd not had more time to talk. On my next visit, she promised, we'd have a few hours to ourselves, and before I read anything fanciful into that, she went on to include Jack. She was full of his plans for Dai Evans. It helped put our relationship into perspective. We were just good friends. No, we were more than that, we were *very* good friends. For instance, she asked a lot about Taunton and was really interested in the life I was living, so much so that she phoned again the following week. Then I phoned Jack and he was out, so instead Ann and I had another long talk. It settled into a pattern after that. Jack was out a good deal, dashing about, rarely with enough time to put pen to paper. Besides, letters weren't really his style – quick phone calls were much more in his line. There were plenty of those over the following months, because working on Saturday mornings and so on kept me in Taunton, while Jack's business never brought him into our neck of the woods, so we kept in touch by phone . . . and when Jack was out I spoke to Ann and sometimes to Gill.

And of course I was busy leading my own life, which was a full time job if ever there was one. People who think country solicitors lead a sheltered existence don't know the half of it. Crime isn't exclusive to cities. At the office I was helping to deal with a case of child abuse which bordered on incest, a wife-battering, several drunken drivings and a whole raft of offences you don't get in towns, like rustling (yes, it still goes on), boundary disputes, poaching, all that sort of thing. Conveyancing, mortgages and drawing up Wills came well down the list. So much for sleepy old Taunton.

Best of all, every day Jumbo and Josh were pumping me full of knowledge, not just about the law, but about people and what makes them tick, who to believe and who not to believe. They were rare teachers. Enthralled by what they were doing, they wanted to pass on their excitement. Above all they had a deep sense of justice, which is rarer than you'd think among lawyers. No legal system is perfect;

justice and the law are often in opposite corners. Too often the law is an ass, which is why it sometimes gets bent by unprincipled lawyers. I should know, my father was one of them. Jumbo was nothing like that.

I remember a meeting with Sam Prentice. *Mr* Prentice to me in those days, but Sam to Jumbo. Sam was our biggest client. We did a lot of work for his businesses which ranged from property development to mortgages and a whole range of financial services. He was a tall, big boned man of about fifty who prided himself on his blunt speech. Self-made was Sam and proud of it. Anyway, due to a technical oversight (nothing to do with us, I'm glad to say) he found he could call in the mortgages on twelve of his houses and then re-sell them for a large profit. Legally he had a water-tight case. In court a judge would have no option but to find in his favour. According to the law, Sam was within his rights, and by heavens, he wanted his rights.

Jumbo didn't hesitate. 'Sorry, Sam,' he said, 'but I don't think I can act for you.'

'Don't be bloody daft,' said Sam. 'We'll have them houses back free. It's a nice little windfall. I'm not passing up on that.'

Jumbo shook his head. 'I won't touch it,' he said. 'If you want to, you'll have to find another firm of solicitors.'

Sam went red in the face. 'What the hell are you on about? The law's on my side.'

'Maybe,' said Jumbo, 'but it's not fair.'

The air was blue after that. 'Fair?' Sam shouted. 'What the fuck's fair got to do with it? This is business, not your bloody cricket.'

Jumbo refused to budge.

Sam gave him another mouthful of abuse, followed by an ultimatum. 'If you don't act on this you can forget the rest of my business,' he shouted, rising to his feet. 'I'll be back tomorrow. If you haven't issued those writs by then, you're finished with me.'

Sam was back the next day. He came in, sat down, and glared. 'Well? You issued those writs?'

Jumbo shook his head. 'Sorry, Sam, I told you yesterday.'

Sam's eyes narrowed to pin-points. A vein pulsed in his neck. He drummed his fingers on Jumbo's desk. 'If I walk out that door,' he said, jerking his thumb, 'everything goes. You'll not get another pennyworth of business out of me.'

'I shall be sorry about that, Sam —'

'What's more I'll tell everyone you failed to look after my interests. That's a lawyer's job, that is. That's why I pay you, to look after my interests.'

Jumbo said, 'I don't think it's in your interests to issue writs. That's my advice and you have it for nothing. I won't take instructions on the matter either, although I'm sure you'll find someone who will.'

'Bloody right,' Sam agreed, nodding. He rose to his feet and turned for the door. Half-way there, he hesitated. 'Since your advice is for nothing,' he sneered, 'perhaps you'll explain why picking up twelve thousand quid is against my interests?'

Jumbo shrugged. 'It's a shit's trick. Those house-holders are paid up to date. They're honouring their arrangements. Now, because they all used the same careless solicitor, an error in their mortgages makes them invalid. Under other circumstances they might be able to go for the lawyer, but he died years ago. They're in a mess through no fault of their own. Only a shit would take advantage. And you're not a shit.'

'I'm not a bloody charity either,' Sam snarled on his way to the door.

We heard no more from him that day. I assumed the worst, he'd taken his business elsewhere. It would be a severe loss to Weston & Weston; about fifteen percent of our business. But Jumbo seemed in no mood to discuss it and I lacked the nerve to press him. Even so, I was worried, and when I called into The Crown for a beer after work Martin and I talked it over. We were discussing the matter in suitably hushed tones, when the door opened and Sam Prentice came in. Peering out from beneath beetle-brows, he advanced into the bar, glaring around until his gaze fell on me. 'Ah, you,' he said, beckoning me over. 'Morton, isn't it?'

I went across to him. 'Mortlake, Mr Prentice.'

'Quite so. Is High and Mighty Weston about?'

I didn't like the High and Mighty, so I said, 'Jumbo's not here tonight.'

'Hmm,' Sam pondered, clearly about to turn on his heel.

'Can I get you a drink, Mr Prentice?' I asked.

Fierce slate grey eyes focused on my face. 'No,' he said, 'but you can give him a message. About what we were talking about, right? At the office.'

I nodded.

'Tell him I want letters out tomorrow giving them people fourteen days to get their paperwork right. Formal notice, understand. A day over that and we issue writs. Understand?'

'Yes, Mr Prentice.'

'At no cost to me.'

'Naturally not,' I agreed.

He stared as if searching my mind. 'Well? Is that fair?'

'Very fair, Mr Prentice. Um . . . well, except I think . . . if you could go to twenty-one days that would be even more fair –'

'Christ! You're as bad as him!'

I broke into a sweat, wishing I'd kept my mouth shut. Not that I minded being compared with Jumbo, that was a compliment, but if the business was back and I'd lost it again . . .

To my vast relief, he nodded. 'Right,' he said, 'twenty-one days from tomorrow. And I want copies of those letters sent round to my office.'

'Yes, Mr Prentice.'

'First thing in the morning.'

'Certainly, Mr Prentice.'

'No cost to me.'

'Quite, Mr Prentice.'

His eyes glimmered for a moment, then he turned on his heel. ''Night,' he said as he went out of the door.

The following morning, Jumbo received the news almost casually. 'Oh good,' he said coolly, 'twenty-one days. That's excellent. Draft the letter and let me have a look at it.'

Astonished, I choked, 'How can you be so calm? You nearly lost fifteen percent of the business.'

'Nonsense. Sam's not a shit,' said Jumbo with absolute certainty. Then a puzzled frown lit his eyes. 'He's getting soft, though. In the old days he'd have come back and told us to give them fourteen days.'

Biting my tongue, I returned to my desk to draft the letter. Twenty-one days later, the mortgagees made a little ceremony of exchanging the correct paperwork; they and their wives gave Mr and Mrs Sam Prentice dinner at the Castle Hotel. The story was in the local paper, complete with a picture of Sam's wife receiving a bouquet. When asked if he'd considered terminating the mortgages, Sam's eyes widened in horror. 'Good God, no. That's not the way I do business. Anyone who takes out a mortgage with me can sleep soundly at night.' And there was a picture of Sam, surrounded by satisfied customers beaming their goodwill and singing his praises.

Jumbo chuckled when he read it. 'That kind of publicity's worth more than twelve thousand, eh Sam?'

Sam was as dour as ever. 'A calculated risk,' he sniffed. 'It's early days yet, but we might turn it to advantage.'

'Reckon you might,' Jumbo grinned. 'Meanwhile you'll be able to live with yourself.'

Living with himself was something at which Jumbo excelled. He did what he thought right, and that was that. Not that he was without his detractors. Detesting the pretentious, he loathed hypocrites and despised bigots, so, not surprisingly, they hated him back. One man (a vicar) always referred to him as 'that damn radical'. He was described as 'Taunton's leading eccentric', by a prominent town councillor, while an ancient in the Rose and Crown always called him 'that fucking cricketer who fancies himself as a lawyer'. For the most part, however, Jumbo was widely liked and respected.

Meanwhile, time was passing, times were changing. The fifties were dead, we were into the sixties, and if Britain wasn't yet swinging, at least it was restless. A new generation was creating new values. Girls were wearing short skirts. Young people had money to spend, and attitudes were changing. And then came the Pill. Bang, crash, wallop! What a catalyst for change that was. Female sexual freedom really took off. Girls burned their bras and tore up the rule books. Even I got laid.

It was after a cricket club dance. This girl Moira and I were necking in the back of my second-hand Ford. We were all over each other on the back seat. I opened her blouse, she unzipped my flies, and so furiously were we thrashing about that her knee cracked my jaw, nearly knocking me out. Then she went berserk. 'What's the matter? Don't you want me?' she panted. Next thing my penis was in her hand and she was guiding me in, and all the time gasping, 'Come on, give it me, give it me.' I was huffing and puffing. She was crying, 'More, more,' and positively shouting 'More!' when I came. 'Oh, Tubby,' she groaned. 'Oh Christ,' I responded.

When we recovered, she said it had been nice for her too. She promised to meet me the following week, but she didn't turn up, even though I waited outside the cinema for an hour and a half. I never saw her again. Not that it mattered. She'd provided me with my first sexual experience and I was suitably grateful. I can still remember her; not what she looked like, but she was wearing a spicy scent, full of cinnamon and cloves, so that whenever I smell bread pudding, Moira comes into my mind.

Looking back, those were my growing-up years,

really growing-up, I mean. People talk a lot of rot about the passing of time. They say this happened on that day, or that happened then. I've even heard people claim to be able to pinpoint when the Swinging Sixties started in Britain. They name an actual day and put everything down to that. Saturday, 14 February 1963. It's rubbish. Change is a gradual thing, it takes time. You're not immature one day and adult the next. It took those early years in Taunton for me to shake off adolescence and advance into manhood. So when self-styled experts place such emphasis on a particular day, they're talking baloney.

As it happens, I remember that Saturday. Among other reasons, what brings it to mind is the weather. That February, indeed the entire winter of '62–'63, was the worst for a hundred years. From December through to mid-March, the entire country lay buried in snow. Scores of old people died from hypothermia, Siberian temperatures froze the English Channel. Most of the south-west was cut off from the rest of the country, and I was cut off with it, trapped in snow-bound, iced-up, deep-frozen Taunton.

I was living in the cottage at the time. For the first year I existed in digs, then I rented a flat, and when I qualified Jumbo helped arrange a mortgage on a small cottage on the outskirts of town. But as for that February being the start of the Swinging Sixties, Jack Webb and such people had been busy long before then . . .

Jack was all over the place. In fact when I next went to London and called round at Gill's, Jack was in Hamburg.

'Hamburg?' I said, hoisting myself on to a stool. 'You mean Hamburg, Germany?'

'How many Hamburgs do you know?' asked Gill, pouring my pint.

Mum would have said 'Fancy that!' and her eyes would have rounded in wonder. I was more sophisticated by then, so I kept a still tongue in my head. Even so, I was amazed. Jack had never been abroad before, neither of us had. I hadn't even got a passport. We'd spoken on the phone three weeks before and Jack had hinted about doing something 'a bit special', but he hadn't said what. And Hamburg! Hamburg was considered even racier than Paris in those days. British soldiers stationed in West Germany came home with vivid tales of the entertainment to be sampled in the Reeperbahn, Hamburg's legendary cabaret district – of women wrestling in mud and live sex shows involving donkeys and pythons and goodness knows what. And Jack had gone there.

'Where's Ann?' I asked, inexplicably nervous.

'Glasgow. She went up yesterday with Janie and The Graduates.'

Talk about jet-setters; Jack was in Germany, Ann was in Scotland. At least Gill was where I'd left him, although something was different even about him. Then I realised what it was. It wasn't Gill, it was the bar that was different. There was a new girl behind the counter. She had red hair and a low-cut black blouse.

'Doesn't Ann work here any more then?' I asked.

'Less and less,' Gill grunted. 'She don't have time.'

'Oh,' I said.

Obviously I was more out of touch than I thought. I would have asked more questions, but lunch times were always busy at Gill's and that day he was rushed off his feet. Besides, I'd only dropped in for a quick sandwich between appointments.

'Just up for the day?' Gill asked when he got back to me ten minutes later.

'That's right, but I'll be finished by four.'

'Lovely,' he said. 'Come back and we'll have a cup of tea before opening time.'

At twenty past four I was back, sitting in the front bar drinking tea while Gill told me lurid tales about Hamburg. He kept his voice low in case it carried to Mary up in the flat. 'Fair makes your hair curl,' he chortled. 'There's one street where all the girls sit in shop windows. If you fancy one, you just go and have her.'

'You don't mean Jack's gone into the sex business?'

Gill looked at my face and burst out laughing. 'In London? Come off it. No, no, there's a lot of music bars in Hamburg. Discotheques, Jack calls them. All into rock and roll. Belting out Elvis like nobody's business. All in German, of course.'

Jack had taken two of his acts across – Dai Evans, who by then had been renamed Jet Storm, and a group called The Post Office Tower.

'Jack got them a very good deal,' Gill said proudly, 'they've all got three-month contracts. Dai's on about five hundred marks a week, with accommodation thrown in, and I think the boys in The Post Office Tower get about six hundred between them. Can't be bad, can it?'

'No, it can't,' I agreed.

I worked out Jack's share and even that came to thirty pounds a week, which wasn't to be sneezed at in those days.

'What about Ann?' I asked. 'You say she doesn't work here any more.'

'She hasn't time. It's not just Janie and The Graduates now, you know. Jack's got eight acts and they're all working.' Gill broke off to go to the end of the bar where he searched under the counter. 'Ah, I knew I had one. Have a look at that.'

He handed me a glossy publicity hand-out, printed in full colour. I imagine Jack mailed them to club owners and such like. Beneath a headline blaring JACK WEBB'S ALL-STARS were pictures of his eight acts, all smiling out from around the edge of the page. In the centre was a caricature of Jack, smoking a big cigar and dressed in the red coat and top hat of a circus ring-master.

It was impressive in a gaudy sort of way, but something about it jarred. Frankly I was still thinking about Ann so I gave it less than my full attention. 'What does she actually do?' I asked.

Gill seemed surprised at the question. 'She's Jack's ears. If she says they've got talent, they're in. If not, Jack gives them the Don't call me, I'll call you routine. Simple as that. Then she helps them polish their acts. And she works with Ossie a lot.'

'Writing his music?'

'That's right. They spend hours together.'

I was wondering how that went down with Jack when Gill read my mind. 'You know Ossie's ginger beer?'

Seeing my expression, he explained, 'Ginger beer. Queer. You know . . .'

I hadn't known.

Gill laughed. 'Takes all sorts, don't it?'

The afternoon was providing revelation after revelation, but before I could speculate further, Gill said, 'Mind you, where all this gets Ann I don't know. Mary's proper worried about her. She reckons Ann should get on with her own life instead of helping Jack all the time.' He lowered his voice. 'He's taking advantage according to Mary, and she don't like it; she's not too fond of Jack at the moment.'

'Oh?' I said.

He shrugged. 'She can see Ann getting hurt all over again. Ann's so unselfish about helping musicians, she thinks everyone's as unselfish as she is, but they're not.'

I frowned. 'But you said Jack's getting them good deals –'

'He is,' Gill agreed, 'that's what I keep telling Mary, but that don't stop her worrying about Ann. Ann's very loyal. Ossie and the others rely on her now, and she won't walk away when they need her.'

I wondered what Gill would say if I told him about AIDA. Probably tell me I was making it up.

He folded Jack's publicity sheet and gave it to me. 'A memento,' he said. 'Frame it as early Jack Webb.'

As I stuffed it into my pocket, he sighed. 'I don't know what to think, and that's telling you straight. I can understand Ann being excited by it all, but Jack's growing too fast. He's even got road managers now, blokes to hump the gear about. And you know he's bought another four vans, don't you?'

'No,' I said, shaking my head.

'Oh yes. And he's talking about getting a proper office. Somewhere in Denmark Street. Tin-Pan Alley, he calls it.'

'He must be making good money,' I said, and tried to work it out. If all of his acts were collecting the same pay as those in Germany, Jack had something like five hundred pounds a month coming in. It brought a low whistle from my lips.

'All very well you whistling,' said Gill. 'But I wish you weren't down in Taunton. This is getting big business. I'll tell you what I think. Jack needs you to keep his feet on the ground. Ann's his ears and you're his best pal. If he keeps both of you, he's made. If he loses either of you, God help him.'

'Don't be daft. Sounds like he's making a fortune —'

'He'll lose a bloody fortune without you and Ann,' Gill said emphatically.

'How can you say that?' I exclaimed, and added grumpily, 'Anyway, he doesn't look like losing Ann.'

Gill sighed as if I was being especially stupid. 'Haven't you heard a word I said? Use your loaf. A clever bloke like you can figure it out. I just told you, Ann thinks musicians are gods. Anyone who treats them half right is a saint in her book. Jack treats them right, so she admires him, that's all.'

I was thinking about that when the red-haired barmaid arrived and it was opening time. It killed the conversation — just as well, perhaps, because I had a train to catch. There was just time for a quick pint before Gill walked me to the door. 'I liked it best when you were around,' he said. 'Jack worries me. He won't be content. He sets his mind on something, then when he gets it it's not enough, he wants something more.'

'That's called ambition. My father was always moaning about my lack of it.'

'Better off without it,' said Gill, shaking hands. 'It changes people.'

Gill's words came back to me when I boarded the

train. After finding an empty carriage, I threw my briefcase on the rack, unfolded my evening paper and was fumbling through my pockets for cigarettes when I came across the publicity hand-out Gill had thrust into my hand. Unfolding it, I stared at the headline. JACK WEBB'S ALL STARS. I disliked it as much as before, but it reminded me of Gill talking about the changes in people. Daft, I thought, people don't change. Jack was always ambitious.

I remembered those thoughts about changes in people some seven months later when I was living in the rented flat in Orchard Street. What reminded me was that I had changed; physically. Nothing dramatic, not like Jekyll into Hyde or anything like that, but I'd lost weight. My middle was several inches slimmer. Still ample, I wasn't wasting away, but for some weeks decency had compelled me to tighten my belt, and finally I had to have my suits altered.

Jumbo came into the office one day, stared hard at the reduced version of me, and said, 'I don't know who you're going to, but does he do ears?'

Playing golf regularly was part of the reason, although Tommy Osborne, a doctor at the club, said the change was mostly due to psychological reasons. 'You've found your right weight,' he told me. 'People do if they're healthy and in control of their lives.'

He made me sound like a contented cat and I said so.

'Don't scoff,' he said. 'You'd be surprised. A lot of people put on weight when they're under stress, especially young people.' He peered at me. 'Did anything upset you in childhood?'

I saw no reason to go into that, and I only mention it here because as I've grown older, everyone except Jack has taken to calling me by my proper name of Peter instead of Tubby. Apart from pleasing Mum, I can't say it's changed my life. I didn't stop being a frog and change into a prince, I simply slimmed down a bit.

The odd thing was that while I was shedding a few pounds, Jack was gaining them, no doubt because he too had found his right weight and felt in 'control of his life'. He began to look less like a blond stick-insect and more like the Jack Webb, Chairman and Managing Director of JWE, whom people began to recognise from their television screens. For at about this time Jack began to appear on the pop shows, of which there were several as television woke up to the youth revolution. First he was on *Thank Your Lucky Stars*, then *Saturday Club* and *Juke Box Jury*, giving his views on the current pop scene. I thought it was terrific. Best friend, crooked-nosed Jack, a bit fuller in the face, was becoming a minor TV personality. He even had a catch-phrase. 'Music's my business,' he'd say directly to camera, 'I know a good tune when I hear one.'

He was right, too, because an Ossie Davidson song 'Echoes' became very popular at the time. Jet Storm recorded it, which was fine in Germany where his three months in the Reeperbahn had gained him a following, but less valuable in England where he was still relatively unknown. However all sorts of other singers recorded 'Echoes' and I remember it well, mainly because Martin Juffs was always whistling it. He refused to believe me when I first told him I knew the composer. Anyway, Martin liked 'Echoes' so much that he actually went out and bought the sheet music. He came back to the office clutching it in his hand. 'I'm fed up with Jumbo's Fats Waller impressions,' he grinned, 'we'll get him to sing this for a change.' And Jumbo did, he fairly belted it out at the rugby club boozeup.

Meanwhile Jack and I kept in touch, and Ann always phoned when he was scheduled to do a TV appearance. 'Six o'clock Saturday,' she'd say: 'Give us a buzz and tell us what you think.'

Jack always wanted to know what I thought. I was his typical viewer so he used me for market research. He was always very concerned with his image. 'It's an image business,' he'd say. 'I've got to project; you know, I've got to look with it. I owe it to my clients to make an impression.'

He was making an impression. In fact, becoming well known. The experts, by whom I mean the same people who claim the Swinging Sixties started in February '63, will tell you Jack Webb started in business in September 1962. That's nonsense. He'd been to Germany by then, and was managing eight acts. What actually happened was that Jack opened his office in Denmark Street.

'We're having a bit of a party to celebrate,' he said on the phone. 'You must come up for the night.'

I imagined a few friends in for a drink, but two days later an invitation arrived, typed on thick notepaper heavily embossed with red and gold letters. Jack Webb Enterprises was pleased to announce a change of address. Not a word about the old address, nothing about living over Gill's pub for the past couple of years, simply that henceforward Jack Webb Enterprises would be located in Denmark Street, London.

The words 'From the Chairman's Office' were printed separately under the address, in case you were silly enough to think it originated in the boiler room.

Martin read it over my shoulder. 'That's posh for you,' he said. '"From the Chairman's Office." That's style.'

'Right,' I agreed. 'That's my friend Jack.'

'You going?'

'You bet.'

The place was heaving when I arrived. Jack's offices were four rooms on the first floor of a very ordinary building, whereas whoever sent out the invitations had Wembley Stadium in mind. Guests propped up the walls and sat on the stairs, balancing drinks and canapés with practised dexterity. Half-way up the stairs my path was blocked by a heavyweight boxer. 'Brian Mann from *Melody Maker*?' he asked. Having said no, I expected him to move aside, but he remained where he was. He had cauliflower ears and fists bigger than hams. 'Harry Andrews from *Music Week*?' he suggested. Hoping to resolve the misunderstanding, I offered, 'Peter Mortlake from Taunton', and tried to get past. Unfortunately he held the high ground and remained where he was. 'Mortlake from Taunton,' he echoed, 'never heard of you.' He obviously thought I was a gate-crasher. I looked about me for a familiar face. 'I'm a friend of Jack's,' I assured him. 'Jack who?' he retorted. I began to think I'd got the wrong address and was at the wrong party. 'Jack Webb,' I said. His eyes narrowed into slits of suspicion. 'Anyone can say that, can't they?

How do I know you're his friend?' In desperation I wondered about telling him of the time at school when Jack and I went through the ceremony of becoming blood brothers by nicking our fingers and letting the blood mingle. Then I saw Jack. He was up on the landing, surrounded by people. 'Jack!' I shouted. Although we were only a few yards apart, naturally he was much higher, in fact my head was in line with his feet. 'Jack!' I bellowed again above the hubbub of conversation. Jack's head bobbed up above the shoulders of his circle of admirers. 'Jack!' I called. Craning and twisting his neck, his eyes darted all over the place before lighting on me. 'Tubby,' he exclaimed impatiently. 'Stop fooling about and come up and join us.'

If nothing else, my arrival at that party illustrates the difference in life-styles opening between us. I was on the verge of becoming a provincial solicitor; Jack was on the verge of the big time-TV 'personality', professional manager, Chairman and Managing Director of JWE, *bon viveur*, entrepreneur, the lot.

'Tubby!' he said, breaking away from the people surrounding him. 'You should have said who you were. What's all this Peter nonsense? How can we keep track if people start changing their names?'

Before I could reply, a petite blonde stuck a glass of champagne in my hand and offered me a choice of sausages on sticks or vol-au-vents. She also explained I was too late for the caviar. 'You should have been here ten minutes ago,' she said, delivering my second reprimand in as many minutes.

By the time I returned to Jack the crowd had closed around him again, like minor planets encircling the sun. He waved to me over their shoulders. 'Get back to you in a minute, Tubby.' Then he returned to answering questions. It gave me a chance to look round. The reception area was very full, full of the sort of people who go to parties given by celebrities. I imagine two were celebrities in their own right, because they too were surrounded by satellites. Jack was the best, though. Carrying on six conversations at once, every now and then he emerged from his crowd with beaming smile and outstretched hand – 'Tony. Glad you could make it.' What amazed me was the sheer volume of people. Hundreds of them. I assumed they were all in the music business. Certainly the talk on all sides suggested they were. And Jack knew them all, not merely those out on the landing and down the stairs, but those in the offices too, through which I wandered in search of Ann.

I found her trapped in a corner, listening to an Australian explain why Neil Diamond needed a new manager. She excused herself with satisfying alacrity. 'Tubby!' Her eyes brightened, lighting her face. 'Hey, you're looking great.' Coming into my arms, she kissed me before stepping back. 'You've lost weight?'

'I know. I'm thinking of entering the Mr Universe contest.'

'Oh funny.' She pulled a face. 'I only meant it as a compliment. It suits you.'

Taking my arm, she steered me away from the Australian who was trying to get back into conversation. 'Isn't this terrific?' she whispered, waving a hand. 'Jack's really cracked it. This rat pack wouldn't turn out for a loser.'

'No. I don't suppose –'

'Shall I introduce you around?' she asked, pausing to collect more champagne as we passed the blonde. 'Or do you want to talk?'

I said I'd rather talk, so we pressed on through the crush until we came upon an alcove near the top of the stairs. It was hardly secluded, just a niche wide enough for us to step back from the main flow of traffic. People were constantly waving to Ann, who responded with, 'How're you doing? Good to see you. Glad you could make it'.

In her own way, she was as well known as Jack. 'So?' she shrugged, dismissing my comment. 'It's a village.' Her single disappointment with the evening was that none of Jack's artists were present. 'They're all working. You know what they say, the show must go on. Still . . .' she said wistfully, 'I wish Janie was here.'

Which led her to bring me up to date with news about Janie and the others. She was very proud of them. 'Aren't they doing well?' she asked, her face flushing with pleasure. We were still talking half an hour later when Man Mountain from the staircase arrived. 'Hi, Tiny,' said Ann. 'Have you met Tubby?'

His scowl travelled from my head to my toes. 'You're not so tubby,' he said.

'You're not so tiny,' I pointed out, returning the compliment, and while he pondered that, Ann explained he was Dai's road manager – 'his roadie', she called him.

'Oh,' I said. 'And how's Dai coping without you?'

I hadn't meant to be critical but Tiny seemed to think it was implied. 'It's all organised,' he replied grumpily before turning to Ann. 'The boss wants everyone in reception for his speech. Can you help round 'em up?'

Jack gave one of the best speeches I ever heard. Some people can make speeches, some can't. I never could. Maybe if I'd succumbed to my father's pressure and joined the debating society, I'd have learned the same skills as Jack, but I doubt it. Jack had a politician's knack of playing an audience. I think he'd always had it, but that night he was special. Once he got to the meat of his subject, he became Moses leading his people to the Promised Land. He became old Ben Johnson penning the Declaration of Independence; and young President Kennedy a year before saying, 'Fellow Americans, ask not what your country can do for you, ask rather what you can do for your country.'

'Having trained as a lawyer,' Jack said at one stage, 'I was appalled when I came into this business. How can something which gives as much pleasure as the music business spawn so many rackets? I can hardly believe the things that go on. A band plays a gig and the guy running the hall siphons off the gate. A band makes a record and gets ripped off by the record company. A composer writes a song and his publisher steals his money. Yet it happens ten times a day, a hundred times a day!' Jack regarded us reproachfully. 'How can artists be treated so badly? You know how! Because they're sitting ducks. Artists aren't businessmen. They're not lawyers or accountants. They live by their hearts, not their heads. They're naïve. They think integrity's a two-way street, they tell themselves if they deliver an honest performance, people will be honest with them. Oh yeah? They get crucified!'

People cheered. A few protested, some laughed, but most people cheered.

Jack held up a hand. 'I say those days are over!'

'Bravo!' shouted Ann.

'It's up to us managers to become more professional,' Jack cried. 'To bring integrity to this business. To create standards. To establish a proper code of conduct . . .' he began counting points off on his fingers as people responded with 'Hear, hear'.

A sideways glance at Ann revealed her excitement. Her eyes shone and she nodded approval. All at once I remembered Gill saying that anyone who treated musicians decently was a saint in Ann's book. And I remembered her parents, those doughty crusaders against injustice. Watching Ann's face I knew she'd worn the same look when she'd listened to her father denouncing McCarthy. This was the same girl who picketed for black rights in New York, who'd marched for SANE, waving her placard about Banning the Bomb.

'It's not enough that artists *hope* for a fair deal,' Jack cried. 'They've a *right* to a fair deal!'

'Absolutely,' Ann called out.

'At JWE,' said Jack, concluding his speech, 'the artist comes first. Then comes the artist. And finally comes the artist.'

And that brought the house down.

I didn't know how much truth there was in that speech. After all, my knowledge of the music business was limited to my contact with people like Janie, and to my friend Jack who was becoming so successful. But I discovered something of the crooked side of the business the following week, when quite unexpectedly I was in London again. A client wanted someone from Weston & Weston to attend a meeting with him in the city, so I went. He and I caught the early train, dealt with his business, lunched with his associates in Moorgate, and by three thirty we were finished. I gave Jack a buzz at his office in Denmark Street.

'JWE, can I help you?' asked the voice on the phone, and I found myself talking to the little blonde, who'd been so concerned about me missing the caviar. When I asked for Jack, she said, 'He's out at the moment, but he'll be back shortly because Ann and Ossie are waiting.'

I spoke to Ann. 'Come over,' she cried.

Jack's offices looked quite different from the night of the party, but then so does Wembley Stadium without the crowds. Brick-red carpet covered the floor in reception, comfortable sofas lined the walls, and the blonde looked up from the desk. 'I'd come back tomorrow,' she said, 'he's in a foul temper.'

'He won't eat me,' I assured her, 'I'm his best friend.'

She was right about Jack's mood. When I went in, his face was black with rage. Ann and Ossie sat across from his desk, looking anxious.

'We've been robbed.' Jack scowled without even saying hello.

I looked round the office. Framed prints still adorned the walls, books lined the shelves, his desk and conference table were still intact.

'Not burgled, you idiot,' Jack snorted. 'Robbed by professionals. Thieving, conniving bastards!'

I sat down next to Ann who gave me a peck on

the cheek. Squeezing her hand, I lowered my voice. 'Who's he talking about?'

'Ossie's publishers.'

Meanwhile Jack was cursing and swearing. Needless to say, he was pacing up and down, bristling with temper. Finally he went behind his desk, but instead of sitting down he put a hand on the back of his chair and glared at me. 'This should appeal to a lawyer,' he said. 'I'll tell you a story about crooks. I'll tell you a story of how publishing works.'

His voice came out as a low snarl, like a volcano smouldering between eruptions. 'This is the story of "Echoes",' he growled, 'a lovely song composed by Ossie Davidson and published by Blanes Music of America, one of the largest music publishers in the world.'

The control he was seeking deserted him. Even to stand still was too much. Slapping the back of the chair, he walked to the door and then back again. 'Guess what Ossie got paid when we signed the contract? Twenty pounds. Correction, they didn't *pay* anything, they lent Ossie twenty pounds against royalties. The way it works is, when the song earns forty quid, they take half for themselves and say to Ossie, "Remember that twenty we lent you? We're taking it back." Result, no money for Ossie. Understand?'

I shrugged. I could understand anyone recovering an advance. After all, an advance is an advance, whether against pocket-money or wages or a discounted bill. In this case the advance was against royalties. What I couldn't understand was why the publisher took half of Ossie's income, and I said so.

Jack scowled. 'Because that's the way it works. You know your trouble, Tubby? You've been conned by Hollywood. All those movies about Gershwin. Or Cole Porter. I can see the scene now. A publisher's office in New York. Enter a young Cole Porter. "Oh boy," he cries, "have I got a great song for you!" He sits down at the piano. He plays, he sings. The publisher springs up from his desk, a big smile on his face, "That's gotta be a hit," he says. Next minute we see the whole world singing this song. Scene after scene; night clubs, radio stations. Suddenly our hero's rich and famous, living in a big house.' Jack stopped to draw breath, 'It's not like that. Publishers don't work that way.'

I hadn't said they did, but there was no point in arguing. Jack was in full flight.

'Stay with the Hollywood version,' he said, 'except the scene changes. Instead of the publisher's office, we're backstage in the Star's dressing room. Enter our publisher, "Oh boy!" he cries, "have I got a great song for you!" He sits down at the piano. He plays, he sings. The Big Star springs up, a big smile on his face. "That's gotta be a hit," he says. Next minute you see him on stage singing it. The camera cuts to the front stalls. We see the publisher and song writer biting their nails. The song ends. The audience rise, everyone applauds. The publisher embraces the writer. The writer embraces the publisher. Cut to the next scene. Our writer is rich and famous, living in a big house . . .'

Jack wasn't only pacing up and down, he was acting all the parts, living his story. He changed his voice for each character. Suddenly he stopped. 'Get the difference?'

'You mean the publisher has to sell the song? That's why he takes half the royalty?'

'You got it!' Educating me was improving Jack's temper. He stopped scowling and gave me a grin. Not that it lasted long. A second later he was glaring again and on with his story. 'Selling costs money. So here's what really happens. The scene stays the same. The Big Star's dressing room. Enter our publisher. "Oh boy!" he cries, "have I got a great song for you!" He sits down at the piano. He plays, he sings. The Big Star looks up from polishing his nails. "How much?" he asks. "You want me to sing that song? You want me to make the writer rich and famous so he can live in a big house? So how much will you pay me?"'

I think I blinked, but even wise old owls blink every once in a while. The truth was, Jack's scenario was a revelation; I had no idea that sort of thing went on.

'Another example,' said Jack. 'Take radio. There's a concert going out live. So what happens? All the song pluggers arrive and the band leader holds an auction. He says straight out, "My boys will play any tune so long as the price is right." So the plugger with the most cash gets his tune played on prime time radio. Get the picture?'

I got the picture. I wondered if the BBC did? I wondered if they knew their band leaders were paid twice, once by them and once by publishers? Publishing sounded a very mucky business, but Jack wasn't complaining about that because he went on, 'That's what a publisher *should* do. Get the song into circulation. Okay, it costs. That's why he takes fifty percent of the royalty. He's got expenses.'

I thought 'expenses' was a mild description of what amounted to bribery.

'Mind you,' Jack muttered as he prowled round the office, 'most publishers are too bloody idle to do a proper job. They just wait for the money to roll in. Then they rip the writer off.'

'There won't be much to rip off,' I pointed out. 'If they don't get the song into circulation people won't buy the sheet music –'

'Punters hear the song elsewhere. Nothing to do with the publisher. Twenty-two singers recorded "Echoes". Dai's version only charted eighteen here, but it was a number one smash in Germany.'

I began to think I'd missed a point. 'So Ossie's rich?'

'Like hell!' Jack snarled. 'We got ripped off. The bastards robbed us.'

It took me a while to understand the manipulations, mainly because Jack kept exploding into further outbursts of temper. What Blanes did was ingenious, but really quite simple. Take Germany as an example. Blanes in Germany had collected the German royalties. Then they'd split the money fifty fifty, half to them, half to the writer. However, because their head office was in the States, Ossie's share had been sent to New York 'for administrative reasons'. Blanes New York had cut the money again, fifty fifty, and sent Ossie's reduced share on to their London office, where Blanes UK had cut the money yet again. Result – what started as a ten percent royalty ended up at one and a quarter percent, and Jack would collect a quarter of that. Ossie got less than one percent.

'It's enough to buy a new pair of shoes,' he said mournfully.

He looked so crushed that I felt compelled to say something. So I asked Jack, 'Can't you dump Blanes and deal with somebody else?'

'Don't be daft. They own the copyright.'

Seeing my blank expression, he explained, 'When you sign a deal with a publisher, they register the copyright. The song becomes their property.'

'For how long?'

'The writer's lifetime plus fifty years.'

I more than blinked at that. I was astounded. 'Echoes' might prove Ossie's most successful song, and he was locked into a rip-off.

Jack saw my expression. 'Don't say it,' he muttered wearily, at last sitting down. 'I'm supposed to take care of my artists. The copyright clause is normal, but Blanes shafted me with their trick of moving money around. I let Ossie down. That's why we're here. I wanted to explain to him what happened . . .' The words dried up and a pained wretchedness came into his eyes as he looked at Ossie. 'Sorry, mate. I let you down –'

'Don't say that.' Ossie shook his head. 'I wouldn't be published at all without you. I'll write other songs, you'll get me better deals –'

'Sure,' Ann interrupted. 'Another manager wouldn't even have explained. He'd have said it was the usual thing. You know what conmen they are.'

'Right,' Ossie agreed, overcoming his own disappointment. 'Forget it, Jack. You'll nail the bastards next time.'

They rallied to him. Sitting there, watching them, listening to Ann and Ossie, I realised how much loyalty Jack's caring manner engendered. The guy in the white hat, I remembered, as Ann said, 'Don't blame yourself, Jack. Everyone's doing fine because of you.'

'Coming up roses,' said Ossie, giving a thumbs up sign and working hard to forget his loss.

I made the only suggestion I could think of. 'Come on,' I said, 'dinner's on me. My train's not until ten.'

So we went out for a meal. The funny thing was that losing that battle was the culmination of AIDA. I watched it happen over dinner. Of course Jack and Ann had been getting closer for months. I'd seen the body language, the eye contact, the nuances every time I came to town. In the old days it had been one-way traffic, with Ann deflecting his openly admiring looks with a laugh and a joke. But lately . . . well, take her reaction to Jack's speech at his office party. When he climbed down from that desk she'd hugged him in a clinch that seemed everlasting, and she'd clung to his arm for the rest of the night. Until then I'd believed Gill's assessment of her feelings – you know, that bit about merely admiring Jack because of his attitude to his artists. But after the night of that party, I'd begun to doubt . . .

And as for that dinner, Ann couldn't do enough for him. He kept cursing Blanes and telling Ossie how sorry he was, and the more he flayed himself, the more pain Ann felt for him. It was in her face, in her eyes. She wanted to console him, to put her arms around him, and to stroke his hair.

I don't think she'd slept with him until then. I really don't. It would have been difficult at Gill's in any case because Mary had very strict, old fashioned values – but that's besides the point. I think Ann had resisted the idea. She didn't *want* to sleep with him until then. But that night she did.

My last lingering hopes for the status quo died over that dinner table. Until then, despite the passing of time and my being in Taunton and their working together, I'd been able to tell myself it was still the three of us. By the time they took me to the station, however, I knew it wasn't.

Going home on the train, I sat in the buffet car and got plastered. Of course it was a selfish reaction. Sure, it was juvenile and dog-in-the-manger. Naturally, I told myself it was bound to happen. Inevitable. Be pleased for them, I said to myself, they're both your good friends. Even so, I got plastered.

I suffered the next morning! The hangover was bad enough, I had a thick head and foul tasting mouth, but everything was made worse by my self-contempt. Cutting myself shaving was predictable, the miracle was I didn't slice open my throat. 'Creep,' I sneered at the mirror. 'Are you going through all that Beau Geste nonsense again? For Christ's sake, grow up!' Strong stuff on an empty stomach, even stronger when delivered while holding a razor in shaking hands. Anyway, the roasting I gave myself would have won marks even from Jumbo. That done, I scalded my throat with hot coffee and took my sore head off to the office, trusting I'd straighten myself out all over again.

It was much easier to forget Ann and Jack at the office. They had their lives to lead and I had mine, and if mine was less glamorous, it never lacked interest. That morning Jumbo and I were negotiating with an insurance company in a claim for compensation. Our client, Glenda Turnbull, had been left

213

crippled after being hit by a runaway truck. Glenda had been nineteen when it happened. That was nearly two years before; since when she'd undergone one harrowing operation after another. I knew a lot about those operations, I'd catalogued every detail. My job at the meeting was to present the medical evidence painstakingly collected over the past twenty-one months. Jumbo's job was to quantify pain – to assess the future for a girl now aged twenty-one who faced life from the confinement of a wheelchair. Money can never truly compensate for a broken body, for the crushed hopes and reduced expectations, but, sadly, money becomes the only available yardstick – and Jumbo was determined upon a great deal of money.

He was at his most tenacious. The insurance company had already raised their offer four times during the preceding months, but Jumbo had refused everything. He was still threatening to go into court. To try to conclude the matter, the insurance company had sent their two most senior officials down to Taunton for the meeting. They made a good team. Watkins, the senior of the two, was a slightly built man, not very tall, whose benign smile and agreeable manner must have saved his company thousands, for he had a knack of appearing generous when in fact giving away very little. By contrast, Roberts, his assistant, was inclined to view as outrageous any suggestion that his company part with a penny.

I admit to being very involved. It was really 'my case'. I'd taken statements from every witness, I'd spent hours at the hospital with Glenda's doctors, I'd assembled surgeons' reports and experts' opinions until I could quote what they said in my sleep. Most important of all, I'd got to know Glenda. I'd watched her struggle through pain and come to terms with her life. She worried more about her widowed mother's health than her own. The two of them lived five miles out of town in a small terrace house on the London Road. Apart from nearly killing Glenda, the accident had damn near finished the old lady. After the initial shock of seeing her only daughter so tragically maimed, had come the sheer hard work of looking after her. I'd raised holy hell at the Town Hall, finally getting a home help on a temporary basis, but it was never enough. Voluntary organisations and neighbours rallied round, they provided aid and did a great deal; but I wanted Glenda and her mother to have money enough to re-establish their lives on a more permanent footing.

Watkins was as slippery as an eel. We battled all morning, winning concessions here and there. They raised their offer by a considerable amount, but it still fell short of what I wanted. I knew exactly how much that was, Glenda and I had discussed it in detail. I'd even helped with the sums. She and her mother would sell their small house and buy a village post office store. We knew which shop, we knew what it would cost, and how much to convert it so that Glenda could manage with the minimum of assistance. We knew the running costs and the income it would provide. I'd checked with the Post Office and they'd agreed to appoint Glenda as post-mistress . . .

At lunch time, Jumbo called a break to enable each side to review its position. Watkins and Roberts went off to the Castle Hotel, while Jumbo and I adjourned to the pub. 'Making progress,' he said cheerfully over a veal and ham pie. We were too. The offer was now far above the figure I'd warned Glenda to expect. It was even above her bottom line, but I wanted a buffer, insurance against the unexpected. I went through the figures again. 'We could just be all right,' I said eventually. 'Glenda seems to have allowed for everything, but . . .'

'How much would make you feel safe?' Jumbo asked through a mouthful of pie.

'Another five thousand,' I said, with more hope than expectation.

Jumbo chewed stolidly. 'They won't be pushed much further, but I've a feeling they don't want this in court. They want it settled today, that's why Watkins himself has come down.'

I nodded.

'So they can have it settled,' Jumbo concluded with a grin, 'but it'll cost them that extra five thousand.'

Back we went and battle resumed. Roberts said they were prepared to make one final offer. 'Take it or leave it,' he said, 'we've wasted more than enough time on this matter.' The offer was for another two thousand. Jumbo began to pick holes, using the same old arguments that we'd battered away with all morning, while I did some more mental arithmetic. I also imagined Glenda's face. She and her mother would be so relieved. All the worry and uncertainty would be over, they could get on with their lives. I'd seen Glenda a few days before, worried to death, frightened that her calculations about the shop would prove to be a pipe-dream.

Watkins rose and strolled over to the window. He wasn't a pacer like Jack, he lacked that kind of energy, but several times during the morning he'd strolled over to the window, turned, leant on the window sill and bent to rub his knees, as if plagued by bad circulation. Which is what he was doing when he launched into his summing up – of how his company had now made five attempts to settle, of how he and Roberts had come down to see us – 'unprecedented for such a simple case' – and of why the offer on the table was their very last word. He compared it favourably with awards made by the courts for similar injuries. He even delicately warned us of the risks we were taking, that if we rejected this offer and a court awarded less, not only would our client lose money, she'd be involved in considerable costs.

I knew we'd reached his sticking-point. I felt a great urge to settle. After all, we'd made vast progress. Glenda's budget might be a bit tight, but she could have her shop and get on with her life . . .

Jumbo gathered up his papers. 'Then we're wasting each other's time,' he said firmly, checking his watch. 'I'll get someone to run you to the station.'

I sweated buckets during the next hour. Back and forth went the arguments. Jumbo announced *his* sticking-point. He didn't want (as I expected him to say) another three thousand, he wanted another *seven*. Roberts came close to having a seizure. Watkins seemed set to walk out. He started packing his briefcase before offering another thousand, 'as my very last word on the subject'. Jumbo reduced his demands by a thousand. Watkins found another five hundred. Jumbo dropped two-fifty. Watkins lost his temper and called Jumbo impossible. What was more, he wanted to be taken to the station. 'Very well,' said Jumbo, flushing with irritation, 'I'll take you myself.' So, tight-lipped with anger, Watkins and Roberts gathered up their things and we trooped out to the car park. We travelled in icy silence. I stared out of the window in numb disbelief: in a fit of pique, Jumbo had thrown it all away. We'd already been offered more than I'd expected, and far, far more than I'd led Glenda to expect. Her life was stalled, waiting for a decision. Going to court would take another four months, and Glenda dreaded the prospect of having every intimate detail of her injuries discussed in public. If she knew what we were doing, she'd never forgive us.

When Watkins realised they were twenty minutes early for their train, he unbent enough to ask if the station had a buffet. Jumbo nodded. 'Naturally,' he said, adding with civic pride, 'a very good one as it happens.'

Watkins recovered some of his earlier geniality. 'Then let me buy you some tea to show there's no hard feelings.'

So off we all went to the buffet. In fact, I bought the teas, and by the time I collected four cups on a tray from the counter, Jumbo and Watkins were at it again. Watkins edged upwards, Jumbo inched downwards, until the total offer gave me my five-thousand-pound buffer and then some.

The London train was announced as Watkins sat back in his chair. 'Well, Mr Weston,' he said wearily. 'Will you accept *that*?'

Jumbo pulled on the lobe of his ear. 'I can't accept anything, it's up to our client —'

Watkins made a hissing sound. Spittle flecked his

lips. His voice shook. 'I thought you had your client's instructions? I thought you were empowered to settle?'

'We're *trying* to settle,' Jumbo explained patiently. 'Naturally I can get instructions –'

'When?' Watkins demanded shrilly, his eyes bright with temper.

Jumbo glanced at his watch. 'Tonight, if I have your written offer.'

The London train arrived. Heaving and shaking, rumbling, hissing even more than Watkins, carriages crept slowly past the buffet window and rolled to a halt. Watkins sat with his open briefcase on his knees, scrawling figures on to a pre-printed form. 'Give me your word you'll *recommend* acceptance,' he said, looking up.

Jumbo nodded. 'Certainly,' he said.

Watkins scribbled another condition and signed with an ill-tempered flourish. 'See that? I've written it. Forty-eight hours. Our offer stands firm for forty-eight hours. Unless accepted by then, I'll see you in court.'

Jumbo accepted the paper and we escorted our visitors out to the platform. I opened a carriage door. 'Thank you for coming,' I said, trying hard to hide my excitement. 'Bah,' scowled Watkins as he climbed up into the coach.

It was too early in the day to buy Jumbo a drink. If the pubs had been open I'd have bought him beers by the bathful. 'Save it for later,' he chuckled. 'Besides, you've things to do. Go and break the news to Glenda and get her written instructions . . .'

Only half listening, I was imagining the joy, the relief, the excitement on Glenda's face. 'Stop the car,'

I said as we passed a florist's. Within minutes I was back with a bouquet of roses and carnations and goodness knows what. 'My word,' Jumbo grinned, 'are you going to do this for all of our clients?'

Back at the office, I flew to my desk for the papers I needed Glenda to sign. I almost ignored the phone when it rang, but I picked it up, anxious not to be delayed.

'Hi,' said Ann, sounding slightly breathless as was her way on the phone.

'Oh, Ann?'

She laughed. 'Don't sound like that. Have I called at a bad time?'

'Er, no . . . I was just going out –'

'Jack had this wonderful idea,' she interrupted. 'He's forming his own music publishing company. Isn't he terrific? He'll do anything to protect our artists. I can't get over it.'

I'd been so absorbed all day I'd forgotten Jack's differences with Blanes Music. I'd even forgotten the images of Jack and Ann coupling naked on a bed, images which had plagued my jealous mind the previous night.

Ann giggled. 'He's come up with a fantastic name. He's going to call it White Hat Music Publishers.'

Thus Jack formed his second company. Jack Webb Enterprises now had a sister-business, White Hat Music Publishers. Like a rocket on full boost, Jack was on his way up. From then on there was an almost awesome inevitability about the way his career gathered momentum.

Meanwhile Glenda and Mrs Turnbull bought their

village post-office stores and their lives took a turn for the better. Mine did too, because the results of my finals came through and I qualified as a solicitor. As did Martin and Austen, so in our own quiet way we were getting our share of excitement. Josh invited us all up to the house for dinner and Jumbo did his Fats Waller impressions.

The following week, I bought Lime Tree Cottage with a mortgage from Sam Prentice. 'No doubt you'll get the paperwork right,' he said with a grin.

I'd seen the cottage when I'd been touring Glenda and her mum around in my car one Sunday, when we were looking for their post-office store. As a matter of fact, it was within a hundred yards of their shop. The property was quite small; originally two up and two down, it had been extended by the previous owner to include a kitchen downstairs and a bathroom above. However, it did possess an inglenook fireplace and a wealth of oak beams, and was set in an acre of land with a drive up the side. I imagined barbecue parties on a summer's evening . . . Mum and Bert could come down and stay for weekends, as could Ann and Jack for that matter. The cottage had only two bedrooms, but having bitten the unpalatable bullet about Jack and Ann sleeping together, I was determined to be as up-to-date as anyone else in the sixties.

Anyway, I bought the cottage, and what with that and being busy at the office, it was November before I next went up to London. I went twice, once on a Tuesday and again the following Thursday, both times with our client who had partners in Moorgate. Dragging me along was a costly exercise, since all I did was to take notes. The fact was, he didn't trust them, and he hoped my presence helped keep them in line. I hoped so too. They were easy days for me because the meetings only lasted two hours and I was free from lunch time onwards. I remember calling round at Jack's Denmark Street offices on the Tuesday, on the off chance of seeing him. The little blonde receptionist greeted me with her cheeky smile. 'Hello. Come for an audition?'

'I've come for the caviar.'

'Caviar's finished,' she said. 'I told you that the first time we met.'

'Then I'll take Ann out to lunch.'

'You'll be lucky. She's in Coventry today, with Janie.'

'What about Jack?'

He was in his office, reading the *Melody Maker* while munching a sandwich. I was reminded of the way he used to pore over the *Financial Times* in the old days at Mortlake, Dingle & Barnes.

'There's more money in this,' he said, tapping the *Melody Maker*.

'Fancy coming out for a beer?'

'I can't. I've got an appointment in half an hour. You can have one of these if you like.'

So I settled for a share of his sandwiches. We drank coffee which he poured from a percolator already warm at his elbow. In his shirt-sleeves, with his tie loosened, he looked unusually careworn and harassed. Shadows showed under his eyes. 'You look weary,' I said.

'It's been that sort of morning.' He shrugged, pulling a jar of pills from his pocket.

'Problems?'

'Pressure.'

I looked at the pills. 'What are those?'

'What? Oh, Prellies. Dai gets them in Germany, they sell them as slimming tablets over there. Try a couple. Get your weight down.'

I shook my head. 'What the devil are you doing with slimming pills?'

'Ah, forget slimming. They're uppers. You get tired, take a few of these. They get you going again.'

He took four while telling me how well he was doing. 'Of course there's bound to be pressure,' he said. 'It's all instant decisions. We're in a hurry business. Take records for instance. A record out this week has a month to make the top thirty. It's dead if it doesn't.'

Next minute he launched into an explanation of how the record business works. As usual, once he got going, he warmed to his theme. 'I'll make it simple,' he said, reaching for the half-smoked cigar in his ashtray. 'Two record companies, right? They issue ten records each. The first sells a steady number of each record. The second has nine duds and a hit. Even so, overall they each sell as many records. Who makes the most money?'

I shrugged. 'If they sold the same there can't be much in it –'

'Wrong!' he shouted gleefully. 'The first company went bust. The second made a fortune.'

His careworn look fell away and suddenly he was the old Jack again, so full of energy that he was out of his chair and pacing the office. No pills on earth work as fast as that; what stimulated him was his fascination with the way businesses worked. He'd been the same when we were employed by my father. He longed to know all the tricks.

'Record companies would starve on ten marginal profit-makers,' he explained. 'What they like are nine flops and one bloody great hit. Why? Because that way the profit comes in faster. That way they know where to invest next time. That way lies glory.'

'Glory?'

'Becoming rich and famous, being top of the heap. You don't get that by producing records admired by the critics. You get it by selling discs by the crate-load.'

The same old Jack, pacing up and down, firing words out like a Gatling gun firing bullets. Onwards and upwards to the success he knew would be his. All the signs were there; true, I'd caught him in a pensive mood, but once he got talking there was no mistaking his air of excitement. Janie and The Graduates were in the charts, Jet Storm continued to wow them in Hamburg, Jack was waiting for a call from Amsterdam about a new deal for the Oakley Hall Trio. Ten minutes later, his appointment arrived. As usual, Jack was in a hurry. 'I told you,' he grinned when we shook hands, 'we're in the hurry business.'

I thought about that on the train going home. The contrast between Jack's world and mine grew more marked all the time. Law is often a slow process. You spend your life questioning, considering options, you ponder and check and move cautiously forward. And life in the country has a similar pace. Everything has a season. 'Can't hurry Spring,' the farmers would say. It would have infuriated Jack, he'd have hauled Spring into January. All that energy! And now he was on pills to make him go even faster. I wondered what was in them. Yet his way of life seemed to be working. He had the entrepreneur's knack of turning every setback into an advance. 'We don't have problems,' he was fond of saying, 'only opportunities.'

Ann was carried away with it all. 'It's just so exciting,' she said when I phoned her the following Wednesday. Knowing I was going up to town the next day, I'd called to see if she and Jack would be free for lunch.

'Jack's in Amsterdam,' she said, 'but I'll be there.'

Next day I collected her from their office. She was wearing a long plum-coloured coat over a black sweater and mini-skirt, white tights and black leather boots that buttoned up to the knee. At the restaurant every head turned when we were shown to our table.

It's easy to remember that lunch. Usually our meetings were part of a larger gathering, but we were by ourselves for once, uninterrupted by strangers or friends, able to concentrate on each other exclusively. Ann told me exactly how she saw me when we sat down. 'Get a look at you,' she grinned, 'my big brother all grown up into a lawyer. Boy oh boy, Peter, why don't we get to see more of you?'

'Because when I'm in London you're always at the other end of the country.'

'Ain't that the truth,' she said, pushing a hair back from her face and puffing as if hurried and harassed. 'Blame old buddy Jack. He's the slave-driver.'

She looked well on it. Confident, assured; a look of amusement lit her dark eyes, as if she was surprised by the amount of satisfaction she was finding in life. Being with her no longer churned my insides.

I could look into her eyes now without my collar feeling too tight. It made me feel virtuous; like an alcoholic passing up on a drink, or a three-packs-a-day man declining a cigarette.

Needless to say, Ann was full of Jack. 'He's a force of nature,' she laughed. 'Dashing around, setting up deal after deal. No one can keep up with him.'

She catalogued what everyone was doing; Janie's progress was followed by a report on Dai, and so forth, all interspersed with her up-dated assessment of London. 'You really must spend more time up here,' she scolded, 'this town's really buzzing.'

Plunging on, she described the night life, the new clubs and discos, the air of optimism, the feeling that anything was possible. 'And we're in the middle of it,' she said breathlessly. 'I mean, you're missing out on so much.'

Any listener would have said she hadn't a care in the world. Yet a few minutes later an unconscious remark of mine made me wonder.

What started it was when I asked, 'Is London more exciting than New York?'

Pulling a face, her tone was dismissive. 'Oh, New York's three thousand miles away. Light-years away.'

I shrugged. 'Even so, that's probably changed too. It's more than three years since you left.'

I don't know why I said it. No special reason, just conversation. But the blush it brought to her face was startling. Her cheeks fairly burned. Pain shone in her eyes, then anger. 'So he told you,' she blurted out. 'He promised he wouldn't. I believed him . . .' Her words faded as she read my expression. I hadn't the faintest idea what she was talking about. Recovering before I could ask what was wrong, she demanded, 'What's this special interest in New York all of a sudden?'

'No special interest –'

'Jack didn't say anything?' she asked, realising even as she put the question that it was needless. 'Oh boy,' she laughed jerkily. 'Goof of the year, right?' Reaching across the table, she patted my hand. 'Sorry. Guilty conscience and all that.'

'I only meant –'

'Sure, sure,' she said, still embarrassed. 'It's just that Jack's been pestering me about New York. You know, about what happened and all that.' Her eyes met mine. 'Why do men always have to *know*? What difference does it make? What happened, happened. I can live with it. Leave it alone, right?'

I nodded without really understanding. 'I only meant if you'd gone back to New York –'

'And taught music in high school,' she interrupted. 'Okay, okay, don't *you* start. I have enough of it with Mary.'

'I didn't know you wanted to become a teacher?'

She shrugged. 'Why not? It's in the blood. My folks were teachers. Sure, I was going to find me a whole new way of life.'

'Oh,' I said.

'Oh,' she mimicked, recovering from her embarrassment, laughter returning to her eyes. 'So what's really different? Janie and the others call me Coach. Jack says I'm his ears. It's my one and only talent.'

'And Mary thinks you're wasting it?'

'Mary thinks I'm wasting. Period. My whole life is down the tube. I'll end up an old maid. You know Mary.'

I didn't know Mary, at least not very well. I'd only

met her two or three times. But I knew Gill and I remembered his worries the last time we'd met. I might have lingered on the subject, but Ann denied me the chance. In fact I'd barely registered that she had told Jack about her past before she began bombarding me with questions about my new cottage.

'It sounds great,' she laughed, 'straight out of *Snow White*. American tourists will kill to be invited –'

'It's not that special,' I assured her, but then found myself telling her about my house-warming party. It had been on my mind for weeks; to have everyone down, Mum, Bert, Jack, Ann, Janie, and as many of the others as could make it. Martin was always asking, 'When do we get to meet these showbiz friends of yours?' A house-warming seemed the perfect answer.

Ann took to the idea with her usual enthusiasm. 'Hey,' she said, 'that's it! If you won't come to us, we'll bring Swinging London down to sleepy old Taunton.'

When we returned to the office, she consulted her diary, Jack's diary, the list of bookings for Janie and The Graduates; she even phoned Gill and invited him, but he cried off on account of Mary not liking to travel. Eventually we fixed a Saturday four weeks ahead and two weeks before Christmas.

Ann said, 'And tell your friend Jumbo to sharpen up on his Fats Waller impressions. If he's any good, we might sign him up.'

In the event, the house-warming was cancelled. Two weeks after my meeting with Ann came the onset of that terrible winter. Icy gales swept the south-west, bringing in their wake the first blizzards. Life changed beyond all recognition. Ferocious winds whipped heavy falls of snow into drifts twenty feet high, roads became impassable, whole villages were cut off. The sheer weight of snow snapped telephone lines and power cables alike, plunging communities into darkness. Without power many people were unable to boil a kettle, let alone cook a hot meal. Unable to warm themselves, people froze to death. The emergency services – police, ambulance crews, doctors, GPO linesmen, gangs of men fighting to open at least some of the roads – were swamped, despite working until they dropped from exhaustion.

At Weston & Weston, Jumbo declared a state of emergency. The legal work – claiming compensation, fighting with the Ministry of Agriculture and insurance companies – would come later. Meanwhile lives were in peril. Farmers were facing ruin; their crops were beyond salvation, their only hope was to save some of the livestock.

From early December until the middle of February, I spent an average of less than a day a week in the office. Jumbo, Martin and Austen spent the same. Our time was consumed in fighting the weather. I lost count of the number of sheep I pulled from the snow. I've forgotten how many miles of road I cleared, how many marooned people we helped to safety, how many bales of hay I flung down from ice encrusted lofts. I remember learning the value of daylight, of cocking an anxious eye at the gathering gloom, fearful that darkness would fall before we achieved our objective. Jumbo would cry, 'One last effort, boys,' and Martin would shout, 'Get stuck into it!' I remember the cold, the biting wind, the misery of wet clothes chafing the skin. I remember being too tired to stand up. But most of all I remember the people and the sense of community, the total lack of selfishness. For me it was another milestone of my journey into adulthood, another lesson in values, of learning what was important and unimportant in life.

I'd moved out of the cottage at the outset. The blizzard cut my telephone line in the first week and life was impossible. Martin, Austen and I moved up to Hedley Hall, Jumbo's mansion, partly for comfort and partly to ensure good communication. Jumbo said, 'Lag all the pipes at your place and get over here. Cook can feed the lot of us, and we've got to heat the pile of old stones anyway.' This 'pile of old stones' quickly became a rallying point for people from miles around. Police, RAF helicopter pilots, ambulance drivers were always trooping in and out of the hall, to warm themselves in front of the blazing log fire (which was never allowed to go out), to exchange information, to eat some hot food, or to use the telephone – for Jumbo's was one of the few not out of order.

We spent Christmas at Hedley Hall. Needless to say, there was a children's party and Jumbo was Santa Claus, so we had some fun amidst the hard physical work.

During those long weeks I had little contact with Ann and Jack, although I knew they had problems of their own, for although conditions in the south-west were by far the worst, life elsewhere was also disrupted. Concerts were cancelled and tours were abandoned, so that Jack was pulling every string he could to find work for his artists. As usual, he triumphed.

He got Janie and The Graduates a booking as entertainers on a liner cruising the Med., Dai Evans went back to Hamburg, The Post Office Tower played Amsterdam for six weeks, the Oakley Hall Trio toured South Africa. I heard about all this in January when he phoned me at Jumbo's. I also heard about his new flat. 'I move in next week,' he said breezily, 'Bolton Gardens, just behind the Cumberland.'

It was an expensive area and I said so.

'Well,' he said, 'time I got something better than this dump. Living over a pub's bad for my image.'

He gave me the address and telephone number and asked when I'd next be in town.

'God knows,' I said. 'Not until things get back to normal.'

They got back to normal on the day claimed by 'the experts' to mark the start of the Swinging Sixties in Britain. That's why it's easy to remember. The country had survived the worst by then, the emergency was at last under control, even in the south-west. Many telephones remained out of order, some roads were still blocked with snow, life was still difficult; but electricity had been restored to a wide area, fresh supplies were getting through, shop-keepers were re-stocking their shelves. Towns and villages had started to function again.

It was my first weekend back at the cottage. Luckily the pipes were unfrozen and I had a mountain of dry logs in the barn at the back. The telephone had been restored along with the electricity. I'd had a busy day moving back and getting the place warmed up: the cottage lacked central heating, and the only means of warming the place was from the living-room fire. But I managed, and by about five o'clock, with a fire blazing up the chimney, I sat down and put my feet up for the first time in weeks. Vaguely, as one does at such moments, I switched on the TV and hence, purely by chance, witnessed the event so beloved by 'the experts'.

It was the pop show *Thank Your Lucky Stars*, on which Jack had appeared. Thinking he might be on again, I stayed tuned, and ten minutes later saw a group I'd not seen before. Neither had I seen anything like them. Their hair fringed their eyes like the busbies worn by the Grenadier Guards. They wore unconventional jackets buttoned up to the neck. The three front figures bounced and jigged all over the place. Even more eccentric, one played Spanish guitar while another held his base guitar like a violin with its neck pointing the wrong way. Screams from the audience made the song almost inaudible, except for one moment when the four voices toppled into falsetto. The resultant 'Whoah yeah!' conquered all. Even I recognised the unmistakable sound of a Number One, and millions of snowbound viewers around the country thought the same, for 'Please Please Me' was destined to climb up the charts, and give The Beatles their first number one hit.

And that show, according to 'the experts' marked the start of the Swinging Sixties. What rubbish! The momentum had been building for a long time, which isn't to decry The Beatles. I thought they were great, which was why I phoned Jack. When I failed to get an answer from his new number, I called Gill's place, intending to speak to Ann if Jack was away. But Ann was at the Harrow Granada with a new singer.

Gill sounded odd on the phone, pleased to hear from me, but worried and upset. When I asked if anything was wrong, he said, 'Of course something's bloody well wrong. I told you not to bury yourself in the country. Where've you been the last couple of months?'

I resented this, considering the state of the weather and all that had happened. Besides, Gill wasn't my keeper, as he realised. 'Sorry,' he said, modifying his tone. 'There's a lot going on I don't like. It wouldn't have happened if you were here.'

'What wouldn't?'

'Jack getting above himself. Behaving like Christ Almighty.'

There was no mistaking his temper. The problem was, he refused to go into detail. The more I pushed, the more he clammed up. However, at one point he said, 'Listen, I know you're fond of Ann. And you're Jack's best pal. You'd better talk to them, they won't listen to me. Someone's got to make them see sense.'

I tried again. 'About what?'

'About Ann ruining her whole bloody life, that's what.'

That's all he would say, apart from urging me to go up to town as soon as possible. The conversation left me baffled and irritated. If people have something to say, they should come out and say it. Afterwards I tried Jack again, intending to ask what the hell was going on, but there was still no reply from his number. Cursing aloud, I replaced the receiver and a second later it rang. To my amazement, Mary Martin, Gill's wife, came on the line. 'Hello,' I said, overcome by surprise. 'How are you?'

Apparently she was as well as could be expected, given the state of the weather and her poor health. Then she said, 'Gill told me you'd been on. We'd like to see you urgently. I know it's a long way, but could you come up tomorrow?'

I'd spoken to Mary about three times in three years! Rarely downstairs in the pub, she spent most of her time up in the flat reading, or watching TV. I knew about her bad health . . . when she wasn't laid low by asthma, she was in pain from an arthritic hip.

'Tomorrow is Sunday,' she pointed out needlessly, 'and all the main roads are clear. It was on the news.'

This was all very well, but to drive to London and back would take ten hours, and I felt in need of a rest. Even so, I couldn't fail to realise something was wrong. Mary had never called me before and Gill had sounded worried to death. 'What's happened?' I asked.

But she refused to discuss it over the phone. The most she would say was, 'There's not been an accident or anything like that.'

By then it was almost six thirty. I wondered if the train service was back to normal. Promising to call Mary back, I checked with the station and learned that trains were again running to schedule. Not that there was much of a service on a Saturday evening; the last train to London was at seven thirty, and by stopping at every hedgerow, was due into Paddington at ten minutes past midnight.

I groaned, and called Mary to say I'd be at their place at about one, or if whatever was troubling her would keep overnight, I'd stay at my mother's and call in the morning. 'Yes,' she said, 'why not do that. Get a good night's sleep and come round here at about ten.'

She wasn't backward in organising my life. I suppose the habit had developed from bossing Gill around. However, she did end by saying, 'And thank you, Peter. I've always said you're such a nice boy.'

That was about my mark. Nubile young things of twenty-five never gave me a second look, but middle-aged ladies with arthritic hips thought I was smashing. I damped down the fire, called Mum and told her to expect me, threw a clean shirt in a bag and dashed out to the car. My devastating charm with elderly ladies worked again, because when I called at Glenda's shop her mother answered the door. Giving her the keys to my cottage, I told her about the fire in the grate and asked if she'd make sure it was all right.

''Course I will, love,' she said. 'Don't worry your head about that. You go off and have a good time.'

So I set off for London, to have a good time.

Next morning I was at Gill's place at ten o'clock. I like London on a Sunday morning; there's room to move on the pavement, and little traffic about. Walking up Tottenham Court Road prompted the thought that if London were always like this I wouldn't have to live in the country.

Opening the door, Gill ushered me in. He shook my hand and thanked me for coming. I felt like a doctor making a house call; an impression heightened by his hushed voice. 'Sorry about this,' he said, jerking his head at the upper floor. 'She only called you because she can't think of what else to do. She's at her wits' end.'

I found myself whispering back. 'What about?'

Instead of answering, he reverted to his normal voice. 'Fancy a pint?'

It was too early, but I said I was ready for a coffee. Gill nodded. 'Come on then, we'll go straight up.' Half-way up the stairs, he shook his head. 'Fine mess this is,' he grumbled sadly. 'Who'd have thought things would turn out like this.'

Mary was waiting for us in their living room. It was a cluttered room full of knick-knacks. Serried ranks of ornaments lined not only the mantelpiece but every other flat surface in sight. Even the television was weighed down by half a ton of china elephants.

'Peter,' she said, welcoming me, 'it's very nice to see you again.'

She spoke from a winged armchair at the far side of an ornamental gas fire. On the floor beside her a magazine rack overflowed with copies of *Woman's Own* and the *Radio Times*. In front of her a small table was already laden with a coffee pot, cups, plates, two racks full of toast and a large jar of marmalade.

'Sit yourself down,' she said when we'd shaken hands. 'Oh, I am glad you're here. I've hardly slept in weeks. I've been that worried.'

Gill waved me into the armchair opposite his wife while he slumped into the matching sofa that took up most of the far wall. There was just space next to it for a bookcase, crammed tight with books bound in the sort of matching jackets favoured by book clubs.

Mary was already pouring coffee. Her face was delicate, small-boned, lightly fleshed, bird-like and sharp-eyed. Possibly she had been attractive when younger, but illness had taken a toll. Now she looked older than Gill. His black hair was only lightly frosted while Mary's head contained more grey hairs than brown. She wore her hair pulled back from her face in an old fashioned bun, giving her the stern look of a schoolmistress.

'I've just this minute made the toast,' she assured me, smiling in a way that banished her sternness. 'Cream? Sugar? Gill, pull that other table over so that Peter can help himself properly.'

Gill was settling another small table next to my chair before I could decline the offer of toast. 'Honestly,' I said, 'thanks all the same but I'm still full from my breakfast.'

Gill asked after Mum and Bert while carrying his coffee back to the sofa. He looked strained and ill-at-ease up here, whereas he always seemed so totally at home down in the bar.

Mary asked, 'And when did we see you last?'

'I was up in November –'

'November,' she interrupted, turning on Gill. 'Didn't we say it was November? Things were all right in November.'

Gill shrugged. 'Dunno about all right. They weren't out of hand if that's what you mean. If you ask me Jack was getting too big for his boots even then.'

Mary said, 'But Ann was all right.'

I wondered where Ann was. I'd expected to see her, hoping she'd explain what the fuss was about. 'Where is Ann? Is she here?'

'No she's not,' Gill snapped.

Surprised, and unable to restrain myself another moment, I asked, 'So what's happened?'

Agitated, Gill turned and put his cup on the bookcase, slopping coffee in the saucer. 'I saw this coming

237

months ago,' he said. 'Jack's carried away with all the money he's making.'

Mary nodded and turned her sharp eyes on me. 'You know we told him to go? Gill threw him out.'

I looked at her in amazement. 'Oh yes,' she said, 'we had to. It got so bad I wouldn't have him in the house another minute, the way they were carrying on. It had to be stopped.'

'We're responsible,' said Gill. 'Anything happens to Ann, and we're responsible. Ever since November she's been . . . well, I dunno what's got into her.'

'So where is she?' I interrupted, already guessing.

Mary gave me a sharp look. 'She's moved in with him. She moved in last Friday.'

It wasn't really a shock. After all, I'd seen the way Ann had looked at Jack that night we went out with Ossie. Events had taken an unexpected turn, but I don't think I was shocked.

Gill said, 'She'll have to come back some time or other. Most of her clothes are still in her room.'

'And Gill's right,' Mary said to me, 'we feel so *responsible*. I keep telling myself none of this would have happened if we hadn't allowed Jack in this house –'

'Huh,' Gill grunted. 'None of it would have happened if Peter hadn't gone down to Taunton. He was the one she was soft on.'

'Nonsense,' I protested.

'It's true,' he insisted, 'or it was until Jack got involved with these pop groups. Since then he's kept Ann so busy she hardly gets time to think –'

'She was going to be a music teacher,' Mary interrupted. 'We thought once you qualified, you and Ann, well, you know, if she got a little job teaching music . . .' Her voice trailed off as she met my eye.

What nettled me was her tone. It was as if she'd explained all this before, and if only I'd paid more attention things would have gone differently. She knew nothing of Jack and me being friends, and him seeing Ann first, and devising his AIDA scheme to go chasing after her . . .

Anger welled up inside me. 'Ann and I are *friends*, that's all. We've never been anything else. And this thing between her and Jack has been growing for ages. They work together, they're excited about what they're doing. I don't know why you're so surprised. You must have seen it coming. I did –'

'But you can't approve,' Mary interrupted, sounding shocked.

'Approve. Disapprove. What does it matter?'

Mary sucked in her breath. 'Well, that's a fine thing, I must say. A young girl living openly with a man –'

'It's 1963,' I said hotly, unable to bite my tongue. 'Sorry, Mrs Martin, I didn't mean to be rude, but people are doing that these days –'

'Not under this roof, they aren't,' she retorted sharply, 'Ann of all people. You'd think she'd know better after that business in New York. She's a very nice girl, Ann is, I'm not saying a word against her, but she picks the wrong type. All this will be over in five minutes, then where will she be? I said to her last week, this has got to stop. It's got out of hand. I told her straight, you're welcome here as long as you like, but I don't want you seeing no more of Jack.'

I blinked. 'You mean you made it a condition?'

Looking uncomfortable, she shifted in her chair. 'We had to do something, Peter. Things couldn't go on as they were. I've been telling her for weeks she's wasting her life.'

More than weeks, I thought, remembering my lunch with Ann. Looking thoroughly wretched, Gill caught my eye. Clearly embarrassed, he would have preferred to be downstairs with a pint, talking things over man to man. This meeting was Mary's idea, not his.

'The thing is,' he said heavily, 'you don't see them as often as we do. Jack's changed. It's do this, do that, all the time. He's the same with them all. Ann, Janie, Ossie. What beats me is they think he's so bloody marvellous. He's making a fortune out of them, yet they act like he's God Almighty. No wonder he treats them like possessions.'

His words reminded me of that publishing hand-out; the one showing Jack in a ring-master's outfit, cracking a whip. For the first time I realised why I disliked it. The emphasis was all wrong. The artists were the principals, Jack was merely their agent. Yet his name appeared top of the bill. JACK WEBB'S ALL-STARS. His picture was largest. Surely it should have been the other way round? Stifling the thought, I said, 'Okay, perhaps Jack gets carried away now and then, but look what –'

'No,' Gill shook his head. 'Sorry, Peter, but I've seen his sort before. He uses people. Oh, I admit he fooled me for a while. Nice as pie until he gets what he wants. And he's got Ann *where* he wants. Jack's got her mesmerised. He keeps her too busy to think straight.'

I'd been too busy to think straight for weeks. I remember returning to Jumbo's one night, so dog-tired I convinced myself I needed a key for the front door. Jumbo's door was never locked, yet I'd stood on that step, shivering in a howling gale, while my numbed fingers searched through my pockets. Even at that moment, I felt heavy-eyed. 'You're wrong,' I said, 'Jack's always been crazy about Ann —'

'Crazy about the idea of her,' Gill interrupted. 'Jack sees images. He don't see people.'

They'd made up their minds. Jack had upset them to a point where they refused to listen. I shook my head in weary resignation. 'What do you expect me to do?' I asked, adding as a truculent afterthought, 'You could have told me this on the phone.'

Mary answered, sitting stiff and upright in her chair. 'We wanted to act quickly. We thought if you went round to see them, they'd listen to you.'

I couldn't face that. The idea was repugnant, it just wasn't on. I said, 'Sorry, Mrs Martin, that's out of the question.'

She saw that I meant it. Her eyes met mine before going to Gill. He shrugged, sad-faced. 'It seemed worth a try. We thought you might intervene for your own sake.'

Had he expected me to horsewhip Jack? Had I changed that much from the insecure, overweight articled clerk who'd gone lovesick to Taunton? Jumbo may have helped transform Tubby into Peter, but not even Jumbo could make me Superman. Especially when Gill based everything on the muddle-headed belief that Ann preferred me to Jack. It was just so totally stupid.

Mary sighed heavily. 'Young people today,' she said, 'you can't tell them nothing.'

It was a funny sort of lunch at Mum's. The talk should have been about what we'd been doing since we last met, and it might have been except for her curiosity about my flying visit. When I told her about the meeting at Gill's, she wanted her say on the subject. Predictably, perhaps, her views coincided with Mary's. 'Ann's being very silly. I'm surprised. She struck me as a level-headed girl.'

'She is level-headed,' I said, defending Ann for the second time that day.

'She can't be,' Mum retorted. 'Not to have gone off with Jack like this. That's *empty* headed –'

'Mum,' I said, 'people lead different lives today.'

It cut no ice. She seemed offended, personally affronted. 'If this is women's lib., I don't think much of it,' she sniffed. 'What happens if Jack tires of her? Where's her security?'

It struck me as a strange argument from someone with her background. What security had marriage given her? Not that I put such a question. She was already pink faced and indignant. Her only difference with Mary was on the question of my involvement. 'I hope you'll have nothing more to do with them,' she said. 'They don't deserve you for a friend.'

Bert had merely listened until then, chewing his way stolidly through a mountain of roast beef, Yorkshire pudding, roast potatoes and peas. But at that he felt obliged to protest. 'Steady on,' he said mildly, expressing concern. 'Poor old Jack's got the whole ruddy world turning against him. He's done nothing to Peter. Peter's got no cause to drop either of them. And Jack's been a good friend in the past.'

'When it suited him,' Mum insisted, going red in

the face. 'I'll tell you what I think. I've always thought it, and now's the time to say so. There's a lot of Peter's father in Jack. They're two of a kind.'

Bert and I exchanged looks of astonishment and bent our heads over our plates. We forked food into our mouths to give us an excuse not to comment. Without saying a word, we shared the same thought: Mum was being totally illogical; there was no reasoning with her in this mood, best change the subject. Mum glared down the table, interpreting our silence as a conspiracy and getting ready to deal with us both. But Bert was too artful. Looking at me, he said, 'I bet the last time you had a meal this good was when you were here.' And when I agreed, he asked the time of my train back to Taunton. So we edged the conversation to safer ground. Even so, as I said, it was a funny sort of lunch. Later, when Mum went out to the kitchen, Bert groaned softly. 'Oh Lord,' he said in a stage whisper, 'we'll have no peace now until Jack pops the question.'

As it happens, Jack already had. The phone was ringing when I got home. Having arrived off the nine-thirty train and collected my key from Glenda, I'd gone grumbling down the path to the cottage, telling myself I needed a rest – and the phone was ringing even as I came through the door.

'Tubby,' Jack shouted, 'where the hell have you been? I've been phoning all day.' Before I could utter a word, he continued, 'Congratulate me. Ann and I are getting married.'

The wedding was a month later and I saw nothing of Jack until the day before, essentially because there were so many problems in Taunton. Everything happened at once. The big thaw which dispersed the snows brought floods in their wake, Jumbo was stricken with influenza, our backlog of work was a mile high, and then, on top of everything, Austen decided to leave. Martin and I were thunderstruck. We had thought of him as content as we were ourselves. I think he was, but the girl he was dating was moving to London and Austen was afraid to let her out of his sight. So he gave notice, and Martin and I were chained to our desks. We worked like Trojans. Jumbo's bout of 'flu was particularly nasty and he was away for weeks. Old Josh did his best to help by coming into the office every Monday and Thursday; the trouble was, he was seventy-seven; still sharp, still alert, but he tired easily and was definitely slowing down, so although Martin and I welcomed his good intentions, we were concerned not to let him do too much. It was the most difficult time ever at Weston & Weston . . . and quite honestly I could have done without so many phone calls from London.

Gill was the first to offend, he called three times in the first week. News of the wedding had not altered his opinion. He grumbled more than ever, even though Ann had mended her fences with Mary. 'Only because of the wedding,' said Gill in a sour voice. 'Mary goes potty about weddings. Getting married is supposed to change everything. Codswallop. Now I'm supposed to give Ann away. I don't want no part of it but Mary keeps nagging. I suppose I'll have to. There's no one else, is there? Mind you, I'd as soon give her away to Hitler . . .'

Mum phoned. Her reservations about Jack and Ann had faded with the news. 'What will be will be,' she said philosophically. 'I'd like to be there, though. Bert and I will be invited, won't we? I mean, you're bound to be best man –'

'Steady on. Jack hasn't asked –'

'Who else would he ask? Of course you'll be best man. You're his best friend.'

And naturally, best friend Jack phoned. Frequently, as a matter of fact, his temper erupting when it became evident that I couldn't drop everything to rush to his side. 'Bloody hell, Tubby, I don't get married every day. The least you could do is get up here and help with the arrangements.'

It was typical of Jack to expect what was important to him to override all other considerations. Eventually I convinced him of the sheer impossibility of my taking time off, and he settled for calling me on a regular basis to up-date me on progress.

But the most extraordinary call was from Ann. It came on the Sunday evening. Martin and I had been in the office all day, ploughing our way through the backlog. After working until eight, we had a meal at the Castle Hotel, still combing through our lists of priorities, wondering how we would cope, and I returned to the cottage exhausted. By then it was ten o'clock; too late to light the living room fire, so I switched on the electric heater, made some coffee, opened my briefcase and settled down for a last hour of paperwork before bed. Which was when the telephone rang.

'Peter?'

'Ann –'

'You mad at me or something? Why haven't you

called? For Christ's sake, Peter, I thought we were close, you and I . . .' She was shouting, angry, tearful, almost hysterical. Her words slurred together, making it difficult to understand all that she said. I tried to interrupt but she shouted over my voice. I had never heard her so upset. Finally, by repeatedly asking what was the matter, I got a response. 'You should have called,' she said angrily. 'You know damn well you should have called. Where have you been all week? Every time the phone rings I think it's you . . .'

Saying everything twice, I stressed how busy I had been, but even that failed to placate her.

'It would only have taken a minute to call,' she scolded. 'At least I'd have known you cared, not like Gill and –'

'Gill cares –'

'He's mad at me for getting married and so are you or you'd have –'

'I just explained –'

'Yeah, you're busy, I know,' she said sarcastically before lapsing into silence.

The pause gave me a chance to collect myself. Her opening words had amounted to an onslaught. Justifiable perhaps, because I should have called. I *would* have, had I not been swamped with work. I began to apologise when she interrupted, 'Okay, you fink,' she giggled. 'How are you anyway?'

'I'm okay –'

'So what about this wedding? Bum idea, huh?'

'You'll be very happy. I told Jack –'

'Yeah, yeah, but what do you *really* think?'

What I was really thinking was that she had been drinking. I could imagine no other explanation, I'd never heard her like this. 'Ann,' I said, 'where are you? Have you been drinking?'

'No,' she giggled. 'I'm in Jack's flat. Ossie left his happy bag behind so I rolled myself a joint.'

'You're stoned.'

'I dunno. When you didn't call –'

'I told you why –'

'Is that the real reason? You're not mad at me?'

'Of course not.'

'You still love me?'

I hesitated, wondering how to respond, questioning why she chose now to ask something she had never asked before.

'Peter,' she said, 'me getting married doesn't stop me loving you. I want you to know that. You and me, well, you know. You and me and Jack, what we've got is a bit special, right?'

'Right,' I agreed.

'This won't spoil it. I mean, Jack and me being married won't change a thing between us, will it?'

'Not a thing,' I agreed, trying to soothe her while my confused brain struggled to interpret her words.

'Promise?'

I promised, and listened to her ramble on until she sounded tired and calm and reassured about what she was doing. Eventually she said a husky goodnight and I was left analysing what had passed between us. Even allowing for her being stoned, her statements had been so extraordinary that I began questioning what I felt for her all over again. I knew one thing, I was no longer jealous of Jack. I was fond of Ann without being infatuated. Looking back, it was easy to understand my earlier fascination, especially remembering Ann at the Green Door and such places. She was at home in an alien world, she was different, with a life in New York about which I knew very little, and a past shrouded in mystery; of course I'd been intrigued. I'd developed the adolescent crush of all time – but had lived through it to preserve Ann as a friend. Now she had a future with Jack, and I felt not the least twinge of envy. Instead, I was pleased for them both.

Finishing my coffee, I went to bed, still thinking of Ann and the telephone call, which I imagined had been prompted by pre-wedding nerves. Not that my thoughts lingered long with Ann, for even before my head touched the pillow the crisis at Weston & Weston was back in my mind and I was scheduling priorities for the next morning.

The next day, the next week and the week after, merged together into one unremitting slog. Martin and I started each day at seven and finished fourteen hours later, but thankfully we kept most clients happy. Even Sam Prentice was impressed. 'You two remind me of me as a lad,' he remarked, conferring the highest praise in his book.

Meanwhile the wedding drew ever nearer and Jack kept me informed with a whole stream of phone calls. As the appointed best man I did feel a bit guilty, even though I thought he was making a fuss. And he was spending a fortune. 'I've got to,' he said. 'Half the pop world and the press will be there. You can't skimp on public relations.' Listening made me wonder if he was marrying Ann or staging a pop concert. Still, that was Jack all over . . .

The wedding was on a Saturday and I went up to London on the Friday morning, arriving at Jack's flat just after lunch. It was the first time I'd been there. Situated in one of those mansion blocks built in the thirties, it consisted of a living room, a bedroom, a kitchen and bathroom. Designed to accommodate two people, it was bulging at the seams with Jack's army of assistants. Ann had returned to Gill's place to live, and Jack's flat had been transformed into Headquarters of Operation Wedding.

'We've got five hundred guests at the reception,' Jack explained, blowing cigar smoke into my face. 'You can't stage something like that without planning.'

'I suppose not,' I said, accepting a four-page typewritten schedule from a girl who introduced herself as Angela. 'I'm Jack's PA,' she said, leading me off to the kitchen. 'There's an awful lot for you to catch up on. See how much of that you can absorb. I'll be back in ten minutes to make sure you understand it.'

'Oh,' I said, squeezing past two men with long hair who were frowning over their copies of the schedule. 'Do we get a written test?'

The schedule read like Eisenhower's battle plans for the D-Day invasion. Every minute was accounted for: '10.45 Bridegroom and Best Man leave for Registry Office – 11.05 Bride and Mr Gill Martin collected from Tottenham Court Road . . .' It was all there, even down to the last buttonhole, and I had just reached the part about the Best Man giving a speech to the five hundred guests at the Reception in the Dorchester, when Angela returned. 'All in order, is it?' she asked brightly.

Feeling weak at the knees, I said, 'I'm not much of a public speaker –'

'Nonsense. Get a few drinks inside you and you'll be fine.'

Maybe that's why my recollections of the next couple of days are incomplete. I had a few drinks inside me most of the time, and while some scenes come to mind with vivid clarity, others are lost in an alcoholic blur. I remember most of Jack's stag party; Dai Evans took over a strip club in Soho for the night. All of Jack's boys were there – Mike and Ossie, Dave and Ray, the boys from The Post Office Tower, the roadies; thirty or forty of us in all. We sang and laughed and told jokes and got tight . . . and awoke in the morning with a hell of a hangover. Jack and I were still swallowing Alka-Selzers when the car arrived to take us to the Registry Office.

That entire day is remembered in fragments. I can recall individual scenes, but often in the wrong order, like examining photographs out of sequence in an album. I certainly remember the crowds outside the Registry Office, girls screaming when Dai Evans arrived, and naturally the radiant bride on Gill's arm. But my mind goes blank when it comes to the actual ceremony. Perhaps weddings are best described by a feminine eye, for even a full account of the reception defeats me. Of the scene in the ballroom at the Dorchester, certain impressions remain. Men resplendent in Moss Brothers' grey, and ladies clad in every conceivable colour; silks and satins, buttons and bows, small hats, large hats, hats bearing every cunning device of the milliner's art, long white gloves, yards of lace, layers of tulle, nylon-clad legs in fine golden slippers. Every couturier from Hartnell to Quant was represented. How can a mere man do justice to that?

But one memory is indelible. It always springs to mind when I think of the wedding. Time leaves it undimmed, so that even now I can see it as clearly as yesterday. An unhappy, jarring incident which might have ruined the whole day had Mary Martin not involved me when she did.

Gill's attitude had been uncertain all day. Even I had noticed his clenched face during the ceremony, and when we arrived at the Dorchester, I was struck by his dark, brooding expression. 'Cheer up, Gill,' I joked, 'it's a wedding, not a funeral.' I should have taken more notice, but I was so busy worrying about my duties as best man and my impending speech, that I ignored his bleak look. Even during the wedding breakfast, I failed to take account of how heavily he was drinking, and afterwards I was on my feet most of the time, reading telegrams aloud and doing my best to be witty. In fairness, I had enough to contend with without worrying about Gill . . .

But later, there was trouble. I don't know who started it, Ossie or Gill, but it got out of hand. I felt sorry for Mary. Red faced, upset and embarrassed, she came directly to me. 'Peter, come quickly, Gill's saying the most awful things about Jack and I can't stop him.' Thank goodness, Mum and Bert were there. Mum took Mary off to the powder room and Bert restrained Ossie, while I steered Gill away and out of the ballroom. We acted so quickly that I doubt if even as many as twelve of the other guests realised what was happening.

Poor Gill. By the time I got him to the men's room, the heat of battle had worn off. He was apologetic about his behaviour, although as firm as ever in his opinions. 'I'd have been all right if Ossie hadn't gone on and on about Jack,' he grumbled, 'but I can't stand the way they all lick his boots.'

He washed and dried his face, combed his hair and looked at me in the mirror. 'Mark my words, Peter,' he said. 'No good will come of this marriage.'

And his words had such a ring of doom about them that I shuddered.

BOOK THREE

GILL WAS RIGHT, AND WRONG, in his predictions
at Ann's wedding. I mean, some of the things he
predicted were right and some were wrong. He was
wrong when he said the marriage would only last
five minutes. What he forgot was that Ann had married more than Jack Webb, she had married JWE and
everyone in it – Janie and Mike, Ossie and Dai and
all the rest of them. They were like a family who,
having always regarded Ann as a sort of big sister,
warmly welcomed her as Jack's wife. In fact so much
so that they rarely left her alone, and the flat behind
The Cumberland became a general meeting place.
Jack moved to a larger flat six months after the
wedding, but it seemed just as crowded when I called
to visit. Not that I visited often.

Austen's departure had left a gap at Weston &
Weston, and Martin and I shared his clients between
us. Consequently we were busier than ever. However, I went to London half a dozen times over the
next eighteen months, and I never failed to call round
to see Jack and Ann. They seemed happy enough. I
remember that by the time of my second visit Jack
had grown his hair longer and put on another few
pounds. The blond stick-insect was coming to re-

semble a plump teddy bear, who wore sharp mohair suits and smoked cigars from morning to night. Next to him, Ann looked sleeker than ever.

I think that what struck me most during my visits, apart from the fact that they were never alone, was their single-mindedness. Momentous events were shaping the world; President Kennedy had been assassinated, Lyndon Johnson was in the White House, the war in Vietnam was escalating and claiming ever more lives – but Jack and Ann were concerned only with music, or, to be more accurate, Ann was concerned with music, Jack was more absorbed by the deals he was making. Both of them lived in a perpetual state of excitement, which was understandable when Dai was never out of the Top Ten, Janie and The Graduates were building a string of hits, and so were The Post Office Tower. To be in the middle of all that absorbed them twenty-four hours a day and seven days a week.

Then one day, out of the blue, Jack phoned to invite me to lunch.

I was surprised at the venue. 'Maidenhead?' I echoed. 'Why there?'

'That's where I've bought a house,' he said. 'Drive up on Sunday and I'll show it to you.'

He tried to sound casual, but I detected his excitement. I couldn't imagine Jack living in a house, especially a house out of London. His life revolved around the West End. He and Ann fitted into their flat as if it was their natural habitat; ten minutes from his office, twenty minutes from her rehearsal stage in the Kentish Town Scout hut. But Jack was quite serious.

We arranged to meet in the car park at Maidenhead

Station. Apparently it was quite close to Jack's new house, and the station seemed a place we were likely to find easily. So I drove up from Taunton, while Jack and Ann drove down from town.

There's a special pleasure in meeting old friends. You may not see them for months, yet when you do, you feel you haven't spent a day apart. There's always so much to talk about, even if much of it is devoted to recalling the past. One of you asks, 'Do you remember . . .?' and the next minute you're clutching your sides, laughing. So I was looking forward to that sort of day as I drove up from the country.

Sadly, it was to prove rather different.

I saw Jack as soon as I drove into the car park. He was smoking a cigar and lounging against the door of a Rolls Royce as if he owned it. He recognised my battered second-hand Ford and came bounding across. 'Tubby, my boy,' he cried as he opened the door. 'Come and have a look at a real motor car.'

He did own it! The green flying-machine had been consigned to the scrap heap. In its place stood a plum-coloured Rolls with Ann waving from the front seat. She was out of the car in an instant, hugging me and looking up at me, her dark eyes bright with excitement. 'I would have phoned you to tell you about it,' she said, meaning the car, 'but Jack wanted it to be a surprise.'

It was a surprise all right, the first of many that day. Dutifully I admired the magnolia upholstery, the walnut dashboard, the drinks cabinet in the back, while Jack reeled off the list of desirable features with the feigned casualness of a salesman in a West End showroom.

'It's splendid, Jack,' I said, 'really splendid.'

He insisted that I left my car parked where it was and travel with them in the Rolls; and when I agreed we set off, purring through the leafy Berkshire lanes while Ann twisted round to talk to me from the front seat. 'You know, Peter,' she said, 'I'm always telling Jack we should see you more often. So when we move into this house you must come and stay every weekend, right?'

I laughed. '*Every* weekend?'

'Why not? There's plenty of room.'

She was right about that. The house was huge. After passing through some majestic white gates – from which the house took its name – we crunched up a long gravel drive flanked by rhododendrons and lilac bushes. Emerald-green lawns sloped down to the river. I was impressed out of my mind even before we reached the house. I think my mouth was agape as Jack parked the Rolls and led the way to the front door. The house was long and low, with a green pantiled roof and green shutters. Inside, the spacious rooms were quite empty, and we went from one to another until we reached the back of the house, where french doors from the drawing room opened on to a terrace the size of a tennis court.

Even then there were more surprises in store. After touring the house, Ann led the way across the gardens to a small cottage partly hidden by trees. She almost skipped along, consumed by excitement. 'And this is for you,' she said, throwing open the door and drawing me over the threshold. 'We want you to come and stay every free moment you get.'

Still holding my hand, she led the way from a living room to a kitchen-cum-dining room, and out again into the hall, past the bathroom to the two bedrooms beyond.

Jack followed, cigar smoke billowing in his wake, seemingly endorsing Ann's invitation while impatient to show me his other possessions. 'See that?' he said, pointing from the living-room window. 'That path leads to the jetty. We've got a frontage on the river of two hundred yards. I'll have a boat out there in the summer.'

I couldn't help but enjoy their excitement. Possessions had always meant more to Jack than to me; I'm content so long as I'm comfortable, and never in my life would I aspire to own a house like Whitegates. But seeing the grin on Jack's face, and Ann flushed with pleasure, gave me a warm feeling inside. I was glad for them both and I said so. Not that we lingered long in the cottage. A minute or so later Jack was ushering me out and locking the door. 'I've booked a table for lunch at a place called Skingles,' he said. 'It's supposed to be good, but you never know until you see it yourself. I want to check it out. If it's any good I can put a lot of business their way.'

By now we were walking back to the car, with Ann in the middle linking arms with us both, in the way she had so often done after our nights at the Green Door. I barely had a chance to look again at the handsome façade of the house before we were accelerating down the drive towards the big gates.

Skingles turned out to be a rather fine establishment, fronting the river near the centre of town. I've no idea what it's like now, but in those days it was a well-appointed hotel, seemingly full of retired colonels and their ladies. Even in the foyer Jack looked out of place, with his hair down to his shoulders and his swaggering gait, and Ann raised a few eyebrows when she removed her long coat to reveal thigh-high leather boots and a skimpy red mini. To my eye she looked delicious, but the sight of her was nearly too much for one old veteran, whose bug-eyed look and crimson face suggested he would have a seizure unless we took Ann away. Accordingly, we left the bar and went into the restaurant. Not that Jack stayed long. As soon as we were shown to our table he began to fidget, craning his neck and looking around. 'I'll just go and see the manager,' he said, getting up from his chair.

Ann and I were engrossed in conversation and inspecting the menu, so it wasn't until Jack returned that I discovered his reason.

'I wanted to introduce myself,' he said with a grin. 'People like to deal with celebrities.'

I felt a pang of dismay that he should feel the need to show off. It seemed to be in such poor taste. Then, as I so often did with Jack, I began to justify it, telling myself that it was probably instinctive in his business. After all, what's showbiz without making a show? And Jack's involvement in showbiz grew all the time. As soon as we had ordered, he delved into a pocket and brought out a folded sheet of paper. 'Read that,' he said, tossing it across the table. It was the draft of a press release due to be issued the next day. Jack was starting his own recording company. 'JWE are proud to announce the incorporation of Apex Records, a new label designed to bring pleasure to millions.' And there was a picture of Jack, puffing away on an eight-inch Havana with the aplomb of a Texas oil billionaire. Reading it reminded me of that day in his office when he had talked of how record companies worked: 'Nine duds and one bloody great hit.' He had been toying with the idea even then. 'But I plan to do better than that,' he said. 'For every ten releases, I'll get *two* bloody great hits.'

He was like that throughout lunch, and for the first time ever I felt uncomfortable in his company. He had always been expansive, given to grand gestures and over-statements, but it was unlike him to brag. I wondered if it was for Ann's benefit, but she seemed not to notice, being too busy telling me of her plans for Whitegates. It seemed that the Kentish Town Scout hut would become a thing of the past. 'We won't need it,' she said. 'We'll do everything at the house, rehearse, make demo tapes, the lot.'

Listening to her was to hear echoes of Jack. They were both so committed to what they were doing. I didn't fault them for that, but listening to them, watching them, noting the interplay between them, I couldn't help thinking they acted more like business partners than husband and wife. When it came to affectionate gestures, Ann displayed as many to me as to Jack, reminding me of the old days in the Whitcombe Street flat. And for Jack's part, although a gleam still lit his eye when he looked at Ann, his expression had been similar when he had shown me his Rolls Royce and toured me round Whitegates. His face had fairly shone with pride of possession.

I was left feeling rather pensive, even though Jack judged lunch good enough for him to consider using Skingles again. Afterwards he suggested I return to Whitegates with them, where Ann had an appointment with a representative from a firm of painters and decorators. I had no choice but to agree, so once more we set off in the Rolls. As it happened, the man arrived just as we did and Ann took him upstairs to discuss colour schemes, leaving Jack and me to wander around the ground floor. Outside it had started to rain, and great fat drops fell against the french windows as we gazed out on to the gardens.

'So you like it?' said Jack, waving a hand round the room.

'Like it? It's a palace.'

'Yeah, well, it's good for the image,' he said, fingering the woodwork. Then he started to tell me what everything was costing. He wanted me to know down to the last penny. The sums made me wince. I wasn't envious, I was pleased he could afford it, I was glad for him, but when he began to gloat, I admit he got on my nerves. Finally I said, 'Steady down, Jack, you're getting carried away.'

His reaction was astonishing. 'Carried away?' he snapped. 'What do you mean? Don't be so bloody patronising. You always have to be Mr Nice Guy, don't you? Well, nice guys get nowhere. If you'd listened to your old man, you might have had something like this.'

Taken aback, I stared at him, and as I did a memory stirred of long ago, of Jack as a boy in my father's house, listening intently as my father explained, 'You've got to be ruthless in life. To hell with the other fellow. Kick him in the teeth if he gets in your way.'

I remembered arguing with Jack afterwards. I kept saying my father was wrong, but Jack had waved a hand round the drawing room. 'He must know what he's talking about. Look at this house. He owns it, Tubby, he *owns* it!' My response had been to cry, 'It's a *thing*, that's all. Things can never be as important as people.'

And Jack, dear old crooked-nosed best friend Jack, had ended the argument with a shame-faced smile. 'No, I suppose not. You're right, Tubby, I know you're right really.'

But at that moment, staring across that room at Jack in his new house, I wondered if he was still of the same mind.

I was about to reply when Ann walked into the room, too busy talking to the decorator to notice our strained expressions. Then Jack grinned a sheepish apology. 'Never mind, Tubby,' he said, taking my elbow. 'Where would the world be without nice guys? Come on, I've got a drink in the Roller.'

Which as far as I remember, more or less, ended my first visit to Whitegates. Ann and the decorator had finished, so we locked up and went out to the cars. The decorator drove off while we climbed into the Rolls. I refused the offer of a drink, less from pique than because I'd had enough over lunch and faced a long drive back to Taunton. So we returned to the station car park, said our goodbyes and set out on our separate journeys.

It took me three and a half hours to drive home. Rain began to fall in the first hour, and after that it lashed down. The clutch began to slip and I had to nurse the car along for mile after mile. All of which added to the irritation I felt about Jack. His sneer about Mr Nice Guy really rankled. I tried to put it out of my mind; and loyalty reminded me of my friend from boyhood – the Jack who had saved me from bullies at school, the Jack whose presence had deflected my father, and the Jack without whom there was no telling what would have happened. I owed him a great deal. Yet I couldn't help seeing the changes in him. Success was making him arrogant, dogmatic, convinced that his opinion outweighed all others. I began to wonder if he'd always been like that. Had I been so in awe of him as a boy that I simply hadn't noticed?

What with the rain and the clutch slipping and Jack falling in my estimation, I was in a thoroughly bad mood by the time I got home. Jack could go to hell as far as I was concerned. Next time he called I'd make damn sure I was busy . . .

Yet such were the complexities of Jack's character, that twenty-four hours later I was ashamed of such thoughts.

Next day, a parcel addressed to me was delivered by special messenger to the office. Unfastening the string, I removed layers of protective brown paper to reveal a briefcase – a very expensive briefcase, hand-crafted in pigskin, with the Asprey label still attached. I certainly hadn't ordered it, a briefcase like that was far too costly for my pocket. For a moment I wondered if Jumbo had treated himself in a rash moment and the parcel had come wrongly addressed. Then I came across Jack's note. All it said was, 'Sorry about yesterday. Jack.'

All my anger evaporated. I mean, how can you remain angry when someone does something like that? It wasn't so much the gift, it was his apology for stepping out of line.

Naturally, I telephoned to thank him, but when I called he was not at his office. So I called his flat,

only for Ann to tell me he was at Wembley, arranging a concert. We got talking, and of course the reason for my call came out.

Ann laughed. 'That's typical. If Jack upsets someone, he sends them a peace-offering.'

At the time I thought I detected wry amusement in her voice. It was only later that I recognised her long-suffering exasperation, and very much later – when I saw him employ the same tactic on others – that I discovered the exact truth of her words. Jack used it almost as standard procedure: the more wounding the insult, the more expensive the gift. He was convinced that money could buy anything.

It was certainly buying him what he considered the good things of life. Whitegates was more than living-space, it became a showcase to emphasise his new status. Three months later, when the builders had finished altering and adding, and the decorators had completed their primping and painting, Jack took occupation and threw a huge house-warming party. Unfortunately I missed it because of a court case in Truro, even so I saw the photographs later, especially those of Jack posing with what the *Sunday Express* described as a 'bevy of stars'.

All the newspapers began to take Jack up in a big way, comparing him with Brian Epstein who managed The Beatles, and pop entrepreneurs like Robert Stigwood. In fact I was as likely to read about Jack in the papers as see him in person, for my visits to Whitegates were spasmodic. Usually the most I could manage was to stop off overnight on my way back from occasional visits to London. All in all I suppose I stayed seven or eight times during the next couple of years, and never once did I find Jack and

Ann by themselves; Janie was there, or Dai Evans, or the boys from The Post Office Tower, or somebody else. Whitegates became the Court of King Jack. Some days he went up to his office, but more and more of his business was conducted from Whitegates. 'It saves time,' he told me. 'Why flog up to Denmark Street when I can call them from here?' And when King Jack called, his subjects came running.

I think that was one of the things which worried me. I never quite understood Jack's relationship with his artists. In law, the artist, Janie for instance, was the Principal and Jack was her Agent. The Principal was *always* more important than the Agent. Yet somehow Jack had turned things upside down. Janie, for example, had become almost deferential towards him. She called him 'Big Daddy' in a seemingly affectionate way, but in a manner that left no doubt about Jack being the boss. Dai and the others were the same, and while they seemed to like Jack, they were careful not to upset him.

If this gives the impression that Whitegates was a joyless and serious place, it would be wrong. There was a lot of fun at Whitegates, especially in the early days. Often when I arrived, Ann would be playing the grand piano in the drawing room, working on a new number with Ossie and Janie or one of the others. One evening I arrived with Jumbo in tow, and within half an hour he was doing his Fats Waller impressions, with Janie joining in the choruses and everyone clapping and laughing. We had a lot of fun that night. And there were plenty of parties, some of which I attended, many that I missed and heard about afterwards.

But as time passed it became impossible to ignore

the fact that Jack was bending the law in his wheeling and dealing. Some of it was relatively harmless. I remember arriving once to the sound of girls' screams coming from the drawing room. Jack had twelve girls listening to one of Dai's records; whenever Dai hit a big note, they screamed, while Jack bawled at them to scream louder. Later he told me they were on his payroll, they went to all of Dai's concerts. 'One of my secret weapons,' he grinned. He had them drilled to jump and scream and shout as soon as Dai came on stage; he actually coached two of them to fall in a dead faint, while the others had to moan and whimper when Dai went into one of his ballads. 'Gets the rest of the audience going,' Jack explained.

I laughed. It was just one of Jack's tricks of the trade, building his bank balance and Dai's reputation at the same time. Where was the harm?

On the other hand, some of the things Jack said told me that he was sailing close to the wind. One night he admitted he was rigging the charts. He came right out and said it. We were playing snooker at the time – the upstairs snooker room was one of his additions, along with the swimming pool and, later, a soundproofed studio at the back of the house. That evening Ann was working downstairs on a new number with Janie and The Graduates, and Jack was playing snooker with me. Our game progressed to the sound of music from downstairs and to Jack's gossip about the pop scene in London.

A lot had changed since the days of the Green Door. Jack regaled me with stories of the new clubs – places like the Ad Lib, the Bag O'Nails near Carnaby Street, and The Scotch of St James. The scene had become much wilder, pop music was now generating big money and a lot of it was sloshing around in the clubs. From what Jack said everyone was either popping pills or smoking hash or playing with LSD (Jack stuck to his cigars but was on pills in a big way).

Anyway, on this particular night, he got to talking about Brian Epstein. Jack detested Epstein. I could never decide if it was genuine dislike or professional jealousy. After all, Jack managed some big names – Dai, Janie, The Post Office Tower and so on – but none was as big as The Beatles. That night he really nagged on about Epstein, and at one point he said, 'Eppy's not a manager, he's a sugar daddy.'

His meaning escaped me and I said so.

Jack shrugged. 'Eppy's so hot for John Lennon, he'd kill for. The Beatles. And Lennon plays him along, one minute he gives him the green light, then he acts hard to get. Poor old Eppy pants along with his tongue hanging out.'

I thought he was joking, but Jack assured me it was perfectly true. 'Eppy got lucky,' he said. 'Chasing Lennon led him to a pot of gold. Can't get luckier than that, can you?'

'No,' I agreed, still wondering if it was true.

Jack laughed. 'I'll tell you a story about Eppy. This will show you his mentality. He's got a record shop up in Liverpool. Someone told him that a record has to sell ten thousand copies to get into the Top Ten, so what does he do? When the Beatles made their first record, he bought ten thousand copies for his shop. Daft bugger. If you want to rig the charts, you've got to be smarter than that.'

He laughed derisively and turned back to the game. After potting a red, he lined up on the pink, his long blond hair almost yellow under the lights suspended over the table. Clad in black sweater and jeans, he looked more like a street-corner hustler than a rich man. I wondered if he was still taking Prellies. If so, they weren't working as a slimming aid; Jack's girth was now greater than mine. 'Eppy's a bloody idiot,' he sneered. 'Still, I suppose I should be grateful. It was his bum idea that started me thinking.'

'How do you mean?'

He walked round the table to reposition the pink. For a moment he just stood there, studying angles, intent on his next shot. Then he came out and said it. He was rigging the charts. It was really quite simple. Apparently charts of best-selling records are compiled from a sample number of shops; whatever is selling in them is assumed to be selling elsewhere. In those days the sample was two hundred and fifty of Britain's five thousand record outlets. If, on the day of the sample, each of two hundred and fifty shops sells two copies of a particular record, it is assumed the other shops sell the same, making a total of ten thousand copies. Jack grinned. 'Ten thousand gives you a hit. So I make bloody sure each of the sample shops sells two of our record.'

'How?'

'How do you think, stupid? I buy them. Tiny gets it done.'

Tiny had been Dai's road manager before he gravitated to being Jack's general factotum. He was always at Whitegates, fetching and carrying.

I said, 'Surely they keep the sample shops secret?'

'Yeah,' Jack agreed, his gaze back on the table as he worked out his next shot. 'I love secrets. They're always for sale, know what I mean?'

He walked round the table, still talking. 'It's easy after that. Once the record is in the charts, DJs give it more air time and the punters really start buying.' He laughed. 'With a bit of luck you end up with a genuine hit.'

He missed his next shot and I missed mine. I think I was too stunned to concentrate. 'Does Ann know?'

'Why should she? It's not her end of the business. She's into music. I'm into money.'

'What about Janie? Dai? I mean, surely they –'

'They're artists with fucking great egos. They think it's their talent.' He laughed. 'It wouldn't help them knowing I can make a hit out of an elephant's fart.'

I suppose it was natural for him to want to share his triumphs. He had come a long way in a short time, and I was his oldest friend. Inside his business, he kept secrets, Dai was given one story, Janie another, Ann knew a little of this, Tiny knew a little of that . . . but Jack alone knew all that went on. Sadly I was a poor audience. Instead of being impressed by the story, I found it worrying. Another thought struck me. Jack was beginning to sound like my father: the same disregard for people echoed in his voice as I remembered from childhood.

'What's up?' he asked, reading my expression.

I shrugged, stifling my disapproval, but he read my mind. 'Don't give me that supercilious look. I got a business to run. You think it's easy –'

'No, but I don't want to hear anything crooked –'

'Crooked?' He flushed. 'Crooked? I'll tell you crooked. Like, we had a gig in Manchester three weeks ago. We had the whole bill, Dai, The Tower, The Oakley Wood Trio . . .' He gulped for breath.

'This hall only had three thousand seats, so I did a deal on three thousand tickets. Know what this bastard promoter does? Rips out half the seats and sells standing-room. He doubles the gate. So we're playing for half price! Not fucking likely. Tiny and I sat this thieving sod down and put the fear of God into him. We got our money. That's what I face every day. That's crooked. So don't you talk about crooked.'

And we didn't after that, because I made a conscious effort to avoid discussing any business with Jack. In fact this proved to be quite easy as generally there were other people around so that, as I said before, most evenings at Whitegates were fun. Invariably Janie and Mike were there, if not Ossie and some of the rest of the boys. I had a soft spot for Janie, and Mike and I had always got on. And, of course, there was Ann, who never failed to make a big fuss of me. Odd though – I couldn't help thinking how things had changed. Once upon a time, Ann had seemed more worldly, more knowledgeable than any of us; now best friend, crooked-nosed Jack, with his new fat face and long hair, had emerged as the master.

I might have taken more note of events in Jack's life if less had been happening in mine. The truth was that Weston & Weston had expanded a great deal since I first went to Taunton, and there were times when we were hard pressed to keep pace. In Josh's day the majority of the firm's clients had lived within twenty miles of Taunton, whereas Jumbo had developed contacts further afield. Many were cronies from his cricketing days who liked to have an old friend dealing with their business. The fees were good, the work was plentiful, but the travelling was getting him down.

I remember one day in particular – Jumbo had just returned from a trip to Bristol. He came into my room looking completely exhausted. 'By God, Peter,' he groaned as he sank into a chair, 'I'm beginning to spend more time dashing around the countryside than I do in my office.'

It was true, he was, and I said as much over a pint with Martin that evening. 'Jumbo's fairly wearing himself out.' Martin stroked his nose and looked thoughtful. Whenever he concentrated he stroked his nose. I used to tell him he'd wear it out, but he took not a blind bit of notice. He was as worried as I was about Jumbo and the following day he started work on what he called his 'business analysis'. Martin was a great lover of statistics, and on the Friday he called Jumbo and me into his office to examine the results of his findings. 'Do you know,' he asked, 'that half of our business is now outside Taunton?'

We hadn't known, in fact we disputed it, but Martin went on to prove all of his figures. Thirty percent of our work came from Bristol, and a combined twenty percent came from even further afield, places like Bath, Chippenham and Swindon. Martin pointed to the map. 'That's where our business is growing,' he said. 'So in future we'll spend even more time travelling.'

Jumbo and I groaned in unison. I had a few clients outside Taunton myself by then, and I disliked travelling as much as he did. Even so, we might have gone on much as before but for two events which occurred within a month of each other. The first, sadly, was that Josh died. Death came suddenly: he went to bed one night complaining of feeling a bit under-the-weather, and passed away in his sleep. It was an understated, dignified death for a wise and considerate man. I always remember him with enormous affection.

People came from all over for the funeral, some even from London. And it was at Josh's funeral that I first met John Lovell. He too was a solicitor, and although his practice was in Swindon, he had known Josh for years. 'One of the finest men who ever lived,' he pronounced, expressing what was in most people's minds. Lovell was fifty-six on the day of the funeral and, in the way that funerals affect most of us, thoughtful about his own future. 'I should have copied Jumbo,' he said ruefully, 'and taken a couple of bright sparks like you and Martin into the firm.'

I saw him only briefly that day. More than two hundred people had gathered to pay their respects to Josh, and although Martin and I had no official duties, we were both anxious about Jumbo. Pale and shaken by the suddenness of his father's death, he preserved a granite-faced dignity throughout the proceedings, but was close to collapse at the graveside. His grief made me realise how strong the bonds could be between father and son. What a contrast to my own filial feelings. I hated my father, whereas Jumbo had lost his best friend.

Understandably, he took a few days off after the funeral, and when he returned he stopped by my office for a chat. He looked sadder and older than at any time since I'd known him, and I regarded him anxiously as he sat down. Even so, once he had fished around for his pipe and got it going, he launched into what was on his mind with much of his former briskness. 'I've decided to sell Hedley Hall,' he said. Then, seeing my surprise, he added, 'No point in keeping it now. Besides it's better to make a clean break.'

'But where will you live?'

'I'm coming to that,' he said. 'I've been thinking about those figures Martin produced. You know, about thirty percent of our business coming from Bristol. I think it's time we opened a branch office.'

Immediately he said it, I saw the sense. The idea was so obvious that I wondered why we hadn't considered it before.

'Of course,' Jumbo continued, 'it will mean me living in Bristol. Be no advantage otherwise, would it?'

And that was the decision he had reached. I must say, if anything demonstrated the strength of Jumbo's character, it was that decision. He had grown up in Taunton, his only place of employment had been his father's law office; everyone knew him. And yet within ten days of his father's death, he had decided to sell the family home and take on a new challenge in Bristol.

Martin joined us and we spent the rest of the morning evaluating the problems of him and me running the office in Taunton while Jumbo established another in Bristol. There was the smell of change in the air, of an old order passing and a new one coming into being. Little did we know that the changes were to be far wider-reaching than those discussed during that meeting . . .

The first hint of something even bigger happening came the next morning, when John Lovell returned to the scene, or rather telephoned Jumbo and invited him to Swindon for a day. Jumbo went on the Friday and events moved rapidly after that. A whole flurry of meetings took place over the following weeks, until eventually it was decided to incorporate Lovell's business into ours and that Martin and I would become partners in what would henceforward be known as Weston, Lovell, Mortlake and Juffs.

It was a proud moment for me. Oh, I know it was small beer by Jack's wealthy standards, but for me it was what I'd always wanted. It was *more*, because never had I thought to see my name over three sets of offices; at Taunton, Bristol and Swindon. There was only one snag: part of the deal required me to move to Swindon.

'Someone has to take over when John Lovell retires,' Jumbo pointed out, 'and it's easier for you to re-locate than it is for Martin.'

This was perfectly true; as well as having relatives in Taunton, Martin was courting a local girl, whereas I had no local ties, and my love-life was spasmodic to say the least. There had been other girls since my 'bread pudding' girl in the back of the car, five to be precise, and every one of them had looked like Ann. The trouble was, they weren't enough like Ann. I'd got a mental picture of my perfect woman – a tall, slim, long-legged brunette whose dark eyes were flecked with gold – and I told myself I would find her if I looked long enough ... Meanwhile Jumbo was right, if one of us had to move to Swindon, I was the obvious choice. There were compensations. Swindon was closer to London, so it would be easier to visit my mother and Bert; it was only an hour from Maidenhead, so I would see more of Jack ...

'Why not give the place the once over,' Jumbo suggested. 'Go up next week and have lunch with John Lovell.'

So I phoned Lovell, made an appointment, and early the following Tuesday morning, set off for Swindon ... without for a moment foreseeing the huge changes about to take place in my life.

My only previous meeting with John Lovell had been that brief encounter at the funeral, so I scarcely knew him when I called at his offices. In appearance he reminded me of a soldier; very straight-backed with the hawk-eyed look of a Commanding Officer inspecting the ranks. Grey-haired and blue-eyed, he had a stern face softened by a wide and generous mouth which suggested his smile would be warm when it came. Unfortunately he smiled very little that morning, being too busy impressing me with talk of his clients, and although he softened a little over lunch, his reserved manner kept me at arm's length. I found him a hard man to warm to. He was as different from Jumbo as chalk from cheese. In fact he as good as said so: 'I'm no match for Jumbo on the social front,' he admitted frankly. 'Naturally, I go along to the Rotary Club and a few other bits and pieces, but I haven't the patience for all this cricket club nonsense.'

Which explained why he had an ageing clientele; the younger crowds of up-and-coming businessmen were passing him by. Things might have been different if his brother had lived, but Harry Lovell had been killed in a motor accident four years earlier. 'Harry had more contact with young people,' said

276

John with an apologetic shrug. 'He was married, with a young daughter; it all helps, I suppose. I keep meaning to do more, but since Harry's death I've been so damn busy there hasn't been time.'

I wasn't sure if I liked him or not; he was stuffy and old-fashioned, set in his ways; I imagined he might be difficult to work with. What encouraged me most was that he had pursued Jumbo about merging the businesses, so he wanted it to work as much as I did. In fact, from what he said, he was really looking forward to partners' meetings. 'It will be a great help to talk things over,' he sighed.

The plan was for us to have a full partners' meeting once a month, alternating the venue between Taunton, Bristol and Swindon. Between times Jumbo, Martin and I would speak on the phone and stay closely in touch. I was convinced of the prospects, but not without realising how much I would miss daily contact with Jumbo and Martin.

I left Lovell after lunch, intending to drive straight back to Taunton. Then I changed my mind. After all, I wouldn't get back to the office in time to do any work, so I decided to make a day of it and go over to Maidenhead. It was a couple of months since I'd seen Jack and Ann, and although they knew about my partnership and the probable move to Swindon, they knew none of the details. Ann had been full of enthusiasm on the phone. 'Swindon! Oh, Peter, that's just down the road. We'll almost be neighbours.'

She was equally enthusiastic when I arrived that afternoon. The drawing-room window overlooked the drive and she saw me alight from my car. Next minute the front door was open and she was waiting for me on the top step. 'Well?' she asked eagerly. 'Is everything fixed? Are you moving to Swindon?'

One of the pleasures of seeing Ann was the welcome she gave me. The uninhibited hug, the kiss on the mouth, standing close, with her arm round my waist. Which was how we were when Jack emerged from his study, a spool of recording tape in his hand. There had been times when coming across us like that would have brought a scowl to Jack's face, but on my two previous visits I had detected a cool indifference. Indeed, there had been a certain scratchiness between him and Ann, hinting at underlying disagreements. But that day Jack was all smiles. 'Tubby, my boy. What's this I hear about Swindon?' So I told him my news and the three of us stood in the hall for some minutes, discussing my meeting with John Lovell. They seemed pleased about the prospect of my living closer to them, but I sensed another excitement. 'What's up?' I asked. 'You're both grinning away as if you've got some news of your own.'

'And how!' Jack nodded and jerked his head towards the drawing room. 'There's a boy in there who's nothing short of a genius –'

'A very rare talent,' Ann interrupted. 'We've been listening to him for the last couple of hours.'

Jack explained that some demonstration tapes had been delivered to his office. 'We get them all the time,' he said. 'Most of them are rubbish. But this one –'

Ann interrupted. 'I couldn't believe these tapes when I heard them last week. Today's the first time we've met him –'

'He's a great song writer,' said Jack, before hesitating, 'but as a performer? I dunno –'

'He's keen,' said Ann, 'he's got a sweet nature. It will take work, but if we can get that across –'

'Come and meet him,' said Jack.

And that was my first meeting with Nick Berkley. Let me admit here and now, he wasn't my idea of a pop star. I couldn't help comparing him with Dai. Dai really looked the part, broad-shouldered, handsome, deep-voiced, very masculine – you could understand why girls went wild about Dai. But poor Nick was nothing like that.

When we entered he was at the piano, playing softly. He stopped and stood up, a short, slender figure, wearing an ill-fitting grey suit.

'Nick,' Jack boomed, leading the way. 'I want you to meet an old friend. Tubby Mortlake, meet Nick Berkley.'

'Hi, Nick,' I said, offering my hand.

'Hello, Mr Mortlake,' he said, giving me a handshake that was as weak as he looked. He had pale grey eyes, no eyelashes to speak of, and biscuit-coloured hair. Possibly his hair was as long as Jack's, but where Jack's was straight and expensively cut, Nick's was a mass of tight curls. His features were regular without being distinguished, and although his smile was pleasant, it was too lacking in confidence to make an impression.

'Nick is coming to live in the cottage,' Ann said unexpectedly. 'He's moving in tomorrow, aren't you, Nick?'

Looking at him, I judged him to be about twenty, certainly no older. His pale eyes shone with gratitude as he looked at Ann. 'If that's still okay with you, Mrs Webb –'

'Ann,' she said, correcting him, 'and of course it's

okay.' Turning to me, she raised her hands in a gesture of hopelessness. 'This poor lamb lives in the original garret. In, er . . . where is it, Nick?'

'Kilburn.'

Ann rolled her eyes. 'A garret in Kilburn,' she said contemptuously. 'Well, that part of your life's over now. You go back there tonight and pack your things.'

Shaking his head in bewilderment, Nick managed an uncertain smile. 'I'll wake up in a minute. Things like this only happen in films. You don't even know me –'

'We've heard your music. Your songs tell us about you –'

'Right,' Jack agreed. He was on the floor next to the piano, fiddling with a large reel-to-reel tape recorder. 'Okay,' he said, straightening up. 'We're ready to roll. Tubby, sit over there. Ann, you going to get us a drink? Then Nick can play a couple more numbers.'

And so for the next hour I listened to Nick Berkley. Ann was quite right, his songs did tell you about him. They were full of youthful indecision, questioning the meaning of life, full of his efforts to understand himself and the people he met. His modest voice was as undistinguished as his looks, pleasing but lacking professionalism. He failed to project. He sang with the shyness of the boy next door, which is what I was thinking when I realised it was part of his charm. He *was* the boy next door; not handsome, not exciting like Dai, not a showman, but sincere and thoroughly genuine. You felt for him. When he sang of unrequited love he sang for every boy in search of a girl. You wanted her to say yes when you knew damn well she would say no. You suffered his pain of rejection, and because of it the poignant, yearning quality of the songs stayed with you. All the frustrations of adolescence were in every note.

He went from song to song, encouraged by his audience. Everything he sang, he had written himself. Four of the numbers were anti-war songs, protest songs I suppose you'd call them, dealing with Vietnam and the dangers of nuclear war. Joan Baez and Bob Dylan were recording that sort of music in the States, but Nick's were the first compositions written by an Englishman I had heard. Ann sat absorbed, her eyes fixed on his face until he finished, when she led the applause. 'Bravo, Nick!' she cried. 'That was magnificent.'

He responded with a shy smile, then his anxious eyes went to Jack, who was lighting a fresh cigar.

'Very good,' said Jack, nodding approval from behind a cloud of blue smoke. 'I like it, except for that political stuff. Maybe in the States –'

'Oh no,' Ann interrupted, 'artists all over the world should make themselves heard –'

'Crap,' said Jack in blunt contradiction. 'Who wants politics when they can get entertainment?'

'Who wants it?' Ann echoed, going pink in the face. 'His market, that's who. The kids asking questions and searching for answers –'

'I don't believe it. It's not commercial –'

'Wrong,' Ann cried, 'it's very commercial.'

They stared at each other and for an instant I sensed the same scratchiness that I'd felt on my last visit, while out of the corner of my eye I glimpsed the dismay on Nick's face. Then Jack was out of his chair and advancing on the piano, his scowl fading as his features settled into a reassuring smile. 'But that's detail,' he said breezily. 'We can sort that out later. Meanwhile we've a lot of work to do. But take my word for it, Nick, we're going to make you a star.'

Nick's face lit up with relief. For an instant he was overwhelmed, so excited that he was speechless. Diminutive beside Jack, he stood up and reached out his hand. 'Thank you, Mr Webb, I won't let you down, really I won't. I'll work and work . . .' Words failed him as he pumped Jack's hand up and down. Next minute he surprised me by releasing Jack and coming over to shake my hand as well. 'Mr Mortlake,' he said breathlessly, 'this is the most wonderful moment of my life, I can hardly believe it.' Stuttering with excitement, he looked at Ann, intent on shaking her hand as well until he realised it was the wrong gesture. He would have kissed her, but lacked the nerve. And Ann laughed, recovering from her momentary hostility towards Jack, and leant forward to kiss Nick on the cheek. 'Remember,' she warned, 'we've a lot of work –'

'I know it,' Nick answered quickly, his eyes shining.

The smile remained on Ann's face. 'Fine,' she said warmly. 'All you need do now is go back to that rat hole you live in and pick up your things.'

'Yes, of course,' Nick stammered, 'I will, Mrs Webb. And thank you, thank you very much indeed.'

Smiling around his cigar, Jack hovered near the telephone. 'Want me to call a cab to take you to the station?'

The boy coloured with confusion. 'Oh no, I couldn't let you do that, Mr Webb. I'll walk –'

'Walk?' Jack sounded horrified. 'It's four miles.'

'I like walking. Honestly. I walk all the time, everywhere –'

I interrupted, 'I'll drop you off. I must be going now anyway –'

'Oh, Peter,' Ann protested, putting her hand on my arm and looking disappointed. 'Stay. Stay over-night –'

'Thanks,' I said, rising to my feet, 'but I need to be at the office first thing in the morning . . .'

She tried to persuade me. 'At least stay for dinner,' she said. But I faced a long drive and it was already six-thirty. So we made our goodbyes, with me agree-ing that life would be easier when I moved to Swin-don, and Nick thanking Jack and Ann all over again. He was so painfully grateful; even when we were in my car, he worried about the inconvenience he was causing. 'Honestly, Mr Mortlake, I can walk,' he protested as I drove out through the gates. 'I don't want to take you out of your way. If you're going to Taunton you want the motorway, and that's up there.' He jerked his thumb in the opposite direction.

'Nonsense,' I said. 'It won't take a minute to drop you off at the station.'

Accepting the inevitable, his thoughts turned back to Whitegates. 'They're the most amazing people in the world. The kindest, most generous . . .' He paused, struggling to express his feelings. 'And that house. I mean, it's a mansion, not a house. To say I could live there, just like that, move into their cot-tage, as if it's no big deal –'

I laughed. 'Your lucky day, eh, Nick?'

'You don't know what it means. My whole life will be different. Mr Webb will make me a star, people all over the world will hear my songs. It's all I live for, Mr Mortlake, you just can't imagine.'

He was right, it was hard for me to imagine his kind of life. I lacked the courage to starve in a garret, waiting for the world to recognise my talent. Not that I have any talent, but even if I had, I wouldn't have that kind of faith. I would be full of self-doubt. I could imagine saying to myself, 'Suppose the world turns me down? I'll starve!' One glance at Nick was enough to know he had seen his share of starving. He looked like a scarecrow, without an ounce of fat on him. And his suit was two sizes too small, his collar was grubby . . .

'I sing in the pub on a Saturday night,' he said unexpectedly. 'They've got a piano, you see.'

'Ah,' I said.

'But tomorrow I won't, will I? I'll be with Mr Webb.' He sounded in awe, still pinching himself about what had happened.

'Right,' I agreed, staring through the windscreen as I realised I had taken a wrong turning. 'Damn,' I said. 'Which way did you come, Nick? When you walked from the station?'

'What? Er . . . I didn't, I mean . . . well, it was light then, things look different in the light.'

Recognising a pub, I began to establish my whereabouts. We were still heading in the right direction. 'Not to worry. We're not far off —'

'Put me down here, Mr Mortlake. Anywhere will do.'

Something in his voice caught my attention. I realised what he had said, that he *hadn't* come from the station. And I sensed his reluctance to go there. The location of the station was unknown to him, yet he had pointed out the way to the motorway when we left Whitegates.

Catching my sideways glance, he realised his blunder. 'I didn't come down by train,' he admitted sulkily, 'I hitched. It saves money, you see –'

'And you intended to hitch back,' I said accusingly, just as the station came into sight.

He coloured. 'It would have been all right if you hadn't insisted,' he blurted out before biting his lip. Then he recovered enough to apologise. 'Sorry, it doesn't matter, really it doesn't.'

As I slowed to a halt in the station yard, I realised he probably lacked money even for his train fare. Instead of helping, I had hindered his journey home. Now, unless I gave him a lift, he would have to walk all the way back to the motorway.

I stopped him as he was about to get out of the car. 'Hang on,' I said, reaching for my wallet, 'you're moving house tomorrow, so you'll have expenses. Believe me, I know about these things. When you're a star, pay me back, okay?'

He looked at the notes in my hand. The money was sufficient for his fares tonight and tomorrow, plus a decent meal in between. Still staring at the money, he hesitated, shaking his head slightly in mute refusal.

'Take it,' I encouraged, stuffing the notes into the breast pocket of his jacket.

The same bemused expression as he had worn earlier reappeared on his face. Finally his eyes lifted with a look of acceptance. 'Thanks, Mr Mortlake, I'll pay you back real soon.'

'I know you will,' I said, shaking hands.

To be honest, I never expected to see the money

again. Not that I worried. I could easily afford it and I'd enjoyed Nick's songs; I was glad to do him a favour, I liked him. So I set off on the long drive to Taunton, pleased to have helped, and with no thought in my mind that he would ever reduce my life to absolute chaos.

The next few months were spent putting Weston, Lovell, Mortlake and Juffs together. Jumbo scoured Bristol for premises, Martin recruited new staff, and I began to reduce my workload in Taunton. Gradually I handed everything over to Martin, and by early March I was spending two or three days a week with John Lovell in Swindon.

In between times, and much to Ann's delight, I was looking for somewhere to live. Ann would have taken over if I'd let her; bought my house, decorated it, furnished it, the lot. As it was, she insisted on coming house-hunting with me. Jack came too, though I wished he hadn't, but they drove down in the Rolls to spend an entire Saturday viewing what Estate Agents described as 'desirable properties'. Of course, by Jack's standards, they weren't at all desirable. 'Pokey little hole,' he growled within earshot of the owner of one cottage. Even Ann had her doubts. 'Don't you think you'd be better off with a flat in the middle of Swindon?'

I knew exactly what I wanted – another cottage like the one I was selling in Taunton, oak beams, inglenook fireplace, and plenty of shelves for my books. I also knew that arriving in a Rolls Royce was not the best way to buy at the right price.

The day was a disaster. Jack grew increasingly

impatient. He sneered at every house and finally, when we returned to my hotel for a drink, started sneering at me. Ann did her best to smooth things over by saying he lacked the patience for house-hunting and suggesting that in future she come by herself.

'Oh really?' Jack scowled, letting his gaze rove round the empty bar. 'Why does Tubby need you to hold his hand all the time?'

Ann caught her breath and a moment of shocked silence elapsed before I said, 'No one's holding my hand, Jack.'

'Yes, well . . .' he muttered, moving off down the counter, tapping a coin to attract the barman who had gone through to the other bar. 'God knows why you want to live here, anyway. Bloody one-horse town. Can't even get a drink.'

Ann threw me a look of apology, and we stood in an uncomfortable silence until the barman returned. With a drink inside him, Jack's temper improved, and by the time I'd bought him another he had thawed enough to start talking about all the money he was making. 'Mind you,' he said, lighting the inevitable cigar, 'it's not easy. Take this kid Nick. He looks like something out of a concentration camp, and I'm supposed to make him a star.'

'He's got talent,' said Ann, a determined look coming into her eyes.

'As a composer, okay –'

'As a performer.'

Jack shrugged. 'Yeah, well . . . remember I'm the poor bastard who's out there trying to sell him.'

Ann opened her mouth to say something, then thought better of it, while I stood there, assessing the friction between them. Some words of Gill's came into my mind: 'Jack's never content. Once he's got something, he's off after something else.' I'd argued at the time; after living through AIDA, I'd never thought to see the day when Jack was indifferent to Ann. Yet there was no mistaking his hostility. Fumbling for a neutral topic of conversation, I plunged into some small talk about Swindon, but it was never strong enough to engage their attention, and shortly afterwards Jack said they had to go. 'I've got a lot of phone calls to make,' he said by way of explanation.

I saw them out to the Rolls and surprised myself by breathing a sigh of relief as they drove off. Jack and Ann were my closest friends, yet a distinct gap was opening between us, or at least between me and Jack. I couldn't help thinking how like my father he was becoming, a comparison that once I would have considered preposterous. But all the signs were there . . . when I looked for them.

Meanwhile I was trying to come to terms with my new life in Swindon. Those were not easy weeks. Having run his own show for so long, John Lovell was as tentative about sharing his clients as they were in accepting a new face – all of which was understandable, but it did make for a difficult time. I spent my evenings familiarising myself with files of past correspondence, I quizzed John to the extent of his patience, and I arrived at the office first in the mornings and left last at night. On top of which, I continued to worry about finding a house. Living in the hotel was a temporary measure; the agents had sold my cottage in Taunton and I was under pressure to remove my possessions. There were days when I thought Martin had got easily the best part of the deal. He was back in dear old familiar Taunton, while I was out breaking new ground.

And then, out of the blue, came Julia.

I was alone in the office one evening, when the bell rang at the front door. Hurrying through the reception area, I opened the door and came face to face with a blonde.

'Oh,' she said in surprise. 'I saw a light on in the office. I was looking for my uncle. I'm Julia Lovell.'

The odd thing was that she looked nothing like Ann. Thick honey-blonde hair framed an oval face, clear blue eyes regarded me steadily, and the wide, humorous 'Lovell mouth' puckered impishly at both corners. Slim and petite, she was shorter than Ann by at least three or four inches. Her powder-blue coat was open, revealing a Paisley print shirt above a navy blue skirt. A blue handbag hung on a strap over one shoulder. Anyone less like my ideal woman was hard to imagine, yet I felt an immediate attraction.

Drawing her into the reception area, I introduced myself, and we talked for a few minutes, although I forget about what – I was too busy trying to think of excuses to detain her. Eventually I said, 'I was just leaving for the hotel. How about joining me for a drink?'

Julia glanced at her watch and looked doubtful.

'It's only over the road,' I pointed out.

She shook her blonde head. 'I've only got ten minutes –'

'Ten minutes is fine,' I said, hurrying to switch off the lights and lock the door. Crossing the road, I realised she only came up to my shoulder. She was tiny, a perfect miniature; slender, lithe and graceful.

Once in the bar, I settled her into a corner and went to the counter for drinks. Such was my hurry that I almost spilled her glass of white wine on my way back to the table.

As soon as I sat down she took a sip of wine, her lips imprinting the glass. 'Nice to meet you,' she said. 'My uncle was talking about you only the other day.'

Vaguely I wondered what John Lovell had said, but mostly I was looking at her. To give myself an excuse, I began to ask questions, polite, but as direct as I could make them. Deep down I felt the wondrous stirring of lust. Why, when she was nothing like my ideal woman? There had to be something, she had to measure up to the specification in some way. Then I stumbled on a clue.

'I'm a teacher,' she said, 'at the local comprehensive.'

'Ah,' I exclaimed, as all became clear. 'You teach music.'

Her blue eyes widened. 'Why on earth should you think that?'

'What? Oh, I just . . . I mean, you do teach music, don't you?'

A look of amusement lit her face, the wide mouth twitched at the corners. 'Nothing so cerebral, I'm afraid. I'm a gym teacher.'

I forget what I answered. Whatever my reply, it dried on my lips as she finished her drink and glanced at the clock. Never had ten minutes passed so quickly. 'That was lovely,' she smiled. 'And I'm sure we'll meet again. Meanwhile . . .' She rose to go.

I put a hand on her arm. 'Stay for dinner.'

She looked at me in surprise before shaking her head. 'Sorry. I've got a date –'

'Break it,' I said, forgetting myself.

I wouldn't have said it if I'd stopped to think. This was me, old stick-in-the-mud Peter Mortlake, behaving like Bogart in *The African Queen*.

Julia hesitated, only for a fraction of a second, but long enough to make my heart beat faster. Her eyes met mine, curious and amused. Then again came a shake of her head. 'I don't break dates,' she said. 'It's very bad manners.'

'Tomorrow then,' I said recklessly.

She smiled, and her smile widened until it took over her face. Blue eyes and soft lips combined to convey warmth as well as amusement.

'Tomorrow,' I repeated urgently, feeling suddenly desperate. 'Let's meet here at seven-thirty.'

Cocking her head to one side, she regarded me with a long speculative look from beneath long eyelashes. 'Are you always so masterful?'

'Always,' I lied.

Her quizzical look reverted to one of open amusement. 'All right,' she laughed. 'If you like. I'll meet you here at seven-thirty.'

I spent the rest of the evening bathed in a warm glow of anticipation. Usually I'm reserved when I meet people, even when I meet good-looking blondes, though I've met precious few of those. Generally I like to get to know someone before I form any sort of judgement, yet something about Julia Lovell had drawn me from the first moment. Good old-fashioned lust was part of it. I don't believe I'd ever seen a body so perfectly proportioned. But it was more than that. There was a frankness, an honesty about her face which had appealed to me deeply.

Consequently I spent the following day in a fidget, waiting for evening to come. I left the office at six, which was a record for me, and hurried over to the hotel to bathe and change into my best suit. And I was waiting in the bar when Julia arrived, looking casually elegant in a blue linen dress.

Everything went right over dinner. We talked about books; other things too, of course, but books kept us going for a long time. Julia had read all my favourites: we discussed Maugham and Steinbeck, Priestley and Burroughs, Shute, Fleming and God knows who else. And in between times I found out a good deal about her. She was twenty-four, had attended the Physical Training College in Loughborough, and had represented Great Britain eight times as a gymnast. She ate well, drank only a little, and smoked not at all. And . . . wait for this . . . when it came to popular music her favourites remained Sinatra, Peggy Lee and traditional jazz.

'Mine too,' I beamed across the table.

She pulled a face. 'What a couple of dinosaurs.'

Over coffee, I told her about my lack of success in finding a house. She was surprised. 'You can't have looked properly,' she said in disbelief. 'There are some marvellous old cottages in the villages around here.'

'Which villages?'

She talked about Wanborough and Pewsey and a place called Wootton Basset, villages she had known all her life – which gave me a perfect excuse to ask for her help the following Saturday.

The same hesitation clouded her eyes as on the

previous evening. For a sickening moment I thought she would refuse.

'Please,' I said, 'I really must find somewhere.'

Doubt lingered in her face. Then she said, 'I can't in the morning. I'm refereeing a school hockey match.'

'I'll meet you for lunch.'

Her misgivings were still there, I could see them, but finally her wide mouth puckered into a smile. 'Okay. I'll meet you here at one o'clock.'

And that's how it started. We met that Saturday, the following Saturday, and the one after that. By the second Saturday I had located the school playing fields, so I collected Julia directly. Saturdays began to develop a delicious routine: from nine until ten I telephoned Estate Agents, confirming appointments for the afternoon, after which I drove to the sports ground, waited for Julia to shower and to change, then took her off to lunch prior to an afternoon spent viewing houses.

It was spring. The days were pleasantly warm and every hedgerow was green with new life; the sun shone, the countryside looked perfect, and suddenly all was right in my life. Julia never tired of looking at houses. We viewed thatched cottages, stone cottages, a converted pub and a dozen old farmhouses. In the evenings we dined, sometimes well, sometimes badly, at a pub or hotel in whichever village we happened to be – 'to get the feel of the place'. And Julia was known wherever we went. Parents would introduce themselves to enquire about their offspring. 'Excuse me,' they would say, peering into her face, 'but aren't you Miss Lovell from up at the school?' Julia met them all with a smile. 'Why, hello, yes, Sarah (or Mary or Jane) is coming along fine.' Their obvious liking for her sprang partly from what their children had told them and partly from the pleasure of meeting some-one that they regarded as famous. Comments ranged from 'Our Betty says you're the most popular teacher at Oakfields' to 'We saw you on television in the Commonwealth Games.'

Julia laughed about her accomplishments. 'It's easy to be a games mistress; I'd hate to teach algebra, that must be hell.' And of her role as an international athlete she would say, 'Goodness, that was ages ago. I'm retired now, you know.'

Retired or not, she moved with the lithe grace of an athlete while I lumbered along beside her; mountainous, clumsy and awkward, like an elephant next to a gazelle.

Ann called during the third week, keeping in touch as usual, and to ask if she should come house-hunting with me. The guilt I felt was partly because I was overdue to call her, and partly because her presence on my cosy expeditions was the last thing I wanted. Three would have been a definite crowd. I felt an inexplicable reluctance to tell her about Julia, and instead talked about someone who was helping me with local knowledge. Stupid really, because Ann wasn't fooled for a minute.

'What's she like?' she asked.

So, of course, I told her. Not that there was much to tell at that stage; after all I had only spent two Saturdays with Julia – even if the third one was booked, along with the following Sunday. Ann responded by saying, 'I feel deserted. Jack's in Amsterdam with Dai and you've found yourself a blonde bombshell. Thank goodness Nick is around.'

Which gave me an opening to move the conversation away from Julia and to ask about Nick. With hindsight, it's easy to say I should have known something was wrong. The clues were there, scattered through Ann's conversation, little nuances of resentment to indicate her dissatisfaction with Jack. Her only enthusiasm was for the imminent release of Nick's first record. But the truth was I scarcely listened. I had no patience for other people's problems. It was Friday evening, and all I could think of was seeing Julia the next day . . .

And it turned out to be a glorious day. Julia's students made her blush when I collected her from the sports ground.

'He's here again, Miss. It's the same one as last week.' They surrounded her as she walked from the pavilion, the braver ones coming up to the car as I got out to greet her. Julia turned on them with mock anger. 'Off you go, you little horrors!' And off they went, shrieking with laughter.

'God,' she groaned, sinking into the seat. 'How do I put up with them?' She so obviously enjoyed them that no comment was necessary. 'That's strange,' she said, giving me a sideways glance as we drove off. 'They don't bother you, do they? Most men would run a mile from a gaggle of schoolgirls.'

'Why? Are they dangerous?'

'Only when they grow up,' she grinned, and began leafing through the particulars of the houses we planned to see.

That day, the third Saturday, surpassed even the others. The rapport which developed between us astonished me. Some men are easy around women – it's an ease I've often envied, the ability to make small talk, to pay compliments without sounding insincere and to make jokes that are rewarded with laughter. Maybe as a consequence of being brought up in the absence of women, such talent had never developed in me. Usually, the prettier the woman, the more tongue-tied I became. Yet with Julia I felt completely at ease, possibly because of the absence of small talk. We had a project in hand, namely to find a home for me, and talking about that, comparing one cottage with another, discussing locations and so on, brought down the barriers – so that by the time the conversation developed along more personal lines, I was as loose-tongued as a drunk.

Certainly I was intoxicated by her looks and her charm. That day she wore a white, low-cut summer dress which revealed tantalising glimpses of her figure. And she wore her hair differently, pulled back and tied by a ribbon.

By the evening we had looked at four houses, one of which had really taken our eye. We discussed it over two very cold bottles of Chablis and the best poached salmon I had ever tasted, before, reluctantly, I drove her home, comforted by the knowledge that I would see her the next day.

A fool would have known he had competition. How many good-looking blondes reach the age of twenty-four without a man in their life? Yet for those first three weeks I imagined I had Julia all to myself. I missed all the clues. After all, she'd had a date the first time I met her; at the sports ground, the kids had identified me as 'the same one as last week'. Of course there was someone else . . . as I found out the following morning.

'How nice to meet you,' said Mrs Lovell as she shook hands and ushered me into her drawing room. 'Julia's told me so much about you.'

John Lovell's sister-in-law was taller than her daughter, taller and imposing, like a duchess. In twin-set, pearls, and a tweed skirt, she was actually quite a fine-looking woman, still gracious and attractive despite the onset of years and the loss of her husband.

'My husband was John's partner,' she said as she poured the coffee. 'But I expect you know that already.'

'Yes,' I said, wondering if I should express condolences four years after the event.

Sensing my awkwardness, she gave me an encouraging smile. 'Life goes on for the rest of us,' she said, 'nothing ever stays the same. After all, you must have thought you were settled in Taunton until a few months ago. How are you finding Swindon? Julia must have shown you every house in Wiltshire.'

Her smile betrayed her. A mite too encouraging, it verged on patronising, or perhaps she meant to convey her disapproval.

'Not quite every house,' I said, 'although that's how it's beginning to seem.'

'How tiresome for you,' she said, sounding suitably sympathetic.

'I'd have been lost without Julia.'

'Mmm,' she murmured, and a speculative gleam lit her eye.

I smiled, and avoided her gaze by admiring the room. Mrs Lovell had been left comfortably off; the family home was a large red-brick house set amid a few acres of well cultivated lawns, and the drawing room was luxuriously, almost lavishly furnished. Framed photographs of Julia abounded; Julia in white leotard, Julia balancing on parallel rails, arcing through space, landing with arms outstretched and feet together. In all of them she looked poised, graceful and altogether quite beautiful.

'Julia keeps telling me to put them away,' Mrs Lovell laughed. 'I'm supposed to condemn them to the attic, along with her dolls' house and the rest of her things. But I enjoy looking at them, so that's where they stay.'

'They're well worth looking at, aren't they,' I said, seizing a conversational opening. Looking around, I saw an alcove gleaming with cups and awards, all testimony to Julia's prowess. More photographs decorated the sideboard, but few of them were of Julia alone; in most she was pictured with a boy, a year or two older. To look at the photographs was to see them grow up together – Julia aged fourteen, the boy aged sixteen, Julia aged fifteen, the boy seventeen, and so on – dressed in matching track-suits, jogging around a running track. One large photograph in a heavy silver frame showed them with their arms around each other's shoulders, each holding a medal while grinning into the camera.

'That's David,' said Mrs Lovell. 'You haven't met him yet, have you?'

'No,' I agreed, feeling strangely apprehensive. My eye fell upon another photograph, this time of David by himself, now adult, wearing the uniform of an Army officer.

'I don't know when he's next on leave,' said Mrs Lovell, 'but I expect Julia told you she's off to see him in Aldershot next weekend?'

'Ah,' I said, trying to sound unconcerned when in fact feeling quite the opposite.

Mrs Lovell smiled indulgently. 'You can understand them taking every chance to see each other. After all, poor David only gets to Aldershot every couple of months. He's in Germany, you know.'

'Ah,' I said again, and gulped the rest of my coffee. Which was when Julia poked her head round the door. 'Nearly ready,' she said breathlessly, and withdrew before I could utter a word.

Having ruined my day, Mrs Lovell gave me another of her encouraging smiles. 'And where are you going this morning?'

'Pewsey,' I said, 'and I've arranged to see two other houses near Marlborough this afternoon.'

'Really? I had no idea so many people sold houses on a Sunday.'

I smiled. 'I promise not to contravene the Sunday Trading Act, Mrs Lovell.'

Mercifully Julia returned at that moment. Sunlight streaming in from the window caught her hair, turning it the same pale gold as her shirt and slacks. 'What time's our first appointment?' she asked, thrusting her arm into a suède jacket. In the sunshine the tan leather looked as gold as the rest of her, so that for a split second she shone like a statue, her nipples showing under the thin cotton shirt as she pulled the jacket around her. Reluctantly I dragged my gaze away and consulted my watch. 'We've half an hour –'

'Is that all? Sorry, no time for coffee,' she apologised quickly to her mother. 'See you tonight. Come on, Peter, let's go.'

As soon as we were in the car, I asked about David.

'Ah,' she said, staring through the windscreen. For a moment that was her only response. Then she sighed. 'Oh dear, Mother's been talking,' she said resentfully. 'Good God, I was only ten minutes. She couldn't wait, could she? I bet David was her sole topic of conversation.'

'Who is he?'

She answered without turning her head. 'The boy next door. We grew up together. He's also a gymnast, part of the reason I got started, I suppose. We joined the same club, trained together, that sort of thing. He captained the British team in Vancouver.'

I cared nothing for his athletic achievements. I forced myself to ask, 'And you and him?'

'Have been going to get married ever since I was four.'

The words fell like a ton of bricks. The car ran on through country lanes dappled with sunshine. It was another glorious day, all that I'd hoped for, except that excitement had turned to bleak disappointment.

Julia threw me a sideways glance. 'There's no need to scowl. After all, you and I are only looking at houses.'

'Sure,' I agreed sarcastically.

It wasn't true. We weren't *only looking at houses*. At least, it wasn't true of me and enough had happened for me to hope it wasn't true of Julia. In four weeks something magical had developed between us; we laughed at the same things, enjoyed the same food, read the same books, listened to the same music. We even looked for the same features in houses, we hadn't seen one property without agreeing about how to convert it – extend a kitchen, heighten a wall, improve the bathroom – that sort of thing. Everyone we met took us for a young married couple. I remember one old man saying, 'This village could do with more young people like you.' And Julia had smiled like a radiant bride. Dammit, we weren't only looking at houses!

When we reached Pewsey, we viewed the property I had arranged to see in almost total silence, avoiding each other's eyes while responding politely to the owners. Afterwards, grim-faced, I drove to the Red Lion at Ramsbury where I had booked a table for lunch. As soon as we arrived I went to the bar. 'Beer?' I asked Julia, offering her no choice in the matter. She nodded and went to sit at a corner table. I carried the glasses over.

'You're not being very fair,' she protested as I sat down.

'Bloody hell! You might have told me –'

'I tried. I was going to tell you last night –'

'I feel such a fool.'

'Why?'

Instead of answering, I took a long pull at my pint.

She regarded me with a mixture of pain and resentment.

'I didn't know it would lead to this. I was only helping you to find a house ... I've enjoyed it ... the subject of David never came up –'

'Oh sure,' I sneered. 'You forgot all about him.' Knowing I was behaving badly made me more bloody-minded than ever. 'I suppose next weekend you'll be looking at houses in Aldershot? Or is he taking you back to Germany with him?'

She flushed. Had she walked out there and then it would have been all I deserved. Instead she contemplated the table for a long moment, before raising her

eyes to meet mine. 'I'll explain if you like, if not . . .'
She picked up her purse.

'No,' I said sharply, before adding more quietly, 'It
was a shock, that's all. Now I know where I stand . . .'
I shrugged and left the sentence unfinished.

Julia's lips compressed to a thin line and we exchanged looks, mine sulky and hers slightly bewildered. Then, ignoring my truculent expression, she
told me about herself and David Watson.

As the photographs had suggested, he was two
years older than her. The Watsons and the Lovells
were friends as well as neighbours, always in and out
of each other's homes, holidaying together, that sort
of thing. The gymnastics had started with a garden
trampoline. 'David was given one for his fifth birthday, so I had to have one too.' To begin with Julia had
simply copied him, determined to equal his daring.
Then rivalry had developed between them, until they
acknowledged their respective skills, and from then
on they had competed against others. Ultimately
they had represented their clubs, Wiltshire, and
Great Britain. 'We were always together,' Julia said,
'until he went into the Army.'

'What happened then?'

She sighed and ran a hand through her hair. 'There
was a lot of talk about getting married. I was nineteen
and he was twenty-one. Everyone said it was the
right time. Then my father was killed and things
ground to a halt.'

'Why?'

A look of pain crossed her face. She stared out of
the window. 'I think I realised I'd been going to marry
to please my father. He'd always been David's biggest
fan. Suddenly he wasn't there, selling me on the idea.

I took another look and decided I wanted more time.'

'Four years?' I exclaimed.

Silently, she bent her head and toyed with her glass.

'What's his view on all this?' I asked.

'He keeps asking me to marry him.'

'And you keep saying no?'

'Worse in a way. I keep saying not yet.'

'Why?'

Again she bent her head over the table, making it difficult for me to see her expression. Finally, in a low voice she said, 'If I could answer that, I don't suppose I'd be here.'

My hopes revived. Excitement surged and my earlier dismay receded, brightening my mood considerably, certainly enough for me to stop sulking. Finishing our drinks, we went in to lunch, and during the meal I delved further. Gradually I established what I was up against. David had always been there. He and Julia were well known local 'personalities'; when they had returned from the Commonwealth Games, each clutching a medal, the Mayor had honoured them with a civic reception; their pictures had been all over the papers. In the main they shared the same friends, all of whom expected them to marry. The Watsons expected them to marry, Mrs Lovell expected them to marry, John Lovell expected them to marry. In David's absence, his friends invited Julia out now and then, but very much as escorts who looked after David's interests; no one ever asked her out on a serious date. It had taken me, an outsider, to do that.

'Any day now I'll be run out of town,' I said gloomily.

Julia smiled. 'There have been rumblings. The Watsons have been on to Mother, Mother has spoken to John.' She met my astonished look with a shrug. 'Sorry, but you know how people are in the provinces.'

We recaptured some of our closeness over lunch, and my mood had improved by the time we left the Red Lion. Even so, as we set off for Marlborough it was hard not to panic. Until then I'd imagined that Julia and I had all the time in the world; we could just go on getting to know each other better and better. I already knew her well enough to know I wanted to keep her. In my mind the houses we looked at were for us, not for me. I'd imagined us putting up shelves, decorating, fixing the place up until it suited us both . . .

And Julia acted the same way. For instance, as we drove off after viewing the first house in Marlborough, she turned to me, her arm along the back of the seat and her hand on my shoulder. 'Now *that* was a possible, don't you think?'

But my mind was elsewhere. 'Suppose he asks you again?'

'Who? Asks what —?'

'Asks you to marry him.'

'Oh, Peter, don't be so boring. I was talking about —'

'But suppose he asks you?'

'He does have a name,' she said sharply.

I stopped at a road junction. My fingers drummed on the wheel. I'd lost interest in looking at houses. 'Let's find a cup of tea somewhere and talk this out.'

'There's nothing to talk out,' Julia said, more sharply than ever. 'Besides, you've an appointment.

These people have turned their Sunday upside-down to show you their house, the least you can do is see it.'

We had reverted to our behaviour in the bar, with me playing the petulant schoolboy and Julia the long-suffering schoolmistress. It was my fault, I couldn't leave the subject alone. After consulting the map, I took the road to the left. 'If you were going to marry him, you'd have said yes ages ago.'

It was the final straw. Slapping the dashboard, Julia exploded, 'Blast you, Peter. Will you shut up!'

'Why bother to see him? Where's the sense –'

'Stop the car. You go and look at this bloody house. I've had enough.'

Pink-faced and boiling, she was not far from tears. I drove on without attempting to stop, but thankfully I had enough sense to shut my mouth on the subject. Even so we were still tense and silent when we arrived at the house; I don't know what would have happened if we hadn't had that appointment. I think Julia would have demanded to go home, and had that happened, things might have been all over between us. Luckily, other people rescued the situation. The need to be courteous to strangers made us at least polite to each other, and the owner of the house, a funny little man in a shapeless brown sweater and baggy green trousers, was full of such abundant good humour that we accepted his offer of a cup of tea. Consequently by the time we left, our good humour had returned. Not that the relationship was as it was before: it could never be that. We had crossed some sort of threshold, and we were both shaken.

Returning to Swindon, Julia refused my offer of dinner, but at least she stopped off at my hotel for a drink. In a quiet corner of the bar, we began to assess what had happened. Julia said, 'I would have told you about David today anyway. I was determined to.'

I tried to respond lightly. 'You would have had to. I planned to ask you on another expedition next weekend.'

She gave me such a searching look that she might have been seeing me for the first time. 'So we find you a house,' she said. 'What happens then?'

I wanted to tell her of my earlier thoughts, of the house being for us, not for me, but I lost my nerve. 'I don't know,' I shrugged. 'What would you like to happen?'

She shook her head and looked away. When she spoke she sounded faintly astonished. 'I've only known you five minutes. I've known David my whole life.'

'I'm only asking for equal time,' I said.

Julia saw the absurdity of my words before I did. Her lips puckered and she started to giggle. 'I'm twenty-four. If you have equal time I'll be forty-eight. You'll have lost interest.'

And I laughed and she laughed and the tension evaporated. I thought she might change her mind about dinner, but she shook her head. 'No,' she smiled, getting up, 'I'm going home to straighten myself out. Right now I don't know if I'm on my head or my heels.'

The best I got was a promise to have dinner on Tuesday, three nights before she went to Aldershot.

It threatened to be a very worrying week.

Next morning, the radio in my room woke me to the sound of Nick Berkley singing 'Broken Promises'. His voice was exactly as I'd heard it at Whitegates; shy and undramatic, but full of sincerity. The disc jockey fairly bubbled with praise, talking about an exciting new talent – 'with "Broken Promises" now riding five in the charts'.

I was pleased for Nick, pleased enough to stop worrying about Julia for a minute or so. But it all came back to me as I was shaving, and I was in an anxious mood when I left for the office.

John Lovell had a word with me before I'd finished opening my post. 'I hear you've been seeing a good deal of my niece,' he said. 'You do know she's engaged, don't you?'

I could have said Julia wasn't *officially* engaged, on the other hand, I thought it best to hear what was on his mind, so I bit my tongue and regarded him with an attentive expression.

'Julia . . . and her mother,' he began awkwardly, becoming embarrassed, 'the fact is they rely on me for advice, ever since poor Harry was killed. Naturally, I take a keen interest, and . . . um, well, I thought I'd just mention Julia's engagement. Nice young chap, you'd like him. Champion gymnast, you know. Friend of the family and all that.'

'Ah,' I nodded my understanding. Even so, I'd heard enough. Glancing at my desk, I picked up the nearest papers to hand. 'By the way, John, could we have a word about this . . .?'

So I changed the subject, quite neatly, I thought – except John's point had been made; he was warning me off.

I said as much to Julia the following night over dinner. 'I sense people conspiring against me.'

'More than you know,' she answered with a troubled look. 'The Watsons were waiting when I got home on Sunday. Mother invited them to supper.'

'Cosy.'

'Embarrassing. They'd obviously been discussing me. They were full of questions about what sort of day I'd had, how many houses did we see –'

'None of their bloody business.'

'Well . . .' She hesitated. 'To be fair that's not strictly true. They've a right to be concerned, I suppose.'

In no mood to be fair to the Watsons, I tried to turn Julia's answer to my advantage. 'Do they have reason for concern?'

She avoided my eye. 'They obviously think so.'

'But what do you think?'

'I think,' she said, moving her hand to avoid mine as I reached over the table, 'that we ought to change the subject.'

'No –'

'Yes,' she insisted.

I disagreed. I sensed she was about to make a decision about the future and I wanted my say on the subject. Besides, I could think of nothing else. Usually conversation flowed easily between us, topics followed each other in rapid succession, but now one single thought dominated my mind: Julia was going away on Friday. It was a regular date, every three months he got a weekend at Aldershot and Julia went down to join him. Images kept forming and re-forming in my brain. I saw them arrive at a small country hotel, watched him take her arm and lead her off to their room . . .

Finally I came right out and said it. 'I don't want you to go on Friday.'

'Peter, please –'

'It has to be said. I don't want you to go. You know I don't –'

'I can't *not* go. The arrangement was made ages ago, before I met you –'

'I don't care.'

Julia looked wounded and hurt. 'Let's talk about something else,' she begged.

'Such as?' I asked, without bothering to conceal the sarcasm. 'We could talk about the weather, I suppose,' I continued, and would have grumbled on but for the look in her eyes. 'Okay,' I sighed, 'I'll think of something in a minute.

And I did. Searching for a neutral topic, I plunged into a story about Jack, drawn from our boyhood. I'm not sure what brought it to mind – AIDA, I think. I'd been asking myself what Jack would do in my situation. Jack would devise an elaborate scheme, he always did. So for the next half-hour I talked about Jack and Ann and the comings and goings at Whitegates. Naturally, I had told Julia about Jack before, but now the whole lot came out – about how we'd met Ann, how Jack had planned AIDA, I even remembered the different stages – Attention, Interest, Desire, Action. Maybe I should have kept it to myself; after all, it was Jack's business, nothing to do with Julia; but she looked miserable enough to make me want to make her laugh. I even told her about the torch I'd once carried for Ann. 'These things happen when you're growing up,' I said, trying to draw a comparison between her and her soldier.

'Oh?' Her lips twitched into a smile. 'I had no idea you were so experienced.'

At least it had got her laughing again, even if she did have reservations about Jack. 'He sounds a very determined character –'

'Oh, nothing defeats Jack,' I said airily. 'He's one of those people –'

'I meant, I'm not sure I'd like him –'

'Sure you would. And Ann. Everyone likes Ann.'

And so we continued, talking about everything under the sun except what was most on our minds. It was so unlike us. Our past conversations had always been so spontaneous. Yet for the rest of the evening we probed each other's thoughts with unsmiling eyes . . .

When I returned to the hotel, there was a message to say Ann had telephoned. I was glad it was too late to call back. I remembered our last conversation, with its underlying sense of insecurity and unhappiness. I was in the wrong mood to listen to more of the same, and unhappy enough with my own problems.

I had a bad night, tossing and turning, unable to find sleep. The more I worried about Julia, the more depressed I became. I even heard my father's mocking voice, echoing down over the years, 'You won't fight. You're a loser. You lose at this, you lose at that . . .'

'I won't lose Julia,' I vowed, more with bravado than conviction. But I needed more time. Except time had run out. Julia was going on Friday . . .

I was awake most of the night, driving myself mad. I even tried to talk myself out of it by telling myself I'd only known Julia five minutes. 'You don't really *know* her at all. How can you? It's only five weeks since you met her. Let her go off with her soldier, there are plenty more fish in the sea . . .'

None of it worked. I wanted Julia. She was right for me and I honestly thought I was right for her . . .

I racked my brains, thinking of AIDA and knowing such schemes were beyond me – where Jack could succeed, I knew I would fail. My brain simply didn't function that way. Besides, there was no time even for AIDA. Julia was leaving on Friday. Bert's words came to mind. 'Pop the question,' he had chortled. 'It works every time.' Did it? It hadn't worked for this fellow David, he'd been asking Julia to marry him for five years.

I suppose I had already been thinking of marriage, but until then it had been a gradual thing. Get the house, settle in at the office, become established, complete every step in an orderly manner. How else would old stick-in-the-mud Peter Mortlake conduct his affairs? Junior partners in firms of solicitors are not renowned for impulsive actions . . .

But on Friday she was going away.

By daybreak I had made up my mind. I remember lecturing myself as I shaved. 'If you've something to say, come out and say it.'

I bought the engagement ring on the way to the office. Crazy, really; I hadn't bought Julia as much as a bunch of flowers, and there I was buying a ring. As soon as I reached my desk I telephoned her at the school, only to be told she was taking a class. Consequently I fretted and fumed all morning, it was midday before she called back, and even then it was to decline my suggestion of a meeting that evening.

'Oh, Peter, I'm sorry. John's coming round to supper and I promised Mother . . .'

I cursed John Lovell under my breath. 'Tomorrow night?'

When Julia hesitated I was sure she had decided against seeing me again.

'Well . . .' she said finally, sounding doubtful, 'if you promise not to argue about the weekend.'

I promised, without being very sure of keeping my word. Then I booked a table at a restaurant at Lechlade, more for its romantic ambience than for its cuisine.

In the event, the food was quite good. Not that either of us ate much, and we were both quieter than usual. I was nervous about what I planned to say, and Julia was still recovering from the previous evening with John and her mother. 'It was a walk down memory lane,' she said with a wry smile. 'Out came all the old photographs, David and me winning our county medals, the pair of us at our first International. Then the Watsons joined us for coffee.'

'Very subtle,' I said, trying to sound sympathetic.

It lessened my confidence to know the world was against me. I needed all the help I could get.

After dinner, leaving the car outside the restaurant, I walked Julia off along the river. Dinner had gone well, but from then on everything went wrong. The plan called for a soft moonlit night, and there had been plenty until then. The weather had been glorious for weeks. It was my luck that it broke that night of all nights; we hadn't walked fifty yards before the rising breeze sent low clouds scudding across a black sky, shrouding the towpath in darkness. Clutching my arm, Julia yelped in dismay. 'Peter, we'll fall in the river if you're not careful. What are we doing?'

I only had the one plan, there was no Plan B for emergencies; I had the one plan and one night in which to implement it. So we stumbled on while I described in glowing terms my prospects at Weston, Lovell, Mortlake and Juffs. Then the rain started. This wasn't ordinary rain; the heavens opened and unleashed a tropical downpour. Separated from the car by two hundred yards of open river bank, I pulled Julia under the shelter of a solitary tree. Within seconds we were soaked to the skin – but I could only think of the words I'd prepared. I remember saying, '. . . as well as my salary, I get a share of the profits.' My teeth were chattering in the icy wind. The rain lashed down. Julia trembled and I drew her close, thinking she was shivering with cold until I realised she was shaking with laughter. 'Oh, Peter, is this your "My intentions are honourable" speech?'

'Well –'

'Don't you think I know you by now?'

'Yes, but –'

'I'm like a drowned rat.'

She was too. We both were. But by then I'd managed to extract the jeweller's box from my pocket and nothing could divert me. The clouds parted and a shaft of moonlight caught the small diamonds set in the gold band. Julia's laughter died. 'Oh, Peter.' The rain beat down and I cleared my throat, phrasing the words in my mind. Then Julia's fingers closed over mine, shutting the box in my hand. She raised her lips to mine and kissed me gently before pushing me away. 'Give me this weekend,' she said huskily. 'I'll know my own mind by Monday.'

As I began to argue, she slipped from my arms. 'Come on, before we get washed away!' she cried, and the next moment she was running back to the car, with me sloshing along behind her, sliding and slipping in the mud. Rain whipped into my face as I ran, leaving me breathless as I reached the car to wrench open the doors. We flung ourselves in, panting and gasping. 'It's freezing,' Julia complained through chattering teeth.

There was nothing for it but to drive her home. Her hair was plastered over her scalp, water ran down her back, her clothes were sodden and she was shaking with cold. And I was equally soaked.

We were half-way to her place before we felt the first warmth from the heater. Meanwhile we squelched in our clothes, steam misted the windows, and the wipers beat frantically to keep pace with the rain.

Then, thank God, Julia started to laugh. Her hand reached over to caress the back of my neck. 'Oh, Peter . . .'

And I laughed as well, though not so much that I forgot what was most on my mind. 'You could phone him. You needn't actually go to Aldershot –'

'You promised,' she said, her hand sliding round over my mouth.

By then we were turning into the drive to her house, and slowing to a halt at the foot of the steps.

'Monday,' said Julia, kissing me swiftly as she opened the door. 'I'll call you, okay?'

'But what –'

She ran up the steps as her mother opened the door.

I faced the longest weekend of my life. How do you fill ninety-six hours? My only thought was of Julia saying, 'I'll know my own mind by Monday.' Meanwhile our future hung in the balance.

Friday dragged. Knowing Julia was at the school until lunchtime made it worse – I wanted to get into the car and go up to see her. And the afternoon was made impossible by the thought of her on her way to Aldershot. In the evening I drove over to Bristol to see Jumbo. He showed me the new offices and took me to a cricket club for a few beers, after which we dined on a hot curry in a Tandoori restaurant and I drove back to Swindon – all the time imagining Julia with her soldier.

When Saturday dawned, I lacked the appetite for house-hunting. Instead I strolled over to the office, opened the post and messed about for an hour. Then I returned to the hotel and read the paper from cover to cover. At twelve o'clock I went out to the yard and cleaned the car. Then I went up to my room to sort out my laundry . . .

The phone rang. It was Ann, first to complain about me not returning her call, then to invite me to a party that night. 'Bring your new friend,' she suggested. 'We're anxious to meet her.'

Nothing would have pleased me more; but even without Julia, the prospect of a party was seductive. At least it would give me something to do, something to think about, people to talk to . . .

Ann's only problem was accommodation. Nick

Berkley was still living in the cottage and Janie and Mike were spending the night in the second bedroom. 'As for the rest of the house . . .' She hesitated before dismissing the problem. 'Don't worry, if you decide to stay, we'll find you a corner.'

So I went to the party, or to be accurate, I *nearly* went. Certainly I drove over to Whitegates that evening. I messed about at the hotel until past eight o'clock, to avoid arriving too early, and reached Whitegates at about nine-thirty. There was no mistaking Jack's party. The house was a blaze of lights and enough cars littered the drive for it to resemble a used car lot for the wealthy; I counted two Rollers, one Porsche, four Jaguars and half a dozen Mercedes. Tiny was acting as car park attendant and arranging them in some sort of order. After a condescending look at my Ford, he peered in the window. 'Why if it ain't Peter Mortlake from Taunton.' I sighed at his heavy-handed attempt at humour. Tiny and I would never get on; for some reason, the words we had exchanged at our first meeting still rankled with him. Even so, I resented his sneer. 'Swindon,' I said. 'It's Peter Mortlake from Swindon.' Which puzzled him long enough for me to get out and give him the key. Then his face brightened. 'Ah,' he said, 'I get it. Changed our name again, have we?'

I left him and walked up to the house. The open front doors revealed a dozen people milling around, and I was delighted to see Janie among them. I quickened my step. Most of the people in Jack's circle would be strangers to me, but Janie and Mike were old friends; and there was Janie in the hall, wearing a low-cut green dress and looking about her as if she were lost. I called as I climbed the steps, 'Janie!' She

316

turned and looked at me without the least sign of recognition. Then the glazed look lifted from her eyes. 'Peter?' Her face brightened, 'Is that really you? Oh, Peter, it's been ages.' As she came into my arms to hug me, she staggered slightly. I gripped her elbow to support her. 'You okay?'

'A bit stoned,' she admitted. Swaying slightly, she craned her neck to look over my shoulder. 'I was making for the cottage. Give me a hand, will you.'

Helping her down the steps, I led her along the side of the house. We had only walked a few yards when she stopped and drew a deep breath. 'Get a load of that air,' she said. 'You get stoned just breathing in the house. All I had were two drags on Mike's joint . . .' She tightened her grip on my arm to stay upright. 'Christ, I feel awful.'

I got her to the cottage by encouraging her every step of the way. 'You're doing fine –'

'It comes and goes,' she said, clinging to my arm, 'know what I mean? One minute I'm okay . . .' She broke off as she reached the door. 'I'll be all right if you stay with me. Will you? Just for a while.'

'Sure.'

After I steered her over the threshold and switched on the lights, she released my arm and wobbled across to the sofa, where she collapsed into an inelegant heap.

'Oh boy,' she muttered, 'I hate these bloody evenings at Jack's.' She sat with her head in her hands for a moment, then she kicked off her shoes and swung her legs on to the couch. 'I'm not going back,' she said, raising a hand to shield her eyes from the light. 'Jack can scream and holler as much as he likes. I've had it tonight.'

'You'll feel better soon,' I encouraged.

'Maybe,' she agreed, squinting at me. 'The room's stopped spinning, that's always a good sign. I'll throw up in a minute, then I'll come back to life.' She managed a weak smile as she re-arranged herself on the couch, as if trying to get comfortable. The attempt must have failed because the next moment she swung her feet back to the floor and sat upright. 'Ugh! I shouldn't bounce around like that,' she said, rising unsteadily to her feet.

I took a step closer and held out a hand, but she turned away to fumble with the clasp at the back of her dress. 'Blasted thing, I can never do it by myself. Give me a hand, will you. Mustn't be sick over my party frock, Jack wouldn't like it.'

The hook and eye met just beneath her shoulder blades. I released the fastening and eased the zip down an inch.

'Thanks,' she said, holding the bodice as she edged past me to the bathroom. 'I won't be a minute.'

'I'll make some coffee,' I said and went to the kitchen. Sounds of Janie retching came through the wall. Searching the cupboards, I soon found some coffee, and after filling the percolator I took a can of beer from the fridge and went to the bathroom door. 'You all right?' For answer I heard the WC being flushed and the sound of water as it gushed into the sink. Returning to the sitting room, I sat down to wait. A few moments later the bathroom door opened and Janie plodded down the corridor in stocking feet. Going into the second bedroom, she was gone for a minute before emerging in a black dressing-gown and clutching a pink flannel to her temple. 'Touch and go,' she said with a wan smile, 'but I'll survive.'

She still looked unwell. Janie could never be described as beautiful; what made men look twice was her bubbly personality and her smile. Nobody was immune to her smile, an illuminated sign couldn't better convey her sunny nature and generous spirit. But at that moment, without a smile on her face, she looked woebegone and ill. As she crossed the room to the chair next to the hearth, she caught my look of concern. 'Don't look so worried. You always look worried. Why's that?'

'Right now I'm worried about you.'

'Don't. I'll be all right. I'm cold, that's all. Aren't you cold? I'm freezing in here.'

I was warm enough, but Janie shivered and drew the robe more tightly about her. Kneeling at the hearth, I put a match to the gas fire, which popped and hissed into life. Then I crossed the room and drew the curtains. 'Coffee will be ready soon,' I said as I returned to the other chair in front of the fire. With the curtains drawn and the gas fire burning, the room looked somewhat more cosy. It had been re-arranged since my last visit. An upright piano stood against the far wall and a stack of annotated paper was heaped on a side table.

Janie followed my gaze. 'Boy Mozart's studio,' she said drily. 'Have you met him yet?'

'Nick? Yes, months ago, when he first —'

'He's not a bad kid,' she interrupted with a faint shrug.

I grinned. 'You sound like a grandmother.'

'I *feel* like a grandmother,' she replied, still holding the flannel to her temple. 'Still, it's good to see you. What are you doing here anyway? You're free, white and over twenty-one, you don't have to be in this snake pit.'

'It's a party, isn't it?'

'At Whitegates?' She laughed derisively, her voice sounding brittle against the distant beat of music from up at the house. 'It might be a party for you. It's a Command Performance for the rest of us.'

There was no mistaking her bitterness. I remained silent for a moment, taking my cigarettes from my pocket. After offering her one, which she declined, I lighted one for myself. Finally I said, 'Command Performance makes it sound as if you're having trouble with Jack.'

She shrugged. 'So what's new?' she asked bleakly, wrapping her arms around herself and rubbing her shoulders, as if still cold.

'I'll get the coffee,' I said.

The coffee was just about ready when I went into the kitchen. I poured two cups, and when I returned to the sitting room Janie was staring into the fire. 'Know what?' she asked with a sad smile. 'Gas fires always remind me of your old flat in Whitcombe Street. Remember?'

I smiled and set her coffee down within reach.

'All those years ago,' she said wistfully, 'it was fun then. Sometimes I look back and wonder how it all got so ugly.'

Ugly seemed an odd word from her. Everything about Janie's life was glamorous, her public appearances, her clothes, she was always smiling, her laughing face adorned a million record sleeves. Except, at that moment she was far from laughing; wrapped in the black robe, staring into the fire, she looked sad and defeated.

'Things were different then,' she continued, as if musing to herself. 'Times change, I guess. People change. Now they don't even want our sort of music –'

'Nonsense –'

'Ask Jack,' she said, looking up quickly, her eyes suddenly brighter. 'Know what he said tonight? I'll tell you. He wants singers who make little girls wet themselves. "I gotta walk in and smell their piss on the floor." That's what he said.' She looked at me, as if challenging me to contradict her, then she tossed the flannel aside and fumbled through the folds of her dressing-gown. 'I will have a cigarette after all,' she said. 'A proper one, I mean.'

Her hands trembled as she accepted it. 'Thanks,' she said, taking a deep drag. For a moment she was silent, then, in a soft voice, she continued, 'He's a bastard at times. You know, everyone's there, and that's what he says, in front of everyone. I don't know why I let him get to me, except I'm frightened. Maybe he's right. Maybe I am over the hill –'

'Rubbish.'

'Really?' Again she fixed me with that hard, challenging look. 'When did you last go to a pop concert? They're not concerts any more. They're events, happenings. You don't play a guitar these days, you smash it to bits. Anything to whip the kids into a frenzy. It's true, they do piss on the floor. Get The Stones, The Animals, The Tower, girls go berserk. They come backstage after and the boys fuck their brains out . . .' Her voice broke and she bent forward to hide her face in her hands.

I went over and sat on the arm of her chair. Resting a hand on her shoulder, I took the cigarette from her trembling hand and stubbed it out. I was a bit lost as to what to do next. Like most men faced with a woman's tears, I was reduced to a feeling of helplessness, of lacking the right words to provide comfort. All I could do was to sit patting Janie's shoulder and hoping to God that no one would choose that moment to come through the door.

Thankfully, she recovered fairly quickly, snuffling into a handkerchief and blowing her nose before taking herself off to the bathroom. She came back smelling of soap and looking fresh faced, if somewhat watery-eyed. I made her drink some coffee, and supplied her with a replacement cigarette.

'Sorry about that,' she apologised. 'I didn't mean to unload on you —'

'Forget it.'

Taking a deep breath, she held it for a minute, then exhaled slowly. 'I'm okay now,' she said with a rueful smile. 'It was partly your fault. Seeing you again reminded me. Remember us opening at the Stork Club? Wasn't that great?'

'Great,' I agreed.

The brief glow faded from her face. 'Those were the good old days. Things are different now —'

'Why? Because Jack's in a bad mood? Come on, he'll be all over you tomorrow, you know that. And what about Ann? She's always been your number one fan.'

Instead of answering, Janie regarded me for a long moment with serious eyes. 'You still got a thing about her?'

Taken by surprise, I spooned sugar into my coffee and tried to think of what to say. Finally, awkwardly, I countered, 'I didn't think anyone knew about that.'

'Everyone knew about that.'

'Oh,' I said, feeling foolish.

A shadowy smile touched her lips. 'Mike and I had a bet about who she'd go for, you or Jack.'

My face muscles stiffened with embarrassment. How strange that an infatuation which no longer meant anything to me should be remembered by others. 'I see,' I said uncomfortably. 'Who won?'

'You did if you got her out of your system.'

Her response was so unexpected that surprise overcame my embarrassment. 'She's still a friend,' I said, 'and I thought you two were –'

'Bosom pals? So did I once. These days . . .' Janie shrugged. 'Like I said, everything's changed. Anyway, you avoided the question.'

'About getting Ann out of my system? Of course I did.' I laughed nervously. 'It was a long time ago. We all act a bit daft now and then.'

Janie continued to stare until I felt obliged to add, 'It's just that, well . . . I thought no one knew. I mean, what about Ann? Did she know?'

'Do you think she didn't? Of course she knew. And Jack. He used to joke about it.'

It was a bad moment. The thought of Jack sneering behind my back was depressing, a betrayal. I wondered if Ann had shared his amusement. I shrugged with a pretence of indifference.

Janie reached for her cup. 'Do you mind if I ask you something? How come you and Jack became friends? How come you *stayed* friends? He's such a shit –'

'Oh, come on. He's difficult at times, I admit, but there are some good things about him. He was a good friend to me once. And take you, he did get you started. You just mentioned the Stork Club.'

'So I should go down on my knees?' Janie responded angrily. 'We started him too, remember? It was a two way street. We were the first on his books. Without us he wouldn't have any of this . . .' she waved a hand round the room as if to include all of Whitegates.

'What gets me,' she continued, 'is his disloyalty. He's not pushing us. All he talks about is Dai and The Tower, and now this kid. He fobs me off all the time. Okay, Dai and The Tower are big box-office, but we've still got a name. Honestly, he could get us plenty of gigs if he tried –'

'What about Ann? Surely she –'

'He doesn't listen to her any more. He doesn't take a blind bit of notice.' Janie shook her head. 'It's not like the old days. These days it's all Jack. Jack the Great I Am, King Jack, Jack the Star-Maker. Ann's opinion counts for nothing.' Concluding with a defeated shake of her head, Janie shrugged, 'Besides, Jack can always shut her up when he wants to.'

'Oh? How?'

'I don't know. Something that happened to her in the States. They were having a row once and Jack turned round and said, "You proved what your opinion's worth back in New York." And Ann went deathly white and shut up like a clam.'

Surprised and intrigued, I waited for her to continue.

'That's all I know,' she said. 'Except Ann's got a thing about New York. Remember when we toured the States? I was sure she'd come with us; you know, go back to New York in triumph, all that stuff. But no way. Annie wouldn't go within three thousand miles of the place. I pleaded with her, I kept saying, "Come on, you know all the clubs, you know the people, we'll have fun." But nothing. Mike got really suspicious. "What's she hiding?" he kept asking. Remember at the beginning? How she was going back until she got involved with Jack, and we had to persuade her to stay? Well one day it all came out. She was *never* going back to New York, she was going to be a music teacher in some school in Kansas.'

Vague memories stirred, but none were relevant to Janie.

'I'm sorry,' she said. 'I'm not having a go at Ann. It's just that she can't help us these days. Meanwhile a year's gone by since our last album —'

'She seems to be helping Nick Berkley,' I said. 'I was here the day Ann invited him to stay at the cottage. She and Jack seemed in agreement then —'

'So long as it suits Jack. If Jack wants it too, that's fine. But if Jack's got other ideas, forget it.'

I felt depressed. Coming to the party had seemed a good idea; it would take my mind off Julia and what was happening in Aldershot. And momentarily, I suppose, it had, but seeing Janie's wretchedness had not improved my spirits.

'Well,' I said, trying to find something reassuring to say, 'I suppose if the worst comes to the worst, you could always get another manager.'

Janie's eyes rounded with surprise. 'You think so? It's not that easy. Jack's not just our manager, he's our publisher, our record company, everything rolled into one. You've no idea of the complications. Even if we tried, we couldn't deal with anyone else.'

For the second time that evening, I was reminded of the Stork Club. I remembered Jack in the lobby, saying, 'I own them,' as his hand closed into a fist, 'I own them, Tubby, I *own* them!'

'Peter?'

I looked up. 'You shuddered,' Janie said with a shadow of her real smile. 'Sorry, I didn't mean to depress you.' She glanced at her watch. 'How long have I been here? I'd better get back.'

To my surprise it was almost eleven. We had been in the cottage for over an hour. 'You said you weren't going back earlier –'

'Earlier I was dying. You saved my life.' Swallowing the remains of her coffee, Janie gave me a brave smile. 'I've got to get back, I've a husband to care for.'

'A husband?' I looked at her in astonishment.

She responded with her first genuinely happy look of the evening. 'Mike and I got married eight months ago –'

'I didn't know.'

'Nobody knows. Jack insisted we keep it secret. Marriage is bad news in our business, according to him. He stopped us before, but finally we insisted. He didn't like it. I guess that's why we're being given the treatment; we're being punished for being so wilful.'

I shook my head in mute astonishment.

She stood up. 'Give me ten minutes and we'll go up to the house. God knows what Mike's doing, probably snorting coke with the rest of the boys.'

'You're joking?'

'Think so?' she asked laconically, raising her eyebrows before turning away.

I watched her go to her bedroom. Her remark about coke jolted me. I suppose I've got double standards on drugs. To be honest I've never seen much harm in smoking a joint; I smoke tobacco which most medical men say is more harmful. But hard drugs are something else.

I sat staring into the fire, thinking over what Janie had said. None of it sat easily in my mind. Jack the Great I Am. King Jack. Jack the Star-Maker. Dimly, from years before, I remembered Gill saying, 'Jack needs you to keep his feet on the ground. Ann's his ears and you're his best pal. If he keeps both of you, he's made. If he loses either of you, God help him.'

But it wasn't only Jack that I worried about. My thoughts turned to Ann, then to Janie, then to me, especially with the news of them snorting coke up at the house. I could see the headlines – 'SOLICITOR CAUGHT IN DRUGS BUST.' With a groan, I imagined John Lovell's reaction . . .

'How do I look?' Janie asked as she emerged from the bedroom. The answer was, transformed; having brushed her hair, applied her make-up, and, most of all, re-introduced her smile to her face, she looked every inch her old self. She turned and offered me her back, and dutifully I fastened the clasp.

'I'm going home,' I said, 'I'm not going back to the house.'

'But why?' she protested.

So I sat her down and explained about solicitors being Officers of the Court and what would happen if I were caught within a hundred miles of cocaine. Without telling any lies, I laid it on a bit thick, and I think she believed me.

Which is how I went to Whitegates without going to Jack's party. Janie and I walked over to the steps, gave each other a hug, and went our separate ways.

I drove back to Swindon, a bit bemused by events. Even now, I don't know if I did the right thing: would I have been better off at the party? At least Ann would have been there and I could have spent the time talking to her, it might have kept me from dwelling on Julia . . .

As it was, selfishly, as Maidenhead fell behind me so too did Janie's problems with Jack. My own problems with Julia surfaced with a vengeance. And when I got back to the hotel it was to find the landlord drinking after hours with some cronies. So I kept them company, boozing away until two in the morning, wondering what tomorrow would bring.

Going to bed late and full of booze seemed a good idea at the time; the prospect of spending another day worrying about Julia filled me with gloom, so the more of Sunday I slept through, the better. Such was the plan, if such negative thinking could ever be described as a plan . . .

But a few hours later the telephone rang. For the first moment of dazed consciousness, I imagined it was Monday, and that the Sunday had mercifully passed me by. I squinted at the clock on the bedside table. Ten-thirty. Daylight penetrating a gap in the curtains announced that it was morning. My mouth tasted foul and I felt tired and hung over. Gradually I realised it was not Monday but Sunday, and I cursed the hotel switchboard for calling the wrong room.

'Hello,' I muttered.

'Peter?'

It was Julia. I sat upright. 'Julia? Where are you?'

'Home. I got back yesterday evening. I did call you.'

My head cleared. Suddenly I was wide awake. 'You called yesterday? I thought you were away all weekend –'

'I couldn't last two days without looking at houses. What did you see yesterday? Anything good?'

Swinging my feet on to the floor, I nursed the telephone in disbelief. Why was she home? What did it mean?

'Did you see anything good?' she repeated.

'Er . . . no, not really. You see, I didn't go –'

'You didn't? Why not?'

'I dunno, it just seemed . . .' The word 'pointless' stuck in my throat. For a moment I was afraid to commit myself. She might have come home to pack, she might be going to Germany, anything could have happened . . .

'Peter, what's up with you? Mother's crying her eyes out, the Watsons are on their way over, John's at the door, and when I call you for help you won't even say a simple word like "pointless"!'

'You mean –'

'Say it!' she shouted angrily.

'Okay, okay.' I burst out laughing from sheer happiness. 'It seemed pointless.'

Only when Julia remained silent did I realise what she had said – about the Watsons being on their way over and John at the door. The tension in her voice was desperation.

'Julia?'

But she had hung up.

Sweat rose on my forehead. 'Hey, Julia!' I shouted. It took me ten minutes to wash and dress. I kept glancing at the phone, wondering if it would ring. The certainty that she would hang up on me kept me from calling her back. Instinct told me to get there. I ran down the stairs and out into the yard. Minutes later, I was edging the car out into the High Street. The sky was blue with another fine morning, church bells were ringing, but all I could hear was Julia's plea for help on the phone.

I blazed up the drive to her house, scattering gravel over the lawn before sliding the Ford to a halt a few yards from John's Daimler. Jumping out, I saw John through the drawing-room window, and beyond him, I could make out the blur of other figures and faces. John jerked his head in my direction, obviously announcing my arrival, and the next moment Julia opened the front door.

She looked no taller than the girls at her school, half waif, half woman, not so much beautiful as forlorn and alone. Relief lit her eyes and her wide mouth trembled with a shy smile of welcome. She remained silent when I reached her, so did I, yet I knew her feelings exactly. I remembered being harried by my father; I knew what it was like to resist and resist until all strength was gone and capitulation seemed inevitable . . . to be saved by that ring at the door.

By way of greeting she touched my arm, before turning away. I followed her into the hall, closing the front door behind me.

'Ah,' said a voice, as John Lovell appeared at the drawing room door. 'I thought it was you. You'd better come in.'

His tone was enough to tell me what Julia was up against – compared to my father, the people around her used velvet gloves, but they were just as manipulative. I could imagine them telling her what was, and what wasn't, for her own good. She had rebelled before by trusting her instincts and delaying her marriage, but the pressure ever since had been relentless. Few understood its insidious nature better than I did. Entering that room was to swim against a tide of hostility; resentful eyes met me wherever I looked.

'Now then,' said John, performing the introductions, 'Evelyn, this is Peter Mortlake.'

The Watsons were cool to the point of being uncivil. Neither of them offered their hand. Mrs Watson nodded an acknowledgement, while her husband said, 'Morning', in a brusque military voice.

Mrs Lovell rose from her chair, a reproachful look on her face. 'I'll get some more coffee,' she said as she passed me on her way to the kitchen.

Watson turned to me with a cold-eyed look. His interrogative gaze was equal to John's, so that to face them both put me in mind of a court martial. 'Just saying,' he coughed, clearing his throat, 'this business has come as a shock.'

'More than a shock,' exclaimed Mrs Watson. 'A bolt from the blue. That's why it's so hard to take. It's always been understood that David and Julia would marry. They nearly did four years ago. Should have. We'd have been spared all this nonsense then.'

She spoke to the room in general, directing her gaze at the mantelpiece. Like her husband beside her, she had a large body, big boned and well-upholstered. Both of them were grey haired, and their clothes – tweed skirt and twin set for her, check suit and brogues for him – suggested a comfortable, middle-class, ex-Army sort of life.

I was still finding a place to sit during these opening exchanges. Julia had taken one end of the sofa nearest the door, and I sat down beside her, leaving plenty of room between us.

John Lovell turned from his position in the bay window. 'This is nothing personal against you, Peter,' he began in the tones of an experienced and reasonable man, 'but you must understand we feel –'

'Disappointed,' I interrupted, seized by an urge to say something. 'Yes, I can understand. You all watched Julia and David grow up and you hoped they would marry.' Pausing, I lowered my voice in an effort to match his agreeable tone. 'But let's face it, John, the days of arranged marriages are over.'

'Well really!' exclaimed Mrs Watson, meeting my eye for the first time. 'That puts us in our place, I must say.'

'It wasn't meant to be rude,' I protested. 'I can understand your concern for Julia –'

'Good,' Watson interrupted, 'and as you've known her no time at all, and we've known her since her childhood, I think we're best qualified to advise her, don't you?'

Glancing at John, I hoped he might intervene with his more reasonable tone, but when he remained silent I was forced to say something. 'Surely it's not a matter of advice. It's what Julia wants –'

Mrs Watson interrupted. 'It's the deceit that gets me. Carrying on behind David's back –'

'I beg your pardon!' Julia gasped, blood rushing into her face. 'How dare you. I haven't been carrying on behind anyone's back. As for David, he knows it's all over. If he can accept it, why can't you?'

Before Mrs Watson could respond, Mrs Lovell returned with the coffee pot. 'Now Julia, you know the answer perfectly well. We *care* about you, darling. We can't stand by and let you ruin your life —'

'And I can't stand these endless conferences. Why involve other people all the time? Phoning John and getting him over —'

'Julia *please*,' Mrs Lovell implored as she sank into her chair. 'You know how I rely upon John. Ever since your dear father was killed —'

'Mother,' Julia interrupted in a cold fury, 'listen to me. I'm going out in a minute and I'm not coming back to face this . . . this Star Chamber ever again. I don't want to hurt you, but never again will you interfere in my private life —'

'Now Julia,' Watson cautioned her, 'don't say something you'll regret later.'

'My only regret is not saying it before,' Julia retorted over her shoulder. Still looking at her mother, she rose to her feet. 'I may not be home tonight,' she said, bending to bestow a placatory kiss upon Mrs Lovell's startled up-turned face. 'So don't wait up —'

'Not home? But where will you be?'

'With a friend. Don't worry, I shall be perfectly safe. I'll see you tomorrow.' She paused, long enough to look at me. 'Peter, shall we go?'

I needed no urging. Rising awkwardly, I followed her to the door, mumbling, 'Er, well . . . goodbye, everyone.'

Nobody answered. In the hall, Julia put a hand on my arm. 'Won't be a minute,' she said, and ran up the stairs.

Left to wait in the hall, I took my car keys from my pocket and bounced them in my hand, scarcely able to believe what had happened. Fidgeting with excitement, I peered at an oil painting over a side table, my attention on that until I realised that John Lovell had followed us out of the room. 'Peter,' he said, startling me, 'a word, if you please.'

I looked at him.

'I think it would have been best if you hadn't come here this morning.'

'Oh?'

'Yes,' he continued, drawing himself to his full height. 'I must say, as your senior partner –'

'No, John,' I interrupted. 'You are senior partner at the office, but we're not in the office now and this doesn't concern the firm. I suggest we leave it at that.'

There are times when I surprise myself. John was certainly surprised; he coloured slightly and a hard look came into his eyes, but before he could respond Julia ran down the stairs carrying an overnight bag. 'Bye, John,' she said, brushing past him to open the door.

As I turned to follow, John made a partial recovery. 'We'll talk more about this tomorrow,' he said.

I shrugged and left him glaring at my back as I hurried after Julia. Opening the car door, she flung the bag on to the back seat and settled herself in the front. As soon as I got in, she said, 'Go Peter, just let's get out of here.'

The edge to her voice was unmistakable, so was the tension in her face. The confrontation had stretched her nerves to the full. I drove out on to the road and headed back towards town without saying a word, giving Julia time to collect herself. Julia too remained silent. Then she surprised me by asking for a cigarette.

'You don't smoke –'

'Peter!'

I gave her a cigarette. The first puff brought tears to her eyes. When she recovered, she stubbed it out in the ashtray. Finally she exhaled a long sigh of relief. 'Sorry about involving you back there. Still, now it's over and done with, thank God.'

'Amen.'

'We can cross it off the agenda. No questions, no explanations, okay?'

There were dozens of questions I wanted to ask, but the time was wrong. Besides, the High Street had just loomed into view and I was wondering where to go next. Julia's unexpected phone call had caught me entirely without plans; we had no appointments to view houses, and I was considering alternatives when I remembered her telling her mother about staying the night with a friend. 'Where are you staying tonight?'

'Anywhere you care to take me,' she said lightly, 'except it had better not be Swindon. I don't want to bump into John over breakfast.'

And so began that marvellous summer. Julia and I were convinced that in finding each other we had found what we most wanted in life. Her mother was difficult and John was tetchy and awkward, but neither of them could spoil our contentment. 'They'll get over it,' we told ourselves. And we believed it, despite their continued opposition.

'With all due respect,' I told John the next morning at the office, 'it's none of your business.'

He went red in the face. 'How can you say that? My own family. Of course it's my business.'

He became difficult at the office, which isn't to say he'd been easy before. But where at the outset he had been enthusiastic about Weston, Lovell, Mortlake and Juffs – indeed, he had largely brought it about – he now gave every impression of resenting the partnership. 'Mr Mortlake is one of our junior partners,' he would say when introducing me to clients. Which was true, but by emphasising it so strongly he did little to help me get established.

Julia fared little better at home. Her mother dripped disapproval like a leaky tap. 'They'll get over it,' we said, firmly repeating what we believed.

Meanwhile I took Julia to Bristol to meet Jumbo, and to Taunton to show her off to Martin. 'She's terrific,' Martin whispered. 'Just what you need.'

Nobody had to tell me, I was convinced. So was Jumbo, who had been forming his own romantic attachments. 'We might even make it a triple wedding,' he grinned, 'with you, Martin and me all going under the hammer as a job lot.' When he heard about my difficulties with John Lovell, Jumbo was sympathetic. 'He'll get over it,' he said. 'Just give him time.'

Which coincided with Julia's opinion. 'Please Peter, be patient. They'll come round to the idea in a few months.' Squeezing my hand, she gave me a grin. 'Meanwhile I don't intend to live like a nun.'

We were discreet. Most Saturday nights found us staying at hotels in Hungerford or even further afield. These days things are different, we would live openly together; but then, in provincial England, the cries of outrage would have rung loud and clear; Julia would have been compelled to resign her teaching position, and as a young solicitor I would have been considered unsound. So we went away at weekends, and pretended to hoteliers that we were 'Mr and Mrs'.

One weekend we went up to town and took Mum and Bert out to dinner. They were enchanted by Julia, but on the Sunday, when we called in at Gill's for a drink, Gill was less than his gregarious self. 'What's up?' I asked when Julia went to the Ladies Room. Gill shrugged, looking embarrassed and awkward. 'She's very nice, Peter,' he said. 'I'm pleased for you, but, well . . . to tell you the truth, I'd always hoped that you and Ann . . .'

No matter that Ann was married, no matter how many times I told him to forget the idea, no matter that Julia was the best thing ever to happen to me . . . Gill persisted in his absurd dream.

We left shortly afterwards. I was determined not to give Gill the chance to say anything which might give Julia the wrong impression. 'See you in a few weeks,' I promised as we shook hands.

In fact more than a few weeks were to pass before I next saw Gill. Most of my time, when not at the office, was spent in looking at houses with Julia, and about a month later we found The Grove. I liked it the moment I saw it, but Julia was alarmed by the size. 'Peter, it's far larger than anything we've looked at before.'

True, but I was beginning to see myself as a family man with a need for bedrooms and playrooms and goodness knows what. My original cottage had been the equivalent of a countryman's bachelor pad, suitable at the time, but not for the future. Besides, to be honest, Jack's sneering condemnation of small cottages had rankled – it stuck in my mind. Although I told myself to ignore his opinion, somehow it still haunted me, and although nothing would ever tempt me to compete with Whitegates, the seed had been sown that I ought to do better.

So I was very taken with The Grove. Eight miles from the office in a small village, it lay back from the road in ten acres of paddock. 'Fine looking house,' I kept saying, blind to the loose slates on the roof and deaf to the warped boards which creaked underfoot. It was quite empty, the owners having gone abroad after entrusting local agents with the business of selling it.

'Mmm,' Julia murmured doubtfully as she followed me around.

'Ignore what it's like now. Imagine what we could make of it.' I pointed out the high ceilings, the wide staircase, the sweeping country views from the windows.

'The kitchen's appalling,' Julia complained in disgust.

'It's a good size. Can't you see it all fitted out with new cupboards and so on?'

Upstairs, Julia asked, 'Why on earth would we want six bedrooms?'

'Four,' I corrected, thumping a wall with my fist. 'Hear that? That's not a load-bearing wall. We'll knock that out and install a bathroom *en suite*. And we'll do the same over here.' I led the way across the landing, banging on walls as I went.

To the rear of the house were a barn and a stable block built at right angles, so that, with the house, they formed a splendid courtyard. Not that it looked splendid the first time we saw it; neglected and full of rubbish, with paint peeling from window surrounds, the area resembled a junkyard. But I saw it differently. In fact I could scarcely contain my excitement. 'Just imagine when we've replaced all the windows and doors. We can paint all the woodwork white and set tubs of plants all over the place . . .'

It got even better – the barn had a big timbered loft. 'Look at this,' I exclaimed, pulling Julia up the ladder after me. 'It's huge. We can convert this into a separate mews cottage for guests. We'll put in a proper staircase and have one bedroom here . . . and a bathroom over there . . .'

For me, the house had magic. The first time we saw it was on a Saturday morning and, after lunching at the local pub, we went back in the afternoon. It was a grey, wet day, and large brown puddles covered the drive. As we splashed our way from the car, Julia grumbled, 'Why call it The Grove? Bleak House is more appropriate.'

I told her to use her imagination – my own was working overtime. In my mind more than the house was being transformed; already the garden had been extended into the paddock. I saw sweeping lawns and a fish pond. 'We could even have a tennis court. And a swimming pool if you like.'

Julia stared in open disbelief. 'Has someone died and left you a fortune? All this will cost –'

'We'll do it gradually. Naturally, the main house comes first, the rest might take a few years. Think of the fun we'll have, imagine the satisfaction.'

It took me seven weeks to convince her. I was afraid another buyer would come along and buy The Grove while we dithered. Meanwhile a surveyor gave me the bad news about the roof, a plumbing engineer produced an estimate for central heating, and a builder costed the other alterations.

Julia grew alarmed at the expense. 'Darling, I know it will be lovely when it's finished, but wouldn't it be wiser to buy something smaller to start with?'

Of course it would have been wiser. My head said it would have been wiser, but my heart took not a blind bit of notice. Something happened to me over those weeks. Until then, it had never bothered me that Jack was a millionaire and that I was a comparative pauper. Content with my lot, I had never wanted more but John Lovell and Julia's mother had needled me by being so in favour of David Watson. The stupid thing was that they had no need to make unfavourable comparisons – I couldn't see what Julia saw in me either. David was an Olympic athlete, David was on the threshold of a glorious Army career, David was this, David was that – but for some miraculous reason, Julia preferred me. I was walking on air, I was light-headed. And for the first time in my life, I wanted to impress.

That was why I bought the MG. The old Ford lacked panache, it was dull, dependable and steady, just like Peter Mortlake. The time had arrived for me to aspire to something more dashing. I didn't tell Julia beforehand because I wanted to surprise her. The first time she saw the MG was when the gleaming red coupé growled to a halt outside her sports pavilion. Even then her students saw it first. 'Miss, Miss,' they shrieked, 'your boyfriend's got a new car.' By the time Julia arrived, I was surrounded by an admiring throng of fifteen-year-olds, all 'oohing' and 'aahing' and asking 'How fast does it go?'

That summer was the happiest of my whole life. Momentous events were happening around the world, but I was barely aware of them. Only the most dramatic impinged on my consciousness. Martin Luther King was assassinated in April, Robert Kennedy was murdered in June, America was in political turmoil. The facts registered without touching my life. Even the student revolution, which was in full flood all over the world – in Paris, in Chicago, in Washington, in London – seemed to have little to do with me. My aspirations were not theirs – where they preached revolution, I aspired to conventional middle-class success with a career, a fine house and a wife.

In fact that was the plan – to survive John's sniping at the office, to buy The Grove, to do it up, then to marry Julia the following Spring. And the plan moved a step forward in July, when my offer for The Grove was accepted. The cost was horrific. Even the first stage, that of renovating the main house, would incur a crippling mortgage, even though I planned to do some of the less skilled work myself, by toiling away at weekends and evenings. Sam Prentice wrote me a mortgage, although not without certain misgivings. 'Eh, lad,' he said, 'I hope to God you know what you're doing.'

Nothing could dent my confidence. What a summer. Nick Berkley's 'Colour Purple' had come out in May, and wherever Julia and I went the song seemed to follow us. Every time we got into the car 'Colour Purple' was on the radio. It became our song, in the way that lovers the world over adopt popular music, and even when Nick had another huge hit with 'Carnival Nights', we remained loyal to 'Colour Purple'.

Odd the way the mind works. Throughout May, June and July I avoided taking Julia to Whitegates, despite a flow of invitations from Ann. It's hard to explain my reluctance. After all, Jack was my oldest friend and Julia was the girl I was planning to marry. Besides, I wanted to show her off, and I had a vague idea that she and Ann would become friends. So I *wanted* them to meet. Yet some deep-rooted instinct made me hesitate. Of course there were some obvious differences. Take drugs, for instance – Julia was ferocious about protecting children from drugs. She would have gone up like a sheet of flame had she known that pop singers, idolised by the girls in her school, were snorting coke at Whitegates. If ever an argument developed, Julia was quite capable of holding Jack and Ann personally responsible for every addict in the pop business. So at least I was aware of the more obvious dangers.

Yet a meeting between them was inevitable, and I took Julia to Whitegates on the first Sunday in July. Contracts were to be exchanged on The Grove during the following week, so I expected that to be the last Sunday I would have free for a long time. 'Come to lunch,' Ann said on the phone, 'then we can spend the afternoon on the river.'

How innocuous it sounded, and yet all my troubles sprang from that day.

BOOK FOUR

EVERYTHING WENT WRONG WHEN I took Julia to White-gates on that Sunday. Looking back I can see the straws in the wind, signposts to further disasters, but at the time I was too shaken to give much thought to the future. The sad thing was that the day should have been perfect. All the ingredients were there. Julia was looking forward to it, though to be honest she was more excited about meeting Nick Berkley than Ann and Jack. Understandably, I suppose; after all 'Colour Purple' remained a favourite of hers, and her students were all agog when she told them who she was meeting. That little bit of name-dropping caused her some embarrassment. 'I should have kept my mouth shut,' she admitted ruefully. 'A couple of girls asked if I could get them signed photos. Naturally, I said I would try. Now it's got out of hand and I want fifty. Do you think he might do it?'

When I phoned Ann, she laughed. 'No problem. Nick will be fine, don't worry.'

So all augured well for our visit. To add to the occasion we spent the Saturday night at our favourite hotel in Hungerford – *favourite* because they always gave us the same room. It was almost a suite: bed-room, bathroom and a tiny sitting room. The bedroom possessed a vast, ornate, magnificent four-poster bed. It was very old; some famous personage was supposed to have spent his honeymoon in it, presumably with his bride, and a good many other couples must have made love in it since. The whole room was mildly erotic; pink wallpapers, a huge chandelier and numerous paintings of nudes. That bed was Julia's favourite place. She once tried to calculate the number of love-makings that had taken place beneath its vaulted canopy. Joyfully we added to the score. In fact it became a challenge to show the bed something new. Julia confiscated a copy of the *Karma Sutra* from one of her students, which came in handy, as did Julia's skills as a gymnast.

So after making love half the night we awoke in each other's arms to yet another beautiful morning, and when she had bathed Julia slipped into her simple white summer dress that she was wearing as a favour to me. Odd really, that dress never failed to turn me on yet the style was so simple; tight waisted with a bodice that cupped her breasts perfectly beneath a scooped neckline which revealed two inches of cleavage. Just to watch her put it on was enough to excite me, so of course I made her take it off again and we went back to bed. Consequently we were late when we left the hotel, not disastrously so, but enough for me to put my foot down to provide us with an exhilarating, pulse-racing dash to Maidenhead. I was never happier. The sky was blue, the sun was shining, the temperature was already pushing seventy. My gleaming red MG flew like an arrow. Beside me was this beautiful blonde, and to cap it all I expected The Grove to become ours the following week. I had it all. No wonder I drove with a grin on my face.

We even arrived exactly on time, dead on the dot of twelve-thirty. Whitegates looked superb. Sprinklers were watering the lawns, the flower beds were vibrant with colour, and the hot sunshine gave the gravel drive the look of pure coral.

To my surprise, Tiny opened the front door. Another surprise was the sweat-shirt he was wearing. It was printed with a lurid picture of Dai in which the colours had run – electric blue hair and smouldering red eyes gave him the look of a maniac. Not that Tiny looked much better, but he did come up with a joke. 'Well, well,' he leered, 'if it ain't Peter Swindon from Taunton.'

Which wasn't bad for Tiny. Not that I let him get away with it. 'Right,' I agreed, 'it ain't Peter Swindon from Taunton.'

'They're out the back,' he said, still enjoying his sense of humour. Waving us over the threshold, he indicated that we should go through the drawing room and find our own way from there. It wasn't difficult. Hand in hand we went through the room and out on to the terrace.

'Tubby!' came a shout from the pool, and there was Jack, heaving himself out of the water to come dripping towards us. He had the wrong sort of skin to go brown. Instead he was a sort of blotchy pink with freckles scattered over his shoulders; a fuzz of gingerish hair covered his chest, and his waist had spread another few inches. Surprisingly, considering his extra weight, seeing him in swimming trunks reminded me of Jack as a boy – we'd both been keen swimmers at school. As he came towards us with a grin on his face, all the old memories returned, all the warm feelings revived – only to be shattered the next minute. Brushing past my outstretched hand, he went directly to Julia. 'So you're Julia,' he grinned, eyeing her appreciatively. 'Well, well, well. Tubby's done it at last.' Putting a wet hand on her arm, he began to lead her towards the chairs round the pool. 'Am I glad to meet you,' he said. 'You know something? I was beginning to think he'd never get a girl of his own. I've been letting him share Ann for as long as I can remember.'

The remark, and his laughter, caught me on the raw. Irritated at being put down in front of Julia, I was about to respond when Ann emerged from the kitchen. She saw me at once. 'Peter!' she exclaimed. 'I didn't hear you arrive.'

The next moment she was in my arms, hugging and kissing me, her white beach robe falling open to reveal a yellow swimsuit and attractively tanned limbs. The warmth of her welcome took the sting from Jack's words, because I forgot them in that moment. Laughing, disengaging myself from her arms, I led her across to Julia, who stood watching with speculative eyes. Introducing her to Ann gave me an odd moment, maybe even one that I feared: I had idealised Ann for so long that – with shaming lack of loyalty – for a split second I was afraid Julia would suffer by comparison. But she emerged from it well. Ann's height served to enhance Julia's diminutive charm, and where Ann's tan was attractive, so too was Julia's immaculate coolness. Feeling lucky and happy, I looked forward to enjoying a beautiful day.

My optimism began to fade even as Jack poured us drinks. Something in his manner jarred. On the surface he was jovial enough – full of jokes and apparent good humour, the perfect host – yet I felt an indefinable tension. Doubts began to form in my mind, doubts which grew when we sat down to eat.

Lunch itself was cold salmon, salad and fruit, eaten at the table by the side of the pool. Eaten and drunk, I should say, for the four bottles of Moselle in the ice buckets were all empty by the end of the meal. Jack drank two by himself, and his voice grew louder and louder, and I found myself wondering whether he had been drinking even before we arrived. He seemed to take issue with everything, becoming more assertive and dogmatic than ever. I began to realise how much he had changed: this was the new, larger than life Jack I had heard about from Janie, and whom I was seeing for the first time. I much preferred the old Jack. He was always full of big ideas, but the new Jack never stopped boasting. For instance, after the meal he said to Julia, 'You know something? Tubby could have been my partner in this.' He waved a hand to indicate the swimming pool and the big house beyond. 'It's true,' he laughed, amused by Julia's surprise. 'I offered him half of JWE, but he wouldn't have it.' Grinning broadly, he blew cigar smoke in my direction. 'Bet you kick yourself now, eh, Tubby old man?'

The best answer I could manage was a pretended nonchalance. 'Oh, I dunno,' I said with a fond look at Julia, 'I think I'm doing rather well at the moment.'

Ann followed my glance and took my meaning. 'You're doing very well, Peter, and now I've met Julia, I can understand why you're so pleased.' Turning in her chair, she smiled at Julia. 'You mustn't mind Peter telling me all about you. That's how we are. From the moment we met, we've been inseparable, haven't we, Peter?'

'Sure,' I agreed without really thinking. Inseparable wouldn't have been my word, after all we often went months without seeing each other, but I suppose the fact of our staying in touch merited some sort of description.

'JWE could have made you rich,' Jack insisted, his face flushed from the wine and the sun. 'That's the point I'm making.' He turned to Julia. 'Now your job, Julia, is to get him out of his rut. He's too easy-going.'

'Oh?' Julia paused, as if considering what he had said. 'I rather like him as he is.'

'He's too bloody soft,' said Jack, wagging a finger. 'He's always been the same. Won't stand up for himself, and I can say this because I'm his oldest friend. I've known him longer than you have.'

'Mmm,' she conceded, with a wicked look in her eye, 'but I've known him more intimately, wouldn't you think?'

It was a good answer, good enough for a laugh and to shut Jack up for a while. Not for long though, and half an hour later, when Ann had donned shirt and shorts over her swimsuit and Jack had dressed in his sailor's outfit of white cap and rope-soled sandals, he led the way down to the river, booming away at the top of his voice about the price of this and the cost of that. Apparently his boat was worth twenty-five thousand. 'And the running expenses would bring tears to your eyes,' he said with mock sadness.

Tiny was on board, running the engines, and it was Tiny who took the wheel when we cast off, leaving Jack to entertain us from a well-stocked bar set aft of a luxurious lounge. I know nothing about boats, and Jack's floating gin palace was my first experience of such craft, but to spend so much for an occasional hour on the river struck me as daft.

When I said as much Jack went up like a sheet of flame. 'Daft?' he echoed, scandalised. 'You don't know what you're talking about. I've struck more deals on this boat than you've had hot dinners. You know your trouble, Tubby? You don't set out to impress people. You've got to get them excited . . .'

And off he went about all the deals he had clinched, which was all very boring for me. There's a limit to the number of times you can listen to someone tell you how clever he is and I was satiated by then. So I spent half my time listening to Ann tell Julia about the Green Door and how she used to cook supper at the Whitcombe Street flat. That was when I made a startling discovery, which helped explain the undercurrent during lunch: Jack and Ann weren't speaking to each other. They hadn't exchanged a word since we arrived; they spoke to me, or to Julia, but they never so much as looked at each other.

I remembered Janie telling me: 'Jack doesn't listen to Ann any more.' Janie was right, things were different from the old days. If nothing else, Jack had listened to Ann about his artists; it was all they ever talked about, their sole topic of conversation; without that, they had nothing to say to each other . . .

Startled by my thoughts, I turned back to Jack just as he was saying, 'Showmanship. Whatever you do, do it with flair –'

'Talking of flair,' I interrupted, 'how's Janie? Is she working on a new album?'

His face darkened to an immediate scowl. 'How can she work on a new album without making new music? I keep telling Ossie to get up to date. They're stale –'

'Isn't Ossie writing anything new?'

'It's the same old stuff. He's locked in a time warp. Without something fresh, they're finished.'

'Oh, surely not. Can't Ann help?' I asked, turning towards her.

Jack grabbed my arm, making me turn back to him. 'I sell our people,' he said belligerently. 'Not Ann. I know the market. Christ, I'm the poor bastard who has to argue with the poxy promoters, I do it every day of my life. If I don't know what's selling, nobody does.' His scowl deepened to a look of real fury.

Ann groaned. 'Oh, here we go. Now you've done it, Peter. Now we're in for a lecture.'

Jack swung round to glare at her, looking at her for the first time that day. 'And what's that supposed to mean?'

Ann replied with a weary shrug, avoiding his eye by watching the river. 'Nothing.'

'I was just telling Tubby –'

'How brilliant you are. Yes, I heard –'

'There's nothing brilliant about knowing the market,' Jack said hotly. 'Janie's lost her appeal –'

'So you say,' Ann retorted sharply, her voice rising. 'According to you. It's *your* opinion.'

'Thank God it is. Some of us know what we're talking about.'

'Steady,' I interrupted, 'steady. I didn't mean to start an argument.'

They both avoided my eye, Ann by staring at the river, Jack by scowling down at his own feet. Not that Jack was embarrrassed for long, he was quick to

352

recover. 'Yes, well,' he laughed, 'someone's got to make the decisions.' He covered his confusion by reaching for my glass. 'Drink up, Tubby my boy. And you, Julia, have some wine instead of that bloody lime juice. Come on, you're supposed to be enjoying yourselves – you've got to on my boat, it's a rule,' he said, raising his voice and looking over his shoulder to where Tiny stood at the wheel. 'Right, Tiny? Everyone enjoys themselves on the *Dolphin*.'

'Right, Boss,' came the dutiful reply.

The afternoon was doomed after that, although some of the tension eased when Julia asked about landmarks on the river bank, it gave Jack a chance to show off his local knowledge and brought Tiny into the conversation. Tiny was only a couple of yards from where we sat, so he must have heard the previous angry exchange, but unless spoken to he remained mute and impassive. Developing into the perfect family retainer, was Tiny, except that Jack and Ann hardly constituted a perfect family.

I breathed a sigh of relief when we turned and headed back towards Whitegates. Meanwhile Jack drank his way through another bottle of wine, even though none of us joined him; Julia had opted for lime juice almost from the outset, and Ann and I had long since had enough. 'For Christ's sake,' Jack moaned. 'You'd think it was a bloody Church outing.'

When finally the house came into sight, my feet itched to get ashore. It was about six o'clock by then and I'd had enough for one day, but even as I began to invent excuses, Ann turned to Julia. 'You haven't met Nick yet. He's signed all your photographs. I told him we'd call in at the cottage.'

'Oh, lovely,' said Julia, genuinely pleased.

'Fine,' I said, revising my plans, hoping to salvage something from the disaster. Julia was really looking forward to meeting Nick Berkley.

'He's working,' said Jack who was by now slurring his words. 'I expect enough material for a new album at the end of the month.'

'Really?' Julia was full of interest. 'He's amazingly prolific, isn't he? I'm dying to meet him.'

Her enthusiasm lifted everyone's spirits for a moment; Ann's pained expression softened into a smile. Jack's scowl eased a fraction, and I sighed with relief. I thought maybe the worst was over . . . only to be proved wrong a few minutes later.

Leaving Tiny messing about on the boat, we walked through the gardens to the cottage, Ann telling Julia about Nick, while Jack pretended not to listen. He slouched along, hands in pockets, the scowl back on his face and his skipper's cap pushed back on his head. I suppose his afternoon had been as unsuccessful as ours, but he had no one to blame but himself. As we neared the cottage, he growled, 'I can't hear the piano. Usually I hear the piano when he's working.'

The curtains were drawn. Ann lowered her voice. 'He might be sleeping. Sometimes he works through the night –'

'No,' Jack interrupted, 'I can hear something. Listen.'

We paused on the step, cocking our heads. Then Jack's face contorted with fury and he fairly burst through the door. I followed, moving more slowly, my eyes adjusting to the gloom. Nick was sitting in darkness watching television. I'd scarcely registered the images of helicopters on the screen before it went blank – Jack had torn the plug from the wall. He was furious. 'For fuck's sake,' he shouted, ripping open the curtains, 'you're supposed to be working!' Sunlight flooded into the room, revealing Ann and Julia just inside the door, both staring wide-eyed at Jack as he ranted. 'Those fucking newsreels. Is that all you're doing? Watching that Vietnam garbage –'

'It is work,' Nick cried, jumping up. His eyes rounded with disbelief as Jack scooped up a pile of video cassettes. 'Jesus, Mr Webb, what are you doing?'

Jack began hurling the cassettes out of the door, throwing them one after the other. 'No more Vietnam,' he shouted. 'Didn't I tell you? No more fucking protest songs –'

'Stop it!' Ann cried, running outside to pick up the cassettes.

Advancing upon Nick, Jack shouted, 'I don't give a shit about Vietnam! Understand? No one gives a shit. Will you get that into your stupid thick head –'

'Jack!' Ann screamed, running back into the room, dropping the cassettes in her hurry to get between Jack and Nick. From the look on her face she clearly feared Jack would lash out with his fists. I moved forward to put a restraining hand on Jack's arm, but he shrugged me off, shaking with rage. 'Will you listen?' he shouted at Nick. 'Listen to me. Do what I tell you. I run this business. I created it, I own it, I make the decisions . . .'

He was ranting, out of control. I don't know what would have happened if Tiny hadn't come in at that moment. He brushed past me and went directly to Jack. 'Telephone, Boss,' he said, pushing his bulk forward. His back was to me so I missed his next words, but I thought I heard him say something about Germany.

'Now?' Jack queried, still breathing hard. 'Did you say they're on the line now?'

Tiny nodded, and stepped back, bumping into me as he did so.

'Okay,' Jack said gruffly. He took another deep breath to regain control, but his face was still red as he turned to Ann. 'I've gotta go,' he said. 'But do us all a favour, will you. Talk some sense into this bonehead.'

With that he made for the door, but not before I reached my decision. I'd had more than enough. 'Jack?' I said, holding out my hand. 'We have to be on our way. If you've a long telephone call . . .'

He stopped and looked at me, his frown fading. Then he nodded. 'You're probably right. This could take a while. There's always something.' He shrugged, turning to Julia with a wry smile. 'Sorry about this,' he said, jerking his head towards Nick, 'but like I always say, a manager's got to manage, right?' Bending forward, he kissed her on the cheek. 'Don't forget what I said about Tubby. He needs shaking out of his rut.'

The relief was almost tangible when he left, hurrying off after Tiny and up to the house.

The shock slowly cleared from Julia's eyes, Ann sank into a chair, and Nick greeted me uncertainly, as if afraid I might continue where Jack had left off. Shaking his hand, I introduced Julia, who did her level best to pretend not to have witnessed Jack's extraordinary outburst. The truth was, we were all embarrassed.

356

After gathering up the cassettes, Nick gave Julia a chair and began fidgeting about, tidying the room, collecting up notepads and loose sheets of music paper. 'Sorry about the mess. I meant to do it earlier, but then I got to watching those tapes . . .' He looked at me. 'I really was working you know, Mr Mortlake.'

'You don't have to explain yourself to us. We're fans, aren't we, Julia?' I said, turning to her.

Which was her opportunity to say how much she liked 'Colour Purple' and Nick's other compositions, and to remind him about his fans at her school.

Shyly he went to a small table and picked up a large brown envelope. 'The photos,' he said, handing them to Julia before turning to me. 'And here's the money I owe you, Mr Mortlake. Sorry it's been so long. Ann . . . Mrs Webb . . . expected you before –'

'He should have been before,' Ann interrupted. 'He's about as reliable as you are, Nick. You let me down. You promised. No more Vietnam until you finish this album –'

'It only needs one more song,' he protested. 'Meanwhile, eighty thousand people are killed every week in Vietnam –'

'And that's what you were working on today?' Ann interrupted.

'It's all I think about,' he admitted, turning to me. 'What do you think, Mr Mortlake? I want to do a rock opera on Vietnam, full of protest songs. I know it defies convention, but it would work. People would go to it, young people would, Vietnam's a young people's war. They're the ones who are outraged, they're the ones protesting all over the States, and here, in Paris, in Germany –'

'Nick,' Ann said, cautioning against his enthusiasm.

'It would sell out. Not that I'm doing it for the money – it's what I want to write – the money could go to charity, the Red Cross could use it for Vietnam orphans, something like that. I've got half the story line. I've written some of the songs . . .' He searched my face for a reaction, 'Well, Mr Mortlake? What do you think?'

Nick could make me feel middle-aged at times. His insistence on calling me Mr Mortlake was partly responsible, but so was his enthusiasm. I was lost for an answer. My knowledge of the Vietnam war was almost as limited as my knowledge of music; Vietnam was America's war. Of course it was on television and in the papers, but I'm not really a political person. And there was Jack to consider. Jack had made his views abundantly clear. Scenting trouble my instinct was to keep quiet.

'It's a wonderful idea,' Julia interrupted, her eyes shining. 'I know you can write it.'

Nick gave her a grateful smile before returning to me, 'Mr Webb's dead against it –'

'The album *is* important, Nick,' Ann interrupted.

'That's not the only reason.' Nick shook his head. 'I'll be ready for the album next week, but all he'll want afterwards is more of the same. I don't want more of the same. It's a question of direction. He insists I go one way, I want to go another. Vietnam's here and now, I've got to write about it now. I can't just ignore it, walk away from it, I want to add to the protest –'

'I know,' said Ann quietly. 'But finish this album

first, Nick.' Worry haunted her dark eyes, and she ran a hand through her hair as she spoke.

'You promised to help me.'

'I know, I will, I promise.'

Something about the look in her eyes tugged at my memory, transporting me back over the years to when we first met in Gill's bar. Listening to Ann made me wonder how much she had changed from the girl who once demonstrated for Black rights in the States, from the girl who'd helped fight McCarthy, from the member of SANE. If Vietnam was America's war, Ann *was* American, which I sometimes forgot. And with rare insight, I thought, 'Jack, you've got a battle on your hands, if Ann believes in Nick's cause as well as his talent.'

Anything could have happened on the way home. After all, I had told Julia so much about Jack, even boasted about him, and the day had been a disaster. Thank goodness Julia had a sense of humour; not that I thought everything she said was so funny.

'Oh boy,' she murmured as I drove towards the motorway. 'So that's Ann.'

'That's Ann,' I agreed.

'Was it strictly for my benefit, or does she always give you that sort of welcome?'

'What sort?'

'Giving you the eye all the time.'

'Oh, come on, we're old friends —'

'And how,' Julia said dryly. 'All that stuff about cooking supper for you in that flat. Did you hear her going on about that? What a cosy little *ménage à trois* that was —'

'Nonsense –'

'That's what she wanted, to dangle you both on a string. No wonder you had a crush on her. A monk would have been hard put to resist that sort of encouragement –'

I started to laugh. 'What are you on about? You've got it all wrong –'

'It's the same now. Look at the way she keeps asking you to stay –'

'We're friends –'

'Dah dah dah dah,' Julia tooted, making trumpeting motions with her hands. 'Listen to this, folks. The oldest show in the world. The man says we're friends, we're just good friends. Roll up, roll up –'

'Will you stop fooling about –'

'Who's fooling?' she asked, squirming around in her seat until her face was dangerously blocking my vision. She rolled her eyes. 'You're finished, Buster. No more good friends for you. The sooner I get you married the better.'

Luckily for our safety, she thumped back into her seat and stayed there for the rest of the journey, muttering about Ann from time to time.

Eventually she turned her comments to Jack. 'Who the hell does he think he is? Why does he call you Tubby all the time? He's got a damn cheek, did you see his waistline? Another year and he'll be positively gross.'

'He's always called me Tubby. It's habit –'

'He puts you down all the time. He spent the whole day bragging about his money and how stupid you were not to join him –'

'I didn't want to –'

'I should hope not, but that's not the point. He's so . . . so bloody patronising!'

I suppose it did look like that to an outsider. Even I recognised it at times, so much so that Jack and I were beginning to clash whenever we met. I was sickened by the way he had bullied Nick. Yet old loyalties die hard. Jack and I went back a long way. He had shielded me when we were boys; at school he had always jumped to my aid; he had diverted my father by spending so much time with us at Wimbledon – many's the weekend when he hadn't wanted to stay, but he always did in the end. I owed Jack, and although Julia had heard it before, I began to remind her.

'Baloney,' she said, 'he's not the type to do what doesn't suit him. If he was a scholarship boy, school would have been miserable for him too – he needed you to bolster his status. Then he wanted to go into the law, and your father made it all possible. You don't owe him a thing. In fact, he owes you.'

There was no arguing with her. Besides, if anything, I was beginning to agree.

Julia was more reflective about Nick. 'He's the one I feel sorry for,' she said. 'He's in the middle, poor little devil. Why does he stay there? He must have made a lot of money this year, he could live anywhere.'

Wondering about that, I reached the conclusion that Nick lived within himself more than in a particular place. His output was so prolific that music was all he had time for. Given shelter and food, a piano and pencils, he had all he wanted. And access to Jack – that's what had drawn him to Whitegates in the first place – the great Mr Webb would make him a star. And Jack had. Now Jack was cracking the whip and Nick was rebelling. Meanwhile, he was Ann's one remaining link with the business.

361

'I can't understand Jack,' I said. 'He's shutting Ann out of the business, but that's what brought them together in the first place.'

'If today's anything to go by,' said Julia, 'they won't be together much longer.'

She sounded so sure that I winced.

'What's the funny face for?'

I shrugged.

'I know what you're thinking,' said Julia, suddenly burying her head in her hands and emitting a low wail. 'Poor Ann. Oh, woe is Ann. Whatever will become of her —'

'Don't be so daft.'

'Mmm,' she murmured, giving me a speculative look.

And so we drove home, relieved to be by ourselves again, luxuriating in our own uncomplicated company. Not that Julia had completely finished with the subject. 'Peter,' she said cautiously as we drove into Swindon, 'I know they're your friends, but we don't have to see them too often, do we?'

Why did agreeing fill me with guilt? I had a sudden mental picture of rats deserting a sinking ship. But that was unfair, I had my own life to lead. I had Julia to consider, and after the day we had suffered, I couldn't blame her for not being in a hurry to sample another. So why did I feel bad about Ann?

Julia grinned. 'Because you're too soft. My friend Fat Jack told me that. But you don't have to worry; if anything happens you'll hear from Ann soon enough; she'll expect you there, holding her hand.'

*

As a matter of fact, Ann did call me the next day. Apparently she and Jack argued bitterly after we left and he had gone up to his office that morning, 'still breathing fire and brimstone. I can't get through to him these days. We don't communicate. He takes more notice of Tiny than me.'

I sympathised as best I could, without ever really finding the right words, fumbling along by saying 'Oh dear' and 'Ah' in what I hoped were the right places. Eventually I plunged to the heart of the matter. 'You don't seem so involved in the business these days?'

'Oh, not for ages, not since we had the row about Ossie. He wrote a number I wanted for Janie, but Jack insisted it was more Dai's kind of song. Ever since then I'm supposed not to know what I'm talking about. I'm thick, you know? Like, I don't know the first thing about music.' Ann laughed, but there was a lot of pain in that laugh.

'That was a bad break,' I said, 'Dai being preferred over Janie –'

'And how, especially as Janie blames me, even though I did what I could. Jack's trying to push her into the wrong mould. He'll do the same with Nick if I let him . . .'

She went on in the same vein for some time. I listened to her talk about Nick's talent, his startling originality, his range and commitment. Most of all she enthused about his idea for a rock opera on Vietnam. I remember her calling it 'a unique way to reach the hearts and minds of young people all over the world'. Maybe it was, but Ann was also describing something else – her forthcoming clash with Jack. I think I saw it more clearly than she did, for although she sounded confident, I knew Jack of old. When his mind was made up, it was made up. Nothing would change it.

I think I did tell Julia about that call. I say 'I think' because Ann rang every week from then on, and I only told Julia about a fraction of them. To have done otherwise would merely have caused friction.

Julia had taken against Ann; beneath all the jokes she really meant it, and nothing I could say would convince her I didn't have a secret longing for Ann, or that Ann wasn't yearning for me. It was my fault, I suppose; I should have kept my mouth shut about once carrying a torch for Ann. But how was I to know Julia would react as she did? Anyone would have thought I was Burt Reynolds or someone . . . I know it was daft, but that's how things were. Meanwhile, Ann called me every week and was forever pressing me to go over to Whitegates, an invitation which I knew Julia would resist with every bone in her body. She had taken to calling Jack 'the fat Führer of Maidenhead' and was quite capable of being equally rude to his face. So Ann's invitations were an embarrassment, and I was glad to have the excuse of my weekend work at The Grove.

It's hard to describe the pull of that house. Some people move house a dozen or more times in their lives, they buy one house, sell it, buy another, go to another district . . . I wanted none of that. Others buy a house as a showplace, a possession with which to impress friends – I wanted none of that either. I was content that The Grove lacked the grandeur of Whitegates or the rich trappings of my father's Wimbledon house. Instead it would be our *home*, Julia's and mine, hopefully for the rest of our lives –

because despite my difficulties with John, I expected one day to take over at the office, and so to live in Swindon for the rest of my days. I hoped Julia and I would raise our children in that house, we would give parties, face problems, laugh, cry, share, grow and develop. Quite simply, The Grove was to be our future.

So every weekend I toiled like a Trojan. Not in the house, which was the domain of skilled men who worked Monday to Friday, gutting and stripping in preparation for the job of rebuilding. Instead, I worked in the gardens, which I had already extended into the paddock. Julia worked too, except for Saturday mornings when she was at the school with her pupils. We bought all the books: *How to Grow The Perfect Lawn*, *Cultivation of Shrubs*, *Professional Rose Growing*. Every Saturday we worked until dusk when, since there was no hot water at the house, I drove Julia back to her place before going back to the hotel to bath and change. Then I collected her for another of our delicious nights in our Hungerford four-poster.

Julia's mother found out about that, or, to be more exact, Julia told her. I was there when it happened.

'Who is this mysterious friend you stay with every Saturday night?' asked Mrs Lovell, and not for the first time. I suppose she had guessed. Even so, she would have been wiser to have left the subject alone – Julia's discretion was as much for her mother's benefit as her own. Until then Julia had avoided the issue, but that day her mother's sniping had been particularly savage.

Turning to me, Julia smiled. 'There's nothing very mysterious about you, is there, Peter?'

Mrs Lovell went pink. 'You mean you stay with *him*?' She could never bring herself to use my name.

'Of course,' Julia replied lightly. 'As you must know perfectly well.'

Then came the dreaded accusation. 'You sleep with him?'

Julia smiled. 'I'm usually too busy enjoying myself, but yes . . . I generally doze off at about four in the morning.'

From then on, I was the Devil Incarnate. Mrs Lovell barely tolerated me when I called at the house. Julia once joked, 'Just imagine, Peter. Next year you'll be able to call her Mother.' And while she giggled at that, I saw the obvious extension. 'And John will be Uncle,' I said gloomily.

The satisfying thing was that I was making progress with John. Or at least, I thought I was. Without blowing my own trumpet, I am reasonably good at what I do, and an increasing number of clients wanted me to handle their affairs – which meant that, thanks to me, John was having an easier time of it. Not that he thanked me for it, but at least he could find no fault with my work, even if he found plenty with me.

The all-important thing was that every week saw more progress on The Grove, and every Saturday and Sunday, Julia and I lovingly inspected the work in the house before toiling away in the garden.

Meanwhile, Ann phoned every week and always with the same invitation. By now it was the end of August, seven or eight weeks since I had taken Julia to Whitegates. Nick's new album had just been released to wide public acclaim, and I wondered if its success might have eased the problems. But the situation was worse, according to Ann. 'Nick's been away a lot lately, doing promotions, but when he's back here all he talks about is Vietnam and his rock opera.'

'Is Jack still against it?'

'He doesn't even know. He goes crazy about protest songs. This will give him a seizure. And it's brilliant. The other day Nick played me some of the stuff he's working on. It's so different, it's weird – heavily political, sinister with corruption, nothing like anything he's ever written before . . .'

I didn't even ask if it would sell at the box office. Maybe it would, maybe it wouldn't, who was I to judge? It was Jack's opinion that mattered, and the more Ann told me, the more I knew Jack would hate it. He had a saying: 'Entertainment comes first, second and third.' Nick's rock opera would never qualify as Jack's idea of entertainment.

'This goes beyond talent, Peter. This is the work of a genius.'

There was awe in Ann's voice, a reverence I'd never heard when she talked of Janie or Dai or anyone else. Oddly, instead of finding it elevating, it filled me with misgivings.

Another thing depressed me when talking to Ann – she kept harking back to the past. With every invitation came references to the Green Door and shared suppers at the Whitcombe Street flat. 'Come over and I'll cook a meal just like the old days.' Naturally Julia was included, but only as one of the crowd. 'I'll get Janie and Mike. Maybe Ossie and Dave. Did you know Janie's just bought a house in Newbury? That's right, it's not far . . .'

Even I could see what she was doing, trying to

recreate how we once were, trying to recapture the closeness which had existed between us. In fact at one point she betrayed her intentions: 'Jack listened to you in those days.' But those days were a long time ago. If she expected me to help plead Nick's case, it just wouldn't work. The past is a different place, populated by strangers; Jack and I had become distant. Talking to Ann made me realise exactly how far we had drifted apart. I no longer carried that obligation inherited from boyhood; time, circumstances and Julia had combined to lift the burden from my shoulders. Julia in particular had shown me that the debt had been paid. I was out from Jack's shadow, living my own life, in which Jack featured as little as I did in his. Our friendship had become so tenuous that only Ann held it together.

'Please, Peter. It would be lovely to see you again. Come on Saturday night and you and Julia can stay over . . .'

With a wry smile, I realised I'd save a hotel bill. The impact of the mortgage on The Grove was beginning to bite. The payments would be more manageable when the house was finished; when Julia and I married we would have our own kitchen and less need to dine out, we'd have our own bed and no need for the magic four-poster. Meanwhile, paying Sam's mortgage left less money for pleasures . . .

Not that saving money was the main reason. The truth was that Ann's weekly invitations made me feel guilty.

'We'll have to go,' I said to Julia, confessing to some of Ann's calls. 'I can't keep refusing.'

Even Julia agreed, though not without making

conditions. 'Okay, we'll go, but if Jack calls you Tubby I shall start calling him Fatty, and if she makes eyes at you, I shall take my clothes off and rape you on the dining-room table.'

So what with one thing and another, it promised to be a difficult evening ... though not even my bleakest expectations equalled the drama about to unfold.

That Saturday I worked alone at The Grove. Julia spent the afternoon at the beauty parlour, having a facial, a manicure and her hair styled. She had already bought a new dress, and when I collected her from under her mother's glacial stare in the evening, I thought she looked even sexier than when wearing her white summer dress.

'Good,' she said when I told her. 'Keep that in mind for the rest of the evening.'

Strange to remember that now. It seems inconsequential, out of place with the events of that night, trivialising something of much greater importance.

When we got into the car, I said, 'It's just us. Ann phoned to confirm we'll be there for eight-thirty. I asked her about Janie, but Janie's not coming.'

Julia gave me a wide-eyed look. 'Oh dear. So it's just us and Fat Jack and Annie the Vamp.' She was in that sort of mood.

'What about Nick?' she asked. 'At least he's someone I like.'

'It's hard not to like him, he's so inoffensive.'

'You mean weak?'

'No,' I said thoughtfully, 'he's not weak, he just

369

doesn't argue about things he doesn't care about. He wouldn't bother –'

'He cares about Vietnam,' said Julia, 'and his music.'

'And how,' I agreed, recounting what Ann had told me about Nick pursuing his rock opera without telling Jack.

Julia shuddered. 'Oh God. Let's hope they don't argue tonight. I could do without another scene like last time.'

'Me too,' I agreed soberly.

In fact that sums up our mood when we arrived, sober and a bit apprehensive, not looking forward to the evening at all. To make matters worse, our misgivings were fuelled almost at once: having parked the car, we were walking towards the steps when we heard the sound of angry voices. Through the windows I saw Jack pacing up and down, waving his arms and shouting at someone. Julia flinched at my side and almost stopped in her tracks. We might have turned tail there and then had Tiny not opened the front door. 'Welcome to the happy home,' he said, bowing and flourishing an arm to invite us over the threshold.

We were duty bound to go in, even though we ascended the steps with all the enthusiasm of the condemned going to the gallows.

Closing the front door after us, Tiny ushered us into the drawing room with the deference of an old-fashioned footman. It was no more than the room deserved for it always made an impression; the Adam fireplace was genuine, as was the Matisse above it; the chandelier was Venetian and most of the furniture French. It was a gracious and civilised room, which deserved better than to be the scene of Jack's obvious bad temper. Pacing up and down in front of the hearth, he greeted us with a wave of his cigar while bawling at Nick, 'The answer is no. No, no, no!'

White-faced, Nick sat at the piano, looking grim and defiant.

Ann rose to greet us. Elegant as ever in green silk, she would have looked the perfect hostess but for her worried expression. Scarcely saying hello, she managed a strained smile while telling Tiny to get us a drink. Then she turned back to Jack. 'You can't say no without further discussion.'

'Oh?' He stopped in his tracks. 'I make the decisions round here. I told you before –'

'This is artistic interpretation,' Ann retorted, 'not a commercial decision –'

'Like hell! A mistake like this could cost a fucking fortune.'

They stood glaring at each other, while Tiny passed me a glass of champagne. 'Cheers,' he said, sounding unconcerned, seemingly oblivious of the row going on. After placing more champagne on a small table next to Julia, he picked up a glass of his own and returned to a chair near the door. He looked so at home that I wondered if he was staying for dinner. If so we would make an odd-looking bunch; the girls were done up to the nines, Jack and I were wearing grey lounge suits, Nick wore his usual jeans, and Tiny was in a black sweater two sizes too small.

Ann gave me another of her strained smiles. 'You can guess what this is about. Nick's Vietnam. We've been trying to explain –'

'Hang about,' Jack interrupted. 'You mean you've discussed this with Tubby?' He sounded shocked, incredulous.

'Yes, if you must know. Peter's been a tower of strength these last few weeks –'

'Oh, that's terrific! Tubby knows, Julia knows, every bugger under the sun knows except me!' Jack gave me a look of disgust. 'Jesus Christ,' he said, gulping the remains of his drink. Crossing to the sideboard, he filled his glass with Scotch.

Ann's voice rose to a shriek. 'What do you expect? Nobody can tell you anything.'

'Damn right,' Jack snarled. 'Nobody *tells* me, they ask. I listen, they ask. I consider, I decide. Me, Jack Webb, not some kid whose head you've filled with dumb ideas –'

Nick rose, protesting, 'It wasn't Ann's idea, Mr Webb . . .'

I listened with mounting dismay. This was even worse than before. Julia tugged my arm, her face pink with embarrassment. 'Peter, I think we ought . . .' She jerked her head at the door. Nodding agreement, I rose to my feet, 'Jack, we're intruding –'

'Don't talk bollocks,' he answered, spilling his drink as he slumped down into a chair. Taking a handkerchief from his pocket, he dabbed ineffectively at his lapel. 'We're having dinner, aren't we? Storm in a teacup,' he said. 'All over now.' Fixing his eyes on Nick, the grim look on his face softened into a shadowy smile. 'Right, Nick? All over. Bum idea, right? Let's forget it. Write me another "Colour Purple". That's what people want.' His smile widened as he turned to Julia. 'That's right, isn't it? Didn't you say you loved that song?'

'Oh yes,' Julia nodded, immediately enthusiastic, her gaze going to Nick.

Ann interrupted. 'Julia also likes the idea of Nick's opera. Don't you, Julia?'

Colour flooded into Julia's face. I cursed under my breath, but before either of us could respond, Jack fairly erupted. 'Will you shut up!' he shouted at Ann. 'I just told you, it's over. Dead! Finished! I don't want another word on the subject!'

Julia flinched on the sofa. My ears rang, Jack's shout was so loud. For a moment there was a little pool of silence, an interlude, then Nick stood up. 'Please, Mr Webb,' he entreated, advancing from the piano, 'if only you'd listen –'

'Me listen?' Jack's face went purple. Next minute he pulled himself up from his chair to face Nick, poking his finger into Nick's chest to prod him backwards across the room. 'Now you listen to me, once and for all. You write the music, I do the deals. Get it? That's how it works. And I do the deals because I know the market . . .'

Jack's brow-beating disgusted me. The chest-prodding was developing into a physical threat. I reached out to put a hand on his shoulder. 'Steady –'

He brushed me aside. 'Sit down, Tubby, for Christ's sake. Tiny, get him a drink.'

Tiny was already at my side, refilling my glass. Agitated, my attention diverted, I swallowed the champagne without thinking. Julia tugged my jacket as I sat down on the arm of the sofa next to her; her eyes conveyed another message about leaving, and I was about to respond when the argument at the piano exploded. Nick shouted, 'I don't want to write anything else. Can't you understand? I *can't*! It won't

373

come. It will take me months to write this, maybe a whole year, but it's the most important thing in my life. I can't let it go –'

'A year!' Jack roared. 'To write some rubbish nobody wants. A whole fucking year! You've got to be crazy. I spend a year building you up and we throw it away –'

'No,' Nick cried. 'We won't throw it away. Please Mr Webb, you won't regret it –'

'I'll tell you what I regret,' Jack snarled, 'letting you live here, that's what. You've had it too easy, it's all been too fast. A year ago you were living in some rat-hole in Kilburn. I took you in and made you a star –'

'I'm grateful. Honestly –'

'Grateful,' Jack mimicked scornfully, 'you don't know what the word means. Taken advantage, that's what you've done. You've had the run of the house, I've given you everything you wanted, and you've abused it. Look at tonight . . .' Jack whirled round to point a finger at me. 'My oldest friend comes to dinner and you ruin his evening by creating this scene . . .'

Nick's eyes met mine in a plea for forgiveness. 'Sorry, Mr Mortlake . . . er, Julia, I didn't mean to –'

'Sorry?' Jack echoed, throwing his half-smoked cigar into the fireplace. He was quite out of control, his voice was hoarse and his hands were shaking. 'It's too bloody late to be sorry. I've had enough of your whining. I've had you up to my back teeth. Once too often this has happened, once too often. In future we'll do our business at the office. Understand? I want you out of this house!'

Nick gasped. His gaze went from Jack to Ann and back again. 'You want me to leave?' he asked, aghast.

'Not want. I'm telling you. You're out. Out of my house until you come to your senses –'

Ann sprang to her feet. 'For God's sake –'

Jack responded furiously, 'And you can shut up. I'm sick of your interference. How many times do I have to tell you? I make the decisions, not you, me, Jack Webb, remember?'

The violence of the outburst left us all breathless. Julia had jumped when Jack shouted.

Jack turned to the mantelpiece, his chest heaving. Putting out a hand to steady himself, he glared balefully around the room as if getting ready to face another show of defiance. When none came, he reached for his glass and swallowed half the whisky at a gulp. Coughing, he wiped his mouth with the back of his hand.

For a moment no one moved, we were like a tableau, frozen, all staring at Jack. Then Nick began to walk to the door. He moved slowly past me, his gaze directed straight ahead.

Jack watched, his eyes gleaming, unnaturally bright in his flushed face. When he spoke his voice was a growl. 'Where are you going?'

Nick stopped and looked around. 'You told me to go.'

'Bloody right. I'll see you in the office on Monday. Ten o'clock sharp.'

Nick stared. I tried to read his expression: bewildered, hurt, sad, frightened, anything but angry. Then he turned away to walk past Tiny and out of the room.

Suddenly Ann laughed; an unpleasant sneering

sound in which incredulity and contempt were evenly mixed. 'Christ Almighty, that's who you think you are. God on earth. The great Jack Webb, star-maker and star-breaker.' Turning her back on Jack, she walked to the sideboard.

I watched her pour a brandy with trembling hands and wished I had something stronger than wine in my glass.

'I made Dai a star,' Jack retorted, 'I made Janie. I made The Tower –'

'All by yourself!' Ann's dark eyes glittered as she whirled round to face him. 'You did it all by yourself? Don't make me laugh. You didn't know the difference between a voice and a cough. What about my contribution? What was I doing when –'

'You helped. I'm not saying –'

'I'll say I helped –'

'I could have hired that help in,' Jack retorted swiftly. 'Voice coaches are two a penny. It's the selling that counts, the presentation, the promotion –'

'You need talent first, and my ear found the talent. Whose ear do you listen to these days? Not mine, you haven't listened to mine for a long while.'

Jack's voice rose with his temper. 'Because you interfere!' he shouted. 'For fuck's sake! You do it all the time. Look at tonight. Jesus! A rock opera on Vietnam. Who wants it? I couldn't think of a more stupid idea if I tried.'

'You don't think. You can't recognise what's under your nose. You talk about Dai and Janie and the others – they're gifted, that's all, they have a talent. But Nick's got genius, and you're too insensitive even to see it.'

'And you can, of course,' Jack sneered. 'Like you did in New York.'

Ann's fingers went white round the glass. For a moment I thought she would hurl it across the room, but instead she slopped brandy over the rim as she answered, 'It's no good, Jack. You can't hurt me with that any more. I've made up my mind. If that boy goes tonight, I'm going with him.'

Jack's jaw went slack. A look of incredulity came into his eyes, complete disbelief. 'You what?'

Ann remained silent, not looking at him, not looking at anyone. Her hands shook as she swallowed more brandy.

My mind reeled. Nick had been gone less than a minute. Julia and I should have gone too, but chance had been denied us. Not that we mattered; we might not have been there for all the notice Jack took.

He erupted with fury. 'You bitch! So that's it. All this crap about genius. Is that when you recognised it? Flat on your back with your legs in the air?'

That was when Ann did look at him. Contempt and loathing filled her eyes. Then she set her glass on the sideboard and walked out. It happened so quickly that the next I heard was the click of her heels crossing the tiles in the hall.

Jack took a pace forward. 'That's right!' he shouted. 'Get out. Out of my house.'

I moved then, coming alive as if from a trance. 'Stop it!' I cried, jumping up. 'Jack, for God's sake! You don't mean it.'

'Bitch,' he muttered, his breath rasping. 'Ungrateful little bitch!' He glowered across the room as the front door closed with a shattering bang.

I needed a strong drink; so did Julia by the look on

her face. Leaving Jack where he stood, I went to the sideboard and poured two fairly stiff brandies. Vaguely I noticed Tiny's empty chair and realised he had left the room. Giving Julia her drink, I downed half of mine, gasping as the brandy seared my throat. Everything had happened so quickly. I resisted the idea of going after Ann, telling myself Jack should do that, but he was back at the sideboard, filling his glass with more whisky. As he turned to face me, there was no mistaking the shock in his eyes. 'How about that?' he said, carrying his drink back to the hearth. 'You take a kid off the streets, you put food in his belly, clothes on his back, and he ends up screwing your wife –'

'You don't believe that,' I said firmly.

He sat down heavily in the chair nearest the hearth, his usual chair, I imagine, because the table next to it bore a box of cigars. Taking one, he began to clip the end.

I said, 'She must have gone down to the cottage. Why not go down there –'

'No.' He shook his head, and when he looked up I saw the shock had already started to fade. In its place was an icy coldness, such as I remembered seeing in my father. The hands wielding the cigar cutter were surprisingly steady. The heat and fury had passed, leaving only an echo in his voice. 'That little bastard. I'll kill him. Who'd have believed it? All this time, him and Ann –'

'Rubbish –'

'That's what people will say,' he growled, putting a match to his cigar. Once it was alight, he stood up and began to pace the floor. When he spoke he sounded not so much angry as a man intent on revenge. 'They'll pay,' he said. 'By Christ, they'll pay. Him first, then her. Nobody runs out on Jack Webb, nobody! By Christ, she'll be sorry . . .'

A shiver ran up my spine. Listening was like listening to my father. Closing my eyes, I was transported back in time, I could hear my father . . . 'I'll see her in Hell for creating such a spectacle . . . God damn her for making a fool out of me.'

Suddenly I heard the front door bang open. Steps sounded in the hall and Tiny rushed into the room. 'The kid's packed his stuff,' he said breathlessly. 'They've gone round to the garage to get her car. Do you want me to stop them, Boss?'

Jack stopped pacing and stared. 'They're taking her car?'

Tiny nodded.

'Jack,' I said urgently. 'Go and talk to her, now, while there's still time.'

He gave me a strange answer. 'She hasn't got any money.'

I shook my head in amazement. 'What the hell's that got to do with it? Go and talk —'

'You don't understand,' he interrupted, returning to his chair. 'She hasn't any money. Where can she go? She'll be back. They've nowhere to go.' He smiled faintly as he sat down. 'You never understand these things, do you, Tubby? They *have* to come back. I own them.' He closed his hand slowly into a fist. 'I own them, Tubby, I own them.'

And as I stared at him, a car crunched past the windows and went down the drive.

*

We left shortly after that. I remember noticing the time, nine-thirty; we had been at Whitegates no more than an hour. I just got into the car and drove, safely I hope, though without much idea of where I was going. Shaken by what had happened, I was undecided about what to do next. We left without dinner. Staying longer seemed out of the question, but as to what to do, Julia was as indecisive as I was. I tried asking questions. Did she want supper? She shook her head. No, she couldn't face a proper meal, just hot coffee and a snack. Did she want to go home? No. Did she want to go to our glorious four-poster at Hungerford? No, she was in the wrong mood. The truth was we were both stunned by events.

After driving aimlessly for a while, I pulled into a motel just outside Reading, and booked in there for the night. The room was clean and well furnished, but distinctly functional compared to the faded decadence to which we had become accustomed. 'Hardly a love nest,' was Julia's wry comment, which was true enough, except the place had been more her choice than mine. Had she not cast her veto, I would have gone to Hungerford like any other Saturday night.

Haphazard though our journey had been, at least it had given us a chance to recover, and by the time we found a table in the coffee shop, we were more in control of ourselves. I was disgusted with Jack, and angry, and worried about Ann. So Julia sat drinking coffee while I let off steam. All sorts of old memories sprang to mind, bits and pieces from way back. For some reason I started talking about Gill. 'He and I could never agree about Jack. I remember telling him

Jack was crazy about Ann, but Gill wouldn't have it. "He's crazy about the *idea* of her," he said. "Jack sees images, he don't see people."'

Julia nodded. 'Shrewd old guy, Gill. Don't you agree?'

Perhaps, with hindsight; most things become clear with hindsight. I even began thinking about AIDA. 'You know,' I said, 'Jack got so wrapped up in that, I don't think he knew what he wanted most, Ann or the success of the scheme.'

'He got both, didn't he?'

'Yes, but somehow schemes became the blueprint for his whole life –'

'Instead of Ann?'

I shrugged. 'You said it wouldn't last the first time you met them. Tonight looked pretty final to me.'

'I don't know why she married him in the first place.'

I did. Or at least, I thought I did. So I explained about the early days when Jack first got his office, all the dashing about, the deals, the excitement, everyone on a permanent high. Thinking about it, things must have been a bit like that for my mother; working for my father, every day in his office, seeing him shine, watching him win battles, always the conquering hero.

'Maybe,' Julia agreed. 'Personally I'm always distrustful of heroes. False gods and all that.'

'Good,' I said, 'because I'm not the conquering hero type.'

On that we went to bed, but it was a long time before I could persuade Julia to relax. The scene we had witnessed at Whitegates had left her edgy and nervy – and pensive. At one point, she asked, 'You don't think there's anything in what Jack said, do you? About Ann and Nick?'

I stopped stroking her thigh and looked up in surprise. 'Are you kidding?'

She smiled. 'I suppose not. It would have been different if she'd gone off with you.'

I kissed her and we made love, less frenetically than in the four-poster bed because of our mood. And afterwards, passion spent, tiredness set in, and with Julia cradled in my arms I drifted into sleep.

It was some time later that I awoke. I'm not sure what woke me, but the bedsheets beside me were cold and my exploring hands failed to find Julia. Coming fully awake, I saw her at the window. The room temperature had fallen and she had slipped my shirt over her bare shoulders; she was quite still, not watching anything in particular so far as I could tell, simply staring out into the night.

Raising myself onto one elbow, I asked, 'What's up? Can't you sleep?'

'Just thinking.'

'About?'

'What happened tonight. Ann. Wondering what she will do.'

I got out of bed and went over to her. 'Sleepless nights about Ann? I didn't think you liked her that much.'

'I don't, but you do.'

'She's a friend.'

'All right she's a friend, but . . .' Julia shrugged, and even in that dim light I could see her troubled look. 'I don't know,' she said, shaking her head. 'I woke up an hour ago with a sense of foreboding, a sort of premonition, if you like. It wasn't a dream, not a proper dream. I mean, I could tell you about a dream; how it starts, where it ends. This wasn't like that.'

I put my arms round her and drew her close. 'Just a bad dream. Come back to –'

'No,' she pulled away from me. 'It wasn't a dream. I just told you.' Her vehemence startled me into silence.

'It was fear,' she said. 'I got very frightened. I mean, we've got so much. I can't wait for The Grove to be finished. I can't wait to get married. I don't want anything to spoil it –'

'What can spoil it? Stop worrying –'

'Ann can spoil it. She's bound to come to you for help. She's *bound* to, Peter, don't you see? And Jack's so totally ruthless. If you get involved, I'm afraid something terrible will happen.'

It's all very well to say that fears imagined in the middle of the night are irrational. That's what I told Julia. I pointed out that she had fallen asleep with the scene at Whitegates still on her mind. 'That's enough to give anyone nightmares,' I said, coaxing her back to bed during the dark, early hours of that Sunday morning.

It's all very well to be logical, but sometimes it's wiser to listen to intuition . . . as I was to discover.

Ann telephoned me at eleven o'clock on Monday morning. Naturally I took the call – I was worried about her. I neither knew where she was nor what had happened since Saturday night.

'Ann,' I said. 'How are you?'

I think I'd expected her to be upset, but she was

more than upset, she was furious, almost incoherent with rage, and when she was coherent the names she called Jack were nobody's business. It took me some time to understand what had happened. Apparently she had gone to Janie's house at Newbury on Saturday night.

'. . . with only the clothes I stood up in,' she spluttered.

As far as I could gather, she and Nick were still at Janie's. That morning she had driven over to Whitegates with the intention of collecting some fresh clothes.

'And that ape Tiny won't let me in. Says he's under strict orders from Jack. Can you believe that creep? Depriving me of my own clothes in my own home! I wasn't even allowed in the door. Tiny even refused to get me a coat . . .'

There was a lot more in the same vein, especially when I suggested she call Jack at his office.

'Call him? I wouldn't lower myself! They're *my* clothes, Peter. For Christ's sake, I should call the police, that's who I should call.'

Involving the police in a matrimonial dispute was not a good idea, and I said so.

'Oh really? So what do I do? Run around naked? All I've got is what I'm wearing . . .'

Under my breath I cursed Jack for being so bloody spiteful, while out loud I continued to try to placate her. 'Calm down, Ann. I can understand how you feel, but not talking to Jack won't solve the problem. The only solution is for you two to thrash things out –'

'I'd like to thrash him. What a shit! What a low-down, miserable, mean . . .'

All this went on for ten minutes, although it seemed longer, but to be honest I think ten minutes is about right. Finally I offered to call Jack myself. Not that I wanted to, but I could think of no other solution. And I really believed I could persuade him to change his mind. 'He'll have had a chance to calm down by now,' I said.

'Well . . .' Ann said cautiously. 'Okay, but don't beg. And don't take any bullshit. He's not doing me any big favours. They're my clothes, let's not forget that –'

'I won't forget –'

'And don't tell him where I'm staying. I don't want Janie getting into trouble.'

I should have known better than to call Jack. I don't know why I did, except Ann was tearing her hair out and even after Saturday night I couldn't believe Jack would be such a bastard. But he was. His response sickened me. I got sneers, jibes and smutty innuendoes.

'Well, well,' he jeered, 'I should have known she'd go running to you. Tubby Mortlake, the faithful admirer. Your big day, eh? Got your reward at last. I bet you've got one hand smoothing her brow and the other hand up her skirt.'

We had a hell of a row, quite defeating what I was supposed to be doing, which was to get Ann her clothes. Jack refused to believe Ann wasn't in my office. He wouldn't listen. Instead he kept calling me Judas and accusing me of turning against him: 'You fucking back-stabber.' I ended up shouting back and we had the fiercest row of our lives. Finally he snarled, 'That's it then. If that bitch has gone to you for a divorce, she can have one, but it will be on my terms, I'll make sure of that.' With which he slammed down the phone.

That was the last time I ever called Jack Webb. The long friendship was finally, irrevocably over. I vowed never to speak to him again.

Meanwhile I had to call Ann back and admit failure. Instead of helping, I'd made the situation worse.

Ironically, she sounded calmer than me when I called her. I was still riled from arguing with Jack, whereas Ann had just finished a long, soothing conversation with Janie, who had lent her some clothes.

'She says we can stay on here,' said Ann. 'It will give me space and a chance to think. God knows what's going to happen.'

I had to tell her that Jack had assumed she was in my office, discussing divorce.

'Maybe that's where I should be,' she said. 'In fact I was going to ask you to see Nick. He'll go mad unless he does something. Honestly Peter, he's making himself ill. If he could talk to you, it would be such a help . . .'

All would have been different had I refused. I did hesitate, I did remember Julia's plea. But Ann only asked me to listen to Nick, she wasn't asking me to help her . . . And Jack had made me mad . . . and I liked Nick . . .

'Please, Peter. Nick's got such a high opinion of you. He begged me to call you. If you could see us this afternoon . . .'

So of course I said yes.

I forgot Nick was a minor celebrity. To me he was someone I knew; a shy, quiet person wrapped up in his music. I forgot he had a public following, so the stir at the office took me by surprise. Within minutes of his arrival the word had gone round, spread by Monica our receptionist and Elaine from the post-room. I even caught Rose, my secretary, giving him a more than curious look when she brought in the tea. Not that she got much of a response – Nick looked exhausted. Anyone more wretched-looking would be hard to imagine. His face contained even less colour than normal, making me wonder if he had slept at all since Saturday. I doubted it from his haggard expression. He was dressed in a blue denim jacket over blue jeans, with a white open-neck shirt and scuffed brown casual shoes. Even Ann beside him was less than her usual elegant self. Janie's clothes fitted reasonably well, but they were the wrong style, too fussy for Ann and not really her colours.

The opening minutes were surprisingly awkward, considering how long Ann and I had been friends. But we had never met in my office before, or under such circumstances. And of course Nick was there, fidgeting and biting his nails, looking from Ann and back to me, as if wishing we would start without him. Which was perhaps why I got off on the wrong foot by asking Ann – 'Did you think any more about phoning Jack?'

'Hell, I'm not calling him. Why should I? It's over. He told you, didn't he?'

'I know what he said . . . but you and Jack –'

'What about us? It's over, Peter. What more do you want?' Distracted, she ran a hand through her hair. 'Maybe it was over before it began. You know, like those thoughts which seem irresistible until you think them through. Then you say, That might be fun, but what about the consequences?' She smiled briefly, her eyes meeting mine. 'And it *was* fun to begin with. You know, chasing around with Janie and the boys, then later, getting the goodies like the Roller and Whitegates, and that Steinway baby grand. Christ, that piano was good. Nick, what about that piano? Wasn't it something?'

He responded with a rueful look while I watched the smile fade on Ann's face. She shrugged. 'Then came all the bullshit. It was always there with Jack. Like with him and you, he always had to be top dog, right? You seemed not to mind. Know something? I've always admired you for that. It never bothered you. It didn't bother me either; you didn't compete with him, neither did I. Leastways I never thought I was competing. I did my thing and he did his. The bullshit was containable then, but later . . . I don't know, something got to him. Maybe it was some*one*. I think Dai said something about me being the brains of the outfit. Jesus, he was never more wrong, but Jack bit it. After that we were on the slippery slope. You know, Jack puffed himself up bigger and bigger – Jack did this, Jack did that. There wasn't room for me any more. Like, suddenly I was some silly *hausfrau* who knows nothing from nothing.'

She broke off to light a cigarette, absentmindedly returning the pack to her bag without offering them. She tried to disguise her nervousness with a shrug of apparent nonchalance. 'That's where we've been the last couple of years, more and more bullshit. The Big I Am, the Great Jack Webb. No one can talk to him, least of all me. Now I don't want to, not any more. I've had it with Jack. You don't know him like I do,

not when he gets vicious . . . the way he can hurt . . .'
She shook her head before raising her eyes to meet
mine. 'Does that answer your question?'

I suppose it did, but it raised more in its wake. Ever
since Saturday night I had been wondering where she
stood in Jack's business. She had helped start JWE,
helped build it up; without Ann, JWE wouldn't exist.
'When you say there wasn't room for you,' I said
carefully, 'I assume you're still involved with the
business in some way? Aren't you a director?'

'Me? No way.' Ann shook her head. 'I'd be hopeless
at anything like that.'

'But you've got shares in it?'

'Oh, come on, Peter. What would I know about
shares and stuff? Jack handled the business –'

'But you worked in it. You were employed –'

'On the payroll, you mean? Something official?
No, I just helped where I could –'

'But you were paid a salary?'

A flicker of amusement lit her tired eyes. I don't
think Ann had been weeping, but neither had she
slept much. 'Cast your mind back,' she said. 'At the
beginning Jack couldn't pay himself let alone me.
There wasn't any bread, remember? Later I got expenses for things I needed, that sort of thing, but I
was never paid wages.' She stared as if trying to read
my expression. 'It just didn't happen,' she said. 'We
weren't like that. It never bothered me, I didn't go
without. It applied even less when we married. I
mean, Jack just paid the bills, simple as that.'

'Yes,' I said slowly, trying to conceal my dismay.
I was shocked. Ann's reward for helping to create a
multimillion pound business was zero. No official
position, no shareholding, no salary, and nowhere to

live. Even her wardrobe had been denied her. She had no assets at all.

My attempted poker-face failed to fool her. 'I need a good lawyer, right?' Despite her shaky smile, there was no mistaking the look in her eyes, a look that cried, Help! 'There's something I want to say before we go further,' she said. 'First, I've never liked lawyers. I don't trust them. They give out about taking care of your interests, when the only interests they care about are their own. Hypocrites, right?' She smiled briefly. 'You're the exception. It's true, Peter, you don't have to blush.'

I don't think I was blushing, but Ann hurried on before I could answer. 'So the second point is you,' she said quickly. 'First there was God, then you and Jack. Like, you've always been close. Of course I could use help, but I'll understand if you don't want to get involved. Okay?'

There it was. I had the perfect out. I could have got off the hook by a nod of my head. With honour. Julia needn't even know Ann had been in the office.

Ann said, 'That's why I asked you to see Nick rather than me. Tell him what to do. Please Peter, he can't go on like this, he's not sleeping or eating, and most important of all he's not working.'

'How can I work?' Nick demanded, interrupting for the first time. 'Sorry, Mr Mortlake, I know you and Mr Webb are friends, but you saw what it's like. I can't work in that sort of atmosphere. It's impossible.'

I restrained an urge to nod in agreement. Instead I suggested, 'Why don't you tell him? Under the circumstances, he might feel the same way. After all, he ordered you out on Saturday.'

'Out of his house, not his business.'

I remembered then that Jack had told Nick to report to the office that morning.

'I didn't go,' Nick said, looking down at his feet, 'but Ann made me phone him before we came to see you. She didn't want to waste your time. So I did, and he just laughed at me.' Nick looked up, a slight colour coming to his face. 'He gave me a bollocking first for not being in the office this morning. So I said what's the point if we're not working together any more? Then he laughed and told me to look at my contracts. "Read the fine print," he said. "Then come and see me."'

Having suffered Jack's sneers, I could imagine his gloating manner with Nick. 'And have you read the fine print?' I asked.

'Ann has,' said Nick, pulling some tightly folded papers from his pocket. 'I'm not much good at these things, but Ann looked at them before we came over here.'

Ann responded to my look with a deprecating laugh. 'Don't look at me. I told you before, I'm no good at business.'

Nick placed the tatty-looking documents on my desk and tried to smooth out the creases with the heel of his hand. 'They were in my jeans for a while,' he apologised, 'I forgot they were there. Sorry, Mr Mortlake, they could be a bit cleaner.'

There were three contracts in all; one with JWE, one with White Hat Publishers, and the third was with Apex Records. Gingerly I began turning the pages. My misgivings began to grow even then. Jack was an expert in such contracts, I was a beginner, it would take me hours to absorb so many clauses.

Glancing up, I asked Nick, 'Did you take advice before you signed these?'

He responded with a blank stare.

'Did you take them to a solicitor?'

'No,' he said, shaking his head.

My misgivings deepened. Pushing the contracts aside, I began to coax him through an account of what had actually happened. Some of it I already knew. After all, I had been at Whitegates on his first visit. I remembered driving him to the station afterwards, when he was numb with excitement. He had moved into the cottage the following day.

'That was when I signed the first contract,' he said. 'The one with JWE. I tell you, Mr Mortlake, that was the biggest thrill of my life. You know, to have Mr Webb as my manager. It was a dream come true.' Even a year later, his eyes shone.

Resisting the urge to say his dream had gone sour, I asked, 'Did Mr Webb go through the contract with you? Did he sit down and explain it?'

Nick frowned and shook his head. 'There didn't seem much to explain. Mr Webb was becoming my manager. It was what I wanted.'

'And he didn't suggest you consult a solicitor?'

'No, we both signed, then went up to the house to celebrate. Ann was there. We drank a bottle of champagne. It was the first time I'd tasted it.'

I glanced at Ann. She flushed as she met my eye. 'It *was* a celebration,' she said guiltily, 'I didn't think . . . I told you before, Jack deals with contracts and things. I've never had anything to do with them.'

My pessimism deepened by the minute. Flicking through the JWE contract, a lot of the clauses struck me as being one-sided. For example, the thirty percent of all gross income which Jack received as Nick's manager applied not only for the five years of the contract, but forever on all deals struck during those years. I couldn't believe such an arrangement was usual.

The contracts with White Hat and Apex bore a different date. They had been signed ten days after the management contract with JWE. 'What about these?' I asked Nick. 'Did you discuss these with a solicitor?'

'No,' said Nick. He was beginning to sound irritated. 'You don't understand, Mr Mortlake. That's what you have a manager for. He fixes up all the contracts.'

'So what happened with these?'

'Mr Webb just showed me where to sign and I signed.'

'Didn't you even read them?' I asked in astonishment.

Nick flushed. He wasn't an idiot, he was more than averagely bright. He simply lived for his music and cared little or nothing about anything else. He shot me a look full of resentment. 'That's how it works, Mr Mortlake. There are things you've got to understand. Contracts and all that are the manager's job, that's what he's there for. He does all the business . . .'

Nick said that a dozen times in the next half-hour as I combed through the contracts. I went through clause after clause, asking questions but getting very few answers. Ann's concern deepened to worry and then to alarm, while Nick grew ever more agitated. So did I, for that matter, shocked that he had signed so much away. He couldn't even talk to the Press without permission from Jack. He was restricted in this and obligated by that.

Finally I said I needed more time to study the papers in detail, but really Nick should consult an expert, a specialist in entertainers' contracts.

Ann's disappointment was obvious. 'But you know the law, Peter. You must know what's involved. All Nick wants is to get on with his work. Now he can't work with Jack and he can't work without him, if Jack's right about these contracts. There must be something we can do?'

I did my best to explain that unless Jack agreed to terminate the contracts, Nick's only recourse was to try to have the contracts set aside in the High Court. 'But you must have a strong case,' I said. 'It's not enough to say you've changed your mind.'

'You saw how things are,' Nick protested. 'How can I work –'

'Did Jack force you to sign the contracts?'

'No, of course not.'

'Did he trick you into signing?'

'No –'

'Correct,' I agreed. 'The truth is you were happy to sign, you wanted to sign.'

'Yes, but –'

'Because you believed Jack would make you a star. And he's made you a star.'

'I'm not complaining about that –'

'So Mr Webb will tell the judge how hard he's worked for you, and that now you're trying to deprive him of a proper reward, which would be grossly unfair . . .'

To Nick's dismay, I went on for some time, not enjoying myself but determined not to bolster false hopes. Nick's case seemed pathetically weak at first sight. I could imagine Jack laughing all the way to the bank. Which brought me to my next point. 'I must warn you that taking a case to the High Court will cost you a great deal of money,' I said sternly. 'Quite apart from the amount of time it will consume. And if you lose, you'll have to pay Jack's costs as well, and you'll *still* be tied to the contracts. It's a good job you've made a lot of money . . .' I stopped, startled by the look on Nick's face. He looked as if he was about to be sick. His face took on a ghastly pallor and he bent forward in his chair.

Ann was at his side in an instant, her arm around his shoulders, uttering soft words of comfort. 'Take a deep breath,' she coaxed, 'and another. That's right, and again . . .'

Gradually Nick pulled himself together, although even then he looked far from well. Rose brought in some more tea and that helped, but it was some time before Nick could continue. Then he said, 'Money might be a problem, Mr Mortlake. You see I'm not very well fixed at the moment.'

I stared in disbelief, trying to remember how many hits he had recorded. 'Colour Purple' sprang to mind, so did 'Carnival Nights'. They must have earned him a fortune. On top of that, there was the revenue from his albums.

'How are you fixed?' I asked bluntly, expecting his answer in thousands.

'I've got about twenty quid,' he said.

I gasped with amazement. I sat back, trying to think of how he could have spent so much money in so short a time.

Nick fidgeted in his chair and began to explain.

395

Apparently he had been broke when he moved into the cottage, and Jack had suggested an arrangement whereby he paid Nick a small sum every week: pocket money against future earnings. 'I don't need much,' said Nick, 'I don't smoke or drink. Everything at the cottage was free, including my food and everything. Mr Webb paid when I went to the studio, Tiny took care of expenses at the two concerts I gave. You see, Mr Webb explained that money's always tight to begin with, what with them ploughing every penny back into more recordings and so on. So I only asked for ten pounds a week.'

I must have looked pole-axed because Ann rose from her chair and came round the desk to reassure me. 'It's not that bad, Peter. There must be masses of money to come. We just need an accounting from Jack, that's all.'

'That's all?' I groaned. 'Can you see Jack passing money over with this going on? He'll wriggle and argue and hedge . . .'

When I stopped shaking my head, I looked at Ann who had nowhere to live, no money at all, and who possessed not even the clothes on her back. I looked at Nick who had twenty quid in his pocket.

And Jack's gloating voice rang in my ears. 'I own them, Tubby, I own them.'

Julia's reaction was not wholly unexpected. When we met for a drink at the hotel that evening, she listened with predictable coolness, fixing her blue eyes on my face and compressing her soft lips into a straight line. Every word I uttered put me in danger of digging my own grave. It might have been wiser to have kept quiet, except that Julia was apt to misinterpret anything in which Ann was involved. So I told her. The only thing I omitted was Jack's snide remark about me comforting Ann with my hand up her skirt.

Julia flushed when I finished. 'My God, she didn't waste time, did she? It only happened Saturday. I said she'd come crying to you –'

'She came for Nick's sake more than her own.'

'Oh, yes, very clever. Oh, Peter, why couldn't you stay out of it? Why get involved?'

'Be fair,' I protested. 'I mean, take this business of Ann's clothes. Who'd have thought Jack would be such a bastard? I had to try to help –'

'So you phoned him and got a mouthful of abuse for your trouble.'

'Yes, well,' I admitted grudgingly, 'he's turned into a bloody megalomaniac. I'm finished with him, he can go to hell from now on. I want no more to do with him.'

'Honestly? You really mean that?'

I looked at her in surprise. 'Of course I mean it,' I said. And I did. It wasn't until I saw the look on her face that I realised its importance to her. She despised Jack, whereas I suppose I'd always looked up to him. He had always been my hero, someone to live up to – crooked-nosed old buddy Jack; he'd been closer than a brother. From the look on Julia's face I guessed I'd told her more than I thought about my boyhood.

'I'll say,' she smiled, when I said as much to her. 'It was Jack did this, Jack did that.'

I shrugged, feeling slightly foolish. 'He was different then.'

'I doubt it. You turned a blind eye to his faults, that's all. You don't any more, you see him as he is –'

'He's turned into a monster,' I said, anger surging through me again as it had that afternoon. 'You should see these contracts with Nick. They're so one-sided they're grotesque –'

'But they're legal?'

'Nick signed them,' I said with a shrug. 'He was of age, only just, I asked him. He was twenty-one two weeks before he signed the JWE contract.' I fell silent, gnawing away at the problem, frustrated and defeated.

Julia traced her little finger round the rim of her glass, her earlier resentment about Ann's visit apparently forgotten. 'So what happens next?' she asked.

'Jack holds all the cards. Nick's best hope is to ask Jack to release him. I told Nick to go and see him, try to end the relationship on an amicable basis –'

'Some hopes. Poor Nick,' said Julia mournfully. 'I bet he was frightened to death.'

'He was, but he promised to try. If that fails, I've given him the name of some West End solicitors. One of their partners specialises in show business matters.'

'So you're not getting involved?' Julia brightened. Hope shone from her eyes.

I shrugged. 'I'm not a specialist –'

'What about Ann? If it does come to a divorce –'

'She'll probably use Carstairs, the people I told Nick about. After all, she'll be there with him, holding his hand –'

'Oh, Peter!' she exclaimed with relief, delightedly leaning over the table to kiss me.

So at least Julia was pleased.

I was the only one who was left nursing a bad conscience.

John Lovell poked his head into my office the next morning. 'I hear a Pop star consulted us yesterday,' he said with obvious distaste. 'Not really Lovell's cup of tea, surely?'

John still referred to the firm as Lovell's, even though the name over the door said Weston, Lovell, Mortlake and Juffs. And by 'Lovell's cup of tea' he meant landed gentry, professional bodies, or commercial enterprises a hundred years old.

I tried to set his mind at rest. 'Only an exploratory meeting. I don't expect anything to come of it.'

'Ah,' he said. 'Chargeable though, eh?'

Every minute of our time was chargeable, according to John; free consultations were definitely out. He had a point of course, the single commodity in which solicitors deal is their time. But I had been nurtured in Jumbo's more relaxed style, whereby all was well so long as the books balanced at the end of the year. I had no intention of charging Nick. Not that he could pay anyway, until he got some money. I wondered if he'd plucked up the courage to go and see Jack. Poor Nick, Jack would bully and gloat. I could see his hand closing into a fist. 'I own you,' he would sneer. The sick-making thing was, he did. According to the contracts, he owned Nick for at least another four years.

And then something happened that made me look at those contracts again. Not immediately, but it happened that afternoon: Jack phoned.

'I have a Mr Jack Webb on the line,' said Rose.

I almost refused the call. After our furious row the day before, I'd vowed never to speak to him again. I wanted nothing more to do with him, but there he was, on the line. I could scarcely believe it. Curiosity got the better of me.

'Hello,' I said, 'and what can I do for you?'

He was boiling with temper. 'Mind your own business, that's what. I've had Nick in here running off at the mouth, asking for money, saying I owe him thousands according to you –'

I bit my lip, wishing Nick had been more discreet. 'I didn't quite say that –'

'What the hell do you know, anyway? It's none of your bloody business –'

'All I said was –'

'Too much, that's what you said. I told Nick straight: if you want a lawyer, at least get a good one. Mortlake's useless, I said. He never was any good, I ran rings round him in the old days –'

'Jack,' I said, 'I'm going to hang up –'

'Oh, typical. First sign of trouble and you run away. You've always been the same. Well, you started this. First my bitch of a wife, now Nick. Bloody interfering little sod. This time you picked the wrong one. Nobody crosses Jack Webb. I'll fix you once and for all . . .'

I replaced the phone. I was sick of Jack's bullying voice, he talked like a gangster. *I'll fix you.* His threats meant nothing. But that gibe nettled me, the one about him running rings round me in the old days. That rankled, and when I left the office at the end of the day, I took the copies of Nick's contracts with me. Julia was giving classes that evening so in any case I faced it alone, and suddenly there seemed no better way to spend the time than in reading those contracts.

By eleven o'clock I could recite every clause. Most of them were one-sided, unfair, and in some cases downright oppressive. I sat in my room making note after note, feeling outraged that Nick had been hood-winked into signing such contracts. Yet – and I came back to it every time – I had to admit he hadn't really been hoodwinked. He had signed them willingly, rushed to sign, virtually begged.

I don't want to get bogged down with the law. Other lawyers might find it of interest, but I would include too little to satisfy them and no doubt too much for those to whom the law is a bore. But a couple of points must be explained. First the matter of consideration. If one party agrees to do something, what does the other agree to do in exchange? White Hat Publishers would pay Nick for the copyright of his work, so there was consideration. Apex Records would pay a royalty, so there was consideration. I was shocked to learn how long it took Nick to get his money, but there seemed little I could do about that. White Hat produced an accounting once a year and sent the details out nine months later, with any money that was due. The problem was that another clause allowed them to set all sorts of expenses against any sums due to Nick, so a clever accountant could have a field day. 'If only Nick had taken advice at the time,' I groaned.

This set me off on a new track. The law expects parties to a contract to be more or less equal in knowledge and experience; inequality of bargaining is regarded unfavourably, and under certain circumstances the law will protect a person who falls under the spell of someone of greater experience.

'Bloody hell,' I muttered, 'Jack's got more experience than Nick will have in a lifetime.'

Pushing the idea around, I went into the bathroom and washed, to wake myself up. That was when the most startling idea of all occurred to me. I realised what Jack was doing, how he was making so much money: he was negotiating with himself – wearing three hats. Like the old three-card trick.

Like most money-making schemes, it was very simple, even obvious, once you realised. Under the JWE contract, Jack was taking thirty per cent of Nick's total earnings for what? For being his manager. But a manager has a duty to act solely in his client's interests – and how could Jack act solely in Nick's interests when he negotiated, apparently on Nick's behalf, with White Hat and Apex? Jack owned White Hat. He owned Apex. To push for more money for Nick meant paying it himself.

And that was when I got really excited, too excited to sleep. So I went back to the office. It was almost midnight by now, and cold in the office, but I only stayed long enough to collect some of my law books. Then I returned to my warm room at the hotel and settled down to work.

I found the reference almost at once. It was in *Armstrong versus Jackson* in 1917. Summing up, the Judge declared, 'No man can in this Court, acting as an agent, be allowed to put himself into a position in which his interest and his duty will be in conflict.'

Jack's *interests* were to ensure that White Hat and Apex made as much money as possible. His *duty* was to get Nick the best deal. How could he achieve one without failing in the other? There was a clear conflict of interests.

My word I was excited, so much so that it was three in the morning before I went to bed. On the table beside me were five pages of notes. I wondered about sending them to Carstairs; not to teach them to suck eggs, after all they were the experts, but since I was sending them a client . . .

If Julia asked, I could say I wasn't involved . . . yet I wasn't exactly uninvolved either.

I was pleased when Ann phoned the next afternoon. I assumed she was calling to tell me she and Nick had made an appointment with Carstairs. My notes had been typed and were ready to be sent to the appropriate partner.

'Hi,' I said. 'Do you know who you're seeing?'

'We've seen him. We went this morning.'

Her voice was enough. I'd heard Ann happy, angry, and most emotions in between, but never so completely depressed.

'What's up?'

It took only a moment to find out. She and Nick had spent three hours with one of the senior partners at Carstairs. He had listened, examined the contracts and looked suitably grave. After which he had warned them of a difficult case and the need to seek Counsel's opinion. All much as I had done, except he had gone a step further.

'He wants money up front,' Ann said helplessly. 'A thousand pounds before he does anything.'

My hopes fell. I remained silent for a moment, not shocked, but a bit surprised by the amount. Finally

I said, 'Did you point out that Nick can afford it when he gets his money from Jack?'

'Of course we did. He suggested Nick ask his bank for a loan.' Ann laughed mirthlessly. 'Nick hasn't got a bank. He's never had any money until now, and even now he hasn't got it, has he? Jack's got it.'

The unfairness of the arrangement began to get to me. Frustration built as I thought of Jack sitting on Nick's money for another nine months, when Nick needed it now. Meanwhile he couldn't even establish how much was due. He had no rights in the matter.

'Peter,' said Ann, and I heard her hesitation, 'did you know this would happen when you sent us to Carstairs?'

Was it reproach I detected, or was it my conscience? 'No,' I said, 'I didn't know, although there was always that possibility. Most solicitors would ask for an advance to cover Counsel's costs, especially with a new client.' I hesitated, not wanting to make matters worse but seeing no alternative. 'The problem is,' I said, 'they'll ask for a lot more to take this into the High Court.'

Ann groaned. 'God knows what Nick will do. He's beside himself now. He broke down yesterday after seeing Jack . . .'

Ann's account of Nick's meeting sickened me. Jack had been at his bullying worst. 'And Peter, Jack was furious about you. He made all sorts of threats. Nick said he seemed so . . . so confident he could hurt you, so sure. Peter, I'm sorry, but is there . . . you know, anything in your past that Jack –'

'Don't be daft –'

'He threatened to fix you any time he wanted. All he had to do was pick up the phone.'

'He's mad. Off his bloody head.'

Poor Ann. I could feel her desperation. She was calling from Paddington Station, and our conversation progressed against a background of shrill whistles and garbled announcements over the public address system. Finally she said, 'We're going back to Newbury now. I'm screwing up courage to ask Janie and Mike for a loan. They might, you know, for old times' sake and all that. They've been very good about putting us up . . .'

Listening made me wretched, even more so when I felt compelled to say, 'Ann, this business between you and Jack. There's no telling where it will end, but is it wise for you and Nick to be staying together?'

The question took her by surprise. I could almost see her expression. Her response was a sort of half laugh, half sigh. 'Oh, it's nothing like that. How could you even think –'

'It's what Jack might say –'

'But you know it's not true. Nick needs my help, he can't cope, he's out of his depth with all this. He's lost, Peter. I've left him having a coffee in the buffet, but you should see him. He's like a walking zombie –'

'I'm sorry, really. But you and him staying together –'

'We have separate rooms, if that puts your mind at rest. Janie and Mike are chaperones. Oh God, Peter, for you of all people to say that.'

I ended the conversation as soon as I could. I said someone was waiting to see me – a lie to cover my guilt for not offering more help. 'Call me when you've spoken to Janie,' I said, 'and good luck.'

That was where we left it, with me not involved, but not exactly uninvolved either.

It was Julia's birthday and we went out to dinner. A week before, it had been an important entry in my diary; now my mind was full of other things, and I was tired from working half-way through the previous night. Even so, I did *try* to be attentive.

First we went to The Grove to inspect progress, then in the fading evening light, I drove to Lechlade, scene of my fumbling proposal. So you see, my intentions were good.

The trouble was, 'Colour Purple' came on the car radio even before we left Swindon, and while Julia's eyes shone with pleasure, all I could think about was Nick fighting injustice. A composer's work played on the radio earns him Mechanical Rights. That's money, for which Nick had a desperate need. Then when we arrived at the restaurant, the pianist was playing 'Carnival Nights'. As I passed the piano on the way to our table, I saw the sheet music propped up in front of him. 'Ten percent,' I thought. 'Nick's entitled to ten per cent on all sheet music.' More money. I thought, 'People are playing his music all over the country and the poor sod is walking around like a zombie.'

So of course it all came tumbling out – Carstairs' request for money up front, Ann's phone call, the lot.

To be fair, Julia was sympathetic to begin with. After all, she liked Nick as much as I did. She was appalled by his plight. 'Poor Nick,' she kept saying, especially when I started to demonstrate exactly what Nick had given away. I quoted great chunks of the publishing agreement.

Anyone else would have had more sense. I should have been plying Julia with wine. It was her birthday! I should have been sweet-talking her into my bed back at the hotel, in which we occasionally made love – not often, for fear of tongues wagging, hence our Saturday nights spent at places further abroad. And Julia looked delicious that night, wearing a frock that showed more cleavage than ever. She was waiting to be invited to bed . . .

Instead I went on and on about Nick, until eventually I plunged into my theories about conflict of interests and inequality of bargaining power. 'Don't you see,' I said, unable to contain my rising excitement, 'if we can win with an argument along those lines, we don't have to argue individual clauses, we can get the contracts slung out in their entirety. Declared null and void. Kaput. Nick gets the copyright back on all of his work, and he's free of Jack once and for all.'

Julia frowned. 'We? *We* get the contracts slung out?'

So I had to explain about going back to the office for my law books in the middle of the night. I told her about my notes.

'I don't understand,' she said, her eyes filling with concern.

'It was just once this idea took root . . .'

But the damage was done by then. Julia's irrational fears rose to the surface. 'You promised not to get involved,' she said reproachfully.

I squirmed. 'It wasn't so much a promise as a forecast. If Carstairs takes the case –'

'But they want money first –'

'Which Ann is going to borrow from Janie –'

'What if Janie says no?'

'She won't say no. They're friends,' I said, dismissing the idea and getting back to the point. 'What I'm trying to get across is that what's happened here is all wrong. Jack's taken advantage. No wonder he's so stinking rich. It's like stealing candy from kids. They *are* kids. Look at Nick, all he thinks about is writing music. He hasn't got the first idea about business. Jack's tied him up with watertight contracts –'

'But if they're watertight –'

'It's the principle. Don't you see? Jack's got no right to bend the law just because he's a smart operator. It's the sort of thing my father would do. The law –'

'Is about rules, not justice.'

'Oh no,' I threw up my hands. 'Don't you start. My father was always quoting –'

'So was mine. He was a lawyer too, remember? Society must have rules, without rules there is chaos.'

'Hitler had rules and courts to apply them. The strong oppressing the weak. That's not my idea of law.'

The words were out before I could stop them. I regretted them instantly, not the words themselves, I believed in them, but the way they had sounded – harsh and uncompromising, with somehow a nasty implication about Julia's father.

She caught her breath. There was a hint of moisture in her eyes. I cursed silently, wishing I could remember that not everybody hated their father.

'He was a good man,' she said, 'a kind man –'

'There you are then. He would have agreed with me. What's happening to Nick is wrong. The law should protect him –'

'Because you say so? Or because Ann asked for your help?'

'Oh, dear God! It's Nick I'm talking about. Why bring Ann into it –'

'Stop shouting. I'm not deaf.'

I suppose I had raised my voice. Certainly the couple at the next table were giving me peculiar looks. I felt like telling them to mind their own bloody business.

What was left of the evening was ruined. We stopped short of having a row, but only just. What infuriated me was that what I'd been trying to say had nothing to do with Ann. Even Nick was almost irrelevant. It was the principle; the law should protect the weak from being exploited. To my mind the law has no greater function . . .

So we finished the meal and I drove Julia home. Some of the tension eased in the car, enough at least for Julia to snuggle against me, although not enough fo her to come back to the hotel. 'No,' she said, 'you've got circles under your eyes as it is. No sex tonight. And no work either. You'll be in a better temper tomorrow if you catch up on some sleep.'

She stopped short of saying, 'That will teach you a lesson,' but the message was there.

I dropped her at her house and went back to the hotel. Actually, she was right, I was tired. Once undressed I climbed into bed and would have gone straight to sleep but for seeing some of my notes on the bedside table. On the top page I had scrawled *Inequality of bargaining power!!!* which was enough

to set me thinking again, and to wonder if Janie
would come through with the money.

Janie didn't. Jack made sure of that. He declared war
the next day. Truth told, he had been at war for days,
but it wasn't until the Friday that I felt the full force
of his blows. I should have expected them; after all,
if I knew one thing about Jack it was that he had an
ingenious mind – present him with a problem and
he always schemed away until a solution emerged.
And Jack's solution was never straightforward; he
would hit when least expected, strike in ways you
couldn't anticipate.

Ann was the first casualty. I'd scarcely cleared my
post when she came on the line. There was no need
to ask about Janie's decision, I could hear it in Ann's
doom-laden voice. It took longer to learn Janie's
reasons and to detect the strength of Jack's cunning.

'He made her an offer she couldn't refuse,' said
Ann, sounding weary enough to have spent the night
weighing the consequences. 'I can't really blame her.
She's frightened. She sees this as a last chance to
revive her career . . .'

Clever, fat-faced old buddy Jack. Even as I listened,
I couldn't help thinking what a devious bugger he
was. Janie's career had been in the doldrums for a
year; now Jack had offered her a big American tour
with maximum publicity, and a promise of making
three albums in nine months.

'She's thrilled out of her mind. Honestly, Peter, I
had to be pleased for her, despite what that bastard's
doing . . .'

People were being forced to take sides. Anyone not

helping Jack was automatically labelled an enemy.

'Janie's terrified he'll find out we've been staying here. Oh Christ, last night was awful, we were up until three. She and Mike were as embarrassed as hell, but they can't afford to get involved, there's too much at stake. It's not just that they won't lend us the money, they've asked us to leave . . .'

Anger welled up inside me, then contempt. I'd always liked Janie and Mike, they were honest, decent, straightforward. They still were, except they were weak. Yet was I stronger? At least Janie had an excuse, Jack had power of life and death over her career. I was only held back by Julia's irrational fear.

Ann was saying, 'I've spoken to Gill. He was pretty marvellous. Not a hint of 'I told you so'. Anyway, Nick and I can move into the pub for a while . . .'

I listened in silence, trying to formulate a response.

Then Ann said, 'God knows where we'll get this money. I'll try, really I'll try. It'll take time, that's all. Meanwhile Nick's suicidal. He can't think straight, let alone work. Please, Peter, isn't there anything you can do? Can we come and see you . . .'

So of course I said yes, come over to the office and talk about it some more. Then I put the phone down and started to scramble through the notes I'd made for Carstairs. And needless to say I cursed Jack, cursed him for using one person to get at another, little realising he was about to employ the same tactics on me.

Jack's attack came with the afternoon post. Ann and Nick had arrived by then, both looking tired and defeated. I sat them down and asked Rose for some tea. Solicitors are used to long faces, half the people who come to our offices are in some sort of trouble; but I'd never seen anyone more troubled than Nick. He had the bemused look of a small boy lost in a shopping mall, in fact so much so that Rose sent out for some chocolate biscuits to serve with his tea. 'There you are then,' she said, making a fuss of him and going quite pink when he raised a tired smile of thanks.

Ann was astonishing. Never for a moment did she mention her own troubles, her every thought was for Nick. Watching her with him was to see not so much a mother-and-son relationship – the age difference of only seven or eight years made nonsense of that – but rather a big sister with a younger brother. A strong big sister and a sick brother; a devoted nurse helping a genius preserve his strength for his writing.

'We must be able to do *something*,' she said, almost pleading, 'Nick can't go on like this. He can't work with this hanging over his head. Even if he could, you know how Jack feels about this Vietnam project.'

Nick joined in the protest. 'He's got no right to do it,' he blurted out suddenly. 'Even Carstairs said that. Nothing in the contracts says I've got to write what I'm told.'

That was true, nothing did, but nothing compelled White Hat to publish what Nick wrote.

'And your work automatically becomes their property,' I said. 'You can't offer it elsewhere. Jack can take what you write and bury it if he likes. He can do that for another four years.'

I admit I was pretty blunt, but there was no point in beating about the bush. Jack *owned* Nick unless we could have the contracts set aside, and the chances of that were not high. I was explaining this when Rose came in with the afternoon post.

'Sorry to interrupt,' she apologised, 'but I thought you might like to see these.'

The fact of her coming in at all during a meeting was unusual. So was the warning look on her face. In a sense I was warned before I even glanced at the letters. Then my heart skipped a beat. The embossed heading came into focus. *Mortlake, Dingle & Barnes*. My father's firm. My father's handwriting was scrawled at the foot of the page. Suddenly I knew what Jack had meant when he had threatened to fix me. He had enlisted my father to fight against me.

Both letters were brief.

Dear Sirs,
We act for Mr Jack Webb of Whitegates, Maidenhead, Berkshire. We understand that Mr Webb's wife recently consulted you and we write to enquire if you know of her present whereabouts. If not, may we ask if you are authorised to accept proceedings against her, since our client is anxious to commence an action for divorce.

The other letter was only a line or two longer:

Dear Sirs,
We act for Jack Webb Enterprises Ltd, White Hat Publishing Ltd and Apex Records Ltd. We write in respect of your client, Mr Nicholas Berkley, who until recently resided at Whitegates, Maidenhead, Berkshire. We understand that Mr Berkley has consulted you regarding his contracts with our

above-mentioned clients. We write to say that there is no truth in Mr Berkley's allegation that he is currently owed monies by any of the above-named companies, and we would draw your attention to the contracts involved. Naturally we confirm that White Hat Publishing will produce an accounting on the due and proper date in accordance with the said contract, and any monies due to Mr Berkley will be forwarded accordingly. However, we would point out that very substantial expenses were incurred on Mr Berkley's behalf and that these sums will accordingly be taken into account.

My brain failed to absorb the letters the first time of reading. I was stunned by Jack's viciousness. Gathering myself, I read both letters again. The letter about Nick told me nothing new; it had been sent for one purpose only – to warn me off, to frighten me, to send me running for cover.

I swallowed hard as I looked up to Ann. 'My father is acting for Jack,' I said.

She stared, not responding until I passed her the letters. Even then I don't think she understood the contents. She barely glanced at them, instead she looked at me, realisation dawning in her eyes. 'He always said you were terrified of your father. That's why he's done it. What a bastard he is! He's never been near your father before, he's not been back since the day you were fired.'

I thought back six, nearly seven years to that day when my father threw us out of his office. After a long moment, I shook my head. 'Jack never understood me and my father. Jack always made it sound simple, when it wasn't. Jack always buttered him up, kowtowed to him. I would never do that. Jack only fought my father once and he lost. I spent my life fighting him. He's a bully –'

'Like Jack,' Ann interrupted.

'Yes,' I said, and I knew she was right. 'Like Jack. But fighting my father taught me a lesson. Never give in to a bully.'

It was only then that Ann read the letters; she smoothed them over her lap and studied them, reading first one and then the other. I tried to imagine her feelings,. Even though she had told me her marriage was over, a letter spelling out divorce must come as a shock. A letter from my father, such as he must once have written to my mother . . .

Ann's hand shook slightly as she handed Nick the letter concerning him. Silently I rose and went to the cupboard. All I had was some dry sherry. Filling three glasses, my thoughts turned angrily to Jack. His tactics were abundantly clear: isolate Ann from friends like Janie and Mike, force Nick to accept the terms of the contracts, neutralise me by involving my father . . .

Ann was still bent over the letter. 'Come on,' I said, handing her a glass, 'remember, never give in to a bully.'

She responded with an apprehensive smile, all of the fight knocked out of her.

'Nick,' I said, giving him a glass. Taking the sherry, his worried eyes searched my face, seeking answers to the letter in his hand.

I took a deep breath. 'Jack and my father seem to think you two are my clients. Is that all right with you?'

Colour flooded into Nick's face. He rose, spilling his drink. 'You mean?'

'I'll be your lawyer,' I said, 'if you want me.'

I heard Ann catch her breath, and sensed rather than saw her stand up. Next minute her hands were on my face and her lips were on mine. She withdrew, gasping, her dark eyes shining. 'Oh, Peter,' she cried, and kissed me again.

Which was when the door opened and Julia walked into the office.

I'm not sure Julia ever accepted the situation. It was partly because she misread Ann's every action, and partly because she had this inexplicable sense of foreboding. 'Something will happen to *us*,' she insisted when we discussed matters later that night. 'I don't know what, I'd tell you if I did. I said Jack was ruthless. Now he's involved your father, don't you see, it will all get so personal and bitter, and somehow we'll get caught up in it. I can't explain, I know it sounds ridiculous, but I just *know*.'

How can you reason when a woman says that? How can someone just 'know'? We talked for a long time, half of it on the verge of a row. What saved us was Julia's choice of language; her urge to tease was irrepressible even when she was indignant. I was explaining that Ann had kissed me because she was worried about Nick.

Julia exploded. 'Oh great! Do Nick a real favour and she'll take you to bed.' Her voice changed to an imitation of Ann, 'Oh, Peter, that's lovely. Let's screw some more. Nick's ever so grateful.'

It struck me as funny, so I burst out laughing, and

finally Julia stopped being mad and joined in. Sadly, however, not even laughter could dispel her fears. No matter how illogical, her apprehension was certainly genuine.

We agreed to differ, eventually. What else could we do? In spite of her fears, Julia accepted that I had taken Nick and Ann on as clients. She also accepted that what happened in the office – short of snogging with Ann – was not really her business. 'But in future I'd rather not talk about it,' she said. 'I'm sorry for Nick, but I hate Jack, and you know what I think about Ann. I'll be glad when it's over, that's all. Meanwhile, I'll keep my fingers crossed and try not to worry.'

So from then on the subject was barred. Ignoring it seemed to work, too, especially for the rest of that weekend, because neither of us mentioned it and we enjoyed ourselves at The Grove, where exciting things were beginning to happen. The interior of the house had looked like a heap of rubble until then; now, alterations were taking shape. We could see which walls had been knocked down and measure the new spaces created, we could see the new bathrooms if not yet the fittings . . .

Julia grinned as we did our tour of inspection. 'When it's finished, we'll open it to the public. Sell tickets to pay off the mortgage.'

'They'll buy tickets for the gardens alone,' I replied.

I was proud of our efforts as landscape gardeners. Not that we were at the stage of planting or sowing, that would come later, but I'd built a picket fence between the extended garden and the paddock, constructed a rockery along one side of the drive, moved a ton of earth to level out what would be the main lawn – and Julia had hacked her way through half an acre of brambles.

I remember that Sunday evening as clearly as yesterday. We were on our knees, sweat-stained and exhausted. Scruffy in gardening clothes, we limped wearily to the car and sat down. I was about to start the engine when Julia stopped me. 'No,' she said, 'let's sit here a bit. Have a cigarette or something, and just look.'

The sun had fallen behind the elms, laying fingers of light across the grass. Ducks clacked down in the brook, a sparrow-hawk circled overhead. The heat had gone out of the day, and Julia and I sat parked in the drive to watch the sun go down.

That was when she fell in love with the place. I'd been enchanted from the first moment, and Julia's excitement had been growing, but until then she had held something back, as if afraid to believe in the plans I had made. That evening, with everything taking shape, she saw The Grove as I'd always seen it.

'Our home,' she whispered under her breath. 'Please God, give us this and we'll be happy the rest of our days.'

Then she hid her embarrassment under a shaky laugh. 'Okay, Mortlake, let's go. I need a hot bath.'

But her grin was false. Worry was back in her eyes, and even without her saying so, I knew that she was once again beset with misgivings.

I had misgivings myself the following week. Ignoring my bleak warnings, Ann and Nick had been euphoric when I'd agreed to act for them. I'd tried to make them see sense. 'Don't expect miracles,' I had said, but, from the look on their faces, I could have saved my breath. Such faith was touching when I was consumed by doubt; the truth was that I was still trying to decide on my first move.

Ann's improved spirits survived the weekend, because she telephoned on Monday, sounding jubilant. 'Our worries about money are over,' she cried. 'We've had the most marvellous idea.'

'Oh?'

'Nick will give a concert, or a couple of concerts. As many as it takes to raise the money to take this case to the High Court.'

It was a good idea, except the contract with JWE barred Nick from giving any public performances without Jack's consent.

Ann groaned when I told her. Then she said, 'Suppose we go ahead anyway?'

'Jack will sue for breach of contract. And he might sue the promoter as well.'

'Can he do that?' Ann sounded horrified.

'Also, I bet he threatens never to let Dai or The Tower or any of the others appear for that promoter again.'

Poor Ann. I hated to disillusion her, but there was no point in encouraging false hopes. For a moment she fell silent, then she said, 'You are going ahead, aren't you, Peter? I'll get the money somehow. People will rally round, you'll see. Guess what Gill said last night? He'll give us five hundred pounds. Isn't that guy something special?'

Far more than five hundred pounds would be needed to go into the High Court, but then was not the right time to say so. Besides, Ann already knew that, and Gill *was* something special. I told her to wish him well from me.

'You bet. And Peter, we've only just started to fight, right?'

'Right,' I agreed and tried to match her enthusiasm. After putting the phone down, I began work on drafting my answers to Mortlake, Dingle & Barnes. What made it difficult was that whatever I wrote would amount to the opening shot in our campaign to free Nick from his contracts. What also made it difficult was that only six months before, my father had been described by the *Sunday Times* as 'the most skilful lawyer in Britain'. Finally I chose to attack the contracts themselves, but without giving reasons.

We refer to Mr Berkley and your respective clients. We have now examined the contracts to which you refer and find them so badly flawed as to be invalid. However, in view of the past association between Mr Berkley and your clients, it is hoped that this matter might be resolved on an amicable basis. Consequently, we propose that these contracts be deemed null and void by mutual consent, and your comments on this proposal would be appreciated in due course.

The odd thing was, I felt a great sense of relief when the letter went off in that night's post. Battle was joined, and I forgot about Julia's irrational fears . . .

The next ten days saw a flurry of letters between me and Mortlake, Dingle & Barnes. Effectively, between me and my father, although all solicitors sign letters as if by the firm and not the individual, so he scrawled 'Mortlake, Dingle & Barnes' at the foot of his, and I answered with 'Weston, Lovell, Mortlake and Juffs'. No one would have known we were related, but of course it was my father; apart from recognising his handwriting, his initials JM appeared at the top of the page. I knew it was him, he knew it was me, and the old fight was rejoined on a new field of battle.

Predictably he rejected my initial letter. He wrote back:

We are surprised you consider the contracts invalid. On what grounds do you make this claim? We consider the contracts to be properly drawn and would point out that Mr Berkley is bound by them, as are our clients, who are anxious to continue their efforts to promote Mr Berkley's career . . .

Changing tack, I used Ann's idea when I replied:

We note your client's concern about Mr Berkley's career. In this connection he is proposing to perform at a concert, or concerts, in London in the near future. Your client's views on this would be appreciated since, although we consider the contracts between Mr Berkley and your clients to be invalid, we should like to resolve the differences of opinion as amicably as possible . . .

I grinned when I wrote that, picturing my father's face when he read it.

His reply bristled with hostility.

We cannot understand your repeated comments

about the validity of the contracts. For our part we are perfectly satisfied that the contracts are valid and enforceable. As to Mr Berkley's proposal to perform at a concert, or concerts, we would refer you to his contract with JWE Ltd, clause 19 (i) and (iv). JWE Ltd advise us that as sole managers of Mr Berkley they cannot give consent for him to appear in any concert not authorised by them . . .

The reply was no more than I had expected. They were rejecting our every move, flexing their muscles, insisting on the validity of the contracts and threatening to enforce them. Which made me wonder if they could? By withholding permission for Nick to perform at a concert, they were denying him the chance to earn a living. That was Restraint of Trade, and Restraint of Trade was definitely not enforceable. Naturally, my father would argue differently; he would say his clients were eager to help Nick earn a living, all Nick had to do was honour the contracts . . .

Even so, the more I played around with the idea, the more I liked it. My hopes rose. Restraint of Trade was at least worth arguing, it was another string to our bow. Now we had Conflict of Interests, Inequality of Bargaining, *and* Restraint of Trade. A good barrister *might* have enough to persuade a Judge . . .

I'd gone as far as I could. I needed help, and the sooner the better. The obvious choice was to talk things over with John, but he was an awkward devil at times. His views on pop stars had already been made abundantly clear. 'Not Lovell's cup of tea,' he had said. So instead of talking to John I went directly to Jumbo, which proved to be a mistake of mammoth proportions ... although eight weeks were to pass before that became clear.

Jumbo grinned from ear to ear when I drove into the office car park at Bristol. 'By God,' he chuckled, 'Martin told me about your MG. I didn't believe him. Here, move over, let me have a drive.'

So Jumbo drove me to lunch at a little place just outside Bristol. Inevitably it was a pub, overlooking a village green. 'Scene of past triumphs,' he chuckled, waving a hand at the cricket pitch.

Everyone knew him, of course. 'Morning, Mr Weston.' 'Lovely day, Mr Weston.' 'Keeping well, I hope, Mr Weston?' The pub was new to me, so were the faces, but Jumbo never changed. Wherever he went, he was known; it took us twenty-five minutes to escape from the bar, where everyone wanted to buy him a drink. Not that Jumbo accepted. The most he ever drank at lunchtime was two half-pints of bitter, but he shook everyone's hand and eventually we made our way upstairs to the small dining-room.

'Have the mixed grill,' he invited. 'It will fill you up for a week.'

Once we had ordered, we got down to business. 'Now then, young Peter, what's this about?'

It took half an hour to tell him, what with having to expound on Conflict of Interest, Inequality of Bargaining, and Restraint of Trade.

He didn't like it. I hadn't expected him to. Jumbo believed our job was to keep our clients out of court. 'A court never resolved anything that couldn't be settled outside faster and cheaper,' was his motto, and I agreed – we resolved ninety percent of client difficulties by negotiation. The problem was, as I pointed out, that it takes two parties to negotiate.

'Daft young fool,' Jumbo called Nick. He referred to Jack as 'an out and out shit' and described Ann as 'that dark- haired girl who can only hear music'.

Over coffee, he puffed on his pipe, scowling furiously. 'You're a bit close to this, what with having been such a friend of Jack's, and now with him involving your father. I have to ask if you're being influenced by the wrong reasons. The need to prove yourself, maybe? Are you fighting for this lad Berkley or for Peter Mortlake? Never forget, a lawyer who acts for himself has a fool for a client.'

'That's unfair. I didn't seek Nick out as a client, but he'll get buried unless we help. We can't turn our backs on injustice. That's not what you and Josh taught me . . .'

And so we argued. He made me go through the whole thing again, just as Josh did in the old days, exerting the same pressure, probing, delving, taking nothing for granted, making me prove every point. The dining-room emptied. Downstairs the landlord called time. Upstairs, the waitress brought us our bill.

Finally Jumbo sat back in his chair. 'All right, I agree. Berkley's got to fight and you've got to fight for him. You need Counsel's opinion on your chances . . .'

I breathed a sigh of relief. No one was harder to convince. If Jumbo believed in my arguments, I had a chance of persuading other people.

But when I drove him back to his office, he insisted

on phoning my father. 'Just in case he'll talk to me *reasonably* about it.'

I'd never known my father be reasonable about anything. 'He won't budge when he thinks he's got the whip hand.'

'So let's test it,' said Jumbo.

Without liking it, I had to accept it. 'All right,' I said grudgingly. 'Then what?'

'If I fail you need to see Counsel. Do you have anyone in mind?'

'I wish I did.'

Jumbo frowned. 'He'll have to be good. You've argued a fair case, but your father will find the flaws faster than anyone. He'll also know the best Counsel.'

Jumbo was still frowning when I dropped him in the car park. 'I'll make a few calls about Counsel, just in case. Leave it with me and I'll get back to you. Okay?'

After thanking him, I was about to drive off when he stopped me. 'Peter,' he said, 'Counsel will cost money, you know. It's no good going for a Junior, we'll have to get a QC for this, a top man, probably someone who's head of his chambers.'

I guessed what was coming.

'John's a bit stuffy about money,' said Jumbo. 'You'd better get that angle sorted.'

I drove back to Swindon, nursing mixed feelings; my relief about convincing Jumbo was now tinged with anxiety. The weather was fine, the roads were dry, yet I had the distinct feeling of driving on ice.

*

We saw Sir Robert Longfellow, QC, in his Lincoln's Inn chambers the following week, at four o'clock on a Thursday afternoon. Jumbo had arranged the appointment and I'd sent Longfellow the papers. In the cab on the way from Gill's place, Ann quizzed me on British law in an effort to keep Nick from fretting about the meeting ahead. He was sick with nerves, literally ill, having developed boils, of all things. His frizzy fair hair lay on his collar, he wore his usual blue jacket and jeans, and he looked like a man under sentence of death. I could have wished for a more presentable client. Thank God for Ann, who was as clean and smart as a new pin. I suspect Gill had provided money for new clothes, for the cream linen suit she was wearing was certainly not Janie's.

'Okay,' she said, 'so we listen to this guy's opinion. What then?'

'We go ahead with the fight, or we don't. It's up to him —'

'Oh?' she said, startled. 'But what about that stuff you told us? Conflict of interest and all that. You said we've got a good case —'

'I said I think we can *make* a case. Longfellow will assess its chance of success —'

'And if he says they're no good, we drop it?' Ann's voice rose in horror. 'Just like that?'

'Ann,' I said in cautionary tones, 'we are here for advice. This man is a brilliant barrister, one of the great legal experts in England. We answer his questions and we listen very carefully to what he tells us to do, okay?'

Her dark eyes glittered with amusement. 'You're nervous, aren't you? Go on, admit it.'

'Just anxious,' I lied. Of course I was nervous. Junior partners in firms of provincial solicitors do not often debate the law with the likes of Sir Robert. When we went in he would have my notes on his desk. He could tear my arguments to shreds, ridicule me, all very politely of course for barristers are invariably respectful to solicitors, but he would know and I would know exactly how far I was out of my depth. Even worse was imagining Nick's reaction if Sir Robert dismissed any chance of success. Yes, I was nervous.

Ann squeezed my arm. 'I always think of you as a great legal expert. He'll have to be good to match you.'

I laughed, and the taxi passed through the gates and into Lincoln's Inn. Ann went all wide-eyed and American, looking at the ancient buildings and murmuring, 'How about this? Straight out of Dickens.'

And of course she was right. The Inns of Court go back much further than Dickens, but the flavour of the place that afternoon was as Dickensian as *Bleak House*. With Nick dragging his feet, I ushered Ann over the flagstones and up the steps to Longfellow's chambers. His name was painted in gold leaf on the black door, above those of his Junior Counsel. Once inside, we were greeted by an elderly clerk who suggested we make ourselves comfortable in the waiting room. 'Sir Robert won't keep you a minute,' he promised. And he was as good as his word, because he had scarcely left when he returned to usher us down the corridor to Sir Robert's room.

From behind a vast Victorian partner's desk, Longfellow rose to greet us. Dressed in a black jacket and pinstripe trousers, he was of medium height and average build; a man of about fifty with exceptional blue eyes – very strong eyes, almost the colour of sapphires. He had a long, intelligent face, an aquiline nose and a mane of grey hair, very thick and stylishly cut.

'This is Olivia Newton,' he said, indicating a woman who sat close to one side of his desk.

Olivia Newton was a junior barrister, one of the ten in Longfellow's chambers. Juniors who serve their masters especially well are rewarded with the gift of a red bag in which to carry their wig and gown and their books; less distinguished juniors make do with a blue one. Olivia's red bag was at her feet, next to her chair.

I made our introductions and we were asked to sit down. Ann took the armchair opposite the desk, Nick and I sat either side, while Longfellow returned to his throne-like chair behind the great desk.

He began unexpectedly. 'Weston, Lovell, Mortlake and Juffs,' he said, holding up the letter I had sent him, while staring at me with those very blue eyes. 'And Mortlake, Dingle & Barnes. Two distinguished firms of solicitors with one name in common. Perhaps I should say, uncommon? I don't know how many Mortlakes are in the London Telephone Directory, but I doubt very many.'

He had a voice developed in the courtroom: clear, strong and well modulated.

'Not many,' I agreed.

He nodded. 'I have known James Mortlake a good many years,' he said, letting my letter fall to the desk as he steepled his fingers, 'but you, Mr Peter Mortlake, are a stranger to me.'

My heart sank.

'May I ask if you are related?'

'He's my father.'

Longfellow's eyebrows rose to his hairline. 'Your father? Well, I'm blessed. I've never heard him mention a son.'

I stifled a groan. Jumbo had warned me about Longfellow. 'You won't like him,' he had said. 'He's a pompous, self-opinionated, theatrical show-off. You'll hate him. But he's bloody good. Nobody better.' Longfellow was probably everything Jumbo said, but even worse, it seemed he was a friend of my father's.

'Father and son,' Longfellow murmured as if musing aloud. 'Well, I'm blessed. Father's on one side, son's on the other. Why on earth doesn't son ring Dad up and say, Our mutual clients are in a bit of a mess? And why doesn't Dad say, Come up to the club and we'll sort it out over a spot of lunch? Simple solution, wouldn't you say? Saves dragging everyone into the High Court.'

I cleared my throat. 'It wouldn't work. Jumbo . . . er, Mr Weston phoned him last week –'

'I didn't suggest Mr Weston phone him –'

'It'd be no good. My father and I haven't spoken in years.'

'Ah.' Sir Robert sounded triumphant, like a magician when all is revealed. He looked across at the window. 'Dad and son don't speak,' he said heavily, as if addressing a jury. Then he swung back to me. 'I'd be obliged, Mr Mortlake, if you would explain.'

Naturally, the notes I had sent contained no mention of personal backgrounds. I had enclosed copies of the contracts, with my comments about them, copies of correspondence between us and Mortlake, Dingle & Barnes, but that was all.

I explained what had happened when Nick first came to see me. 'I advised him to go to Jack . . . Mr Webb . . . and try to negotiate a way out. Things between them had reached a low ebb, Nick felt he couldn't work –'

'Very good advice,' Sir Robert interrupted, turning to Nick. 'And did you follow that advice, Mr Berkley?'

Nick swallowed hard. Longfellow's laser-like stare was disconcerting. 'Yes,' said Nick, 'I went to see Mr Webb . . .'

Longfellow listened, nodding now and then while making notes with a gold pencil. 'You definitely asked him to release you from these contracts?'

'Yes,' said Nick, nodding his head.

'And you would swear to that in court if need be?'

'Yes.'

Longfellow turned back to me. 'Then what happened?'

'When Mr Webb refused, Nick and Mrs Webb went to see another firm of solicitors –'

'On your advice again?' he asked as his eyebrows rose.

'Yes. Jack Webb and I have been, or rather we were, friends for a long time. I thought it best if –'

'You disqualified yourself for that reason?'

'Partly for that reason, and partly because ours is a general practice. One of the partners in Carstairs, the firm I recommended specializes in –'

'Yes, yes, I know Bannerman,' Sir Robert interrupted impatiently. 'And what happened then?'

I hesitated. 'While Carstairs were sympathetic, they were concerned about fees, and ... well, as you've seen from the contracts, Jack can hold on to Nick's money –'

'So he came back to you?'

I nodded.

'Go on.'

'Well, next was the letter from Mortlake, Dingle & Barnes.'

'Quite a coincidence,' Sir Robert said dryly. 'Your old friend turning to your father. Had he used him before?'

'I don't think so.'

'Mortlake, Dingle & Barnes are not JWE's usual solicitors?'

'I don't think so.'

'And James Mortlake doesn't usually act for White Hat Publishing or Apex Records?'

'Not to my knowledge –'

'Whereas your old friend knew of your relationship with your father?'

'Oh yes, since we were boys.'

Sir Robert digested that with the faintest of smiles. 'Tricky chap, your old friend. Very well, let's press on. Mr Berkley returns to you after seeing Carstairs. You get the letter from Mortlake, Dingle & Barnes, which we can presume was designed to push you out of the action. You decide you may as well be hanged for a sheep as a lamb and answer it, thus bringing about the exchange of letters of which I have copies. After which your senior partner intervenes with his telephone call to your father. In other words, you try to disqualify yourself again. Is that about it?'

'Not quite. To be honest, I didn't ask Mr Weston to –'

'He insisted, perhaps? He tried to disqualify you?'

'He thought –'

'He stood a better chance of talking James Mortlake into a deal than you did?'

'Something like that.'

'And what did you think?'

'I thought my father would tell him to go to hell.'

'And did he?'

'Not in those words –'

'But to that effect. Then what happened?'

'Then Jumbo ... Mr Weston, told his office to contact your clerk and we made this appointment.'

The fingers of Sir Robert's left hand drummed on the desk while his right hand gripped on the gold pencil. 'So three separate attempts were made to arrive at an amicable settlement? Mr Berkley with Mr Webb, you in your first letter to Mortlake, Dingle & Barnes, and Mr Weston on the phone to your father. And all were rebuffed.'

'Correct.'

He added a line to his notes, and when he looked up he was smiling at Ann. 'Now I must apologise for my arrant bad manners,' he said, his voice growing warmer. 'Forgive me for not addressing myself to you before.'

Ann was charmed, I could see it in her eyes. She smiled at him and was still smiling when he asked, 'And why, I wonder, does the glamorous Mrs Webb closet herself with her husband's enemies at a time like this?'

Colour rose in Ann's face. She turned to me for help.

'Ah,' I said, intervening, 'I'm sorry, look, I should have explained –'

'No need,' said Sir Robert without taking his gaze from Ann's face, 'Mrs Webb will explain. Now then, Mrs Webb, how did this all come about?'

And so the entire story came to be told, including the way in which Ann had left Whitegates on that Saturday night. Longfellow was alternately friendly and aggressive, gentle one minute and savage the next. He explained he was only seeking to establish what might come out in court, but he pulled no punches. And after her initial surprise, Ann recovered, and she and Longfellow had some heated exchanges. He attacked her hard at one stage. 'You left your home and went to Newbury with this man,' he said, pointing at Nick. 'Then you left there and went to London with him. Come, come, Mrs Webb, we are all mature and sensible people. I put it to you that you are having an affair with this man –'

'Not true,' Ann protested.

Longfellow pressed on. 'And that this sordid affair began while you were both under your husband's roof –'

'Bullshit!'

'Then why leave a dutiful husband who gives you a luxurious life –'

'Built on a lie! Exploiting artists instead of nurturing their talent –'

'Which you went along with,' Longfellow said harshly. 'You condoned it, until –'

'No! I never condoned it. Jack always said the artist came first, second and third. I didn't know the first thing about the contracts until Peter explained –'

'And that's why you left your husband?' Longfellow sneered scornfully. 'Is that what you want me to believe?'

'I don't care what you believe!' Ann shouted furiously.

Longfellow smiled. 'Ah, but you must,' he said quietly, taking the heat out of the argument. 'I must believe, Mrs Webb. In court, the Judge must believe. Don't you see?'

After that he began to coax her through the story of how she and Jack had met and how they had come to marry. Listening and watching, I hated Longfellow for the way he drew out even intimate details, yet I had sense enough to realise that I was watching an expert at work. Longfellow knew the entire story by the time he had finished. Finally he sat back in his chair. 'And now,' he said softly. 'What of the future when this is all over? A reconciliation with your husband, perhaps?'

'Never,' Ann said flatly. 'I never want to see Jack again. It's finished.'

They stared at each other, Ann defiant as she returned Longfellow's searching look. Then he nodded and turned to Olivia Newton, as if inviting her to ask questions, but she shook her head and merely made a note on her pad. In her mid-thirties, she was fresh-complexioned with brown hair, homely-looking rather than attractive, and although she had scarcely spoken, I still remembered her voice when she had greeted us; a warm, comforting voice. In court, I imagined, witnesses would underestimate her, so relieved to be spared Longfellow's thunderbolts that they would fall hook, line and sinker for Olivia Newton's more gentle approach.

Satisfied with Ann's story, Longfellow turned his

attention to Nick, using the same tactics, abrasive one moment and gentle the next. It was painful to witness, yet at the same time intensely revealing. I learned more about Nick in the next thirty minutes than at any of our previous meetings. An orphan, he had been brought up by foster-parents who had treated him more like a slave than a child; after a lifetime's deprivation, no wonder he had been bowled over by Whitegates; no wonder he had seen Jack as a god. Fidgeting with embarrassment, often scarlet of face and not far from tears, he resisted Longfellow's more intimate probings, but never with much chance of success – Longfellow stripped him bare, revealing a timid soul who had known little of the love he wrote about in his songs. Maybe that's what gave them their yearning, aching quality; maybe the violence he had suffered as a child was why he felt so strongly about the mindless violence of Vietnam. I only know I became angry as I listened, and Ann grew upset; Olivia Newton stopped making notes and simply stared at Nick, absorbed by his story. And still Longfellow persisted, as relentless with his questions as an incoming tide.

Outside, the sky darkened into evening, while inside the room we ached for the pitiless examination to end; and when at last it did, we breathed a collective sigh of relief. I felt exhausted, wrung out, and a sideways glance at Ann revealed the pain in her face.

Sir Robert Longfellow sat back in his chair. Deep in thought, he was silent for several minutes. He stroked his nose and ran a hand through his hair. Finally he looked up at me, and I was struck by the coldness in his eyes. The severity of his expression gave a bleak cast to his face. 'You came here for an opinion,' he began, in such sombre tones that I immediately feared the worst. 'Very well,' he said, 'in my opinion, taken one by one, these contracts' — he paused to tap the papers in front of him — 'these contracts are essentially valid, and from what I have heard of Mr Webb, he wouldn't change as much as the date. Perhaps *especially* the date, for if Mr Berkley can be brought to heel, Mr Webb can expect to receive a vast sum over the next four years. Indeed, in the case of the publishing agreement he will go on receiving money even *after* four years. From what you tell me, he won't easily let go of that. Obviously Mr Berkley is a talented young composer at the outset of his career. Who knows what his contribution to music will be? And who knows how valuable in terms of money? If Mrs Webb agrees with her husband on one thing, it is that Mr Berkley possesses a rare gift. And Mr *Webb* owns that gift. It is his to exploit, his to control, and quite clearly he will not relinquish control. Furthermore, he has turned to one of the most distinguished solicitors in London to help him retain that control.'

Longfellow paused to let his gaze pass from me to Ann, then to Nick, no doubt to register our collective dismay.

Ann sucked in a breath. 'Are you saying there's no chance?'

Longellow frowned. 'I'm saying your husband —'

'Please don't call him that,' Ann interrupted, a faint blush coming to her cheeks.

Longfellow's shoulders twitched in the faintest of shrugs. 'Very well. I'm saying the other side have a very strong case.'

Nick groaned. Hunched up in his chair, elbows

on his knees, he stared down at the floor in utter dejection.

'On the other hand,' Longfellow continued, 'along comes the younger Mr Mortlake who says it's not fair. He claims Mr Webb is wearing two hats when he should only wear one. I agree with him. He claims Mr Webb took unfair advantage when the contracts were negotiated. I agree. He says Mr Webb's current conduct towards Mr Berkley amounts to Restraint of Trade, and in my opinion he's probably right.'

Ann stared, a puzzled look in her eyes. 'So if Peter is right –'

'Mr Berkley has a case to take to the High Court,' Longfellow concluded.

Nick glanced up at the mention of his name. His eyes brightened with hope. Longfellow looked at him. 'The choice is yours, Mr Berkley. Mr Mortlake has had some ingenious thoughts, I can mount my strongest attack, but everything hangs on whether you've the stomach to fight – I warn you, it will be a fight. I suspect that Mr Webb and Mr James Mortlake between them will give us a most furious battle.'

His eyes gleamed as if relishing the prospect, and even Nick did his best to look determined. He straightened his shoulders and stuck out his chin. 'You mean we've got a chance?'

'A very good chance,' Longfellow laughed. 'Nearly as good as theirs, I should think.'

Ann's puzzled objection came quickly. 'Are you telling Nick to fight even when their chances are better?'

'What choice does he have?' Longfellow countered. 'To be brought to heel like a dog? For that's what it amounts to. Either he works in harness with Mr

Webb, or he can forget music altogether, at least for another four years. Is that what you want?'

'No,' Nick interrupted. 'I *must* write music –'

'Then you must gird up your loins. You have some good friends,' said Longfellow, pointing to Ann and then me. 'Draw strength from them. If you want to rid yourself of this bully, you must buckle on your armour and fight him.'

Nick nodded slowly before turning to Ann. She smiled and held out a hand.

Clearing his throat nervously, Nick faced Longfellow across that vast desk. 'Yes,' he said. 'Yes, we must fight, if you and Peter will help me.'

So much happened in the next eight weeks that it's hard to be exact about the sequence of events. I suppose the first red letter day came when Mortlake, Dingle & Barnes again refused to release Nick from his contracts and we issued the writs. After that, the battle was on in earnest, with Sir Robert doing all that he could to get the case into the High Court as soon as possible. 'Frankly,' he said to me in private, 'unless we resolve this by Christmas, I think Berkley's health will pack up.' I could only hope he was wrong, although Nick looked more haggard every time we had a meeting in chambers. Ann, as usual, tried to protect him. 'Why does Sir Robert keep bullying him? For God's sake, Peter, *do* something!'

There wasn't much I could do, especially when I knew Longfellow was trying to prepare Nick for the tough cross-examination he might face at the trial. Under those circumstances, bullying was necessary, although I never said so to Ann for fear of worrying her about her own appearance in court.

My most fervent hope was that Jack would cave in, or rather my father would cave in – because I knew he would be calling the shots. I could imagine him and Jack together. They had always got on; Jack was the son my father had wished for. Now he had got him. I could picture the two of them at Whitegates or Wimbledon, Jack pacing up and down, my father's voice vibrant with enthusiasm as they plotted and planned. Yet I still hoped they would give in; I still hoped we would be spared the trial. After all, Jack couldn't *force* Nick to write or to perform at a concert, so what good was the contract with JWE? The answer to that was 'not much', but if the High Court set the JWE contract aside, the odds were they would also veto the contracts with White Hat and Apex. The White Hat contract was vital to both sides; Nick's compositions earned money day and night. Jack's rake-offs on that money were helping him build a fortune – whereas, if the contract with White Hat was overturned, Nick would get immediate money and his copyrights back, giving him an ongoing income. He could plan his life all over again . . .

A constant worry was money. Jack had the advantage. Jack could afford to fight a case in the High Court, Nick couldn't. Jack could let us go right up to the day and settle on the steps of the court. But if he *refused* to settle, Nick had to be ready to meet the costs of the action.

'Don't worry, Peter,' pleaded Ann, 'I'll raise the money somehow.'

'How?' I kept asking. With Longfellow and Olivia

Newton and me working more and more hours, costs were mounting up fast.

'Please, Peter,' Ann begged, 'I'll get the cash together, really I will.'

So we went on, with me hoping all the time that Jack would cave in.

Meanwhile Ann and Nick lived at Gill's pub and existed on Gill's charity. Gill was a tower of strength. I saw a lot of him over those weeks, for it was at his place that we held our 'councils of war', often upstairs, with Mary presiding over cups of hot coffee. More arthritic than ever, she had taken to Nick. 'He might be nothing to look at,' she said, 'but he's all right, is Nick. A nice boy. He reminds me of you, Peter.' Which I assumed was a compliment, although with Mary there was no telling.

Down in the bar, Gill would question me over a pint. 'This bloke Sir Robert. Knows what he's about, does he, Peter? He reckons we've got a good chance?'

I said what I could to reassure him without raising his hopes. 'My big fear,' I confessed, 'is that they'll starve us out. Cases like this cost money, Gill, and a lot of it.'

'I know,' he said, 'it's all Ann talks about at the moment. She's just the same as she always was, never a thought for herself when she's got a musician to help.' He grinned. 'Know what I think, Peter? I should have been born a genius like Nick, then I'd have someone like Ann to run around after me.'

And Ann *was* running around. Within a week of that first conference with Longfellow she had started her 'Fighting Fund'. I was reminded of when I first met her, when she had made my spine tingle with talk of fighting McCarthy and about petitioning for the rights of underprivileged Blacks. Maybe that's what gave her the idea, or maybe the idea was born out of sheer desperation.

It was Gill who first told me about it. 'She says if Nick can't give concerts to raise the money, there are plenty of musicians who can. That's what she's doing, you know. Calling up her old contacts. They had a gig in Soho last night, raised fifty-five quid. Ann gets up and gives a little speech.' He chuckled, 'Tell you what, she'd have made a bloody good Trade Union leader.'

I grinned as well, though I couldn't help thinking we'd need a lot more than fifty-five quid.

'What she really needs,' said Gill, 'is Janie to give a concert, or Dai. Bloody hell, when you think of all the people she's helped, it fair makes me sick.'

Gill's predictions about Jack had come true, but never once did he say 'I told you so', which is more than I can say for my mother: Being so often in London, I sometimes stopped overnight at the flat. Snippets of our action against Jack were beginning to find their way into the papers, and Mum and Bert were full of the case, especially when they found out about my father's involvement. 'Didn't I tell you?' Mum sniffed. 'Of course, you and Bert thought I was daft. I saw the look on your faces, so don't say otherwise. I remember saying there was a lot of your father in Jack. Well, if you ask me, they deserve each other, two nasty pieces of work together, that's what they are.'

Pictures of the 'two nasty pieces of work' appeared in the *Express* the following morning. ROCK AND ROLL BOSS HIRES LONDON'S TOP LAWYER ran the headlines, above a photograph of Jack and a separate one of my father. It gave me a jolt to see him staring up from the paper. Older than my image of him, his cold eyes were still enough to make my heart miss a beat.

The *Daily Mail* ran a big picture of Nick: 'POP STAR ISSUES WRIT. Pop phenomenon Nick Berkley, who set the nation's feet tapping with such hits as "Colour Purple" and "Carnival Nights" is taking his Boss to the High Court in a case bound to make headlines . . .'

Our lives changed with the Press on our heels. Nick's whereabouts were tracked down to Gill's pub and from then on you couldn't go into the bar without bumping into a reporter. Naturally I warned Ann and Nick against making statements or attributable comments, but that's easier to say than to do, as anyone who has dealt with the Press will confirm. It was yet another hardship for Nick. From the day the *Mail* ran its story, Nick's trips with me to see Longfellow were the only times he went out. Even the bar was off-limits. He spent most of his time upstairs with Mary, or up another flight in his rooms in the attic, ironically living in what had been Jack's office when he had started JWE.

The Press caused trouble for me as well as for Nick. Both of Swindon's local papers pounced on the story, and without a picture of me on their files, they ran a photograph of the office. LOCAL SOLICITOR IN POP STAR'S HIGH COURT BATTLE blazed the story on page one.

John Lovell was furious. 'What will our other clients think? Lovell's has always been the most highly respected firm in the district. I warned you against taking this business on in the first place . . .'

He really lost his temper and said all sorts of things which had obviously been boiling up for a long time. His venom came as a shock. I'd given up with Julia's mother — short of dropping dead, nothing would please her — but I had eased John's life a good deal at the office, and I honestly thought I'd made progress with him. I'd forgotten the angry words we had exchanged when Julia dumped David Watson in favour of me, but it quickly became evident that they were still in John's mind. He and the Watsons were old friends, together with Julia's mother they played bridge every Friday — all of which I'd known in a vague sort of way without paying it much attention, after all, to my mind, it was none of my business.

'This sums you up,' John shouted, pointing at the newspaper. 'You've got no proper values. Imagine mixing with people like that. I suppose you expect Julia to mix with them too? Good God, I shudder at the thought of her being involved with a crowd of drug addicts and long-haired layabouts. It wouldn't have happened with David. Never! David would take proper care . . .'

I shut the door. John was shouting loud enough for the whole of Swindon to hear, let alone the staff in the office. Mind you, I was shouting back by then, so neither of us behaved very well.

Two days later, John raised the matter of Nick's case again. I'd been to London in the interval, again to see Longfellow, as John knew perfectly well because Rose told him when he asked where I was.

'I understand you've had another meeting with Counsel,' he said, poking his head into my room.

'Yes.'

'And when, may I ask, do we see some money?'

Ann had given me Gill's contribution but was waiting until she had collected a sizeable sum before sending me more money.

Ignoring the spiteful look on his face, I said, 'We've had five hundred –'

'That's a very modest sum for such big ideas,' he answered waspishly. 'Counsel's fees must already be over a thousand. We'll need a lot more than five hundred –'

'It's coming –'

'It better had, most certainly it better had!'

With that he went out, leaving his words hanging in the air like smoke in the wind. At any other moment I might have recognised the warning. *Most certainly it better had!* There had been a threat in his voice. But I had a mountain of work on my desk, and I was still disgusted with John from two days before . . . so the warning went over my head.

I saw little of John during the following weeks. Of course, now I know what he was doing, he was biding his time, waiting to make his move against me, leaving it until the last possible moment. I know now, but at the time I was dealing with our clients as usual, and dashing up and down to London for meetings with dozens of people. Part of our attack in the High Court would be to demonstrate that other recording companies would have given Nick more generous royalties than Apex, thereby proving that Jack was more interested in getting a good deal for himself than for Nick. So I saw record company executives, agents and managers, and as many people who would see me, gathering more ammunition for Longfellow. It all took time, but it seemed to me that our case was growing stronger and stronger.

With so much going on from Mondays to Fridays, I saw less of Julia, so weekends became precious. And we had some marvellous weekends. The onset of autumn signals a busy time for gardeners; every weekend saw Julia and me planting something. We had everything planned, young cherry trees, rose bushes, standard roses, daffodil and crocus bulbs for the spring. And the building work in the house was running ahead of schedule, which meant deciding on fittings for the kitchen and bathrooms and so on. Sam Prentice was paying the builders and adding the costs on to my mortgage, so at the time I wasn't too worried about money. I had my salary and a share of the end-of-year profits, as is usual between partners in firms of solicitors. In our case, Jumbo and John Lovell took thirty-five percent each, and Martin and I shared the remainder. In time, when Jumbo and Lovell retired, Martin and I would have most of the profits. Financially everything was fine; the mortgage was burdensome, but Julia and I knew we could manage. The important thing was to start married life in the house of our dreams. So when we weren't planting shrubs in the gardens, we were visiting showrooms and altogether having a marvellous time.

That was when we decided to bring everything forward. 'If The Grove is finished in January,' said Julia, 'we could get married straight away. Why wait until spring?'

To our delight, all of our plans were maturing at once.

Weekends were a welcome relief from my worries.

445

At weekends I spent money, during the week I worried about the money Ann had managed to raise. Of course there was a big difference: the money I was spending wasn't mine, it was Sam's, which I would pay back over twenty years; the money Ann was looking for was *immediate* money, and as October slipped into November, the need became increasingly urgent. Every day, Ann called me. 'Hi, Peter. We got another sixty pounds last night. Isn't that terrific? Aren't people wonderful?'

It was terrific, and people were wonderful, but by now the date of the trial had been set. We were to go into Court on December the eighth. Four weeks to go, and Ann's 'Fighting Fund' still looked pitifully slim.

Ann's confidence kept us going. 'It's building, Peter, honestly. The word is spreading. And if we go to court, we'll get a lot of publicity and sympathy . . .'

Meanwhile she was dashing all over the country in her bid to raise money.

Nick collapsed on the tenth of November. Longfellow had been anxious about Nick's health from the outset. His fears had been justified, just at a time when I was becoming more hopeful. Living with Mary and Gill had made a great difference to Nick. He was much more at home there than at Whitegates, Mary fussed over him, Gill grumbled in his soft-hearted way, and Nick had responded. He'd become devoted to them. He was company for Mary, putting her old piano to use for the first time since arthritis had ended her playing days for ever. And he talked to her, about everything under the sun; I'd never known him chatter so much, he forgot his shyness completely. He was even beginning to respond to Gill's little pep talks about our meetings with Longfellow. 'Chin up, lad,' Gill would say as we set off for chambers. 'Remember, this Sir Robert bloke is on your side. He and Peter know what they're doing. Just think, once this business is over, you'll be able to get on with the rest of your life.'

But on the tenth of November, Nick collapsed.

Gill phoned me. 'The doctor says it's nervous exhaustion. He's been bottling it all up, trying not to seem worried for our sake. The doctor says he needs complete rest in peaceful surroundings, and lots of fresh air. He don't get much of that here, does he? The poor little devil can't go out without being jumped on by nosey-parker reporters.'

The trial was four weeks away, and Nick would need all his strength to face that. I groaned. 'What does Ann say?'

'She's not here, is she? She's in Manchester, trying to raise money. Then she's going to Birmingham. I don't expect her back until the end of the week.'

Meanwhile Gill had a pub to run and two invalids on his hands. I was at a loss. If The Grove had been finished, Nick could have stayed there. I thought about asking Mum and Bert to put him up, they had a spare room, but they were out all day and in no position to look after him. Besides, the Press might track him down in London; he could become a prisoner just as much in Bayswater as in the Tottenham Court Road. I was searching round for a solution when Glenda Turnbull and her mother sprang to mind, in their village stores just outside Taunton, a few yards from my old cottage. They had a couple of spare rooms which they let out Bed and Breakfast in the summer. Peace and quiet, the doctor had said, and fresh air. There was nowhere better, and few people kinder.

Surprised to hear from me, Glenda agreed at once when I explained the situation, and an hour later I was on my way to London in the MG. Nick protested when I arrived, saying he was feeling better, but one look at his grey pallor left me in no doubt. 'Come on,' I said, 'you can spend a few weeks hidden away in the country.'

It took the rest of the day to drive him down to Taunton, but I felt quieter in my mind once he was installed with Glenda. Another crisis was under control, thanks to help from a few friends.

Meanwhile Ann was drawing help from dozens of friends. In clubs and coffee bars, pubs and dance halls, she was retracing the route she had taken on tours with Janie. Some people shunned her: news of her 'Fighting Fund' had reached Jack and he was using his influence. But musicians always responded to Ann. They talked the same language, as I remembered from the Green Door and such places.

In Manchester alone, Ann raised a staggering seven hundred and eight-five pounds. She was delirious when she came on the phone. 'It's even better than that,' she said breathlessly, so excited that her words were falling over each other. 'People are organising things themselves. They're making collections at a dozen gigs next week and I won't even be here. They'll send the money on . . .'

The same happened in Leicester and Nottingham. Wherever musicians congregated, they were having a whip-round for Nick.

The money was coming in. Some of it came directly to me at the office, cheques made payable to

Weston, Lovell, Mortlake and Juffs, with 'The Nick Berkley Fighting Fund' printed in brackets, cheques for ten pounds, twenty pounds, postal orders too – often with little notes attached: 'Here's some bread. Love to Ann from Bert Lomax and The Hot Shots.'

With time running out, every day counted. In London, Gill's pub, once Jack Webb's first office, became the Fund's London collection point. Gill called me every day. 'Some bloke just brought in another thirty quid. Bloody marvellous, ain't it?'

Two and a half weeks before the trial, Ann had raised an incredible thirteen thousand, four hundred and twenty two pounds. Which, in these inflationary times, may not seem a tremendous amount, but, for example, The Grove in its original form had cost me only thirteen thousand. Money was money at the end of the Sixties.

I still hoped Jack would cave in. Every time another letter arrived from my father, I looked for a softening of their position. Alas, they remained as unyielding as ever. And with ten days to go, Jack attacked on another front. He delivered divorce proceedings against Ann, claiming adultery with Nick Berkley.

'You bastard!' I swore, guessing he would release the news to the papers. And, of course, he did. Liking nothing more than a juicy divorce, the tabloids leapt on Jack's allegations. ROCK AND ROLL BOSS CITES PROTÉGÉ screamed the *Mirror*; NICK NICKED MY WIFE said the *Mail*. When I called Longfellow, his gloomy assessment was much the same as mine. 'It's window-dressing for the trial,' he said. 'They'll create an atmosphere of scandal to discredit Berkley even before he goes in the box. That's why they've left it so late . . .'

I cursed my father for playing his usual devious game.

It was a bad morning, followed by a worse afternoon, capped by a terrible evening and a disastrous night, for as if I didn't have headaches enough, John Lovell chose that day of all days to unleash his attack. He came into my room at four-thirty, with his hat and coat on, ready to leave. 'I've called a special Partners' meeting for the morning,' he said. 'Jumbo and Martin have agreed to be here at ten.'

'A special meeting?' Taken by surprise, I looked up from the pile of work on my desk. 'Why? What about?'

I was about to complain about the time meetings take up, when I stopped, distracted by the look on his face. His expression was as spiteful as when we had argued a few weeks before, except that this time his eyes gleamed with triumph.

'I'm exercising my veto,' he said, 'on the matter of Berkley versus Webb's businesses. We're pulling out of the case. You'd better tell your long-haired friends to find another solicitor.'

With which, he walked out.

Naturally, I called Jumbo. All he knew was that Lovell was complaining bitterly about me and had called an emergency meeting 'and he's muttering about some clause or other in the partnership agreement'. I went scurrying through my filing cabinets, trying to find my copy of the Partnership Agreement, before realising it was in my room at the hotel, along with the rest of my personal papers.

I worked until seven, forcing myself to concentrate

when all the time my mind kept straying. Finally I finished and hurried over to the hotel and up to my room. Julia was giving a class, so she and I weren't meeting that evening. Just as well, perhaps, for half an hour later I found my copy of the Partnership Agreement. And there it was, in black and white, hidden deep on page nineteen, clause one hundred and three, or something like that, a time bomb about to explode in my face:

In the event of a client, or a prospective client, being unacceptable to either of the Senior Partners, it is agreed that Weston, Lovell, Mortlake & Juffs will not act for such client.

Lovell came straight to the point the next morning. We had scarcely sat down in his office – Jumbo and Martin puzzled and a bit sheepish-looking, me hollow-eyed from a night full of worry – when John launched into his attack. He described me as wilful, insubordinate, difficult to work with, and 'a young man whose values are likely to bring this firm into disfavour in the community'.

I had to listen to this clap-trap. My blood boiled. Jumbo and Martin protested about some comments, but Lovell was determined to have his say, and he had it. Not a word about me lightening his work-load; not a mention about him rarely arriving before ten, by which time I'd been in the office a couple of hours, or that he usually left at four when most nights I was there until seven. Just so much hypocritical bullshit. The truth was he was still sulking about his precious David Watson, but he could hardly admit that, so he struck at me with whatever else came to hand.

'I have been constantly misled,' he complained, looking at me. 'You don't deny that I expressed reservations about this fellow Berkley when he first came into the office? You said nothing would come of it.'

'Which was what I thought at the time –'

'But you changed your mind later. Without consulting me. Right or wrong?'

I shrugged, trying to think of an answer.

'And now you've cobbled together a case of very dubious value –'

'Not according to Sir Robert –'

'He says it stands a chance, that's all. No more than that –'

'Oh come on. Anything can happen in court, we all know that. He can't guarantee –'

'Exactly! And you can't guarantee we won't be left with massive Counsel's fees because you've got a penniless client –'

'What about the money coming in?' I asked hotly. 'You've seen what comes through the mail –'

'Hang on, you two,' Jumbo interrupted, puffing on his pipe and waving a hand to calm us down. 'Let's make sure we know what we're arguing about . . .'

After which, Jumbo struggled to introduce a note of sanity, only for Lovell to disrupt all reasonable argument. 'There's nothing to discuss,' he kept insisting. 'Under the terms of the partnership agreement, I can bar any client I want. I'm merely exercising my rights . . .'

Poor, patient Jumbo, his every effort was rebuffed. At one point, he asked Lovell, 'If you felt like this, why didn't you say so before?'

'I wasn't asked,' Lovell retorted indignantly: 'Mortlake just steam-rollered ahead, constantly misleading me . . .'

He said a lot more in the same vein, causing me to regret my decision to consult Jumbo instead of him. I'd given him a stick, and he was beating me with all his might.

'I'll tell you what this case is about,' he said waspishly. 'It's about Mortlake showing off to his friends, pretending he's some sort of Perry Mason on English law. He'll look damn silly now, won't he, when he writes to them saying he can no longer act for them.'

'I can't do that,' I gasped in dismay.

'You've no choice,' Lovell snapped. 'I'm exercising my veto –'

'We can't pull out now,' I said in dismay, appealing to Jumbo for help. And Jumbo tried to help; again and again, but Lovell was resolute, completely disregarding the effect he was having on future working relationships. This was his chance to bury me and he was taking it, irrespective of protests from Jumbo and Martin.

Round and round we went, covering the same ground, with me becoming increasingly desperate. The only semblance of logic in Lovell's arguments related to money. 'I will not let you expose this firm to financial risk –'

'For God's sake!' I protested. 'Look at the money that's been raised. It's coming in all the time. Every post brings more –'

'Pennies. You're talking pennies when I'm talking pounds, thousands of pounds. I've spoken to Longfellow's clerk about their likely fees. My estimate is that another ten thousand will be needed –'

'How can you say that? We might not even go into court. The other side could settle –'

'I doubt it –'

'Okay, we could go into court and *win*. It won't cost us a penny –'

'Very unlikely,' Lovell sniffed, 'and I told you before, I will not let you risk this firm's money in a reckless battle of wills with your father –'

'To hell with my father,' I shouted, losing my temper. 'What about our client? What about this poor sod who's been ripped off? What about –'

'I have a rule. Never go into court without being sure of the firm's money.' Lovell turned to Jumbo. 'Surely you support me on this?'

Jumbo threw me an uneasy glance. He had warned me about the money. With a shrug, he asked Lovell, 'Is that your sole concern? That the firm should not be at risk?'

Lovell responded with a virtuous look. 'My concern is always the interests of this firm.'

I groaned, 'How many times must I tell you. The money is coming in –'

'But it's not here *today*,' Lovell sneered, 'and we're taking the decision now to avoid further risk.'

Jumbo cleared his throat. 'Would you remove your objections,' he asked, 'if the firm had the money today?'

I groaned again and buried my head in my hands. 'Not a hope. No chance. Ann's performed miracles already . . .'

Lovell watched me squirm, apparently considering Jumbo's idea. Eventually he said, 'Very well. I don't wish to be unreasonable. After all, it's the firm I'm thinking about. Mortlake could amend his letter to

Berkley saying we can only continue to act if we're put into funds by another ten thousand –'

'They haven't got it,' I cried. 'They might get it if we go to court. Don't you see? All the publicity –'

'Raising money for a lost cause?' Lovell sneered. 'I can't think many will have the stomach for that. No, I'm sorry. Today is the deadline and that's my last word on the matter.'

It was, too. Jumbo tried, Martin tried, but Lovell wouldn't budge. I could have murdered him. Looking at the sneer on his face, I thought of Nick plagued by ill health, and of Ann's desperate race around the country, and of all the people who were helping; like Gill and hundreds of others, maybe thousands of others, all putting their hands in their pockets simply to help right a wrong. And I thought of what my father and Jack would get away with, and the injustice of life when a miserable bastard like Lovell can foul everything up, and I got more and more angry, and more and more determined, until the words came tumbling out. 'I'll guarantee the money,' I said.

Lovell reacted with astonishment. 'Guarantee ten thousand pounds? I'm sorry, but I don't think you have the means.'

'Take my share of the profits. You're right, I haven't got the money, but you could use my share of the profits.'

'Your share . . .' Lovell choked, 'but your share only amounts to about three thousand a year –'

'At least you'll get it. I'll sign it over, here and now. Draw something up, and I'll sign it,' I said desperately. 'I know it will take three years, but –'

Jumbo stirred in his chair, 'Steady on, Peter.'

'No!' I was shaking with anger. 'He agreed if we got the money –'

'Today,' Lovell interrupted, 'I said if we had the money *today*. I don't see why the firm should wait three years.'

'You bastard! You won't give an inch, will you?' I pushed my chair back from the table. 'You mean-minded bloody hypocrite,' I shouted on my way to the door.

I forgot my own needs, forgot Sam's mortgage needed my annual share of the profits. It must have been at the back of my mind, but all I could think of was Nick and Ann and the need to keep fighting.

'I'll get you your money,' I said and slammed out.

'So I went straight to the bank,' I said, to Julia's astonishment.

'Which bank?'

'My bank. In the High Street.'

We were in the bar at the hotel, having the most peculiar, most difficult conversation. I'd already downed a couple of pints before she arrived.

I struggled to explain. 'There was no other way. John insisted on the money today. There was nothing else I could do.'

The baffled look in Julia's eyes deepened to total bewilderment. 'But what did you *do* at the bank?'

After taking another mouthful of beer, I cleared my throat and plunged on. 'We had to have the money, right? Today. So I borrowed it.'

She stared, mute with disbelief.

'It will be all right,' I said with all the confidence I could muster. 'It might not even be needed. Jack could settle before we go into court.'

'They lent you ten thousand pounds,' she whispered softly, awed by the sum. 'Just like that, without strings?'

'Ah, well,' I laughed, trying to make a joke. 'Not without strings exactly. They are a bank, after all. They'll want it back, won't they?'

Frowning, Julia looked round to make sure we were not overheard, unlikely anyway because we were the only people there except for the barman and three old men at the far end. Even so, she lowered her voice. 'Peter, I don't understand . . .'

Explaining was even more difficult than I had imagined. I was sure I'd done the right thing, the *only* thing, I'd been left with no choice. But explaining to Julia was developing into the worst experience of my life. She listened intently, never taking her eyes from my face, occasionally shaking her head very slowly from side to side. I explained about all the money Ann had raised, and that Longfellow thought we had a good case. 'So you see, we won't need a penny if we win.' I explained about her uncle being an absolute bastard. But I couldn't avoid telling her what had happened at the bank; Julia had a right to know, so I had to tell her.

'They've got their head office to think of,' I said. 'I mean, *they* understand, but naturally they had to put things on a businesslike basis.'

Julia's face was like alabaster. Her eyes showed incredulity and mounting concern as I explained what she was already working out, that to repay ten thousand pounds as well as Sam's mortgage was

beyond my resources. 'Not that it will come to that,'
I assured her, 'there's no chance –'

'But if?'

'It won't happen –'

'But if?'

I tried to make her understand we were discussing
a totally hypothetical situation.

'Yes, yes,' she said impatiently, 'but if the worst
were to happen?'

I took a deep breath. Then I told her. 'The Grove
will have to be sold when the builders finish in
January.'

The pain in her eyes tore at my heart. Julia meant
more to me than any person on earth, and she was
looking at me as if I had betrayed her.

'But that won't happen,' I promised, willing her to
believe me.

'No,' she whispered. 'Oh, no.'

I reached for her across the table. 'It won't
happen –'

Pulling away from me, she fumbled in her bag. Her
voice broke to a sob. 'How could you do that?' she
asked with a groan of despair.

'Please,' I begged. 'Don't worry –'

Her eyes were bright with tears. 'Our home,'
she whispered, 'all our dreams, our hopes . . .
we've worked so hard, I can't believe you would do
it –'

'You don't understand.' I ached with the need to
comfort her. 'Please –'

'All the promises, all the plans . . . didn't they
mean anything?'

'Of course they meant –'

'Why?' she sobbed as tears coursed down her

cheeks. 'Why did you do it? Does she mean that much to you? That you throw us away –'

'Oh, no.' My heart sank. 'No, you've got it all wrong. I didn't do it for Ann –'

'Then why?' she cried, her words muffled by her handkerchief.

I lacked the right words. I knew what I felt, but conveying such complicated feelings defeated me. I tried. God, how I tried. But nothing I said sounded convincing.

'Because it was the right thing to do, don't you see?' I said despairingly. 'What Jack is doing is wrong, and John was so bloody impossible –'

'He must have his reasons –'

'Please, Julia, trust me on this –'

'Trust you?' she gasped, dabbing her eyes with shaking hands, struggling to regain control. 'I don't *know* you, I don't understand you. You didn't even tell me. You've thrown our future away and you didn't even tell me –'

'I told you as soon as I could.'

She took a deep breath and let it out with a shuddering sigh. Her tears had stopped flowing, leaving her face wet and smudged. 'Too late,' she said softly, 'you told me too late.' Closing her eyes she sat back in her chair, breathing deeply, clenching her trembling hands in her lap.

'Nothing's been thrown away,' I pleaded. 'Nothing's changed . . .'

But it had. I knew when Julia opened her eyes. Her look was different from the fond look to which I'd become accustomed. Without being angry or even tearful any longer, it was hurt and a bit empty, the trust had gone, the look was cautious and neutral.

'I'm going,' she said, rising quickly and handing me off. 'No, you stay –'

'Don't be daft –'

'I don't want you –'

'You're upset. If you must go, let me drive you home –'

'No! I don't want to talk, I can't even look at you –'

'Julia, *please*.' I put a hand on her arm, trying to stop her as she made for the door.

Resisting, she pushed past me. 'Leave me alone,' she cried. 'You threw it all away. I never want to see you again.'

BOOK FIVE

BY THE TIME WE REACHED the High Court the following week, I had endured some of the most dispiriting
days of my life. I'd not seen Julia since she ran from
the hotel that night. Every time I telephoned, her
mother answered, growing increasingly terse until
finally she threatened: 'If you don't stop pestering
us, I shall inform the police.' Not that I took any
notice. I tried to waylay Julia on her way to the
school, but she avoided me by having a car collect
her every morning. When I telephoned the school,
she was always taking a class. When I delivered a
letter to her house, I received no reply . . .

It was a hell of a time, made worse, by the atmosphere in the office. John and I scarcely spoke. Clearly,
he knew how things stood with Julia and me – her
mother kept him informed. No doubt the Watsons
had also been told, and the precious David was
already winging his way home.

Meanwhile the telephones on my desk never
stopped ringing. Sir Robert Longfellow's clerk was
on every day, wanting to dot every 'i' and cross every
't' before we went into Court. Ann was on the phone,
upset by press reports about her alleged adultery with
Nick. Nick was on the phone, demanding we sue the

Mail for libel (as if I didn't have enough on my plate). Gill was on the phone, reporting the receipt of more money. Jumbo was on the phone, pledging four hundred pounds for the Nick Berkley Fighting Fund. Martin called and promised to send fifty quid. Mum was on the phone, so was Bert . . . everyone called except Julia.

Saturday morning found me exhausted. I tried to reach Julia again, only to be thwarted once more by her mother who this time couldn't disguise her pleasure as she announced: 'Julia's gone away for the weekend.'

Without work, I would have gone mad. Luckily Rose had offered to come in to help dispose of the bits and pieces which had accumulated, so I dragged myself into the office and we made a day of it. Work was therapy. Apart from anything else, it kept me from going to The Grove to inspect progress. I had no appetite for that, or for gardening, or anything to do with the future. So Rose and work saved the day – but nothing could save me from Saturday night; enveloped in a thick cloud of depression, I sat in the bar and got steadily drunk.

I think the hangover was the turning-point. God, I was ill on the Sunday! An hour went by before I could see straight; two hours passed before I could shove shaking hands into a shirt. Sitting on a bed, nursing an aching head, you either feel sorry for yourself or you snap out of it – and then was no time for self-pity. I could almost hear my father sneering. I admitted out loud, 'Carry on like this and I'm finished. All will be for nothing; Nick's sessions with Longfellow, Ann's race round the country, me raising the ten thousand pounds . . .'

With the trial starting on Thursday, I *had* to put Julia out of my mind. I had to forget my quarrel with John. In my cups the previous evening, I'd even had thoughts of resigning and moving away from Swindon to start all over again . . . but it would all have to wait until after the trial.

Monday dawned and I was in the office by seven-thirty. The same on Tuesday, which was the day Ann got back to Gill's from touring the country. She called me in the morning, anxious to confirm last-minute arrangements. 'You can't bring Nick here,' she said. 'Reporters are three deep in the bar.'

'You're moving out,' I told her. 'I'll bring Nick up to town from Taunton tomorrow and take him to my mother's place. We'll be there by about seven. You join us there, we'll have something to eat, then stay at an hotel round the corner. I've booked you and Nick in under false names . . .'

Methodically I worked through my check-list, hoping that I'd thought of everything. Having organized Ann, I called Nick, who sounded nervous but determined, and after that I contacted Sir Robert's clerk and we completed our arrangements for Thursday. So that, what with one thing and another, I spent most of the day on the phone . . .

I cleared my desk and packed my case, heavy-hearted about Julia, nervous about the trial, trying not to worry . . .

Then an amazing thing happened. Half the people in the office appeared at my door. Rose came in, bearing not just a cup of tea but a huge cake decorated with a horseshoe and the words 'Good Luck' in white icing.

'We all chipped in,' she said with a smile. 'We all think what you're doing is wonderful.'

How they found out, I don't know, but the whole office knew about me raising the ten thousand.

So I cut the cake, shared it out, and we had a sort of good luck and farewell party rolled into one. 'We'll all be thinking of you,' Paula from the post-room assured me. 'Everyone's crossing their fingers.'

Everyone, of course, with the exception of John, who was like Scrooge the day before Christmas. I heard him grumbling in the lobby as he left. 'This case doesn't stand a dog's chance,' he said, 'I don't know what all the fuss is about.' He was the only person in the office not to shake my hand and wish me luck in the High Court.

'Never mind,' said Rose, 'he'll find out what the fuss is about when you win.'

Fuss is something at which my mother excels. It works wonders at times, and having seen the way Nick responded to Mary, I knew I was right to involve Bert and my mother. 'What I'm trying to do,' I told Bert on the phone, 'is to stop Nick worrying. Try to take his mind off the High Court in the morning.'

Of course, there wasn't much chance of that. Nick fidgeted every mile of the way on the drive up from Taunton. He kept finding something new to worry about.

'Nick,' I pleaded, 'relax –'

'But what about all this stuff about Ann and me in the papers?'

'Don't let it get to you. It's spite, that's all. Jack's got a weak case and he's trying to blur the issue –'

'What about the jury? They'll all be sitting there –'

'There won't be a jury,' I sighed, and went through it all over again. Longfellow and I had covered the ground at least twice, but Nick's mind went blank at times. Hating the very idea of a court, he refused to contemplate what would happen. His imagination ran riot. Some people are like that; they become gripped by an irrational fear, like claustrophobia, agoraphobia or any other phobia. Nick had a phobia about courts that had worried Longfellow from the outset.

'A jury decides on facts,' I said, 'but in this case both sides agree on the facts: the facts are the contracts. They exist, okay? There's no argument about that. The dispute is about whether they're valid or not, and that's a matter of law. So we take them to an expert and let him decide –'

'You mean the Judge?'

'That's right, but he's not judging *you*. Remember that. He's judging the contracts. That's why it's best to think of him as an expert. In fact,' I said, 'it's very boring most of the time, just a lot of stuffy old lawyers arguing among themselves.'

This vast over-simplification was to be shot full of holes when we went into Court, but I was less concerned with legal niceties then than with easing Nick's fears.

Just as I had hoped, Bert and my mother rose to the occasion. By the time I arrived with Nick, they had created almost a party atmosphere. Although I'd expected to see Ann, I was surprised to find Gill and Mary there as well.

'It was nice of your mum to invite us,' said Mary, embracing me with her arthritic hands.

'Not half,' grinned Gill. 'And I'll tell you something else, Peter. I've got someone in to look after the pub for a few days, so we'll be in court to cheer you on.'

'And us,' said Bert. 'Your mum and I are taking a week of our holidays, starting tomorrow.'

It was a funny kind of atmosphere. A stranger would have said we were a family. Bert and Gill could have been brothers, while Ann and Nick were like adopted children to Mary. It was a closing of the ranks to face the battle ahead; which made my heart ache for Julia, and I was wishing she had been there even before Gill asked, 'Where's Julia, then? I thought she'd be with you.'

'Working,' I lied. 'She couldn't get the time off. You know what schools are like before Christmas.'

My mother knew I was lying. She didn't say so, but she gave me an old-fashioned look as she ushered us into the dining room.

The spread laid out was enormous. 'Got to keep your strength up,' said Bert, slapping my back as he led me to the table. Meanwhile Mary and Mum were making a great fuss of Nick, and Ann was telling him about the people she had met on her travels. She looked tired, worn out by the effort she had made, but other than that, in good spirits.

So we gathered at the table and had a fine meal, with Bert and Gill talking about football and films and goodness knows what, to keep Nick from fretting about the trial. And they largely succeeded, even though the trial was never far from anyone's mind and bound to surface again before the evening was over.

468

It was Ann who brought it up first. Opening her handbag, she took out an envelope. 'Peter,' she said, 'here's the rest of what we managed to raise. Six hundred and ten pounds. There might be a bit more, but it won't be much. We've about scraped the barrel.'

They were short. In my heart I think I'd always known they would be. Despite Ann's magnificent efforts and the generosity of Gill and Jumbo and so many others, the Fighting Fund had failed to reach the target. The Grove would be sold if the Judge found against us. All the dreams and hard work, all the plans made with Julia, all my hopes would be gone.

Everyone looked at me. 'Is it enough?' Ann asked anxiously.

There was only one answer I could give. 'Yes,' I said, 'it's enough.'

Gill insisted on making a speech. 'You know,' he said, rising to his feet and addressing my mother, 'the first time I met your son and Jack Webb, I don't deny it was Jack who impressed me. Cowboy Jack, I used to call him, because he came in one day wearing a big white stetson. Knows all the angles, does Jack. Sharp as a knife, if you know what I mean.'

'I should say I do,' Mum interrupted. 'When I was young and silly I married a man like that.'

'And we all know where *he* will be tomorrow,' said Bert heavily.

'Helping Jack,' Gill agreed. 'That's what I'm saying. Young Nick here couldn't have got this far without Peter. Now Peter's not just up against Jack, but his father as well –'

'His father's always been against him,' Mum said emphatically.

'Then shame on him,' Gill pronounced, 'because I'll tell you this about Peter, he'll always do the right thing. He follows his conscience. It didn't take me long to realise I was wrong about Jack; I worked that out years ago, and I said so to Peter. But what I never said was that he should have been the one in the white hat. Remember those old Westerns?' he asked, cocking an eye at my mother. 'The hero always wore a white hat? That's what the joke was about that night in my pub: the good guy in the white hat. Well, I'm putting that right tonight . . .' Gill broke off to collect a large paper bag which he had left on the sideboard. 'Peter,' he said, 'if ever anyone should wear this, it's you, for you truly deserve it.'

'Bravo!' cried Mary as Gill came round the table with this huge white stetson in his hands; and everyone shouted and clapped as he set it on my head.

It was worse than embarrassing, there was a real danger of the evening turning into a celebration. 'We've a long way to go yet,' I cried. But they seemed to think we'd already come a long way. I think they were reacting against the tension, like troops on the eve of a battle. All of them were so sure we would win; even my mother got carried away. 'I know it's your fight against Jack tomorrow,' she said, patting Nick's hand, 'but it's also father against son, and Jack will learn he's put his faith in the wrong man.'

'Hear, hear!' Bert cried, waving his glass.

I sat there in that ridiculous hat and tried to explain that solicitors take a back seat in the courtroom. 'The barristers take over tomorrow,' I said. 'It will be up to Sir Robert.'

'Hooray for Sir Robert!' Gill bawled enthusiastically. 'Sir Robert will show them, eh, Nick?'

'He frightens me to death,' Nick admitted, looking quite bleary-eyed after one glass of white wine. 'Every time I speak to him he tears me to pieces –'

'He won't do that tomorrow,' said Gill, 'he's on your side. Right, Peter?'

'Right,' I agreed, thinking it was just as well. In exactly the same way as I had gone for a top man, so had my father, and Sir Emlyn Griffith, QC, would not be on our side. Olivia Newton had phoned me about Griffith. 'He's ferocious,' she had said. 'It will be a battle of Titans in court.'

In chambers, Sir Robert had been dismissive of my plan to send Nick and Ann to the High Court in the hotel laundry van. As we crossed the Strand, he changed his mind. 'Good God!' he muttered. 'Just look at that crowd.'

Hundreds of people, mostly young girls, spilled across the pavement outside the Royal Courts of Justice. Soaring one hundred and sixty feet above, the bell tower can rarely have looked down on such scenes as policemen linked arms to clear a passage to the entrance.

'I've sent the van to the Carey Street entrance,' I said breathlessly. 'The crowd might be thinner round there.'

In front of us the crowd shrieked as Dai Evans alighted from a taxi. My stomach lurched as I saw Jack with my father. I glimpsed Janie and Mike as they struggled to reach the protective police cordon. Then we were in the thick of it ourselves, pushing and shoving, deafened by the piercing screams from all sides. The crowd surged forward against the policemen's linked arms. A few yards to my left a girl of no more than sixteen sank her teeth into a constable's hand. Pain mingled with outrage as he roared, 'You bitch!' Like an eel, she wriggled past him; like an avalanche, he responded, throwing himself after her, his outstretched hand catching her foot. Unbalanced, she pitched forward, her skirt rucking up as she fell. The constable rose to one knee, retaining his grip on her shoe, only to be thwarted as she twisted away, leaving the shoe in his hand, throwing herself forward like a sprinter. Despairingly he hurled himself after her, catching the hem of her skirt. Checked in flight, the girl staggered and fell again. Rolling and kicking, her hands went to her waist, releasing the clasp. Next moment she was up, leaving her skirt in the constable's hands, kicking off her remaining shoe, and running up the steps into the great mosaic-paved hall, thin, unformed legs pumping like pistons beneath her pink knickers. Flashbulbs popped on all sides and the pressmen had their picture for the afternoon papers: NICK BERKLEY TRIAL OPENS TO WILD SCENES the headlines would scream.

The courtroom was more than a room with walls, a floor and a ceiling like any other: the courtroom had enough majesty to make most people nervous. Taking my place at the solicitors' table, my gaze wandered from the vast Queen's Bench itself, set on its raised dais, to the chandeliers suspended from the vaulted stone ceiling. High up on the balcony level, shafts of wintry sunlight penetrated the leaded panes of cathedral-like windows. The heavy oak panelling which clad the walls and almost every other surface in sight, was relieved here and there by the inclusion of some wrought-iron railings, a row of law books, and a clock which ticked loudly.

Behind me, the public gallery was beginning to fill as people filed in through the green drapes which concealed the doors. Craning my neck, I saw my mother and Bert, both looking anxious. I saw Mary, stiff and awkward in her movements as Gill helped her to a seat. In vain I looked for Julia's blonde head, telling myself not to expect her, yet unable to stop hoping that she would be there to lend her support.

How supportive had I been to Nick, I wondered? Could I have done more to prepare him for this? I'd left him in the conference room across the passage, recovering with Ann from their journey in the laundry van. If nothing more, it had provided some light relief, another diversion to occupy Nick's mind, to keep him from worrying. Perhaps I should have brought him into London earlier, taken him to another court to witness another trial, to see for himself at first hand what went on. I'd considered the idea, only to reject it for fear it might make him even more nervous . . .

Sir Robert Longfellow and Olivia, both wigged and gowned, arrived to take their places in front of me. Sir Robert looked troubled and uneasy. Turning to me, he lowered his voice: 'I had a chat with Griffith in the robing-room. He was as unyielding as stone. He believes he can win.'

I swallowed hard and said nothing.

Longfellow frowned. 'My impression is that he's

got something up his sleeve. Something we don't know about.' His hard blue eyes bored into mine. 'You don't think they can spring a surprise?'

My mouth went dry. It would be typical of my father to conceal his hand until the last minute. Unpleasant surprises had littered my boyhood. But surely not this time? Clearing my throat, I whispered, 'I can't believe it's anything like that. I know this case inside out. Griffith must be bluffing.'

'That wasn't my impression,' Longfellow muttered grimly. 'Here he comes now. Judge for yourself.'

I turned as Griffith entered, flanked by his junior on one side, and by my father on the other. They were all smiling; my father said something by way of a joke and Griffith responded with a deep-throated chuckle. A plump man of medium height, Griffith had the rosy face of a cherub beneath his wig. Seeing the amused brown eyes, the button nose and mobile lips, I wondered why Olivia had described him as ferocious. He looked as tame as a pet rabbit to my eyes. But I had to admit that the vast confidence he conveyed made me decidedly nervous.

Suddenly my father and I were staring at each other. All the old authority was there in a look that had once filled me with dread; the same expression around the eyes that told of fresh torments in store. It was a smug, self-satisfied look that said as clearly as words, 'I'll get to you in a minute, and God help you when I do.' But I was neither a boy any longer, nor an articled clerk in his office. Squaring my shoulders, I held his gaze until he looked away. He glanced up at the public gallery. I wondered if he had seen my mother, I wondered what she had made of the exchange. But most of all I wondered if Longfellow was right to suspect my father of baiting a trap.

'Silence in court!' shouted the usher.

We rose as the Honourable Mr Justice Hunter entered from a door behind the Queen's Bench.

Longfellow's words raced round my mind: *My impression was he's got something up his sleeve.*

We bowed to the Judge as he took his place in his deep-backed leather chair. He nodded, and we subsided into our seats.

Something we don't know about, Longfellow had said.

I threw a sideways glance at my father, studying the lines in his face. *You don't think they can spring a surprise!* Surely not. I'd checked everything, checked and double-checked. Vaguely I heard Longfellow talking to the Judge, estimating that the trial would last six or seven days. Vaguely I heard Griffith agree. Staring at my father brought to mind all the traps he had set in the past. It was his favourite game. As if from a distance, I heard Longfellow tell the Judge what he would attempt to prove, I heard Griffith explain what he would seek to refute, while I kept asking myself *What trap!* Defeated, I risked a final glance over my shoulder, only to be confronted by a sea of faces with Julia's not among them.

'Very well, Sir Robert,' said Mr Justice Hunter. 'Let us begin. Please call your first witness.

'Mr Nicholas Berkley.'

I watched Nick take the stand. The witness-box stood to the left of the Queen's Bench, almost directly over the seats provided for the press, every one of which was occupied.

'On which Bible do you wish to be sworn?'

'I'm a Roman Catholic,' said Nick.

'The Douai Bible, please.'

Listening to Nick take the oath was reassuring. He spoke quietly but firmly, and without hesitation. On my orders he was wearing a white shirt and a grey suit instead of his usual blue jeans. I relaxed a notch and settled back to listen.

Step by step, only asking questions to which he already knew the answers, Longfellow took Nick through his story and was soon at that fateful first meeting at Whitegates.

'So you played the piano all afternoon. You gave Mr Webb a recital, in fact. Is that right?'

'Yes.'

'How many songs did you sing?' Longfellow asked. 'Approximately? After all, there must have been a lot of them for the recital to last all afternoon.'

'About twenty, I think.'

'Twenty? As many as that? All of which you'd written yourself?

'Yes.'

'And did Mr Webb like them?'

'Well, yes,' said Nick. 'I think so –'

'Mr Webb didn't jump up and cry "Stop! That's awful. You're wasting my time"?'

Nick smiled. 'Oh no, nothing like that. He liked them. He said so.'

'He liked them,' Longfellow echoed, rolling the words around his mouth with great satisfaction. 'Very well. Mr Webb listened to your songs and he liked them. And what did he propose to do about liking your songs?'

When Nick frowned, Longfellow immediately

came to his rescue. 'Did he make a suggestion about your career?'

'Oh yes,' answered Nick, his face brightening, 'he said he would become my manager.'

'I see.' Longfellow glanced down at his notes on the table in front of him. 'And did he give you a contract to sign?'

'The next day,' Nick nodded, 'when I moved in –'

'The next day?' Longfellow affected surprise. 'That was quick. He must have liked your songs a great deal.' Pausing, perhaps to count the number of times he had emphasized Jack's liking for Nick's songs, Longfellow continued. 'Giving you a contract so quickly suggests he was afraid you would sign with somebody else –'

'Objection.' Griffith bounced up from his chair. 'My lord, the witness is being asked to speculate –'

'Sustained,' the Judge responded, admonishing Longfellow with a baleful stare.

Longfellow tried again. 'Is it true that Mr Webb put you under contract at breakneck speed for fear of losing you –'

'My Lord!' Griffith protested, rising again.

'Sir Robert, please,' Mr Justice Hunter sighed.

As Griffith sank back into his seat, Longfellow bowed from the waist. 'I beg your Lordship's pardon,' he murmured, turning back to Nick. 'It is correct, is it not, that within twenty-four hours of your meeting, Mr Webb gave you a contract to sign?'

Nick nodded. 'Yes, that is correct.'

'Were you familiar with such contracts?'

'No –'

'Had you in fact ever seen a contract of this type before?'

'No.'

'But Mr Webb wanted you to sign it there and then?'

'Yes.'

'And you did sign it?'

'Yes.'

'You didn't take advice on it first?'

'No.'

'Perhaps Mr Webb said, "Take this contract to a solicitor and ask his advice on the wisdom of signing it." Did he suggest anything like that?'

'No,' said Nick, shaking his head. 'He didn't say that.'

'Perhaps he went through it with you himself, explaining clause by clause what he was asking you to sign?'

'No –'

'For instance, did he point out that under the terms of this contract he receives thirty per cent of your total earnings, whereas other managers take only twenty per cent?'

'No.'

'Did he suggest that you took the contract away to study at your leisure?'

'No.'

'In fact the very opposite happened, did it not? He gave you a pen and told you to sign there and then. Isn't that true?'

Scowling at Longfellow for leading the witness, Griffith nonetheless remained in his chair.

'Yes,' Nick replied.

'And you signed without even reading it?'

'Well, yes, that's what happened.'

Longfellow went on, stacking up points. Knowing

478

the story so well, I found I could listen with half an ear while my attention wandered elsewhere. I watched the Judge. He was a short, solidly built man: as moon faced as an owl under his wig, whose bored expression concealed an unfailing alertness. From time to time he made a note on his pad; other than that he seemed scarcely to move. Yet while his body remained still and his face was impassive, his eyes missed nothing as they flicked back and forth between Nick and Sir Robert.

Longfellow was like a miser gloating over his hoard, picking up each nugget of evidence and polishing it before passing on to the next.

'We come now to the contract with White Hat Publishing,' said Sir Robert. 'How did that come about?'

'Mr Webb said he would publish my songs.'

'All of them? Including the songs you wrote before you met Mr Webb?'

'Yes.'

'Including, for instance, the songs you sang when you met him for the first time?'

'Yes.'

'And as your manager,' said Longfellow, 'looking after your interests, I expect Mr Webb took your songs to all sorts of publishers, trying to get the best deal. Is that what he did?'

Nick shrugged. 'I don't know.'

'He didn't inform you of progress?'

'No.'

'So what did he do?'

'He just gave me this contract to sign.'

'The contract with White Hat Publishing?'

'Yes.'

'And you signed it?'

'Yes.'

I risked a glance at my father, hoping to see some faint stirring of alarm. Instead I saw the familiar sneer. He looked totally confident. Longfellow's earlier words played on my mind: *Griffith was as unyielding as stone. He believes he can win.* My heart sank at the memory of past defeats inflicted upon me by my father. I racked my brains in search of a trap.

Longfellow proceeded as relentlessly as the ticking clock. 'What about the contract with Apex Records?' he asked. 'Did that come about after Mr Webb had tried to persuade other companies to offer you a recording contract?'

'I don't know.'

'Because you assumed Mr Webb would get the best deal for you. Is that what you assumed?'

'Yes.'

'You assumed he was looking after your interests. Is that right?'

'Yes,' Nick nodded, 'he was my manager –'

'And you trusted him?'

'Yes, I did.'

'In fact,' said Longfellow, 'you trusted him with your money, your career, everything. It was as if he were your bank manager, your solicitor, your booking agent, all rolled into one. Isn't that right?'

'Yes.'

'Which was why you signed the contracts with White Hat Publishing and Apex Records without even reading them. You left all of your business affairs in Mr Webb's hands. That is correct, is it not?'

'Well, yes, he was my manager.'

To my mind, Longfellow was proving Conflict of Interest as clearly as ever it could be proved, but not a line of worry showed on my father's face. Neither did Griffith look disturbed; he sat back in his chair apparently as cheerful as when he had walked into court.

For the next hour, Longfellow demolished the contracts, clause by clause, line by line. The clock ticked on. The Judge made his notes, my father smiled and I worried. Yet Longfellow was presenting an immaculate case and Nick was responding better than I had imagined. He seemed quite relaxed. From time to time his eyes met mine, and I gave him a little nod of encouragement, but for the most part he seemed fully at ease.

Longfellow wound up by asking Nick about his rock opera. 'I don't want to dwell too long on this,' he said, 'or go into it too deeply, but is it true that you and Mr Webb argued about the direction your career should take?'

'Yes,' Nick nodded. 'That's right.'

'In other words, Mr Webb tried to dictate what you should write?'

'Yes.'

'And you objected because, apart from Mr Webb's lack of musical talent or qualifications, you felt he had no right to interfere with your work?'

'Correct.'

'Indeed,' Longfellow nodded, 'even the contracts which you signed, appallingly onerous and one-sided though they are, even *those* contracts do not give him the right to dictate to you in such a fashion, do they?'

'No.'

'Exactly,' Longfellow smiled, and turned to Mr Justice Hunter. 'That concludes my questions, my Lord.'

Hunter nodded and glanced at the clock. 'Very well,' he said. 'It is a little early, perhaps, but I think we might take this as a suitable moment to adjourn.'

And so we rose as the Judge went off to his lunch, leaving us free to do likewise. All in all, I felt we had made a good start. If the morning had been undramatic, at least it had been satisfactory. The worry was that Griffith and my father appeared to have found it equally satisfactory. They looked positively smug when they walked out of the courtroom, leaving Longfellow to stare after them, a puzzled look in his eyes.

'I would remind you,' Mr Justice Hunter told Nick when we resumed after lunch, 'that you are still under oath.'

Nick nodded gravely and turned to face Griffith, who greeted him with a welcoming smile. 'Mr Berkley,' began Griffith in his Welsh lilt, 'this morning you told his Lordship about signing that first contract, the one by which Mr Webb became your manager. Do you remember?'

'Yes.'

'You did want to sign it, didn't you?'

'Oh yes,' Nick agreed readily.

I settled back in my chair and watched and listened to Griffith. There was nothing we could do to stop him. Predictably, he dealt with the implications Longfellow had planted in the morning. Step by step

Griffith demolished any suggestion that Nick had been bullied into signing the contract. His eagerness to sign became as transparently obvious to the court as it had that day in my office.

Griffith never seemed to stop smiling. 'As for the suggestion made by my learned friend,' he said, with an amiable nod in Longfellow's direction, 'that Mr Webb snapped you up from under the noses of his competitors, perhaps you could tell us, Mr Berkley, how many other people offered you a contract?'

'Well, none, because –'

'No one else was interested. It was Mr Webb's contract or nothing, wasn't it?'

'I agree there were no other contracts –'

'Of course you do,' Griffith smiled, 'because it's the truth and you're telling the truth. That's right, isn't it?'

'Yes.'

'Exactly.' Griffith nodded, as gentle in his way as Longfellow had been in his. 'And after that, Mr Webb took you into his home and made you comfortable, did he not?'

'Yes,' said Nick.

'You were a lot more comfortable there than in your draughty attic in Kilburn, would you say?'

'Much more comfortable, yes.'

'In fact,' Griffith went on agreeably, 'Mr and Mrs Webb created an atmosphere in which you could compose away to your heart's content. Surrounded by luxury, encouraged by a powerful man and his beautiful wife, your every need was taken care of, was it not?'

'Yes, it was.'

'And you were very happy, weren't you?'

'To begin with, yes.'

'One could say Mr Webb was your benefactor as well as your manager?'

Nick shrugged. 'Yes, I suppose so –'

'Oh, come now,' Griffith admonished gently, 'don't be so grudging. Here is a man who transports you from a miserable garret to a luxurious mansion. He feeds you, he encourages you. What else was he but your benefactor?'

'I said yes already –'

'Of course you did,' Griffith beamed his full agreement. 'And under this benevolent guidance, your music went from strength to strength. Isn't that true?'

'I'd already written some of the songs before I went –'

'Quite so,' Griffith nodded pleasantly, 'but it was at Whitegates that your talent blossomed, thanks to the help provided by Mr and Mrs Webb. You agree on that, I take it?'

'In a manner of speaking –'

'And while Mr Webb was out promoting your career, Mrs Webb was at your side encouraging you to write. Isn't that how it was?'

'A bit like that,' Nick agreed.

'A bit?' echoed Griffith. 'I submit it was *exactly* like that. You don't deny Mrs Webb encouraged you to write, do you?'

'Oh no,' Nick said quickly.

'There you are, then,' Griffith agreed and cocked his head to ask, 'She knows a lot about music, does she? Mrs Webb?'

'An enormous amount,' Nick agreed, smiling at

the chance to praise Ann. 'I've never known anyone like her.'

Peering down at the table, Griffith rearranged his papers and made a note with a gold pencil. Then he looked up and smiled. 'Go on,' he said, 'tell us more.'

A faint frown creased Nick's brow. 'What more do you want? Ann . . . I mean, Mrs Webb, knows more than anyone I've ever met.'

'You've not met the like of her before. Is that it?'

'That's what I said –'

Griffith's eyes positively twinkled. 'And I believe she is even more fulsome in praise of you. Doesn't she describe you as a genius?'

Nick shrugged and looked vaguely uncomfortable. 'It's just her way of talking.'

'Is it, indeed?' said Griffith, an edge coming into his voice. He stared for a long moment without saying a word, a steady, silent look which was designed to embarrass – and embarrass it did, for although Nick returned the gaze, he grew visibly more uncomfortable.

I shifted in my chair as worries began to gnaw at my stomach.

Clearing his throat, Griffith said, 'You were impressed by her, she was impressed by you, and the two of you spent a lot of time together, growing closer and closer –'

'My Lord,' Longfellow was on his feet, 'I really must protest before my learned friend goes further. This fishing expedition has no relevance to the issues before you.'

'I'm inclined to agree,' said Mr Justice Hunter, adjusting his spectacles as he peered down at Griffith.

'Sir Emlyn, although you have not yet asked a question, I am at a loss to see the purpose of this line of reasoning.'

Contriving to look more like a cherub than ever, Griffith responded in a placatory tone, 'If I may crave Your Lordship's indulgence for a few moments more, I am sure my purpose will become clear.'

'I think it's clear now,' Mr Justice Hunter said dryly. 'What I'm questioning is its relevance.'

'My Lord, it's relevance goes to the heart of this case.'

Mr Justice Hunter stroked his chin and answered carefully, 'Very well, Sir Emlyn, you may proceed, but please do so with caution.'

'I'm obliged to your Lordship,' said Griffith with a slight inclination of his head. He turned to fix his gaze on Nick. 'Isn't this what happened?' he began. 'You moved into Mr Webb's home. Mr Webb was away a good deal promoting your career, and you and Mrs Webb were thrown into close contact with each other.'

Longfellow fidgeted but remained in his chair.

'Consequently,' continued Griffith, 'you and Mrs Webb became very friendly, did you not?'

'We became friends,' Nick agreed.

'Good friends?'

'Yes, good friends.'

'And isn't it true that while you became ever more friendly with Mrs Webb, her relationship with her husband deteriorated?'

'Objection,' Longfellow leapt to his feet. 'My Lord, the witness is –'

The Judge shook his head. 'I will allow the question.'

Griffith resumed his attack. 'I put it to you again, Mr Berkley: while you and Mrs Webb were growing closer, was a distance opening between her and her husband?'

'I don't know –'

'You don't *know*? You were there! This was taking place in front of your eyes –'

'No,' Nick shook his head. 'You talk as if I lived in the house. I was in the cottage most of the time.'

Griffith cast his eyes upwards in an expression of disbelief. 'Very well,' he said, 'let me put this to you. Understandably you were excited with the success of your compositions. Thanks to Mr Webb, everything in your life was working out right. There you were in this grand house, flattered by the attentions of the attractive Mrs Webb. Naturally, you were sympathetic towards her. Isn't that so?'

'Sympathetic? I liked her, yes –'

'More than liked.' Griffiths picked up his notes. 'I quote your own words: "I've never known anyone like her." That's what you said. You were bowled over, infatuated –'

'No!' Colour rushed into Nick's face as he shook his head. 'We're friends –'

'Just good friends,' Griffith sneered.

I remembered Julia mocking me with exactly the same words, yet I was sure the innuendo was no more true of Nick than it had been of me. I watched as Nick tried to recover, but his composure was badly shaken.

'Isn't it true,' Griffith demanded, 'that Mrs Webb interfered in her husband's business affairs –'

'My Lord,' Longfellow was again on his feet, 'the

witness is being asked to speculate about matters which were none of his concern.'

'But they *were*,' Griffith insisted. 'My Lord, they were very much his concern, as I shall demonstrate if your Lordship permits.'

'Very well,' said Hunter. 'Proceed.'

Griffith bounced on the balls of his feet like a boxer. The smile had long since gone, and his voice sounded angry. 'I put it to you, Mr Berkley, that Mrs Webb was constantly trying to interfere in her husband's business affairs, and that you had knowledge of this.'

Nick shook his head. 'I don't know –'

'Isn't it true,' Griffith bored deeper, 'that when Mr Webb resisted his wife's interference in his business, she came running to you –'

'No!' Nick replied, looking hot and distressed.

'And that you comforted her –'

'That's not true –'

'And you colluded with her –'

'No!' Nick's voice rose to a shout.

Griffith shouted back, 'Then why did Mrs Webb leave Whitegates with you?'

'I don't know,' said Nick in confusion. 'I mean, there was this terrible row –'

'Exactly! A row about you. And Mrs Webb ran off with you, and –'

'She didn't run off with me,' Nick countered hotly. 'Not the way you make it sound –'

'She left her husband, did she not?'

'Well . . . yes, but –'

'And she ran off with you to a house in Newbury. Isn't that true?'

'Yes, but –'

'And after that you went to London together. Isn't that so?'

'We went to a friend's –'

'Where you now live together under the same roof!'

'No, we don't, not any more, I'm not living with Ann any more.'

I caught my breath, cursing Nick's clumsy words.

'Ah, but you *were*!' Griffith pounced. 'And while you were living together, you concocted this miserable little scheme. This case has nothing to do with contracts. That's just an excuse for you to try to discredit a man who befriended you – a man who plucked you from oblivion and made you a star –'

'No, that's not true –'

'You deny you were plucked from oblivion?'

'No, I accept that –'

'And Mr Webb made you a star. You deny that?'

'It's not about that –'

'Exactly. It's not about your career at all, is it? It's about Mrs Webb. That's why we're here. A woman scorned. Scorned by her husband because she interfered, she turns to her lover and brings this trumped-up case –'

'No!' Nick shouted. 'That's not true!' Looking ruffled and dishevelled, his knuckles showed white as he gripped the edge of the witness-box. 'None of it's true.'

Griffith taunted him. 'Not true, you say. Hasn't Mrs Webb supported you all the way with this case?'

White-faced, Nick swayed slightly as he clung to the box. 'Yes, she's helped me –'

'Helped you? I should say she has. Hasn't she toured the country with a begging bowl, asking musicians to part with their hard-earned money –'

'Yes!' Nick choked. 'Yes!'

Griffith looked triumphant. 'I'll put it to you this way,' he said. 'Without Mrs Webb we wouldn't be here today, would we?'

'In one sense, no, but –'

'Come now,' Griffith softened his tone and began to coax, 'you wouldn't have done this by yourself, would you? Think back to the early days. You and Mr Webb got along fine, didn't you?'

'Yes, to begin with –'

'Then Mrs Webb came between you –'

'No,' Nick protested, 'we began to argue about the music I wanted to write –'

'And didn't Mrs Webb *encourage* you to argue?'

In his confusion, Nick hesitated.

'You see!' Griffith pounced. 'Without Mrs Webb, you and Mr Webb would have patched up your differences. None of this would have happened –'

'But he was so ... so ...' Nick searched for the right words.

'So positive about your best interests?' Griffith suggested. 'Of course he was! Look what he's done for you in a year. Twelve months, that's all. In no time at all, he established you. He could see a glorious future for you. Then he saw it being thrown away because you were taking bad advice. No wonder he was upset. Come now, Mr Berkley, in his position, *you* would have been upset. Be honest now. You take an unknown composer, let him live in your house, you make him a star, then see him in danger of throwing it all away. Wouldn't that upset you?'

'Well ... yes –'

'Wouldn't you try to stop him?'

'I suppose so –'

'And isn't that what happened in this case?'

I squirmed in my seat as Griffith moved the argument further and further away from the contracts. They were forgotten, hidden by his sleight of hand. From then on, Nick went from bad to worse. Longfellow was up and down protesting, but Griffith survived the interruptions and led Nick into one trap after another.

'Why did you go to Mr Webb in the first place?'

'Because . . .' Nick swallowed. 'I'd heard about JWE . . . I'd seen him on television —'

'Him?'

'Mr Webb.'

'Ah,' Griffith nodded. 'On television, was he? And what was he doing?'

'Talking about records.'

'As an expert?'

'Yes.'

'It was *Mr* Webb you saw?'

'Yes.'

'Not *Mrs* Webb?'

'No.'

'So *Mr* Webb is the expert, isn't he?'

Sneaking a sideways look at my father, there was no mistaking the sadistic gleam in his eye. No mistaking it because I knew it too well. I wanted to scream as I had once screamed as a boy — *It's not like that, not the way you're saying it.* How many times had I sweated through such inquisitions?

Nick sweated. Poor honest Nick, trying to give straight answers to slanted questions. Griffith was merciless. Longfellow objected vigorously and Hunter upheld countless protests, but nothing deflected Griffith as he thundered to his finish.

'Wouldn't you agree you've been disgracefully ungrateful?'

'No, I *was* grateful –'

'But you stopped being grateful?'

'Not that so much as –'

'Gratitude ceased to matter. You got what you wanted –'

'No –'

'This benefactor – your words, Mr Berkley – this benefactor gave you food and shelter and comfort, did he not?'

'At the beginning –'

'This expert – your words, Mr Berkley – this expert started your career, did he not?'

'Yes –'

'And you threw it back in his face!' Griffith snarled in disgust. 'No further questions,' he concluded, spitting the words out contemptuously as he sat down in his seat.

It was over. At last it was over. Nick's face was the colour of oatmeal. He swayed in the box, gripping the sides from sheer exhaustion. Unable to help him, I avoided his eye. Drained and anxious, I waited for Longfellow to rise, knowing in my heart that the damage was done. Throughout the barrage of questioning I had been watching Hunter's face; the feigned look of boredom had slipped now and then, enough for me to guess at his thoughts, and it seemed to me that Mr Justice Hunter thought Nick every bit as greedy and grasping as Griffith had suggested.

Longfellow took his time getting up, no doubt to give Nick a chance to recover. In the public gallery a woman coughed, and people fidgeted to release the tension which Griffith had created. Even so, Nick

flinched when Sir Robert finally rose. Nick's apprehension was pitiful. His eyes begged, *Not more, I
can't stand much more.*

The mute appeal drew an immediate response
from Sir Robert. 'I have very few questions,' he said,
softening his stern expression to an encouraging
smile. 'My learned friend,' he said, with a sideways
look of distaste at Griffith, 'has implied a great deal.
However, we need only concern ourselves with the
matter of your relationship with Mrs Webb, since all
implications flow from that. Do you follow?'

Nick nodded.

Longfellow looked grave. 'I want you to consider
your answers very carefully. Take your time and
remember you are on oath.'

Nodding again, Nick moistened his lips with the
tip of his tongue.

'Think back to when you and Mr Webb argued
about your work. Did Mrs Webb automatically side
with you?'

'Not automatically, no.' Nick shook his head. 'She
was anxious for me to finish the album I was working
on. The thing was, she could see what I was trying
to do, what I wanted to do, she understood. She . . .'
Nick hesitated. 'Well . . . she did say she would help
try to persuade Mr Webb.'

Longfellow raised his eyebrows. 'So my learned
friend was right to suggest she encouraged you to
argue with her husband?'

'I would have argued anyway. That's the difference, don't you see? With or without Mrs Webb, I
can only write what I feel, it's useless otherwise.
Mrs Webb didn't put me up to it, if that's what you
mean.'

I breathed a little more easily. I could see where Longfellow was going, but he was treading a dangerous path. Nick had a knack of saying the wrong thing.

'Mrs Webb didn't put you up to it?' Longfellow said heavily, relieved to have obtained a beneficial response.

'No. That's not how it happened at all.'

'Very well.' Longfellow nodded. 'Then there was this terrible row and you left Whitegates for good. And Mrs Webb left with you. In view of my learned friend's questions, I must put this last question to you. Are you and Mrs Webb lovers?'

Nick blushed crimson. Colour rushed up his neck and flooded his face. 'No,' he said, 'we're not.'

'And have you ever been lovers?'

'No, never.'

Unconcerned about Nick's embarrassment and more likely pleased with the effect he had created, Longfellow nodded his satisfaction. 'I have no further questions,' he said, resuming his seat.

Mr Justice Hunter sat with his chin cupped in one hand. I tried to read his expression, but the owl-look had returned and he was giving nothing away. It was hard to assess whether Longfellow had regained any of the lost ground. My hunch was, some, but not all.

Hunter glanced at the clock. 'I think this would be a good time to recess for the day.'

We all rose as he walked out. My eyes went to Griffith, who had turned to whisper to my father. Unlike Longfellow they looked pleased. 'At least now we know their line of attack,' Longfellow grumbled, 'but we shall have to do better tomorrow.'

*

It was a difficult evening. As a witness, Ann had been barred from the courtroom until she had given her evidence, so she had spent a frustrating day in the waiting-rooms. 'I bumped into Dai and Peter Ellis from The Tower. Neither of them would talk to me, they're both too frightened of Jack.'

I got Ann and Nick back to the hotel and had dinner sent up to my room. Nick was upset about his encounter with Griffith. 'The questions came so fast there was no time to think.'

I said he had done well and that Longfellow was pleased with him.

'Really? Honestly?'

'Honestly,' I lied.

'My turn tomorrow,' said Ann with a brave grin.

'You'll be the star of the show,' I told her.

We went early to bed, and I dreamt my father had imprisoned Julia in a tower. Around the base of the tower was a moat, and in the moat were some sharks. They were all there, swimming along, Griffith was a fat shark with enormous teeth, Jack was more like a killer whale the way he thrashed through the water; John Lovell was a blue shark and Julia's mother was a piranha. Every time I tried to swim across, they attacked in unison and drove me back to the bank. Meanwhile my father stood beneath the portcullis of the tower, dismembering Nick and feeding him to the sharks limb by limb. They were all there but for Julia, and she was nowhere to be seen. Asleep or awake, my heart ached for her, and when I awoke I prayed she would be in court in the morning.

*

My prayers went unanswered. Bert was there with my mother, Gill and Mary were there, with Nick sitting between them. I was surprised to see Jumbo and John Lovell in the back row. The public benches were full of people, but Julia was not among them. It was a dispiriting start to a day destined to turn into a disaster.

Ann at least began well. Wearing a pale yellow knitted suit which contrasted splendidly with her glossy black hair, she cut an attractive figure in the box. Watching her take the oath, I wondered what the Judge was thinking as he formed his important first impressions. Perhaps he was speculating on the suggestions Griffith had made, and not blaming Nick if Griffith were right. Longfellow had decided that Olivia Newton would lead Ann through her story, and I knew he was right as soon as they started. Olivia, warm and matronly; Ann, crisp and assured; they sounded like two professional women discussing a matter of mutual interest, creating an atmosphere in which the very suggestion of an affair with Nick would jar as much as raucous laughter in church. Reassuring, even if Griffith did loll in his chair, devouring Ann with his eyes as he waited his turn.

Skilfully Olivia drew out the importance which had been attached to music in Ann's upbringing. At one point, listing the qualifications she had gained as a child, Ann smiled. 'I can play six instruments competently,' she said, 'but not one with flair. I can tell you how a singer should sound, yet I can't hit a true note. On paper I'm technically perfect, but you need ear-plugs to listen to me. Therefore music is both my greatest sorrow and my greatest joy.'

Hunter's eyes gleamed with the appreciation of a small boy skipping piano practice.

With a few swift questions, Olivia revealed Ann's knowledge of the music world in New York. 'And then you came to London?'

'That's right,' Ann agreed. 'It was just starting to happen here. There was so much talent, I couldn't believe it.'

Olivia was good. While not really doubting her, I had been understandably anxious, but she had struck the right note from the start, encouraging Ann to respond naturally while at the same time enhancing her stature as an expert. Briefly we heard about Ann's coaching of Janie and The Graduates, Dai Evans, and The Post Office Tower during the early days of JWE.

Olivia smiled. 'I believe Mr Webb referred to you as his ears.'

Ann nodded. 'And everyone else called me "Coach".'

'An accurate description. That's what you were, weren't you?'

'Yes.'

'Were there any other coaches?'

'No.'

'So they owe their success to you?'

Anne shook her head. 'Don't flatter me. They owe their success to themselves. It was their talent and hard work. I just helped where I could.'

It gladdened my heart to watch Mr Justice Hunter. Ann was making such a good impression that he was almost nodding agreement. I glanced sideways at my father, who looked as calm and as unruffled as ever. So did Griffith. I tried not to worry . . .

'And in what way,' Olivia was asking, 'does Mr

Berkley differ from the others? What makes him so special in your opinion?'

'His range. I don't want to take anything away from the others; they're mostly performers anyway, whereas Nick's future is as a composer.'

'Isn't Mr Ossie Davidson a composer?'

Ann nodded. 'Sure, and Ossie's a dear friend, or at least I hope he is, and he's very good at what he does. But he'd be the first to agree that, musically speaking, Nick is a hundred times more literate. What we're talking about here is an incredibly rare talent. Someone like this comes along maybe once in a generation . . .'

Ann's enthusiasm was inexhaustible. I'd heard her talk about music before, so it wasn't a new experience for me, except for the circumstances. And the circumstances were exceptional. If the past weeks had been hard on me, they had been gruelling for Ann. She had walked out on Jack, abandoned her home, been labelled an adulteress, faced a messy divorce case . . . yet without thought for herself she had stormed round the country raising money for Nick. And there she was in the witness-box, glowing with excitement as she described a talent that comes along once in a generation! The odd thing was that listening to Ann made me yearn for Julia all the more. Julia and I were two of a kind, just as, in a way, Jack and Ann were two of a kind. The thought had never struck me before, but it was true: they were both driven by obsessions. Gill was right when he said 'Jack sees images, not people', but so was Jumbo when he called Ann 'that dark-haired girl who only cares about music'. Where Jack was single-minded about money and power, Ann was single-minded about music and musicians. Of course, there was a difference: where Jack was selfish and grasping, Ann was the opposite. Yet when it came to musicians, she was as uncompromising in her pursuit of *their* best interests as Jack was in pursuit of *his*. No wonder the marriage had failed. There was none of the give and take between them that I had thought existed between Julia and me . . .

And so the clock ticked on until the judge declared a recess for lunch. Griffith had been surprisingly quiet all morning, not rising to his feet once, letting Olivia have it all her own way. And without doubt Ann had made a good impression on Hunter. My hopes rose. If Hunter believed Ann, he had to believe Nick, because they were telling the same story, they were telling the truth . . .

Our prospects were improving, although a great deal would depend on the afternoon, when Ann would face Griffith.

Griffith rose to his feet. Where his questioning of Nick had commenced with a smile, there were no smiles for Ann. Having cast her as the villain of the piece, Griffith meant to continue in the same vein. Even as he started, his black Welsh hair fell across his brow and his voice rasped with aggression. 'You have been represented as an expert,' he said. 'A sort of glorified talent scout. Is that how you see yourself?'

Ann replied without hesitation. 'I don't see myself as a glorified anything.'

Mr Justice Hunter's mouth twitched as he repressed a smile.

Griffith narrowed his eyes and rocked back on his

heels. He scowled. 'But you have a high opinion of your ability to select musical talent, do you not?'

'I have a high opinion of musical talent,' Ann answered.

A faint stirring arose in the public gallery as people whispered, anticipating perhaps that Ann would fare better than Nick against Sir Emlyn. I crossed my fingers and hoped.

'For instance,' said Griffith, 'it's been suggested that you discovered Janie and The Graduates. Is that true?'

'It's not been suggested by me.'

'So it's untrue?'

Ann frowned. 'How can anyone discover anyone? It's like saying Columbus discovered America when it was there all the time.'

In the gallery a man laughed, and the rising murmur caused the amused look on Hunter's face to darken into a reproving frown.

'Very well,' Griffith conceded heavily, 'I'll put it another way. Do you consider yourself instrumental in their success?'

'I like to think I helped.'

'Really? Even though you said their success was due to their own talent and hard work? Are you now claiming the credit?'

'No.' Ann shook her head. 'I would never do that.'

'Because you know that such credit wouldn't be deserved, don't you?'

Ann frowned. 'I said earlier –'

'What you conveyed earlier was an impression. An impression of modesty. You said their success was all due to their talent and hard work. But that's not how you feel, is it? You just admitted as much. I helped, you say. Without my help none of it would have happened –'

'That's not what I said,' Ann protested sharply.

'But it's what you *think*! Take the matter of coaching. Earlier you told my learned friend that everyone called you "Coach". You were asked if there was another coach and your answer was no. Is that correct?'

'Yes,' said Ann, 'I mean, no, there wasn't another coach –'

'Would it surprise you to learn that Janie Marsham had been coached in singing since she was nine years of age?'

Ann responded with a startled look. 'I knew she'd had lessons, yes –'

'And Dai Evans sang at the Royal National Eisteddfod, for which he was coached –'

'That was years before –'

'And that Tommy Bleeson of The Post Office Tower had been soloist in school choirs and chapel choirs and goodness knows what. Do you think he could have done that without lessons?'

'I was talking about when we started JWE!' Ann retorted hotly.

'So all of these . . .' Griffith paused, as if suddenly struck by her answer. Quickly he made a note on his pad. Then he resumed. 'So all these people were *trained* singers and musicians. Some were already *professional* musicians. Yet you would have us believe it was your training –'

'All I said was that I helped!'

Griffith sneered his contempt. 'I daresay whoever made tea for Christopher Wren could claim to have helped build St Paul's.'

'I more than made tea,' Ann said stubbornly, going pink in the face.

'Ah!' Sir Emlyn's voice rose in triumph. 'There it is again. Pride. Your contribution must be recognised –'

'My Lord,' Sir Robert Longfellow rose to his feet, 'the witness has clearly defined her contribution. She would no more claim to have coached these people since birth, than to be responsible for their God-given talent. With respect to my learned friend, is he not labouring –'

'I rather agree.' Hunter nodded. 'Sir Emlyn, the witness has said she helped these artists. Can't we leave it at that? After all, you're not contending she hindered them, are you?' He smiled at his wry joke.

But it was no joke to Griffith. 'With respect, my Lord, that is *exactly* what I shall contend in respect of Mr Berkley. That she has severely damaged his career.'

Hunter was taken aback. 'I see,' he said. Frowning slightly, he removed his spectacles and began to polish them with a handkerchief produced from under his robe. Without glasses his face looked younger and less owl-like, despite his thoughtful expression.

'My Lord,' said Griffith, 'as for the other artists, I only seek to establish what contribution this witness made to their careers because my learned friends have represented her as an expert.'

Staring down at his spectacles, Hunter considered for a moment. Then with a final polish, he replaced them on his nose. 'I understand,' he sighed. 'Proceed, then, although I hope we shall not get bogged down on this point.'

But Sir Emlyn had every intention to bog us down. He wanted to wallow. Over the next twenty minutes he attacked every contribution Ann had made to

JWE. Longfellow objected four times, and the judge ruled in his favour, but Griffith side-stepped and retreated and counter-attacked. I was appalled. Without Ann, JWE wouldn't have existed, but to listen to Griffith was to believe Ann was a know-nothing little gold-digger who had ridden to Whitegates on Jack's coat-tails.

'You see,' said Griffith at one point, 'what these trained musicians needed was a manager. Isn't that right?'

Wearied by the attack, Ann nodded. 'Yes, but –'

'I put it to you that Mr Webb established their careers. For example, you didn't go out and get them engagements, did you?'

'No.'

'Mr Webb did that, didn't he?'

'Yes he did, but –'

'Mr Webb negotiated with the owners of night-clubs and concert halls and such places, didn't he?'

'Yes.'

'Exactly! It was his energy, his drive, his enthusiasm which put Janie and The Graduates on the map. You don't deny that, surely?'

'I don't deny it entirely –'

'And the same holds good for Mr Evans?'

'Yes, it does –'

'And The Post Office Tower, and all the others?'

'Yes.'

'It was Mr Webb who negotiated with publishers and such people, wasn't it?'

'Of course –'

'And Mr Webb who dealt with the recording companies, correct?'

'Naturally.'

Sir Emlyn paused in his rapid-fire questions. 'You say "naturally", Mrs Webb, but with your husband doing so much the point becomes clear, does it not? Your own contribution was negligible –'

'I like to think it more than that.'

'Exactly!' Griffith bellowed in triumph. 'You like to think! I know you do, I said so earlier. You like to think everything was your doing –'

'I never said that –'

'I'll tell you *exactly* what you said,' Griffith pounced, reaching for his notebook. 'These are your very words. *I was talking about when we started JWE*. That's what you said. When *we* started JWE. Not when Mr Webb started JWE. When *we* started it. Do you see the difference?'

'That's how it was –'

'A partnership, was it? You and Mr Webb, fifty-fifty?'

Ann gave a resigned shake of her head. 'No, nothing like that –'

'When Mr Webb formed JWE Ltd, did he appoint you as a director?'

'You know he didn't.'

'Did you become a shareholder?'

'No,' Ann conceded wearily.

'Were you a director of White Hat Publishing Ltd?'

'No.'

'Or a shareholder?'

'No.'

'What about Apex Records Ltd. Were you a director –'

'No, and I wasn't a shareholder either,' Ann cried, losing her temper. 'What's the point of these questions?'

Griffith affected surprise. 'Surely, that's obvious? I put it to you that had Mr Webb considered you so valuable, he would have appointed you to the boards of all of these companies –'

'Well he didn't, did he?'

'No, he did not. Neither were you a shareholder –'

'He dealt with all of that stuff –'

'While you concentrated on grooming the artists. Is that right?'

'Right,' Ann nodded.

'I see,' said Griffith softly. 'So let's go back to when you were doing all this work at JWE. What sort of salary were you paid?'

Ann groaned and lowered her head. Gripping the edge of the box, she stood, head bowed, her black hair falling forward on to the yellow suit, a posture of utter weariness. 'I don't believe it,' she muttered not quite under her breath.

Griffith cocked his head. 'Sorry, could you repeat that?'

'She doesn't believe it,' Hunter interrupted sharply. 'That's what the witness said, Sir Emlyn.'

'I'm obliged, my Lord,' said Griffith.

Hunter's faint look of distaste was almost indiscernible. Turning away, his expression softened as he looked at Ann. 'Would you like to sit down, Mrs Webb? You've been standing much longer than I anticipated.'

Raising her head, Ann accepted with a grateful smile. 'Thank you, my Lord.'

A court usher hurried forward with a stool and Ann moved aside to allow him to set it in the witness-box. Thanking him, she sat down. The interruption lasted only a couple of minutes, but from the look on Ann's face, the respite was welcome. Griffith was wearing her down and scoring some valuable points. I hated to admit it, but a stranger might easily have believed Ann's contribution to Jack's success was as marginal as Griffith was suggesting. Even the Judge was beginning to waver, despite his act of consideration . . .

Next minute, Griffith was attacking again. 'What we've established so far, Mrs Webb,' he said, 'is that you were neither a director nor a shareholder in any of your husband's companies. That is correct, isn't it?'

'Yes.'

'And we were talking about the salary you received –'

'I received no salary.'

Griffith feigned disbelief. 'No salary? What, none at all? Nothing?'

'Nothing.'

'Perhaps you were paid through White Hat Publishing?'

'No,' Ann shook her head. 'I was not paid by White Hat, Apex or JWE. I didn't need a salary and I didn't ask for one.'

Griffith rubbed his chin, apparently nonplussed. 'You see, Mrs Webb, this is how it strikes me. Far from being a valuable expert, you simply helped out now and then because your husband . . . husband-to-be as he was then . . . liked to have you around. You were a sort of lucky mascot.'

Ann's eyes burned with defiance but she said nothing.

'No harm in that,' Griffith shrugged, 'mascots are fun. No harm, except for what went on in your head, and instead of seeing yourself as a sort of Girl Friday, you wanted credit for the success of the people around you. Isn't that how it was?'

'No, it's not –'

'Isn't it true that you began to interfere in your husband's business decisions?'

'How can you say that?' Ann's frustration erupted. 'How could I interfere? It was our lives. We started JWE together –'

'No!' Griffith interrupted harshly. 'You did not start it. Mr Webb founded the business. You weren't a director, a shareholder; you didn't even rate a salary. You consistently exaggerate your importance.'

A look of desperation began to haunt Ann's face as Griffith pressed on with his attack. By now Ann had lost her earlier composure; frustrated and harried, she teetered on the verge of losing her temper. Griffith goaded her more and more until suddenly she blurted out the most damning admission.

Griffith asked, 'Did you interfere between Janie Marsham and your husband?'

'I took her side –'

'Exactly. You know best, don't you? You're the expert –'

'Right! Okay. You're right. If you want the truth, I've forgotten more about music than Jack will ever know. He knew nothing until he met me!'

The words hung in the air. Griffith immediately fell silent. The impact of the outburst was dramatic. My heart sank. Ann had sounded shrill and spiteful. It didn't matter that there was truth in her words – Griffith had succeeded in portraying her as a woman scorned. I was afraid to look at Hunter.

Griffith stared. 'All that resentment,' he said softly, 'all bottled up inside you.'

Ann bit her lip and returned his stare.

'So what happened?' asked Griffith, 'about this difference of opinion? Did Janie Marsham run off to a lawyer to try to get out of her contracts?'

Ann shook her head.

'No,' said Griffith, 'because she knows perfectly well that Mr Webb will look after her interests. There's no doubt in her mind about who is the expert. But Mr Berkley is younger, less experienced, more impressionable. Instead of listening to Mr Webb, he listened to you, didn't he?'

Ann passed a hand through her hair, tired to the point of exhaustion. 'Jack doesn't understand –'

'And you do? That's what it's all about, isn't it? When it comes to musicians, you've always believed you know best.' Griffith paused before asking sharply, 'What does the name Bruno Katzman mean to you?'

Ann swayed in her chair. Shock marked every line of her face.

'Answer the question, Mrs Webb!' Griffith persisted.

Longfellow and Olivia were both on their feet, but their protests were needless because Hunter had already seen the look on Ann's face. 'You look ill, Mrs Webb,' he exclaimed. 'Are you all right?'

Ann stared at Griffith as if seeing a ghost.

'The court will adjourn for ten minutes,' Hunter announced, before realising the time was close to four o'clock. 'No,' he corrected, 'as it's so late I think we may as well recess for the day.'

'My Lord,' Griffith rose quickly, 'we beg permission to add Mr Bruno Katzman to our list of witnesses . . .'

Ann's face was ashen. I heard Griffith say it was not possible to include Katzman before – 'but I am now informed he will arrive from New York this weekend . . .'

Alarmed by what was happening to Ann, I absorbed what Griffith was saying only in snatches.

'. . . information only made available to me as I came into court this afternoon . . . I need to confer with my instructing solicitor . . . should we consider it desirable, we shall seek your Lordship's permission to add Mr Katzman to our list of witnesses . . .'

I heard Longfellow object, I heard Hunter say he would make a ruling on Monday, I heard the court rise – indeed, I stood up with everyone else, but I saw only Ann's white face as Longfellow's warning exploded in my mind – *He's got something up his sleeve. Something we don't know about.*

We went directly to the hotel, Ann and Nick, Gill and myself. In her crisis, Ann had turned to Gill as a daughter would to a father, and within minutes Gill had organised two cabs at the Carey Street entrance and was ushering Bert, Mary and my mother into one before joining us in the other. Dazed and still shaken, Ann travelled in silence, clinging to Gill's arm, while I sat on the tip-up seat, with Longfellow's angry words ringing in my ears: 'You'd better find out what the hell this is all about.'

At the hotel, we went in through the staff entrance at the back and were very quickly up in my room.

'Ann could use a drink,' said Gill. 'In fact, we all could.'

I sent down for a bottle of brandy and some coffee,

while Ann went into the bathroom. It was some time before she emerged, and when she did it was clear she had been crying. 'I'm okay now,' she said in answer to Gill's anxious look. 'How can anyone sink so low? I can't get over Jack being such a shit. God, people like him and Katzman are a breed all on their own.'

'Who's Katzman?' I asked.

They ignored me. Gill sat Ann down in one of the room's two armchairs and poured her a brandy. Then he gave her a cigarette and some coffee, and all the time he was saying things like, 'Calm down' and 'It's all right now'. Meanwhile Nick had perched himself on the hard-backed chair in front of the dressing-table and I had sat down on the bed.

Finally, when Ann looked at least partly recovered, Gill said, 'You'd better tell Peter.'

And so, after all that time, I came to learn what had happened to Ann before she arrived in London. Odd the way life turns out. I'd had all sorts of theories once about what it could be; I remember I even asked Gill at one time, only for him to shrug his shoulders and say, 'Maybe she'll tell you herself one day.' And now she was telling me.

Some of it was as I had imagined. There had been a love-affair with a musician.

'His name was Tommy Barton,' she said, directing a sad smile at Nick. 'Ever hear of him?'

Nick frowned and shook his head.

'Played the sweetest guitar you ever heard. No one ever played better guitar. No one, I swear.'

After the death of her parents, Ann had moved in with him. 'He didn't have a dime and we lived on my parents' insurance money . . .'

Any witness would have been moved by the ache in her voice and the look in her eyes. Ann's eyes had never shone like that for Jack Webb. Within five minutes it was obvious that she had harboured different and far stronger feelings for Tommy Barton.

The world she talked about was one I could scarcely imagine; the New York music scene of the Fifties was as foreign to me as the planet Mars. Except for one item; apparently Tommy had got himself involved in a contractual mess with Bruno Katzman, much as Nick had with Jack.

'. . . it used to tear me apart. Tommy would be playing to crummy joints, getting nowhere, earning peanuts. And this was a real talent, someone so special the whole world should have heard him. Katzman and I had some real screaming matches. I'd go round to his office and he'd give me all this bullshit about looking after Tommy's interests. The only interests Katzman cared about were his own. Typical screwing manager. One day I made him so angry, he threw me down the stairs. Correction, *he* didn't, his goons threw me down the stairs while he stood and laughed. Oh Jesus, you wouldn't believe the stand-up fights I had with Katzman . . .'

Once embarked on the story, Ann couldn't stop. She chain-smoked as she told it, her hands shook now and then and sometimes her eyes glistened with tears, but it was clear that while her life with Tommy Barton was years in the past, it remained fresh in her memory.

'. . . never a day passes when I don't think of him. We used to sit around, dreaming about him playing the Hollywood Bowl or somewhere, spending hours planning the numbers . . .'

Meanwhile he was bound hand and foot by his contracts with Katzman.

'. . . the infuriating thing was, Katzman could have done something. He was big enough, even I had to admit that. He had all the right contacts, did business with powerful people. He just had too much going for him. You know, there was always something bigger than Tommy, to claim his attention. So I pleaded with him. "Let Tommy go," I begged, "there's a guy I know who can take Tommy places." There was, too. There was this guy Lou Martello who was really hot for Tommy, always going on about the things he could do for him . . .'

Gill had heard the story before, but he listened intently, occasionally staring down at his big, red hands, while for the most part watching Ann, his eyes reflecting her pain.

'. . . in the end I said to Tommy, "Let's go to Martello anyway. What can Katzman do? Sue us? So let him. Like, we can prove you're starving to death being tied up with him . . ."'

Katzman did not sue them. Instead he made it difficult for Tommy to find work.

'. . . Martello kept his end of the bargain. To begin with he got Tommy some real classy bookings, you know, smart places full of people ready to listen. Tommy would open and go down a storm. I'd think, he's on his way now, here comes the big-time. Then the next night they would tell him to go. No explanation. Audiences loved him, but all of a sudden managements were too scared to book him. It had to be Katzman. I knew it, and Martello knew it, but he was a gutsy little guy; he believed in Tommy as much as I did so he kept trying . . .'

Then Martello had an accident.

'. . . to be honest, I think it was genuine. I mean, I suspected Katzman at first. One night Martello's driving home and gets hit by a truck. I was sure it was Katzman. Then I found out the truck driver was hurt even worse than Martello. They ended up in the same hospital . . .'

Without Martello, Tommy Barton had no one to represent him.

'. . . there was always the *hope* of something happening when Martello was around – slender, I know, but I could use it to keep Tommy going. Meanwhile we lived on the insurance money. We had enough, not big bucks or anything, but we could get by. The roughest part was dealing with Tommy's fits of depression. Even before Martello's accident, he was getting pretty desperate. Keeping his spirits up was a full-time job, believe me. Tommy would get so down, sometimes I thought I'd never get him to smile or laugh or see anything funny ever again. Then when Martello finished up in hospital . . .'

Ann swallowed and took a deep breath. 'It's hard to explain. Tommy was full of ambition. So ambitious it hurt, and when he couldn't find work, the frustrations built up. He used to go into these deep black moods . . .' Her voice faded and she lowered her eyes to watch her hands fidget on her lap.

I looked at Gill who shrugged. 'There's no easy way to put this,' he said. 'Tommy took an overdose, he killed himself. Ann got home one day and it was all over.'

Nick gasped. I sat in shocked silence, trying to think of what to say.

Gill sighed. 'It was a hell of a business for a young girl –'

'I still miss him,' Ann said quietly, still looking down at her lap. 'Even now I miss him. Such a waste of a lovely man, and all that talent. Twenty-three years old. We would have made it happen for him one day, I know we would . . .'

Gill got up and gave her some more coffee and let her talk herself out. Finally, when Ann had regained her calm and fallen silent, Gill turned to me. 'The thing is,' he said, 'she told Jack about it, before they got married.'

'Oh,' I said.

Ann looked up. 'I more or less had to tell Jack. He kept asking me what happened in the States. And what with him wanting to marry me, it seemed only fair.'

Her choice of words sounded odd. Encouraged by her wan smile, I said, 'You make it sound as if you didn't want to marry him.'

'I don't think I did,' she answered, shaking her head. 'Not *want* to. It wasn't the way it was with Tommy. But well, I suppose what with working with him, and he kept asking me all the time . . . it was important to him, he said it didn't matter that I'd felt more for Tommy than I did for him, everything would work out. Perhaps it did for a while . . .' She shrugged. 'Anyway, you know the rest; now you know the whole story.'

At that moment I thought I understood Ann for the first time in my life. Casting my mind back to the days in the London flat, I could understand, now, all that scathing bitterness she had vented on musicians' managers. I understood her initial reluctance to help Janie, and to get involved all over again; I understood how impressed she must have been with Jack in his white hat . . .

And Jack? To have won the prize only to find he was living in the shadow of a dead musician . . . Jack of all people. He couldn't stand being in anyone's shadow. Jack had to win. But how did you compete with the dead? Was that why this fight had become so bitter?

Gill went over to the table and poured himself another brandy. Tilting the bottle, he looked at my glass, but I shook my head. 'So you see,' he said, 'Jack knew all about Katzman.'

'But why send for Katzman now? What possible evidence can he give?'

'There was an inquest,' said Gill. 'Naturally, with a suicide —'

Ann sucked in her breath and went very white.

'You all right?' Gill asked. 'Why not —'

'Tommy left a note,' she interrupted. 'A letter, really, it went on for pages, saying he loved me and couldn't go on letting me down . . .' She buried her head in her hands. '*Him* letting *me* down.' She choked, and hurriedly rose from her chair.

'Ann!' said Gill, but Ann rushed off to the bathroom.

Gill rubbed the worry lines in his forehead with the heel of one hand. 'I could have told you all this without her being here,' he sighed. 'Anyway, Katzman told the inquest that Tommy was a moderately useful musician who could have earned a steady living if Ann had left him alone. According to Katzman, Ann encouraged him to believe he was more talented than he was. So what with Katzman, the note and everything else, the coroner gave Ann a hard time. More or less said her ambition had driven Tommy to his death. "This will be on your conscience the rest of your life," he said, and a lot more besides.'

A minute before, I'd imagined I understood everything. Now it was even worse than I thought. The great wave of sympathy I felt for Ann was swamped by the horror of Jack using this against her.

Gill saw the look on my face. 'That's right,' he said. 'They'll put Katzman in the box, let him tell his story, then say it's happening all over again. They'll say she's encouraged Nick the same way. Today was bad enough, but Ann won't have a scrap of credibility left. I'm sorry, Peter, but I can't see a snowball's chance in hell of winning this case now.'

Never have I been so totally depressed as when driving back to Swindon the next morning. Everything had gone wrong. Longfellow had been as shaken as me when I called him about Katzman – and angry. 'If Hunter wasn't so weak, he'd throw it out as inadmissible evidence. I'll do what I can, but you'd better prepare Mrs Webb for another hard time on Monday.' Poor Ann. And poor Nick. Few of the papers gave him a chance. NICK BERKLEY ACCUSED OF BRINGING TRUMPED-UP CASE cried the *Mail*; DID WIFE ACT FROM SPITE? asked the *Mirror*.

Worrying so hard about Ann and Nick had left me little time to think of my own problems, but they closed in on me as I drove into Swindon. I'd lost Julia. I'd lost Nick's case in the High Court. I'd lost The Grove – not that I wanted it without Julia, but I'd have to find somewhere to live. I'd have to take a small flat . . . if I stayed in Swindon . . . if I could stomach John Lovell in the office . . . if I didn't resign . . .

Such were my thoughts as I drove down the High Street and into the yard behind the hotel. Parking the MG, I carried my bag up to my room, wondering what the hell to do with myself.

As soon as I opened the door I saw something was wrong. Books left on the coffee-table had been moved. The chair by the wardrobe had been transferred to the window. Then I saw the suitcases, two of them, one was blue, the other was brown, and quite definitely neither was mine.

I groaned aloud. As if I wasn't plagued by enough troubles, the hotel had let my room to somebody else . . .

Then Julia emerged from the bathroom in a striped woollen dress. She looked serene and unruffled. 'Hello,' she said, 'I expected you earlier. I phoned your hotel in London and they told me you'd left –'

'What are you doing here?'

'Ah,' she said, 'now that's a good question. I don't know if you'll think it's good news or bad news.'

Still standing in the open doorway, I dropped my bags and gaped at her.

'I've left home and moved in with you. I was just about to put my things in the wardrobe.'

I stood and stared, too surprised to say anything.

'John came round last night,' she said, 'he couldn't wait to tell us you'd lost. Full of it, he was, until I blew my top. Partners should support each other, I said, which made me feel a complete hypocrite because I hadn't supported you either . . .' She swallowed hard and her apparent calm deserted her. The next moment she was trembling. Then we were in each other's arms, and she was saying how she'd let me down and that I'd been right all along . . .

And all this was going on with the door wide open and people gawping in from the corridor. Even after I closed the door, it took me some minutes to realise what had happened. I was overjoyed, but I did try to be sensible. 'You can't move in here,' I said. 'What will people say?'

'Who cares?'

'What about the school?'

'I'll be expelled.'

'What about your mother?'

'She can come for tea on Sundays if she behaves herself.'

'Julia, be sensible. You know I've lost The Grove. I'll have to move out of here into a small flat —'

'You mean *we'll* have to move out to a small flat.'

We went to bed then. Eleven o'clock in the morning. In fact, truth told, we spent much of that weekend in bed. 'Saving money,' Julia joked. 'It's cheaper up here than down in the bar.' But later we did have a drink in the dining-room, running the gauntlet of speculative looks. And we talked and talked, as much about events in the High Court as our wrecked plans for The Grove, as if we had to get the case over before we could get on with our lives.

Julia fell silent when I told her about Katzman. Eventually she said, 'I'm sorry about Ann. I'm still not sure I like her and I know that's unfair; the truth is, I don't really understand her —'

'Who does? Except that I'm closer to understanding her now than before. But believe me, she's a generous spirit. There's no harm in her. Not like in Jack. And my father makes things a hundred times worse. He's pulling the strings, teaching Jack a new set of tricks . . .'

We speculated on every issue. 'What they've done,' I said, 'is move the goal posts. Hunter's let them get away with it so far, but eventually Longfellow will get back to the contracts. That's what this case is really about . . .'

It was easier to see rays of hope when Julia was with me, and with her encouragement I began to feel better. Even if we had lost The Grove, we had a future together. I would have lost Buckingham Palace for that. Meanwhile, after two bad days in court there were at least two more to come . . . the battle wasn't yet over.

Monday was another bad day. The best thing about it was that Julia was in court with Bert and my mother and the others.

It soon became clear that Sir Emlyn would have no need to include Katzman when the time came to call his witnesses; his own searching questions were enough. Ann had no option but to reveal all that had happened in New York.

'So yet again,' Griffith sneered, 'it was a matter of your knowing better than the experts. You always have to be right, don't you, Mrs Webb?'

But having absorbed the shock over the weekend, Ann had recovered some of her strength. 'It's more a matter,' she retorted, 'of always being on the side of the artist.'

'Your misguided opinions led to a man's *death*!'

Griffith thundered in outrage. 'Wasn't that the coroner's verdict?'

Longfellow refused to allow that. Shaking with fury, he pointed out that a rebuke delivered while summing up did not amount to a verdict. And Hunter was angered enough to admonish Sir Emlyn with startling firmness.

So the morning wore on, the courtroom ringing with angry exchanges. My father sat back, looking well content with his tactics, caring not a jot for the pain he had indirectly inflicted on Ann. What did it matter, compared with the success of his scheme? And without doubt his scheme had damaged Ann's credibility: when Griffith finally sat down, the seeds of doubt had been well sown. Had I not known better, I might have been asking questions myself. Was Ann a wilful, manipulative woman who had set out to turn Nick's head? Had she urged him to bring this case merely to strike at her husband? Was Nick so besotted that he had no mind of his own? While Longfellow set about repairing the damage as best he could, I found myself watching Hunter. His face gave no clue to his thoughts, yet I clung to the hope that he had not lost all sympathy for Ann. Hope was all I could do . . .

Longfellow called our penultimate witness. Howard Nesbitt was an executive with a record company, who had supplied me with a good deal of information during my hectic researches. His time in the witness-box was brief.

'Yes,' he said, in answer to Longfellow's question, 'given the chance, we would have offered Nick Berkley a contract.'

'At what rates of royalty?'

'Two per cent higher than he was getting from Apex.'

Longfellow nodded and pressed on with his other questions, which were all designed to demonstrate the harshness of the Apex terms and conditions. Nesbitt obliged with some very satisfactory answers. I breathed a sigh of relief to have reached safer ground.

Our last witness was Harry Saunders, a one-time singer who now managed several pop groups and at least one composer. Nesbitt had mentioned him to me, and when I had met Harry I'd been well rewarded.

'Mr Saunders,' Longfellow began, 'are you the manager of Mr Danny Williams, the song-writer?'

'I do have that privilege,' Harry answered with a grave bow. He was a dapper little man, dressed in a pale grey suit and a polka-dot bow tie.

'Yes,' he agreed in answer to Longfellow's next question, 'White Hat published a number of Danny's songs: of course, that was early on, before Danny got established . . .'

Keeping Harry to 'Yes' and 'No' answers was hard work, even for Longfellow. Harry would have volunteered his life history given the chance. Gently but firmly, Longfellow brought him back to what was relevant.

'The contract,' Harry echoed. 'Yes, I remember the contract. The first time Jack Webb gave it to me I thought he was joking. I said to him, "You can't be serious. No one in his right mind would sign this." There was no way I'd allow Danny to put his monicker on that. No way.'

'So you went to another publisher?'

'Not then, I didn't. To be honest, I was just starting

and feeling my way around. This business is all contacts. Not so much what you know as who you know. So then I didn't know enough other people – but I knew enough not to sign that contract. Not the way it was written. I said to Danny, "You sign this, and Jack Webb might as well sleep with your wife because he's got everything else."'

'So what did you do?'

'Rewrote the contract. Cut great chunks out of it. Jack Webb put some back in, I took 'em out, he put 'em in again. It went on for months. But finally we got a contract a bit more to my way of thinking. Not ideal, but we could live with it until Danny was a step or two further down the road . . .'

Griffith did his best to paint a different picture when he rose to his feet. 'You don't deny that Mr Webb helped your client get started?'

'No, but –'

'In fact, without Mr Webb your client might still be completely unknown. Isn't that right?'

'I'd have got Danny started somehow –'

'But you hadn't any contacts. You went to Jack Webb and he took a chance. Isn't that true –'

'Yes, but –'

'Thank you. No further questions.'

And that was our case. Longfellow said he had no further witnesses and Hunter adjourned the court for lunch. No one on our side felt very happy – unlike Griffith, who gave me a big beaming smile as he left.

The afternoon went largely against us as well. The first witness Griffith produced was another record company executive. He was their *expert* witness, to counterbalance Howard Nesbitt. He did, too, claiming that in his experience the terms and conditions of the Apex contract were eminently fair. And then came the parade of the stars: Dai Evans, Janie, Ossie, Mike, Dave, one by one all the boys in The Post Office Tower, went into the witness-box and sang Jack's praises. What he hadn't done for their careers wasn't worth doing – according to them. By now Ann and Nick were sitting in the row immediately behind me, and the three of us could scarcely believe what we were hearing – especially from Janie. My mind went back to that night in the cottage when she had sobbed her heart out. Jack had been every kind of shit under the sun. Now she might have been describing a different person entirely.

I got cramp in my fingers from writing notes to Longfellow. Each note was more desperate than the last, but all had the same theme: 'Ask them about all the help Ann gave them in the early days.' 'Ask Janie how JWE started.' 'Ask Mike about the time he was going to pack his bags and go home to Bristol.'

Longfellow took not a blind bit of notice. Leaning forward, I whispered urgently into Olivia's ear. Finally back came a note. *We're concentrating on the contracts.* As if I didn't know that? I agreed, let's concentrate on the contracts, but was that any reason to sit through this rubbish?

I expected Longfellow to be as rough to their witnesses as Griffith had been to ours, but not a bit of it. He barely rose to his feet, and when he did it was only to ask the most mealy-mouthed questions. In fact, the few which he did ask simply underlined what Griffith had already established. Of Janie, for instance, he asked, 'And are you quite sure that Mr Webb has always acted in your best interests?' To which, of course, Janie replied with a big positive

Yes. The question he put to Dai Evans wasn't much different: 'Do you think you would have been a wealthier man if another manager had handled your business affairs?' To which, of course, Dai answered with a very firm No. Even Hunter threw Longfellow several curious glances. 'Have you no further questions, Sir Robert?' And Longfellow merely bobbed back with a meek smile. 'No thank you, my Lord, no further questions.'

I seethed all afternoon, a condition not helped by the close proximity of my father, who kept throwing me triumphant sideways looks. Finally, thankfully, at four o'clock the court rose and the torture was over.

'We must talk about this,' I said immediately.

Longfellow reacted to the temper in my face with a smile. 'Come along then, let's go back to chambers.'

Leaving Julia to go to my mother's with Nick and the rest of them, I followed Longfellow and Olivia back to Lincoln's Inn.

I started even before he took his seat behind his vast partner's desk. 'I can't understand you,' I said hotly. 'Look at how rough you were on Nick in this office. You frightened him to death –'

'I was simply trying to prepare him for what Griffith might do to him. I wasn't far wrong, was I?'

'No, but what about their people today? You could have given them the same treatment.'

'I got what I wanted from them,' he said, accepting a glass of sherry from Olivia. 'Have a drink and let's talk this through in a calm and reasonable manner.

I have to admit his behaviour was better than mine. So was his reasoning. 'I'm sorry about Mrs Webb,' he said. 'In my opinion Hunter let Griffith go too far, but he did, so we have to accept it. Her value as an expert witness is now virtually nil, although I suspect Hunter might give her full marks for her courage.'

'Hear, hear!' said Olivia softly.

'But our case has never depended on Mrs Webb,' said Sir Robert. 'Neither would it have been helped by my thrashing those poor unfortunates who were committing perjury to protect their careers.'

'Sir Robert,' I said, still agitated despite the drink, 'we've had three days of this case and there's not a lot left –'

'I should think two or three days more. We'll have Jack Webb most of tomorrow, then Griffith and I will present our final submissions on Wednesday. With luck, we'll get a result the day after.'

'And at the moment we must be behind –'

'Oh definitely,' he agreed with a smile, 'but you must try not to worry.'

And so, after a night spent worrying despite Longfellow's advice, came the day I shall never forget. We were all there in the now-familiar courtroom; Julia and Ann, Nick and Mary and Gill, Bert and my mother. So too were Janie and Mike and Dai, and the boys from The Post Office Tower.

Jack arrived like a conquering hero to take his place in the witness-box. He and my father exchanged confident smiles, and a few minutes later Griffith rose to his feet.

The opening question set the tone for the next hour. 'Mr Webb, I believe you have a motto within your organisation. Would you tell us what it is?'

'Yes,' said Jack. 'It's the same now as the day I started JWE. "The artist comes first, second and third." Everyone will tell you about it. These days we even have it printed on our letterheads . . .'

There was no stopping Jack after that. At ease in the witness-box, he expanded on every well-rehearsed question. Jack had always been able to give a speech at the drop of a hat, and Griffith fed him all the right lines. The court heard how Jack had thrown up a promising career in the law . . . 'with the firm of Mortlake, Dingle & Barnes actually, who are my solicitors these days' . . . because 'Janie Marsham asked me to help her.'

I wrote Longfellow a note . . . *My father fired him* . . . but Sir Robert made no effort to read it. Instead he watched Jack intently, taking his measure.

There was no mention of Ann, no credit for her work, no credit for anyone save the mighty Jack Webb. It sickened me to listen. I doodled on my legal pad, drawing matchstick figures of Jack swinging by the neck from the end of a rope.

Meanwhile the clock ticked on and Jack was made to sound the greatest expert on music who ever lived. Not once did Longfellow interrupt. *Try not to worry* he had said the previous evening. Few of us could take that advice, especially Nick, who sat behind me biting his nails.

Finally, having run out of praise for Jack's industry, his integrity, his talent and renowned reputation, Griffith sat down well pleased with himself. His performance almost drew a round of applause from members of the public, who muttered and buzzed with conversation until Hunter tapped his gavel for silence.

Griffith had generated so much admiration for Jack that even Longfellow seemed affected by it when he rose to his feet. His early questions were all about the size of Jack's businesses, the awards won by his artists, the number of gold discs, silver discs, platinum discs . . .

I kept thinking . . . *We're losing, they're winning, Jack's the last witness, unless we strike now it's all over* . . . but Longfellow just went on and on in a voice which conveyed unmistakable approval. Then, at last, he began talking about the contracts given to artists by JWE, White Hat and Apex.

'We use a standard form of contract,' said Jack.

Longfellow nodded. 'I was wondering about that,' he said, 'after all, the expression "standard form of contract" can be used in two ways, can it not? For instance, there are those contracts used in transactions of common occurrence, such as bills of lading, insurance policies, contracts of sale in the commodity markets. The standard clauses in those contracts have been settled over the years by negotiation between the representatives of the commercial interests involved, and have been widely adopted because experience shows them to be fair and reasonable.' Longfellow smiled. 'I'm sure you became familiar with many such contracts in your early days at Mortlake, Dingle & Barnes?'

Jack nodded. 'Yes.'

'Whereas,' Longfellow continued, 'in some cases, what is fair and reasonable cannot be established because the activity is so new that the years of negotiation haven't had time to take place. In which case, unable to refer to established forms of contract, the participants must draw up their own. Is that right?'

'Yes.'

'And I suppose the making for sale of gramophone records might fall into that category, might it not?'

'Yes,' Jack agreed, looking faintly bored.

Longfellow tried a lighter touch. 'For instance, I don't suppose there have been many mass meetings between the managers of record companies on one side and recording artists from all over the world on the other, to work out a universal contract. I don't suppose that would be practical, would it?'

'Hardly,' said Jack dryly.

Longfellow nodded. 'So each recording company produces its own contract. Is that right?'

'Yes.'

'And that's what you did for Apex?' Longfellow asked agreeably.

'Correct.'

'And I suppose you did the same sort of thing for White Hat Publishing?'

'That's right.'

'Quite so,' Longfellow nodded approvingly. 'I wondered how it worked. I imagined it would be something like that, because without standard contracts being available – I use "standard" in the sense of insurance policies and so forth – you didn't really have any choice, did you?'

'Not really.'

'And they became the *standard* contracts adopted by White Hat and Apex. In other words . . .' Longfellow paused to inject an apologetic little smile . . . 'so that it's quite clear in my mind: the contracts drawn up by you are what you refer to when you use the expression "standard contracts"?'

'Correct.'

'My word,' Longfellow murmured with clear admiration. 'No easy task drawing up contracts.' A friendly grin appeared on his face. 'Just as well you were trained as a lawyer. I'm sure there were times when you blessed Mr Mortlake for the thorough training he gave you, eh?'

Jack smiled but he made no response.

'After all,' Longfellow went on, 'these contracts would have to protect White Hat and Apex from every eventuality, wouldn't they?'

'Naturally.'

'That was of the utmost importance, was it not?'

Jack frowned impatiently. 'Well, yes, I just said so –'

'Yes, of course,' said Longfellow by way of an immediate apology. 'Of course you did. And . . . er . . . with these standard contracts, you commenced business . . . publishing music, making records, and so forth . . .' Sir Robert faltered as if losing his train of thought. 'I have understood everything properly, haven't I?'

'Yes,' said Jack, without bothering to conceal his impatience.

Jack wasn't the only one with a frown on his face. Turning in my seat, I glimpsed Gill looking anxious and worried, obviously unimpressed with Longfellow's lack-lustre performance.

Indeed, there was even a frown on Longfellow's own face, which seemed to express annoyance not at Jack but at his own inability to clarifiy his thoughts. 'I think I've understood everything now,' he said. 'I'm a bit bemused by the speed of your success. For instance, I believe I read somewhere that Apex Records now produce records made by more than a hundred artists —'

'Nearly two hundred,' Jack corrected proudly.

'Two hundred!' Longfellow exclaimed. 'I do beg your pardon, I hadn't realised JWE had so many clients —'

'They aren't all JWE clients,' said Jack. 'In fact most of them aren't.'

'Oh, I see. So how many are? About fifty per cent?'

'No, no,' Jack sighed, exasperated to have to explain such basic matters. 'Apex is a big operation. JWE clients are possibly only twenty per cent of the turnover.'

'Twenty per cent,' echoed Longfellow, 'I see. And the same applies to White Hat, I suppose? Not all of the compositions published are written by clients of JWE?'

'Right. Only about twenty percent.'

'I'm obliged to you,' said Sir Robert, making a note. Bending forward, he studied his papers for a moment before exclaiming, 'Yes, of course. Stupid of me. I should have realised companies the size of White Hat and Apex . . .' He straightened up, a rueful expression on his face. 'Just let me get one final thing clear. All of these artists come along and sign the standard contract. Is that right?'

Jack nodded. 'That's right.'

'Exactly the same contracts?'

Jack shrugged. 'A word or two here and there might be different, but basically the same standard contract, yes.'

Longfellow looked relieved. 'Thank goodness. I

think that's what was confusing me. So they don't vary a great deal, these standard contracts?'

'Not a lot,' said Jack, shaking his head.

'A word or two here and there,' Longfellow mused. 'What sort of words would vary, do you think?'

Jack shrugged. 'Well,' he said cautiously, 'it all depends.'

'On what, Mr Webb?' Longfellow asked politely.

Jack fidgeted with the cuff of his grey mohair suit. 'It varies,' he said. 'It's hard to be specific.'

'I understand,' said Longfellow agreeably. 'I suppose some managers make all sorts of outrageous demands for their artists,' he chuckled. 'Have you serve them breakfast in bed if they could, eh?'

Jack smiled. 'Something like that.'

'I can imagine,' Sir Robert nodded cheerfully. 'So I suppose you make some small concession here and there. Instead of breakfast in bed you might give them tea in the kitchen, so to speak.'

Jack hesitated and threw a glance at my father.

Sir Robert offered an encouraging word. 'Just now and then.'

Jack nodded.

'Only a little concession,' said Longfellow. 'Like another half percent on Apex royalties, something like that?'

'Something like that,' Jack agreed.

'Perhaps more than half a per cent,' Longfellow speculated. 'Say, even another three or four per cent?'

Jack shook his head vigorously. 'Not another four percent. No way. That would be definitely out of the question –'

'Whereas an extra two or three per cent is quite common?'

'Not three per cent, no –'

'But two per cent?'

'Not common, exactly –'

'But not unusual either?'

'No, I suppose not.'

I began to breathe more easily. Longfellow had succeeded with the thin edge of the wedge. I wondered if Jack realised? Throwing a quick glance at my father, I saw only the familiar look of complacency. How alike he and Jack were; only years separated them; hard and smooth, with thin lips and eyes which betrayed their meanness of spirit.

Longfellow continued with the same earnest expression. 'I see,' he said. 'And would these small concessions extend to clauses elsewhere in the contracts? Not just the rate of royalties, for instance?'

'Not often –'

'But sometimes?'

'Now and then,' Jack admitted reluctantly.

As stealthily as a poacher bagging game, Longfellow began to tighten the net. With Hunter's permission, Jack was given a blank copy of a White Hat contract, and with a copy of his own in his hands Longfellow began to examine clause after clause. Reading them out, he paused after each one. 'What about clause three, for instance? Have you ever made a concession on that?'

Jack shrugged. 'It's hard to remember.'

'But you may have done? Let's suppose you want this very special composer. Bert Bacharat, for instance. If his manager said, "It's a deal if you reduce the effect of clause three from five years to four years", would you agree?'

'I might,' Jack conceded.

My father began to flick through the papers on the table. In front of him, Griffith lolled in his seat, as amiable as ever except for the look in his eyes. Next to him, his junior cupped his chin in his hands, while in front of me Olivia Newton sat absorbed. And above us, staring down from the Queen's Bench, Hunter watched as an owl might watch for mice. Lawyers all, each following with keen concentration as Longfellow probed with his questions, perhaps wondering where he was going and weighing the consequences of what would happen when he got there. Griffith had few opportunities to interrupt, save for one point where he rose to his feet. 'My Lord, surely my learned friend is not going to ask this witness to examine *every* clause in the contract?' But if Hunter had been tolerant of Griffith with earlier witnesses, he was equally tolerant now of Longfellow, who was quick to reply, 'Not every clause, my Lord, but with your permission I should like to pursue this line of questioning a little further.' And pursue it he did, through the White Hat contract and then the Apex contract, with Hunter making note after note and Jack becoming flustered in the box.

Finally Longfellow had established enough. 'Correct me if I'm wrong,' he said in the almost deferential tone he had adopted from the outset, 'but it seems to me that at least a third of the clauses in the publishing contract are amended from time to time. Would you agree?'

Jack had little choice but to agree. Longfellow was merely summing up what had been established. The best Jack could do was quibble. 'A third is a bit high,' he said.

'A quarter, then,' said Longfellow, prepared to be generous.

'About that,' Jack nodded.

'And the same might be said of the Apex contract. One in four of those clauses might be altered during the process of negotiation. Correct?'

'I'd think it more like one in five,' said Jack, still quibbling.

'Very well. One in four for White Hat, one in five for Apex. Is that about right?'

'About right, yes.'

'And those clauses would be changed for the benefit of the artist, would they not?'

Jack hesitated, as if seeing a pit opening before him and trying to find a way round.

'Surely,' said Longfellow, 'it's obvious these managers would want to negotiate a better deal, not a worse one, for their artists. Isn't that so?'

'That's what they'd want, yes.'

'And White Hat and Apex would amend these standard contracts to accommodate them. Yes or no, Mr Webb?'

'Yes.'

Feelings of relief swept over me as the pit opening before Jack deepened into a chasm. I felt no pity. This battle was of his making. He could have released Nick from the contracts without any of this. Instead he had tormented Nick, abused Ann, and run to my father who had complicated the issue with a shoal of red herring. But the law could be used by the weak, as well as bent by the strong, and as Longfellow proceeded relentlessly, I felt a great stirring of hope.

'The reason,' said Longfellow, 'why I wanted to be so clear about this concerns Mr Berkley who, a little over a year ago, came to you and asked you to be his manager. That's right, isn't it?'

'Yes.'

'Indeed, from what my learned friend has helped us to understand, Mr Berkley almost *begged* you to become his manager, did he not?'

A faint smile came to Jack's face. 'You could say that.'

'Because he believed you to be a very good manager. Indeed, he has told this court that he believed you to be the best in the business. Were you aware that he held you in such esteem?'

'Perhaps then he did, but —'

'There are no buts about it, Mr Webb. He trusted you completely. For instance, when you gave him a contract to sign, and I refer now to the contract with JWE, did he say, "I must take this away and show it to a solicitor to see if it's fair?"'

'He didn't have a solicitor —'

'Answer the question, Mr Webb,' said Longfellow with a new sharpness. 'Did he take it to a solicitor?'

'No.'

'Did he negotiate with you? Did he try to change anything?'

'No.'

'In fact he just signed it. Without reading it. He signed it as a blank cheque, as a demonstration of his trust. Isn't that so?'

'I suppose so —'

'Yes or no, Mr Webb.'

'Well, yes —'

'And shortly after that, did you give him a contract with White Hat Publishing to sign?'

'Yes.'

'Which again he signed without reading, isn't that so?'

'He could have read it –'

'But did he?' Longfellow asked more sharply than ever.

Jack began to bluster. 'I don't remember. It was a long time ago.'

'No matter,' said Longfellow, anxious to press on. 'And at the same time did you give him a contract with Apex Records to sign?'

'Yes.'

'And I suppose you don't remember whether he read that either,' said Longfellow with withering scorn.

Jack went red in the face. 'Like I said –'

'It was a long time ago.' Longfellow nodded scornfully. 'Not that it matters, because trusting you as he did, counting himself lucky to have you in charge of his affairs, he would have expected you to know exactly what he was signing. And you *did* know, didn't you, Mr Webb?'

'Of course I did –'

'Of course, because as his manager it was your job to know. Correct?'

'Obviously –'

'And you're a very good manager, Mr Webb, aren't you? The best in the business.'

'I don't know about the best –'

'Oh, come now, don't be modest. You've built up a very successful business. You're good at what you do. Do you know of a better manager, Mr Webb?'

'Well, put like that, no –'

'Therefore you knew exactly what Mr Berkley was signing, didn't you?'

'I just said I did!'

'Very well. Please tell his Lordship *exactly* what your client Nick Berkley was signing.'

Jack threw a hurried glance at Hunter. 'I just explained. He was signing the contracts with Apex and White Hat –'

Longfellow pounced. 'Which you as his manager had negotiated on his behalf. Correct?'

Jack swallowed hard. 'I arranged them –'

'Arranged?' Longfellow laughed. 'That's a good word. These contracts that you *arranged* were in fact nothing more than the standard contracts such as we have just examined. Is that correct?'

'Yes,' said Jack, now well aware of his danger and looking at my father for help.

'Contracts which other managers refused to let their clients sign!' Longfellow said triumphantly. 'Isn't that what you told the court?'

'They signed them eventually,' Jack protested.

'After they'd struck out twenty-five percent of the clauses. Isn't that true?'

Jack was the picture of misery. His eyes begged Griffith to intervene, but Sir Emlyn had no excuse and Mr Justice Hunter was in no mood to entertain anything less than the most solid objection. The Judge sat with his chin resting on steepled fingers, staring at Jack as if he had just slid out from under a rock.

Longfellow's voice was like ice. 'I repeat. Is it not true that other managers struck out twenty-five per cent of these contracts?'

'Yes,' Jack choked.

'Because those clauses were against the interests of their artists. Yes or no, Mr Webb?'

'That's what they said –'

'Yes or no!'

'Yes,' Jack admitted with bowed head.

'But what about the artists you represent? All Mr Berkley was given was the standard contract, wasn't he?'

'Yes, but –'

'Because the poor devil had you for a manager!' Longfellow thundered. 'Because you were earning at both ends. You were confronted by a conflict of interests of your own making, weren't you?'

Jack responded with a dull red-faced stare.

Longfellow struggled to control his temper. 'In fact what's been happening is that you've been negotiating with yourself. For White Hat to give any of your artists better terms will cost you more money. To make the terms less restrictive would reduce your hold over them. Isn't that true?'

'It's one way of looking at it –'

'They trusted you, Mr Webb!' Longfellow shouted, shaking with fury. 'They gave you thirty per cent of their earnings to look after their interests. In effect, you were a trustee, yet the only interests you've been concerned about are your own. My God, you behaved as if you owned them! Hasn't anyone ever told you that you can't own people!'

Griffith was on his feet, roaring his protest, while Hunter hammered his gavel for order. For a moment both barristers stood before the Queen's Bench, red-faced and angry.

My spirits soared. *You can't own people!* Turning in my seat, I stared my father full in the face, and for the first time in my life he lowered his eyes. Not for him the defiant look I'd had to muster all the years of my boyhood. It was beyond him. Fumbling with his papers, he averted his eyes and pretended to be oblivious of my presence.

Reprimanded by Hunter, Longfellow was now trying to regain control of his temper. Scornfully he resumed his attack upon Jack. 'These documents,' he said, pointing disdainfully to the papers before him, 'these so-called contracts aren't worthy of the name. Contract is an honourable word. A contract is an agreement freely entered into between two equal partners. There was no such equality here, was there, Mr Webb?'

Jack flinched under the lash of the words. He looked wretched and defeated. In vain he turned to my father for aid and encouragement.

'In fact there was gross inequality,' Longfellow thundered, unleashing his temper again. 'Even worse, there was blatant, bare-faced conflict of interest. Contracts such as these exist only in the devious minds of the people who draft them. I am confident that his Lordship will say they have no place in his court. They're unenforceable, Mr Webb. They're null and void . . .'

It didn't matter that Griffith was again on his feet, voicing his protest. It didn't matter that the Judge was hammering his gavel. The look on Hunter's face was enough. There would be no going back now. Hunter's face said it all. In my excitement I nearly cried aloud, *We've won!* I clung to the table to keep myself in my seat. *We've won!* I looked at my father slumped in his chair. I saw Jack white-faced in the box, Griffith still on his feet protesting; turning in my chair, I saw the tears in Ann's eyes and the relief on Nick's face, and I realised that they too knew. *We'd won!*

Another day and a half was to pass before our victory became official. The next morning, Longfellow and Griffith delivered their final submissions, and the Judge took the rest of the day to consider his verdict; so we endured some more anxious hours, but for me the real nail-biting ended when Longfellow concluded with Jack. Not even Griffith at his most eloquent could repair the damage. Jack had been totally discredited and we had witnessed the fall of a tyrant; perhaps more than one tyrant because even my father bowed his head when the Judge found in our favour.

We held the celebration party at Gill's place, which was appropriate considering that was where this story began. The consequences of the Judge's verdict were enormous – Nick got his career back, I kept The Grove, and Julia, thank God, was on hand to share it. And believe it or not, Ann had found yet another musician.

She was full of him at the party; her enthusiasm was irrepressible. 'He'll be here any minute. I met him in Manchester the other week. He played at a gig to raise money. I tell you, Peter, this guy is terrific. He and Nick will do tremendous things together. I mean, Greg, that's his name, Greg was actually *in* Vietnam a year ago. Can you imagine him writing the lyrics for Nick's music . . .'

Ann was full of plans to return to New York, taking Nick and Greg with her.

'I'll tell you something though,' she confessed with a wry smile. 'Nothing's for nothing in this world. Jack gave me a lot of pain, but he sure taught me about what not to do. After what I've been through I'll give even that creep Katzman a run for his money . . .'

Without knowing it then, I was never to see her again. With her protégés in tow, she left for New York within the week, and although we corresponded for a while, inevitably the letters faltered with the passage of time. Nick did finish his rock opera on Vietnam. The show failed in New York, I think because the Americans were still trying to come to terms with their role in the war, but it did well enough in Paris and London and elsewhere to justify Ann's faith in his talent – a talent applauded by the whole world when he wrote *Inferno* the following year, and *Surfers* a year after that.

To the best of my knowledge, Ann never married again. Last year I read she was living in Los Angeles and was very much involved with Clyde Martin, the young composer who wrote the musical score for the film *Treasure*. I have no idea where she is now, but of one thing I'm certain. Someone, somewhere, is being buttonholed by a woman whose dark eyes sparkle with excitement as she says, 'You've got to listen to this guy. His music is tremendous.'

As for Jack, after that last day in court, I never saw him again either. The thread which had bound our lives together had finally broken. Our long friendship was as dead as Jack's career in the pop business. Within a year, Janie and Dai and all the others had left him; freed from their bonds because of Nick's victory in the High Court.

Odd, how life works out. My old nightmares, inherited from boyhood, might never have been erased had Jack not turned to my father. As it was, defeating him in court, seeing my values triumph over his, reduced him from a giant to a pygmy. Had Jack not involved Katzman, Ann might never have laid the ghost which had kept her from returning to New York. And most of all, had Jack as a boy not listened to my father, we might not have fought in the High Court. But that's life . . . which sometimes has an odd way of delivering justice.

Fontana Paperbacks: Fiction

Fontana is a leading paperback publisher of fiction.
Below are some recent titles.

- ☐ CABAL Clive Barker £2.95
- ☐ DALLAS DOWN Richard Moran £2.95
- ☐ SHARPE'S RIFLES Bernard Cornwell £3.50
- ☐ A MAN RIDES THROUGH Stephen Donaldson £4.95
- ☐ HOLD MY HAND I'M DYING John Gordon Davis £3.95
- ☐ ROYAL FLASH George MacDonald Fraser £3.50
- ☐ FLASH FOR FREEDOM! George MacDonald Fraser £3.50
- ☐ THE HONEY ANT Duncan Kyle £2.95
- ☐ FAREWELL TO THE KING Pierre Schoendoerffer £2.95
- ☐ MONKEY SHINES Michael Stewart £2.95

You can buy Fontana paperbacks at your local bookshop or
newsagent. Or you can order them from Fontana Paperbacks,
Cash Sales Department, Box 29, Douglas, Isle of Man. Please
send a cheque, postal or money order (not currency) worth the
purchase price plus 22p per book for postage (maximum postage
required is £3.00 for orders within the UK).

NAME (Block letters) _____

ADDRESS _____

_____